BREAKING THE NEWS

EXPOSING THE ESTABLISHMENT MEDIA'S
HIDDEN DEALS AND SECRET CORRUPTION

ALEX MARLOW

THRESHOLD EDITIONS

New York   London   Toronto   Sydney   New Delhi

To Wynn and Robert

Threshold Editions
An Imprint of Simon & Schuster, Inc.
1230 Avenue of the Americas
New York, NY 10020

Copyright © 2021 by The Jobin Group LLC

First Threshold Editions hardcover edition May 2021

THRESHOLD EDITIONS and colophon are trademarks of Simon & Schuster, Inc.

For information about special discounts for bulk purchases, please contact Simon & Schuster Special Sales at 1-866-506-1949 or business@simonandschuster.com.

The Simon & Schuster Speakers Bureau can bring authors to your live event. For more information, or to book an event, contact the Simon & Schuster Speakers Bureau at 1-866-248-3049 or visit our website at www.simonspeakers.com.

Interior design by Jaime Putroti

Manufactured in the United States of America

10 9 8 7 6 5 4 3 2 1

Library of Congress Cataloging-in-Publication Data
Names: Marlow, Alex, author.
Title: Breaking the news : exposing the establishment media's hidden deals
   and secret corruption / Alex Marlow.
Description: First Threshold Editions hardcover edition. | New York :
   Threshold Editions, [2021] | Includes bibliographical references. |
   Summary: "From the editor in chief of Breitbart News, a firsthand
   account of how the establishment media became weaponized against Donald
   Trump and his supporters on behalf of the political left"— Provided by
   publisher.
Identifiers: LCCN 2021009229 (print) | LCCN 2021009230 (ebook) | ISBN
   9781982160746 (hardcover) | ISBN 9781982160753 (paperback) | ISBN
   9781982160760 (ebook)
Subjects: LCSH: Mass media—Political aspects—United States. | Press and
   politics—United States. | Right and left (Political science)—United
   States—History—21st century.
Classification: LCC P95.82.U6 M365 2021 (print) | LCC P95.82.U6 (ebook) |
   DDC 302.230973—dc23
LC record available at https://lccn.loc.gov/2021009229
LC ebook record available at https://lccn.loc.gov/2021009230

ISBN 978-1-9821-6074-6
ISBN 978-1-9821-6076-0 (ebook)

CONTENTS

PREFACE

This is not a book merely about liberal media bias. Since Donald Trump descended that escalator and announced his candidacy for president in 2015, "bias" is far too benign a word for the establishment media's collective tendencies. The notion that our mainstream press is merely reporting the news with a subtle tilt away from a neutral viewpoint seems quaint in the year 2021. No, in our modern media landscape, advancing chosen agendas drives America's newsrooms far more than fact-finding or truth-telling, and examining newsrooms using a liberal/conservative dichotomy is too simplistic. Leftism, globalism, and corporatism have emerged as the dominant ideologies that drive major content decisions by leading news outlets. More and more, newsrooms in recent years have gravitated toward stories that advance the notion that an interventionist government combined with powerful, well-funded global bureaucracies provides the path forward for America. Rarely do newsrooms, increasingly owned, financed, and operated by the world's biggest companies, provide a check on the corporations that control so much of our lives and culture.

Yes, our media is on the attack, looking to harm and even destroy the personal lives of their perceived adversaries. And they've gotten nastier. Much nastier.

The American media is the principal player in our modern day "cancel culture," the recent phenomenon where a person is banished from polite society, or at least social media, for offending popular culture's prevailing consensus.

Their ultimate goal is to cancel America, at least in the traditional sense. Next they'll replace it with a woke-topia where political correctness, corporatism, and globalism replace liberty, In God We Trust, and *E pluribus unum.*

Breaking the News is about the modern era of political media. In this book, I track the evolution of the "Democrat Media Complex," which was Andrew Breitbart's expression for the incestuous nature of the establishment media elite and America's ideological Left. I explain why and how certain stories are covered—or not covered—and who benefits from those coverage decisions. I examine the deals cut, the corporate connections, the family ties, and the global ambitions that are shaping the news that you consume every day, even if you can't always see it in plain sight.

And in the spirit of Andrew Breitbart, I'll give you some tools to fight back.

And we must act now, because a free American press hangs in the balance.

A Brief Note on Style and Format

While I believe *Breaking the News* covers more ground than any book on this particular moment in media, it doesn't cover *all* of the ground that there is to cover.

This is, at times, a pity. So many of the hundreds upon hundreds of stories I reviewed during the research process are worthy of discussion, but I simply couldn't make them all fit.

For example, *Newsweek* published a piece in 2019 suggesting it could be time to rethink cannibalism.[1] It's undeniably compelling and alarming, but it gets just this one mention.

Another amazing story that didn't fit elsewhere: CNN legal analyst Areva Martin accused my SiriusXM Patriot colleague David Webb of "white privilege" during a radio interview. If only I could have seen her face when Webb told her that he is black.[2]

And what about when CNN's Jake Tapper suggested that longtime Trump associate Roger Stone "might like" going to prison; the consensus among some in the Internet commentariat appeared to be that this comment by Tapper was a homophobic joke about prison rape.[3] (A CNN spokesperson claimed the comment was about Stone's love of attention.)[4] Tapper also anchored an entire television segment on Trump's penis.

All of these stories cry out for additional discussion, and there are seemingly half a dozen more like them that occur each day.

In the chapters dedicated to specific news outlets, I chose to focus my research and analysis on three "case studies": Bloomberg News, because of their subservience to China and the uniqueness of Michael Bloomberg's presidential run; MSNBC, because it was the ultimate media arm of the anti-Trump "Resistance"; and the *New York Times*, because it was the most influential establishment media outlet in Trump's America. I think taken together, these three outlets use nearly every tool in the media's kit that can be used to advance the interests of big corporations, the political establishment, and the globalist left. I believe after reading those chapters, you'll agree.

That's not to say that other news outlets aren't covered in great detail. If you picked up the book hoping for a beat-down of, say, CNN, or the *Washington Post*, I don't think you'll be disappointed, but they don't get the full "case study" treatment.

Maybe I'll take those on in the sequel!

I mention this at the outset for one specific purpose: just because it doesn't appear in *Breaking the News*, it doesn't mean it isn't fake news. The corporate media establishment is constantly trying to manipulate their audiences and the world to serve their political, personal, and financial ends. Nearly every major outlet is doing this, and they'll never stop. Ultimately it is on the citizens of the United States of America to be conscientious consumers of the news media. Only then can we begin to fight back.

THROW YOUR BODY ON THE GEARS

[Alex Marlow] is the most consequential countercultural figure to come out of UC Berkeley since the Free Speech Movement.
—*San Francisco* magazine

I grew up in an upper-middle-class neighborhood in West Los Angeles, on a quiet street, with happily married parents, and a sister and assorted cats. I attended terrific schools, excelled in clubs and sports, and was fairly well liked by my peers and the faculty (at least that's how I remember it).

So, nothing in my backstory screams "counterculture."

Still, I always felt like I was an outsider.

Growing up, I began to notice a disconnect between the well-reasoned articulateness of the talk radio hosts my parents listened to in the car and what I was reading in our media and learning in the classroom. I came to believe that core institutions were not providing Americans the full spectrum of ideas. I considered this a grave injustice and a dereliction of civic responsibility.

For high school, I went to Harvard-Westlake, which is the most competitive—and perhaps the best—private school on the West Coast. It is usually the top choice for prominent families in Los Angeles and Hollywood and has a list of noteworthy graduates that bests most top-tier universities. (People connected with the school have tried to disown me at least once.)

Most HW families are one-percenters and are on the left. My family was neither of those things. This reality made me feel like I was inside of one of the greatest social experiments imaginable. I was getting all the essential beats of what life is like for powerful, elite liberals without actually having to be one.

This became addictive.

When no Division I baseball offers came in and I got accepted to the University of California, Berkeley, I knew I needed to take this social experiment to its logical next step.

I was going to live in the heart of the Left, the epicenter of the Free Speech movement.

While at Berkeley I studied political science and music, and the overall experience was a big success. I participated in clubs, played intramural sports, and worked at a sustainable/local/organic restaurant. Don't laugh, hippies make the best goat-cheese-based appetizers. But my real major was in leftism. I didn't just get to study my political opposites, I got to live with them, work with them, make friends with them.

But these hippies were not there for my amusement; they were there to be part of the beating heart of the American Left: people fully committed to stopping anything conservative or traditionalist, and most will stop at nothing to bring down their target, even if their tactics are less than ethical.

At UC Berkeley there is a club literally called "By Any Means Necessary," or "BAMN." Our college Republicans club would debate them regularly with aggravating—but undeniably entertaining—results.

While on campus, I tried my own hand at activism: organizing on historic Sproul Plaza, running a modestly successful blog focusing on a combination of campus and national events, as well as podcasting. I even appeared on the cover of *Time* magazine, along with several other politically active students.

Just as I was about to begin my last semester, I met a man named Andrew Breitbart at an event for young conservatives in Santa Barbara hosted by Young America's Foundation (YAF), a prominent and still powerful group that owns the Ronald Reagan ranch, Rancho del Cielo. YAF is best known for bringing conservative speakers to campuses.

I recognized Breitbart's name from the many, many, many Breitbart .com articles I had clicked on while reading the Drudge Report over the years. I had made DrudgeReport.com, the world's most important news-aggregation website, my home page in the tenth grade on my father's recommendation. I was stunned when I found out that "Breitbart" wasn't a giant media conglomerate in Düsseldorf with hundreds of reporters tapping out hundreds of articles a day. It was actually just one man in his West Los Angeles home office compiling news wires and RSS feeds into one convenient place.

But Andrew wasn't an ordinary newsman. He had two qualities that spoke to me as a middle-class Hollywood native and a soon-to-be Berkeley graduate: he was a showman with a compelling counterculture sensibility, and he was a true populist.

He gave a speech that night in late 2007 that was quite radical at the time: he proclaimed that culture is upstream from politics. Or, in other words, America's entertainment industry, media, and academy are guiding policy and precipitating big societal changes. Hollywood leads, Washington follows.

After childhood on the Westside of Los Angeles and college at Berkeley, I knew he was speaking the truth. But I had never heard anyone describe it as clearly or as confidently as Breitbart.

Nowadays, virtually every conservative believes Breitbart's axiom about politics being downstream from culture, but in the fall of 2007, it was a revolutionary gospel and only one man was preaching it: Andrew Breitbart.

I had to talk to him. But how?

Well, Andrew being Andrew, it wasn't difficult. He was hanging out in the hotel lobby bar after his speech, holding court and drinking red wine with anyone who wanted to talk to him about news, or baseball, or music, or anything else really. I was interested in all those things and we were practically neighbors, so we became fast friends. He told me that he was about to expand his news empire into original content and offered me a job by the end of the weekend.

We were about to enter the glamorous world of blogging!

I believed the time was ripe for a center-right news organization to emerge that would hold the powers that be accountable, to tell the stories the establishment wouldn't, and to hunt down the scoops "respectable journalists" didn't have the interest (or balls) to track down themselves. It seemed clear to me right away that Andrew was the exact person to do it.

He had the brains, the experience, and the intensity. He also had a terrific sense of humor, a thick skin, and seemingly endless stores of energy. His website was going to have a unique attribute at the time that I found incredibly compelling: while still focusing on truth and accurate reporting, we were going to state our biases openly and allow consumers to judge us accordingly. This is a massive differentiation from establishment media publications who still insist they are neutral while their reporting reveals an obvious agenda.

He saw this as an opportunity to gain credibility. By admitting he was a conservative, he was attempting to redefine what it meant to be a credible journalist in the modern era. Could you picture a prime-time CNN anchor or a White House correspondent for the *New York Times* admitting they are on the left? It's unfathomable—and remarkably dishonest.

I thought this approach was visionary and it suited me perfectly.

In January 2008, I became Breitbart.com's first employee. I worked part-time at first and began full-time when I graduated a few months later.

In the thirteen years I have worked at Breitbart, I've not only had a front row seat to the new media revolution, but I've also been lucky enough to have had a hand in shaping it. I was mentored by one of the best who ever lived, Andrew Breitbart. I was a part of the teams that took down ACORN and Anthony Weiner. Andrew Breitbart promoted me to managing editor when I was twenty-five years old. In 2013, a year after Andrew's death, our president and CEO Larry Solov and then-executive chairman Steve Bannon made me editor-in-chief when I was twenty-seven.

Journalist and fellow UC Berkeley alum Scott Lucas wrote in 2017 that I was "every bit the culture-jammer, throw-your-body-on-the-gears, power-to-the-people agitator that '60s free speech icon Mario Savio was." This is the highest possible praise from a Bay Area liberal.

Savio, the quintessential Free Speech movement hero, is best known for his "Bodies Upon the Gears" speech. The key moment:

> There's a time when the operation of the machine becomes so odious, makes you so sick at heart, that you can't take part! You can't even passively take part! And you've got to put your bodies upon the gears and upon the wheels . . . upon the levers, upon all the apparatus, and you've got to make it stop! And you've got to indicate to the people who run it, to the people who own it, that unless you're free, the machine will be prevented from working at all!

This is the essence of the spirit of the counterculture in one paragraph. I've lived it for my entire adult life. It has been a wild ride so far, and it's just getting started.

CHAPTER 1

THE RISE OF BREITBART
AND THE FAKE NEWS HALL OF SHAME

Just after Trump's victory and his appointment of former Breitbart News executive chairman Steve Bannon as "Chief Strategist," Breitbart began to receive scrutiny unlike anything we had ever seen before. We'd certainly seen our share of good news cycles and bad, but we were on a roll of late. I had just gotten back from the United Kingdom, where I had spent much of the summer covering the British referendum to leave the European Union, otherwise known as Brexit. Nigel Farage, then the leader of the United Kingdom Independence Party (UKIP) and figurehead of the anti–European Union movement, said that "Brexit would not have happened without Breitbart."[1] Reporting on Hillary Clinton by Breitbart staffers, especially *Clinton Cash* author Peter Schweizer, had become imbedded in the consciousness of the American electorate. And of course, Breitbart was the first major American media outlet to take Donald Trump seriously as a presidential contender.

With the elevation of Bannon, the smears were flying at a rate that we hadn't seen in our history. Here were some of the most common falsehoods that were repeated about our merry band of grassroots journalists:

Breitbart news is anti-Semitic. Perhaps the most oft-repeated smear on us is also the most absurd. Andrew Breitbart and Larry Solov, both Jewish, conceived of the idea for Breitbart.com while on a sojourn in Israel, where they visited holy sites and met with Prime Minister Benjamin Netanyahu. The first editor-in-chief of the website and current senior editor-at-large, Joel Pollak, is an orthodox Jew. Many of the top editors past and present are Jews. My mother was raised Jewish. Breitbart News has a Jerusalem bureau where we cover the Jewish state from an over-whelmingly pro-Israel perspective.

The preponderance of evidence against the claim we're anti-Semitic raises the question, where did the smear come from? Almost certainly it is based on this single headline: "Bill Kristol: Republican Spoiler, Renegade Jew."[2]

That's it. Certainly, that's an intense headline, and one that normally wouldn't get published on our virtual pages. But the article, a takedown of apostate Republican magazine editor and "Never Trump" pundit Bill Kristol, was written by prominent *Jewish* intellectual David Horowitz, and this was his preferred headline. What's more, in the article, Horowitz criticizes Kristol for not being sufficiently pro-Israel. Israel, of course, is the only Jewish state on earth.

Rarely do media hit pieces on Breitbart give any of this context. So, a single opinion headline from a Jewish thought leader is used to cancel out thousands of pro-Jewish articles written by Jewish writers and editors.

This isn't bias. This is weaponized political media designed to destroy us.

Breitbart news is racist and sexist. This one is nearly as easy to debunk, if you use the traditional definition of racism (discriminating against people based on their skin tone). As it happens, Breitbart News' entertainment editor is black (Jerome Hudson), our copy chief is a black woman (Adrienne Ross), our world editor is a Latina woman (Frances Martel), our chief defense correspondent is an Asian woman (Kristina Wong), and our top video editor is also a woman (Amand House). Not to mention numerous Jewish staffers including those mentioned above. And those are just examples from middle management. Journalist Wil S. Hylton reported in the *New York Times Magazine* that I personally have "a pretty good record of promoting women and minorities."[3]

Since 2015, Breitbart News has published the Cartel Chronicles. This series is designed to be a channel for citizen journalism and other reporting on cartel activity throughout Mexico, the United States, and beyond. The Cartel Chronicles gives a voice to the Mexican citizens who are the greatest victims of cartel violence, as well as countless Americans who are harmed by the illegal drug and human smuggling trade. We publish the Cartel Chronicles in both English and Spanish.[4]

For years, publicly traded SiriusXM has given Breitbart News between

23 and 38 hours of live national radio a week. At least 2 of those weekly hours are hosted by a black woman, Sonnie Johnson. It would be quite a feat for a racist network to produce two thousand hours a year of original broadcasting without producing even a single racist sound bite, yet we somehow manage!

As for me, my first job in conservative media was with my first favorite talk show host: a black man named Larry Elder, who now hosts a nationally syndicated show for the Salem Radio Network.

So, Breitbart is a pro-Jewish website with a reputation for treating women and minorities well and publishes many articles in Spanish. Yet we were branded racist. Why? It's because the Democrat Media Complex, which has been weaponized against the Right and traditional American values, has changed the definition of racism to mean, in essence, anything associated with or supportive of Donald Trump or conservative America. Occasionally, even being insufficiently anti-Trump or politically correct is enough to get you branded with the scarlet "R."

So, everyone on the right is now "racist" to one degree or another. Thus, the Left has to invent new language to distinguish between the *really* bad people and your garden-variety rubes. Thus . . .

Breitbart News is "the platform for the alt-right." The expression "alt-right" is relatively new and if you asked ten people to define it, those who have even heard of it would likely give you differing answers. That said, they would probably associate the term with racism and Jew-hatred.

Luckily for us, this one might be the easiest to refute of them all: professor and noted Israeli-American author Yochai Benkler, who has studied Breitbart with interdisciplinary colleagues at Harvard and MIT, literally told the *New York Times Magazine* in 2017 that "Breitbart is not the alt-right."

Case closed, right?

Well, no, because Steve Bannon once told *Mother Jones* that we are "the platform for the alt-right."[5] Though Bannon has a genius and a magnetism that is often productive and usually compelling, he is also prone to using declarative language when he is entirely incorrect. Occasionally he's a visionary; other times he's a WWE professional wrestler. This was an example of the latter. I wasn't there for the conversation, nor do I know exactly what Bannon was thinking, but he certainly wasn't telling a reporter that our pro-Israel outlet, owned and edited by Jews, is also anti-

Semitic. Yet, if you read news reports about Breitbart, that's exactly how the comment is portrayed.

At that point in time, we had published the most thorough reporting on the alt-right and its various factions earlier that year in a piece titled "An Establishment Conservative's Guide to the Alt-Right."[6] The article was widely read and generally well received; Bloomberg News included it on their 2016 "Jealousy List" of the stories they wished they had written.[7]

So, Breitbart certainly popularized right-wing ideas that were an alternative to establishment conservatives, and we had written comprehensively about the "alt-right," so it's easy to see how Bannon could have made this flub.

But a flub is all it was, as confirmed by Harvard's Benkler.

Yet, our weaponized media never let the facts get in the way of a favorable narrative. So, they have used that single phrase to define us instead of examining the tens of thousands of pieces of content or the thousands of hours of radio we produce each year.

All's fair in love and war, as the saying goes.

And this is war.

Breitbart News peddles conspiracies. Of the smears on Breitbart News, this is the one that has gotten the least traction. But still, it merits a quick review.

Wikipedia in their wildly inaccurate entry on Breitbart News (remember, it's not bias, it's weaponized media) lists four total conspiracy theories we have allegedly peddled over the years (remember, Breitbart News was founded well over a decade ago and publishes about one hundred original articles each day). Here they are:

1. Wikipedia falsely connects Breitbart News with the "birther" conspiracy theory that Barack Obama was born in Kenya. We have always presumed Obama was born in America. In fact, even when we broke the story of what we believe to be the origins of birtherism (a promotional pamphlet used by Obama's literary agency in 1991 that states he was "born in Kenya and raised in Indonesia and Hawaii"), we clearly stated within the piece that we believe he was born in the USA anyway. From a disclaimer we tacked at the top of the article: "Andrew Breitbart was never a 'Birther,'" and Breitbart News is a site that has never advocated the narrative of "birther-

ism." In fact, Andrew believed, as we do, that President Barack Obama was born in Honolulu, Hawaii, on August 4, 1961."[8]

2. Wikipedia claims we promoted Pizzagate, a bizarre conspiracy that key members of Hillary Clinton's inner circle ran a child sex ring through a northwestern D.C. pizza parlor using coded emails. Wikipedia states flatly that we hyped the absurd story and, as of spring 2020, cited four source links to back up their claim: one to the *New York Times,* one to Snopes, one to PolitiFact, and one to the *Daily Beast*, all frequent targets of Breitbart News's media reporters.[9] Of the four, the word "Breitbart" appears only in the *Daily Beast* piece; none of the four link to a single article where we promoted "Pizzagate." Breitbart's Wikipedia page is "locked," which means it is nearly impossible to get this blatant falsehood removed from our page.

3. The third "conspiracy theory" we allegedly peddled is simply because we quoted Roger Stone accurately. Breitbart transcribed an interview between Steve Bannon and Roger Stone in which the conservative provocateur alleged that Huma Abedin had ties to a "global terrorist entity." Our reporting does not confirm nor deny Stone's claims. If reporting accurately on what a prominent figure says is considered an endorsement or even a promotion of "conspiracy theories," Breitbart is also guilty of pushing *thousands* of conspiracy theories lobbed by the ladies of *The View* and CNN hosts we post on a daily basis.

4. Wikipedia says we published "claims that Hillary Clinton and the Obama administration supported ISIS." This is an exaggeration. Breitbart published a single article by a former junior reporter who misconstrued a memo Hillary Clinton received that he believed indicated the Obama administration was supporting ISIS *specifically* in the chaotic and confusing Syrian civil war against the Bashar al-Assad regime. As it turned out, our writer misinterpreted the memo and we have since retracted the story. It wasn't our best work, but it hardly makes us "conspiratorial."

So, the establishment media's narrative about Breitbart has been wrong the entire time. If you're taking time to read this book (and an organization funded by George Soros isn't paying you to do so), this probably isn't a surprise to you. But what might be a surprise is the extent to which the establishment media has so clearly put their agenda ahead of the truth. Breitbart is far from the only group of people smeared by a belligerent media class. Recall some of these classics from my personal Fake News Hall of Shame:

THE CHARLOTTESVILLE HOAX

The media insists to this day that President Trump said that neo-Nazis were "very fine people" after the protests and riots that took place in Charlottesville, Virginia, in August 2017. The lie stems from a press conference held on infrastructure at Trump Tower on August 15; toward the end of the presser, a reporter questioned Trump as to whom he blamed for the violence that day, considering that neo-Nazis were in attendance. Trump reacted as follows (emphasis mine):

> Excuse me, they didn't put themselves down as neo-Nazis, and you had some very bad people in that group. **But you also had people that were very fine people on both sides.** You had people in that group—excuse me, excuse me. I saw the same pictures as you did. You had people in that group that were there to protest the taking down, of to them, a very, very important statue and the renaming of a park from Robert E. Lee to another name.

This was all the media needed to claim that Trump is literally a Nazi. Conveniently, they left off the rest of the discussion. Full transcript (emphasis mine):

REPORTER: George Washington and Robert E. Lee are not the same.

TRUMP: Oh no, George Washington was a slave owner. Was George Washington a slave owner? So will George Washington now lose his status? Are we going to take down—excuse me. Are we going to take down, are we going to take down statues to George Washington? How about Thomas Jefferson? What do you think of Thomas Jefferson? You like him? Okay, good. Are we going to take down his statue? He was a major slave owner. Are we going to take down his statue? You know what? It's fine, you're changing history, you're changing culture, and you had people—**and I'm not talking about the neo-Nazis and the white nationalists, because they should be condemned totally**—but you had many people in that group other than neo-Nazis and white nationalists, okay? And the press has treated them absolutely unfairly. Now, in the other group also, you had some fine people, but you also had troublemakers and you see them come with the black outfits and with the helmets and with the baseball bats—you had a lot of bad people in the other group too.[10]

So not only is Trump not literally Hitler, he flat out condemned Nazis a mere minute after his infamous "fine people" comment. In fact, CNN reported the story accurately in August 2017 but went on to become one of the most prominent proponents of the hoax as time went on.[11] The establishment media echoed this falsehood for years all because, it appears, it helped frame the president as a racist.

Not only was Trump's answer to the reporter a good one, but it predicted the eventual cancellation of Washington and Jefferson. ("Cancellation" is the expression for widespread ostracism or even banning of figures, past and present, from polite society and social media.) A short time after Trump's comments, it became fashionable to rename schools that honored Presidents Washington, Jefferson, and even Lincoln.[12] These presidents are simply too controversial for the woke moment in which we find ourselves.

Assemble the renaming committee! We need a few Colin Kaepernick Middle Schools to open up and some Jussie Smollett Highways anyway.

The fake news narrative that Trump said there were "very fine people" on both sides followed him around to the end of his presidency. Joe Biden regularly cited the Charlottesville hoax as part of his inspiration to run for the highest office. Biden, himself a white man with a checkered history when it comes to race, rode this smear all the way to the White House.

THE BRETT KAVANAUGH HOAX

Then-judge Brett Kavanaugh's nomination to the Supreme Court was never going to be an easy process even though he had virtually a perfect resume. He was squeaky clean. He had a Yale education and a terrific reputation in the community. He coached girls' youth basketball and served hot food to the homeless in soup kitchens. And he was hardly a right-wing radical. While on the D.C. circuit court, he voted with his liberal colleague Judge Merrick Garland 93 percent of the time. (Garland was Barack Obama's pick to replace Antonin Scalia after the latter's death in 2016 and would become Biden's attorney general.)

But, Kavanaugh was replacing Justice Anthony Kennedy (for whom he had clerked), who was often the court's swing vote. This meant his confirmation would create perhaps the most conservative Supreme Court in generations.[13] *Roe v. Wade* now in play? The Democrat Media Complex certainly wasn't going to take that chance. They had to stop the confirmation.

The first tactic from the Democrats (who quickly began hurling invective at Kavanaugh) was a fishing expedition: one million pages of documents would be examined before the Senate would vote, by far a record.[14] This was less likely to yield controversial dirt than it would buy time for a strategy to reveal itself. And it did. Brett Kavanaugh was going to be painted as a sexual predator.

In the era of #MeToo (an anti-sex-abuse social movement that led to many high-profile public firings and arrests), men accused of sexual assault were guilty until proven innocent in the court of public opinion, which meant this vector of attack could maybe succeed despite a seeming lack of actual proof. The Democrat Media Complex was certainly determined to find out.

First, the Intercept reported that Senator Dianne Feinstein had obtained a letter alleging a sexual assault by Kavanaugh against a woman (later identified as Christine Blasey Ford) that supposedly took place in 1982.[15] Ford's story was published in the *Washington Post*. Drama ensued, there were demands the FBI to look into the matter, and the Kavanaugh confirmation vote was delayed.[16]

NBC published a report from one of Kavanaugh's former classmates, Christina King Miranda, that supposedly backed up Ford's story.[17] But upon scrutiny, there were significant discrepancies in Miranda's and Ford's stories.

Next, the *New Yorker* ran the story of Deborah Ramirez, who claimed that someone had thrust a penis in her hand while she was at Yale thirty-five years prior; it had recently dawned on her that that person was Brett Kavanaugh. But no credible witnesses could even place Kavanaugh at the party, much less recall the incident. Ramirez also acknowledges that she had been drinking. The *New Yorker* article indicates that she might have been hesitant to come forward due to her hazy recollection; only after six days of reflecting and discussions with her attorney did she speak to reporter Ronan Farrow.[18]

The *Times* tweeted at the time, "Having a penis thrust in your face at a drunken dorm party may seem like harmless fun." They deleted the tweet and apologized.[19]

Ford eventually testified in front of the Senate Judiciary Committee. Within the span of a minute or two, questioner Rachel Mitchell, a sex crime expert and Maricopa County, Arizona's deputy county attorney, got the Democrats' star witness to say that she had to "get up the gumption with the help of some friends" to fly to Washington for the hearing—but that she also regularly took flights to places like Hawaii, Costa Rica, South Pacific islands, and French Polynesia to surf.

Mitchell remained preternaturally calm through this surreal exchange, so much so that to many in the establishment media, Christine Blasey Ford remains credible to this day. Despite the seemingly contradictory testimony, she received praise from every corner of the media, from *Time* magazine to Fox News to *Marie Claire*. She even inspired a book about the #MeToo era, which was endorsed by *Publishers Weekly* and Ashley Judd.[20]

There would be at least one more accuser. NBC reported that Julie Swetnick claimed she witnessed the future Supreme Court justice participate in gang rapes when he was about fifteen years old (the network included a disclaimer that her report was contradictory).[21] Swetnick was represented by disgraced lawyer and flash-in-the-pan cable news celebrity Michael Avenatti.[22] The pair never produced a single witness, but a former boyfriend said he believed Swetnick had psychological problems and was a group-sex enthusiast.[23]

This was an embarrassing end to one of the media's most disgraceful sagas.

Brett Kavanaugh was confirmed to the SCOTUS on October 6, 2018, on a 50–48 vote, the narrowest in U.S. history.[24]

Russian Collusion: The Fakest Fake News

The story that garnered the most attention from our establishment media during the Trump presidency was a 100 percent bogus one: the story that the president had colluded with the Russian government to rig the 2016 election and that the president of the United States himself is a Russian asset. For conservative audiences, this notion always seemed kind of absurd. After all, we had read how it was Clinton World that was intertwined with the Russians in Peter Schweizer's 2015 book, *Clinton Cash*.[25] Among the revelations in the book is that while Hillary Clinton was secretary of state, the U.S. approved a sale that effectively transferred 20 percent of the United States' uranium reserves to a Russian government–owned company. The transaction was approved by the Committee on Foreign Investment in the United States (CFIUS), a government interagency that includes the State Department. (Clinton has repeatedly denied approving the deal, insisting that the decision was delegated to lower-level officials.)[26] Uranium is not only an important strategic metal, but it is nuclear-weapon-usable and naturally radioactive.[27] Thus, handing it over to the Russians wasn't just potentially corrupt, it had serious implications for our national security.

Around the time this deal went down, the Clinton Foundation received $145 million from investors in the uranium deal, according to bombshell reporting by the *New York Times*. (The *Times* was trashed for daring to report unflatteringly on the business dealings of the Clintons while Hillary was our nation's top diplomat.)[28] Additionally, a Kremlin-linked bank paid Bill Clinton half a million dollars for a brief speech that took place in Moscow around that time. Putin reportedly thanked Clinton for delivering the speech.[29]

After quickly brushing over evidence of possible corruption unearthed about the Clintons, our establishment media were attempting to gaslight Americans into believing Trump is Putin's puppet. It wasn't going to work unless they delivered the goods, which they never did.

Though Trump has certainly praised Putin, his policy toward Russia was quite tough, much more so than his predecessor's.

• Trump treated Russia as a major cybersecurity threat, imposed numerous tough sanctions, and banned Russian cybersecurity software within the U.S. government.[30]

• Trump signed sanctions against Russia that the Russian prime minister Dmitry Medvedev described as a "full-scale trade war."[31]

• Trump expelled Russian diplomats and shuttered their consulate in Seattle.[32]

• Trump cracked down on Russia with even more sanctions over a violation of a Cold War–era nuclear arms pact.[33]

• The Trump administration sold arms to Ukraine in December 2017; this gave the Ukrainians the capability to defend themselves from Russian aggression. Obama could have done this but he didn't, and Trump reportedly made this call personally.[34]

• Trump's Justice Department indicted twelve Russians on charges of election meddling, with Trump himself deciding to announce the indictments just a few days before a planned summit with Putin.[35]

All of this was subtext as the Russian collusion investigation played out—at least for folks who get news from non-establishment sources. While CNN was reporting breathlessly and repeatedly on Trump saying nice things about Putin and other dictators, they apparently did not consider that this was all Trump's strategy.[36] It's not like he wrote a famous book about negotiations called *The Art of the Deal*.

When we learned that the entirety of Big Scary Russia's method for overturning an American presidential election was basically to buy $100,000 of Facebook ads and hack John Podesta's emails, I knew the witch hunt was doomed to fail.[37]

I was on Bill Maher's HBO show *Real Time* in the summer of 2017 when I predicted that there would ultimately be no evidence the Trump campaign colluded with the Russians to rig an election *and* that no one in the establishment press would get held accountable for misleading the public and wasting our time. "You guys continue to talk about this story in the establishment press instead of talking about the president's agenda, which is by design. Because you guys won't apologize if it turns out there's nothing, no one will come out on MSNBC, they'll just move on to the next hysteria," I told Maher.

Sadly, my predictions came true.[38]

The levels of deception and delusion carried out by our activist press to misinform the public on Trump and Russia were unfathomable. Nearly every single establishment media newsroom got the crux of the story wrong, and they published well over half a million articles on the subject (and that's counting only from May 2017 to March 2019).[39] Here is an extremely truncated list of fake news lowlights among infinite examples:

• October 2016. *Slate* circulated a rumor that President Trump was communicating with Russia using a secret server.[40] This story was weaponized by the Clinton campaign, but it was never substantiated.[41]

• November 2016. The *Washington Post* smeared a number of outlets, including the Drudge Report and WikiLeaks, as being a part of a network of 200+ websites promoted by a sinister and clandestine Russian propaganda operation.[42] The story was wildly misleading at best, and the *Post* eventually appended an editor's note, distancing itself from its own reporting.[43]

• December 2016. The *Washington Post* falsely reported that "Russian hackers penetrated the U.S. electricity grid through a utility in Vermont."[44] This story was echoed throughout establishment media and hyped by Democrat politicians, but it has remained unsubstantiated.[45]

• June 2017. CNN published—based on a single anonymous source—that both the Senate Intelligence Committee and the Treasury Department were investigating a Russian investment fund with ties to Anthony Scaramucci, who was briefly Trump's White House communications director. Democrats weaponized the story, until it was debunked by Breitbart News and others.[46] Though they never explicitly admitted that it was false, CNN retracted the story, and the three reporters responsible for the story were asked to resign.

• June 25, 2017. The *New York Times* claimed that seventeen intelligence agencies reported that Russia had orchestrated hacking during the 2016 election. This false claim was repeated throughout the media, despite the fact that it was four intelligence agencies, not seventeen.[47]

• December 2017. ABC's Brian Ross falsely reported on-air that during the campaign, Trump had directed Michael Flynn (who would later become the president's national security adviser) to make contact with the Russian government and that Flynn was prepared to testify about it.[48] The report was false and it led to Ross's resignation.[49]

• December 2017. Bloomberg and the *Wall Street Journal*, among other outlets, reported that some of Donald Trump's financial records had been subpoenaed by Robert Mueller's special counsel from Deutsche Bank, which the Trump family used.[50] As it happens, the subpoenas concerned "people or entities affiliated" with Mr. Trump (whatever that means), not the president himself.[51]

• December 2017. CNN reported "exclusively" that Donald Trump Jr. may have conspiried with WikiLeaks, which had hacked documents. The CNN story by Manu Raju and Jeremy Herb was based on emails "described" to them.[52] However, WikiLeaks was directing Team Trump to emails that were already public.[53] This story led to an embarrassing correction.[54]

• May 3, 2018. NBC News reported that federal investigators wiretapped Michael Cohen, then Trump's personal attorney, and presumably there were tapes of the calls. This was false.[55] NBC acknowledged the error in a lengthy correction.

• November 2018. The British newspaper the *Guardian* posted an anonymously sourced bombshell allegation that Trump's former campaign manager Paul Manafort held secret talks with WikiLeaks founder Julian Assange inside the Ecuadorian embassy in London just prior to the release of hacked DNC emails.[56] (Assange had taken refuge there from U.S. extradition several years prior and had never left.)[57] There is no other evidence Assange and Manafort ever met, and the "secret talks" were not even hinted at in Robert Mueller's special counsel report.

• December 2018. McClatchy reported that Trump consigliere Michael Cohen had a secret meeting with Russians in Prague during the summer of 2016.[58] The Mueller report notes that "Cohen had never traveled to Prague."

• January 10, 2019. *New York Times* star reporters Maggie Haberman and Ken Vogel, along with Sharon LaFraniere, falsely reported a "bombshell" that Paul Manafort passed polling data to the Kremlin.[59] In fact, Manafort wanted data sent to two Ukrainians. The *Times* issued a humiliating correction.[60]

• January 18, 2019. BuzzFeed falsely reported that Trump directed then-attorney Michael Cohen to lie to Congress on his behalf, citing two anonymous sources.[61] Robert Mueller's special counsel office took the rare step of releasing an outright denial of the BuzzFeed report. (Anthony Cormier, one of the reporters on the story, delivered a TEDx talk in 2017 on "Combatting Fake News"; in the twelve-minute speech, he accused Breitbart of peddling falsehoods on three occasions.)

For years the establishment media falsely insisted the bogus "pee pee" dossier, which had been financed by a law firm that represented Hillary Clinton, had been corroborated at least two times.[62] The dossier, according to Justice Department inspector general Michael Horowitz's famed report released in December 2019, "played a central and essential role" in the FBI's decision to seek Foreign Intelligence Surveillance Act (FISA) authority to surveil Trump staffer Carter Page.

Alisyn Camerota, former DNI James Clapper, Representative Ted Lieu (D-CA), anchor Jim Sciutto, and many others hyped the credibility of the clearly bogus document on CNN's air.[63]

Rachel Maddow, Nicolle Wallace, John Harwood, and others on NBC's cable news properties clung desperately to the notion that none of the dossier had been *disproven*. (Little in life can be *disproven*, which is why our legal system relies on "innocent until proven guilty" as opposed to the inverse. I could accuse Rachel Maddow and Nicolle Wallace of murder, animal cruelty, or intentionally lying to moderately large cable news audiences every weekday for years in order to undo the 2016 election of Donald Trump, and it would be impossible to disprove any of it.)

The establishment media seemed to have no introspection about how wrong they were about Donald Trump and Russia. In fact, quite the opposite. The *New York Times* and the *Washington Post* won Pulitzer Prizes for Russia panic reporting, even though it ultimately amounted to nothing.[64]

The award-winning articles have aged very poorly. They rely on vast amounts of speculation, endless cover-your-ass caveats, and an array of wishful thinking that in retrospect looks more like a Hollywood fantasy—or a large-scale hoax to brainwash the public.

During this fake news cycle, literally dozens of celebrities accused the U.S. president of treason, a crime punishable in the United States by death.[65]

Meanwhile, the *Times* and much of their establishment media cohorts missed what was a much, much larger and contemporaneous story about U.S. government corruption: the surveillance of the Donald Trump campaign by the Obama administration.[66]

Perhaps the Pulitzer has become akin to a "participation trophy," a booby prize for the privileged journalism establishment class to reward to each other, regardless of whether their reporting actually *informed* the public or *misinformed* it.

In July 2017, political journalist Joshua Green, who writes primarily at Bloomberg, wrote (fittingly) at the *New York Times* that "No One Cares About Russia in the World Breitbart Made." After a dramatic opening that included the claim that "Mr. Trump's presidential campaign had, at the very least, been eager to collude with Russia to influence the 2016 election," Green wrote, "You'd have had to travel to the political fringe of right-wing talk radio, the Drudge Report and dissident publications like Breitbart News to find an alternative viewpoint that rejected this basic story line."

He continued, "The Breitbart mind-set—pugnacious, besieged, paranoid and determined to impose its own framework on current events regardless of facts—has moved from the right-wing fringe to the center of Republican politics."[67]

The only problem is that Breitbart had the narrative correct all along. It was an incorrect assumption shared unquestioningly by all of the establishment that Russia would have preferred a Trump presidency to a Hillary Clinton one. It was absurd to believe a germophobe like Trump had a urine fetish, and that he traveled to Moscow to indulge it. And it was, above all, idiotic to believe that Trump was simultaneously the biggest buffoon in the history of American politics but also savvy enough (despite having zero political experience) to rig an American presidential election with the help of a geopolitical adversary and not leave a trace of incontrovertible evidence.

Yet, this is exactly what you were told to believe, and if you dared to question the media's Russia narrative, you were "besieged, paranoid and determined to impose [your] own framework." At least according to an author featured in the *New York Times*.

Green's article concluded, "If special counsel Robert Mueller finds evidence of Russian collusion, it will be followed by a bigger test measuring just what it takes to snap out of a mass hallucination."

Perhaps Green hadn't considered it was the media establishment that was doing the hallucinating.

Or maybe they were simply at war.

The Covington Hoax, or When the Fake News Targets Children

Late Saturday night, January 19, 2019, I was rushed back to my desk to watch a viral video from the March for Life (an annual anti-abortion march that takes place in Washington, D.C., each year) that appeared to show white teens in MAGA hats taunting an old American Indian man while he beat a sad little drum.

The man, sixty-four-year-old Nathan Phillips, said that the boys chanted "Build that wall, build that wall," among other supposedly horrible things.

The public conviction of the pro-life boys from Covington Catholic High School in Kentucky—especially then-sixteen-year-old Nicholas Sandmann, who grinned silently at Phillips—was instant.

The *New York Times* tweeted: "Boys in 'Make America Great Again' Hats Mob Native Elder at Indigenous Peoples March."[68] (Phillips was reportedly participating in a march for American Indians at roughly the same time as the March for Life.)

CNN "conservative" S. E. Cupp lectured the boys, their parents, and the country in general over our collective awfulness.[69]

Then-congresswoman Deb Haaland (now interior secretary) harshly condemned not only the boys, but President Trump as well, tweeting, "The students' display of blatant hate, disrespect, and intolerance is a signal of how common decency has decayed under this administration. Heartbreaking."[70]

New York Times reporter Maggie Haberman (more on her later) expanded the scope, tweeting that "dozens of students" were "laughing and egging on" the behavior and that "officials suggest" there could be expulsions.[71]

Actor Chris Evans wrote out an eight-sentence tweet that reads like beat poetry but can be summed up as "MAGA boys bad, Native American man good."[72]

Rosie O'Donnell called Sandmann a "horrible smug asswipe."[73]

Actor, former Screen Actors Guild president, and 9/11 conspiracy nut Ed Asner tweeted, "This is not America."[74]

Former CNN talking head Reza Aslan tweeted of Sandmann,[75] "Have you ever seen a more punchable face than this kid's?" *Slate*'s Ruth Graham repeated the "punchable" face line.[76] CNN's Bakari Sellers agreed: "[Sandmann] is deplorable. Some ppl can also be punched in the face," he twittered.[77]

Actor Tim Robbins mused, "How does this behavior reflect the life and lessons of Jesus Christ?"[78]

Actor and Dell Technologies spokesman Jeffrey Wright fantasized about the students getting beaten. He rage-tweeted: "Since they're in DC, they should take the phucking red hats and #MAGA bullshit and get up in some faces over Congress Heights way. The reaction won't be so dignified. They'll relocate that smug grin to the back of his pencil-dick neck like he's asking for."[79]

The government-funded news media was typically awful. NPR's headline read, "Video of Kentucky Students Mocking Native American Man Draws Outcry."[80]

Comedian, former CNN personality, and national basket case Kathy Griffin (who is famous for a photo in which she held a bloody severed head of President Trump) called for the children to be publicly named.[81]

NBC News interviewed another young man from the same region of the country—a gay person who had been valedictorian of another local school—who trashed the Covington Catholic students without evidence that they had done anything wrong.[82]

The New York *Daily News* and the British *Daily Mail*, among others, portrayed Covington High School in an unflattering light with years-old photos of kids at a school basketball game allegedly wearing "blackface." (They were not in blackface, nor were they making racial taunts.)[83]

Even the diocese of Covington condemned the kids and apologized to pretty much everyone.[84] The *Washington Post* used the statement to tarnish the entire pro-life movement. They connected the event to President Trump's "Pocahontas" nickname he uses for Senator Elizabeth Warren, a white woman who identified as an American Indian nearly her entire adult life.[85]

Also to the *WaPo*'s delight, the mayor of Covington condemned the boys soon after.[86]

Even prominent media conservatives piled on. Radio talk show host and NBC News contributor Hugh Hewitt wrote in a tweet that is beyond satire that it would be "great if Covington Catholic invited Philly Archbishop Chaput, a member of the Prairie Band Potawatomi Nation, to visit the school for some teaching on respect, forgiveness, courtesy." Hewitt also signaled his virtue by tweeting "train every high schooler in Proverbs 15:1" ("A soft answer turneth away wrath: but grievous words stir up anger").[87] Ironically, Sandmann gave the softest answer to Phillips possible: a smile. He used no words at all. If only Hewitt had done the same.

Republican establishment pundit and magazine editor Bill Kristol seemed to imply that President Trump(!) should call Phillips to express regret.[88]

The most over-the-top, self-righteously irresponsible coverage of the Nicholas Sandmann saga came from the *National Review*, which published an article literally titled "The Covington Students Might as Well Have Just Spit on the Cross." The author, Nicholas Frankovich, savaged the children, repeatedly invoking religious language and principles to do so. Apparently, there was extreme urgency to get the rebuke of the pro-life teens in MAGA hats: the article was published at 2:55 a.m. The hit piece on children was so urgent it couldn't wait until daybreak.[89] *NR* ultimately retracted the piece and apologized.

The establishment media's narrative turned out to be pure fake news, of course.

Nathan Phillips, the narrative's victim/hero, wasn't simply a kindly old native person: he is a career activist who fights on behalf of left-wing causes. While the March for Life has been an annual event since 1975, the first Indigenous People's March launched that year (it did not return in 2020). Coincidentally, it was scheduled at the exact same time as the March for Life. This is either a wild coincidence, or Phillips was there that day specifically to stir things up.

Phillips also has a criminal record. He had pled guilty to assault and has several alcohol-related charges, a negligent driving charge, a driving without a license charge, and was charged with trying to escape jail. Phillips also touts his Marine Corps service, claiming he had served "in theatre," but according to the *Washington Examiner,* he had never been deployed outside of the United States and his main job was as a refrigerator mechanic.[90] The *Washington Post* had to issue a substantial correction after incorrectly reporting that Phillips fought in the Vietnam War.[91]

According to retired Navy SEAL Don Shipley, an advocate against stolen valor, Phillips had been AWOL (away without leave) on three occasions.[92] Phillips left the military after a series of disciplinary issues.[93]

He also appeared to be prone to making up stories seemingly out of whole cloth. In one instance, Phillips claimed that he had been "spat on" by a "blonde-haired, blue-eyed hippie girl" who called him a "baby killer"; he then bragged about beating up her boyfriend.[94]

In other words, the media's hero, Nathan Phillips, appears to be a bit of a fabulist.

There was a third group also in attendance that day: the Black Hebrew Israelites, a relatively obscure and radical religious sect who believes they are descended from lost tribes of Israel.[95] Even the left-wing Southern Poverty Law Center has called them "black supremacists" and "militant" and reported that they have a racist and anti-Semitic worldview.[96]

You wouldn't know that, though, if you got your news from the *New York Times.* The Gray Lady published a puff piece titled "Hebrew Israelites See Divine Intervention in Lincoln Memorial Confrontation."[97]

Initial reports indicated that the Covington boys had initiated the confrontation, verbally accosting both Phillips and the Black Hebrew

Israelites. But it wasn't the Covington kids who started it, it was the Hebrew Israelites. Extended footage revealed them referring to the students as "school shooters" and "a bunch of incest babies." [98] Video shows the Hebrew Israelites verbally attacking the American Indian marchers and the March for Life participants, hurling an array of racial slurs.

More in-depth footage also makes it clear that Phillips approached the Covington boys, banging his sad little drum. It is also clear he was not cornered, as suggested by our press.

Phillips said repeatedly that the students had chanted "build the wall" or "build that wall," a favorite chant among Trump devotees. The media found this irony particularly delicious because, as CNN's Cupp put it, the American Indian population has "literally zero illegal immigrants." To this day, though, there is no video of the Covington Catholic kids chanting anything remotely close to "build the wall," despite the fact that there were a number of cameras present filming the confrontation. However, video did emerge that appears to show Black Hebrew Israelites mockingly shouting "build that wall" at the "dirty ass crackas."

In fact, additional footage provided by Sandmann's attorney shows an indigenous demonstrator suggesting that the students should go back to Europe because America is "not your land." [99]

Soon after, the Covington Catholic students' bus arrived and they left the steps of the Lincoln Memorial. Nathan Phillips did not continue up the steps of the memorial—despite telling multiple national news outlets that the students were blocking his path.

In an incredibly telling moment on ABC's daytime talk show *The View*, Whoopi Goldberg lamented how yet again the media had rushed to draw conclusions about a viral Internet video before the facts were in. "Why do we keep making the same mistake?" she asked the panel. [100]

Joy Behar responded instantly and with certainty: "Because we're desperate to get Trump out of office. That's why."

Precisely. The media and celebrity establishment, even some political conservatives, waged war on minors without the slightest bit of due diligence because they had MAGA hats on.

The character assassination of Nicholas Sandmann was not bias; it was weaponized media.

Sandmann brought lawsuits against many of the responsible parties. In January 2020, he and CNN agreed to settle a $275 million lawsuit. [101]

Though the terms were not publicized, they are widely believed to represent a clear victory for Sandmann. On July 24, 2020, Sandmann settled a $250 million defamation suit against the *Washington Post*. The settlements were for undisclosed amounts.[102]

He has additional suits pending.[103]

"Justice for Jussie": A Hate Crime Hoax

Over the past half century or so, American law enforcement and popular culture have conferred an extra level of seriousness and gravity to "hate crimes" as opposed to regular crimes. The definition of a hate crime, according to the FBI, is a regular crime with an added element of bias. "A 'criminal' offense against a person or property motivated in whole or in part by an offender's bias against a race, religion, disability, sexual orientation, ethnicity, gender, or gender identity," the FBI.gov website states.[104]

Hate crimes are sure to grab headlines across international news because the victimhood is *doubled*. The victim was a casualty of whatever crime had been committed, *and* they're a victim of racism/sexism/homophobia/bigotry, etc.

This explains why the media instantly was whipped up into a frenzy when a gay, black actor was allegedly attacked in Chicago in late January 2019. Jussie Smollett, an actor on the popular Fox show *Empire,* had supposedly been attacked by two men while walking home from a Subway sandwich shop at around 2 a.m. on January 29. According to Smollett's original report, two white men beat him badly,[105] fractured one of his ribs, and wrapped a noose around his neck (a symbol for lynching). The assailants also allegedly hurled racial and homophobic slurs, asking him if he was "that f***ot 'Empire' n***er?" They even poured bleach on his dark skin, according to Smollett, in what would have been an unspeakable act of abject racism.[106]

If the attack wasn't dramatic enough, the two supposedly white attackers were also wearing red "Make America Great Again" hats, the iconic sartorial symbol of Donald Trump supporters. As they left a broken Smollett at the scene, they had supposedly shouted "This is MAGA country," despite the fact that they supposedly were in Chicago.

This all happened on one of the coldest nights of the year with an overnight windchill well below zero degrees.

Smollett later posted to his Instagram a photo of himself in a hospital bed, scratched and bruised, providing ample evidence for would-be supporters to draw bold conclusions about the veracity of his account.

Smollett's story was immediately embraced by the media and Hollywood establishments.

A gay black man had been a victim of a racist and homophobic attack by Trump supporters! This was way too good to check!

Or was it? Since, of course, this hate crime turned out to be a giant hoax.

Still, the media was inundated with virtue signaling on behalf of Smollett, accepting his claims wholesale. Some examples out of an infinite list:

• Then-senator Kamala Harris (D-CA) tweeted praise for Jussie and called the (hoax) attack "an attempted modern day lynching."[107]

• New Jersey senator Cory Booker called the fake attack "vicious" and "an attempted modern-day lynching." He tweeted an endorsement of an "anti-lynching" bill in Congress.[108]

• The NAACP blamed Donald Trump for the (hoax) attack and a general atmosphere of terror in the United States.[109]

• Maxine Waters (D-CA) said she knows and loves Jussie and his family and called him a "fantastic human being." She suggested President Trump deserved some of the blame.[110]

• The New York Times took Smollett's story as gospel, reporting Smollett "was attacked in Chicago by 2 assailants who yelled racial and homophobic slurs." Joe Biden quoted the tweet— uncritically—and predictably added some generic sanctimonious lecturing to Americans about bias: "We must stand up and demand that we no longer give this hate safe harbor; that homophobia and racism have no place on our streets or in our hearts. We are with you, Jussie."[111]

• CNN's Don Lemon said in an interview that he texted Smollett every day following the phony attack, asking if he was okay.[112]

• Yamiche Alcindor, PBS's White House correspondent and NBC News fixture, tweeted, "We have to do better as a country. This is disgusting." [113]

• *Rolling Stone*'s Jamil Smith declared the attack "terrorism." [114]

If the journalism class was irresponsible, the celebrity establishment was downright reckless. Transgender nonbinary actor Elliot Page (who at the time was a lesbian actress named Ellen Page), Cher, pop star Katy Perry, actress Olivia Munn, actor Billy Eichner, Rosie O'Donnell, Rob Reiner, *Moonlight* writer/director Barry Jenkins, *Frozen* actor Josh Gad, *Star Trek* actor George Takei, and many others rushed to defend Smollett and/or attack MAGA and Trump before the evidence was in. [115]

Nearly all of these reactions were instantaneous, tweeted or grammed soon after initial details emerged, despite the fact that the story's main sources were Jussie himself and celebrity gossip blog TMZ.

Meanwhile, local news reporters were left with little concrete evidence to back up Smollett's wild story. On January 30, about thirty-six hours after the purported attack, reporter Rob Elgas of ABC 7 Chicago reported that "no obvious people that could be assailants" had been discovered by local law enforcement, and that "detectives have poured [*sic*] over hundreds of hours of surveillance video." [116]

But this still didn't dissuade the media that Jussie had been victimized.

The *Chicago Tribune* blared a headline that in retrospect looks downright comedic: "Week before reported attack, Jussie Smollett got threatening letter with 'MAGA' written for return address." The article details that Smollett was sent a letter filled with white powder that spelled in "cut-out letters"—so corny! "You will die black f*g," it allegedly said. The *Tribune* pointed out that the letter was also stamped with American flags. [117]

If this hate crime had been real, it would certainly have been the lamest, most ham-fisted, most uncreative hate crime in American history.

As the days wore on and there was still only circumstantial evidence and no credible witnesses to affirm Smollett's story, he needed to do damage control, so, with (crocodile) tears in his eyes, he sat down with Robin Roberts on ABC's *Good Morning America*. The interview is largely incoherent and borderline embarrassing, but he says he is "pissed off" at his doubters for refusing to see the truth. [118]

Hours later a report emerged that there were two "persons of interest" in the alleged attack. Charlie De Mar of local Chicago CBS sent a tweet that must have given the Jussie fanboys and girls a cold sweat: "Police raided the home of two persons of interest in Jussie Smollett case last night. Both men are of Nigerian decent and have appeared as extras on the show. Police took bleach, shoes, electronics and more." [119]

This was the beginning of the end of the latest woke hate hoax.

The two men, brothers who had been background actors on Smollett's Fox television show, were detained by Chicago police.[120] Police suspected Smollett paid them to stage the attack.[121]

Around this time, social media ramped up its censorship game. Instagram deleted a post by Donald Trump Jr. that was skeptical of Smollett. The Facebook-owned platform later said it was removed "in error." [122]

On February 20, 2019, just three weeks after the alleged incident most definitely did not take place, Jussie Smollett was charged with disorderly conduct and became the suspect in an investigation for filing a false police report.

Still, as of February 20, 20th Century Fox TV and Fox Entertainment still backed Smollett, describing him as a "consummate professional." [123]

That sentiment didn't last long, though. Smollett was arrested on February 21. Chicago police superintendent Eddie Johnson said Jussie falsified the hate crime (and the MAGA letter) because "he was dissatisfied with his salary" he was earning from *Empire*.[124]

Fox announced he would no longer appear on the show a day later.

Smollett was eventually indicted for sixteen counts of disorderly conduct by Cook County, all of which were eventually dropped.[125] Joe Magats, an assistant state attorney, did state shortly thereafter that it was not "an exoneration." "We believe he did what he was charged with doing," Magats told the local ABC affiliate.[126]

That didn't stop CNN's Brian Stelter, host of the ironically named *Reliable Sources,* from suggesting that Jussie was now in fact the "victim," concluding that he was "triumphant" and could return to work on Fox television.[127] Apparently it was wishful thinking on Stelter's part, as Smollett never did film any new *Empire* episodes.[128]

He was charged for a second time related to the hate crime hoax in February 2020. This time six new charges were brought against him by a special prosecutor. He pleaded not guilty.[129]

Bubba Wallace and "Very Fake Noose"

At Breitbart News, we were skeptical of the Jussie Smollett story from the start. This is because we have reported on a number of "very fake noose" hate crime hoaxes throughout the last decade.[130]

A few examples of many:

• September 2015: Three "nooses" hung on the University of Delaware campus were actually just parts of some lanterns.[131]

• May 2016: Some rope found on the ground (not in a tree) before a Milo Yiannopoulos speech at DePaul University turned out not to be a noose but merely some rope on the ground.[132]

• June 2017: Discarded plastic wrap tied into a loop found on the University of Maryland campus definitely was not a noose.[133]

• August 2017: Cops determined that a "noose" at a Washington, D.C., construction site was rope used to do construction, not threaten minorities.[134]

The list goes on. And the media breathlessly reported them all as potential hate crimes.

The "very fake noose" stories continue: In June 2020, ropes tied by *a black man* in an Oakland park were treated as a noose by law enforcement, even though the man said he used them for exercise.[135] In an incredibly important moment representative of the national Woke Panic of 2020, Oakland mayor Libby Schaaf whitesplained the non-nooses to black Oaklanders: "Intentions do not matter. We will not tolerate symbols of hate in our city. The nooses found at Lake Merritt will be investigated as hate crimes."[136]

Actually, when it comes to ropes tied to trees, intentions are the *only* thing that matters.

In June 2020, black NASCAR driver Bubba Wallace was allegedly targeted with a "noose" placed in his stall of the garage at Talladega Superspeedway for the GEICO 500.[137] Wallace has used his NASCAR success to push far-left politics, including racing with "Black Lives Matter" painted on his car, wearing an "I Can't Breathe" shirt, and lobbying to get the Confederate flag banned from NASCAR (this effort succeeded).[138]

Unfortunately for Wallace, the "noose" wasn't a noose (notice the pattern?) but was a garage door-pull that had been in place since October of the previous year.[139]

It was "unfortunate" for Wallace because he seemed to want to be a victim of a hate crime, as evidenced by an appearance on CNN with Don Lemon. When Lemon asked his thoughts on the FBI's findings that he was *not* targeted for his race, Wallace reacted by saying he, like Jussie, was "pissed" and went on to defend his character from attacks.[140]

Perhaps a more appropriate reaction to the news that you weren't targeted for a hate crime would be relief, but in 2020 America it means you miss out on savoring the sweetness of public victimhood.

"It was a noose," Bubba told Lemon. "Whether tied in 2019 or whatever, it was a noose. So, it wasn't directed at me but somebody tied a noose. That's what I'm saying."

No, it wasn't a noose. It was a rope used to open a garage door.

Hate crime hoaxes—hyped by the media until they unravel, then quickly forgotten—aren't simply confined to nooses. Breitbart News documented at least a hundred hoaxes in all between 2007 and 2016.[141] The College Fix, a right-of-center blog that covers academia, reported on at least fifty pieces of very fake hate crime news between 2012 and 2018.[142]

The Most Meaningless Impeachment

"Could Trump Be Impeached Shortly After He Takes Office?" This was a headline published in *Politico* on April 17, 2016, a full six months before Trump was even elected.[143]

On January 20, 2017, the *Washington Post* published a headline "The Campaign to Impeach President Trump Has Begun." This was on Inauguration Day.[144]

If there was any doubt in your mind that eventually President Trump would be impeached, impeached again, and if he ever wins another term, impeached a third time, I submit these two headlines as evidence that impeachment was always a goal for the Democrat Media Complex.

Democrats called for impeachment throughout 2017 and 2018. Texas representative Al Green (not the terrific soul singer, the not-so-terrific congressman) came clean about the real reasons behind the impeachment obsession and in a candid moment said, "I'm concerned if we don't impeach this president, he will get reelected."[145]

So, the Democrats knew they would impeach, but for what? In late 2019 we got the very odd answer: Trump was impeached for urging Ukraine to look into whether Joe Biden's son was actually corrupt.

It has been said that All Roads Lead to Breitbart, and impeachment is no exception. The lineage of the narrative goes back to our own senior contributor Peter Schweizer and his book *Secret Empires: How the American Political Class Hides Corruption and Enriches Family and Friends*. In the book, Schweizer uncovered Hunter Biden's ties to a shady Ukrainian energy company, Burisma. Hunter was hired to Burisma's board in 2014 despite not having any background in energy and having no known ties to Ukraine. Hunter had some investing background, but it simply didn't stack up against the other members of the board.[146] There was only one reason anyone would hire Hunter Biden into such a role: his dad was vice president of the United States. Hunter was compensated well for the work he was or wasn't doing for Burisma: $83,000 per month, Schweizer reported. It seemed as though the primary if not sole purpose of having Hunter Biden in this role was his Rolodex: he was likely being paid specifically for being well-connected to political elite. "We now know with emails that have been released that he was working at Burisma's direction to try to deflect investigations into Burisma," Schweizer told me in an interview.[147]

In January 2018, Biden claimed bragging rights for getting top Ukrainian prosecutor Viktor Shokin fired. Shokin was known to be investigating Burisma, and the then vice president threatened the Ukrainian government to "take action" against him or they wouldn't get a billion dollars in aid. Biden admitted all this on tape at an event at the Council on Foreign Relations.[148] The audience of foreign policy sophisticates laughed along with Biden as he regaled them with the story.

This seems to be the definition of quid pro quo: fire the guy investigating my son's suspicious business deal or you don't get a billion dollars.

Seems pretty scandalous. Unless, of course, you live in the alternate reality of the Democrat Media Complex.

As they often (always?) do, they figured out a way to make Donald Trump the villain of all this. On July 25, 2019, President Trump had a phone conversation with newly installed Ukrainian president Volodymyr Zelensky that would eventually lead to impeachment.

(Zelensky, unbelievably, was formerly a comedic actor who had portrayed the Ukrainian president on the popular satirical television program *Servant of the People.*)

During the call, President Trump encouraged Zelensky to look into what had actually happened with the Bidens, Burisma, and the fired prosecutor. The key line from the transcript of the call, which was made public by the Trump administration:

> The other thing, there's a lot of talk about Biden's son, that Biden stopped the prosecution and a lot of people want to find out about that so whatever you can do with the Attorney General would be great. Biden went around bragging that he stopped the prosecution so if you can look into it . . . It sounds horrible to me.[149]

Zelensky agreed to "look into the situation" with no obvious or explicit tie to military aid. This makes sense since the White House had already decided to review and delay (not withhold) the aid from Ukraine.[150]

Enter the "whistleblower." The "whistleblower," who wasn't actually a whistleblower since he seemingly heard about the call only secondhand, is almost certainly a CIA analyst named Eric Ciaramella.[151] Ciaramella was hired into the Obama administration and had previously worked with Russia-hoaxer John Brennan and anti-Trump DNC operative Alexandra Chalupa, as well as Joe Biden himself. RealClear-Investigations reported that he had been accused of working against Trump from within the government.[152] The official intelligence community inspector general even found that the not-really-a-whistleblower had "political bias" against Trump.[153]

The whistleblower logged a complaint with Senate Intelligence Committee chairman Richard Burr (R-NC) and his house counterpart, Adam Schiff (D-CA), that the Trump phone call was interfering in the 2020 election, but in the complaint he admits that he was getting at least some of this information secondhand (at best) and from other anonymous officials in the deep state.[154] It is unclear from the complaint if he had firsthand knowledge. As it turns out, whistleblowers needed to have firsthand knowledge of alleged wrongdoings to qualify for whistleblower status. That is, until the rules were quietly changed just prior to the Trump impeachment.[155] That's quite a coincidence!

Reading the complaint, I was left with the impression the whistleblower was operating under one of two premises: 1) There is no legitimacy to what Donald Trump suggested to the Ukrainian president, and thus the president of the United States was soliciting a foreign leader to help him rig the 2020 election by investigating an opponent's family, or 2) Trump might have had legitimate reasons to want the Hunter Biden investigation restarted, but he shouldn't have even obliquely suggested it to Zelensky on the call, because Joe Biden was a potential political rival.

And it's possible he was drawing these high-stakes conclusions without having the benefit of having been on the phone call in question.

And we're to assume it's merely coincidental that the "whistleblower" previously worked with Joe Biden, a Trump opponent.

If Congress and the political establishment were to accept the whistleblower's premise—that it is political meddling to investigate the potential corruption of one of America's most powerful families because it's too close to election time—the implications are profound. America's elite would officially be entitled to different rules and laws than ordinary people. This is something you're only supposed to see in the third world.

Want your family to avoid scrutiny? Just run for office! It's that easy.

The media and Democrats framed the impeachment around the concept that Trump had made a quid pro quo offer to Ukraine: relaunch the investigation into Hunter Biden or you don't get your aid. This is absurd for a number of reasons.

First of all, Trump wasn't exactly insistent that an investigation into Hunter resume. Though reporting on this has been spotty, there is no solid evidence that Ukraine relaunched an investigation into Hunter Biden. Ukraine wasn't even aware that the aid had been delayed until months after the call.[156]

Second, a quid pro quo isn't just legal, it is the standard when it comes to foreign aid. Foreign aid is not a welfare program for sh*thole countries paid for by U.S. taxpayers; the purpose of aid is so that we get cooperation and/or intelligence from the country that receives the aid. If they don't behave the way we require, they shouldn't get more aid.

Argubably, quid pro quos are inherently good, or at least a necessary evil. Maybe we should investigate foreign aid that is not offered up as part of a quid pro. If not a quid pro quo, why give out the money?

Zelensky himself said there never was a quid pro quo with Trump anyway.[157] What's more, then–European Union ambassador Gordon

Sondland said that Trump had said, "I want nothing. I want nothing. I want no quid pro quo. Tell Zelensky to do the right thing." [158]

So what were we even impeaching Trump for, anyway?

Perhaps the media saw the writing on the wall, because they eventually ditched the quid pro quo narrative. [159]

The results of the impeachment ritual were never in doubt. Trump would be impeached and the Senate would acquit him. The Democrat Media Complex was okay with this because it meant that more of Trump's time was wasted and his administration would have less energy to dedicate toward actually executing an agenda.

Adam "Pencil Neck" Schiff led the impeachment charge. [160] Though he was short on substance, he was long on theatrics. His witnesses testified in secret and Republicans weren't allowed to question them. They weren't even allowed to question the *not*-whistleblower; meaning, Team Trump wasn't allowed to cross-examine his accuser. Hunter Biden, the catalyst of it all, also never testified. The media received selectively leaked information and enthusiastically reported every meaningless detail. The public was never allowed to see the full witness transcripts from the secret testimony, which is remarkable considering the end goal was to remove a duly elected president.

At one point, Pencil Neck performed a dramatization of President Trump's call with Zelensky with fabricated quotes like, "I want you to make up dirt on my political opponent, understand? Lots of it." [161]

Why would he make up quotes if he really had the goods?

Schiff even revived a Russia collusion allegation during the hearings. [162]

It was a jubilee of fake news. And not only was our media okay with all this, they were participatory, cheering it on every step of the way.

CNN political analyst Joe Lockhart tweeted details of a fake conversation that he had "overheard" between Republican senators on impeachment. [163] It was retweeted more than thirteen thousand times.

CNN covered the impeachment obsessively, round the clock, despite the fact that they were hemorrhaging viewers. [164]

But they *had* to cover the impeachment obsessively, because it was "historic." [165] The media constantly reminded news consumers that this impeachment was, if nothing else, "historic." Bloomberg, *Politico,* Reuters, the *New Yorker,* the *Washington Post* . . . everyone who is anyone described the impeachment as "historic." [166]

On December 18, 2019, the inevitable came and President Trump was impeached.[167] Article one, which accused the president of abuse of power, passed 230–197; Republicans all voted against the resolution along with two Democrats, Representatives Collin Peterson (D-MN) and Jeff Van Drew (D-NJ), joining them.

(Legal scholars are divided on whether abuse of power is sufficient grounds for impeachment. After all, which president hasn't abused power? Maybe William Henry Harrison, who was in office for a month. James Madison was obsessed with not abusing power, so he might be off the hook, too. But who else, honestly?)[168]

The second article of impeachment—essentially that Trump obstructed Congress's ability to conduct the bogus impeachment process—passed the House with 229–198 votes. Van Drew, Peterson, and Representative Jared Golden (D-ME) voted against it. Justin Amash, now an Independent, voted in favor of article one. Representative Tulsi Gabbard (D-HI) voted present for both articles.

Five *Washington Post* reporters celebrated with a "Merry Impeachmas" dinner.[169] Shameless reporter Rachel Bade said her tweet (that literally said "Merry Impeachmas from the WaPo team!") was misinterpreted. (Fake news about fake news!)[170]

Many impeachment bombshells led to embarrassing corrections, including one from ABC that claimed a Zelensky adviser was informed that discussing Joe Biden was a "precondition" of a Trump call with Zelensky. Not only did the story turn out to be false, but ABC's Zelensky adviser wasn't actually a current Zelensky adviser.[171] It was just more blatant fake news weaponized against Trump.[172]

CNN's Jake Tapper worked himself into a lather defending Hunter Biden from Representative Jim Jordan (R-OH) on his show *State of the Union*. Tapper accused Jordan of making "wild allegations" against Joe Biden's son, then the anchor misrepresented the facts around the firing of Ukrainian prosecutor Viktor Shokin. "Joe Biden was trying to get a prosecutor who was not pursuing corruption fired," Tapper said.[173] However, he testified in a sworn affidavit that he was fired because the vice president was upset he was nosing into the Biden-connected company and that it could cost Ukraine aid.[174]

Paul Callan, a CNN legal analyst, got even more carried away than Tapper, openly fantasizing about Mike Pence getting removed from office for being a "co-conspirator" who reinforced Trump's quid pro quo.[175] This would clear the way for—President Nancy Pelosi.

Fox News's Chris Wallace enthusiastically hyped the impeachment news cycle.[176]

But the real steroid boost for all of these fake news stories came from social media companies. While the impeachment saga allegedly was about Donald Trump trying to manipulate the 2020 election, it ended up being a dry run for the tech establishment to manipulate it on behalf of Joe Biden. New censorship tactics and strategies emerged during the impeachment saga that were later deployed during the 2020 election.

For one, a YouTube "error" took down the livestreams of both Breitbart News and the pro-Trump Right Side Broadcasting Network while we covered the Senate trial.[177] Establishment and left-wing channels (redundant?) remained online during that time.

A couple of weeks later, Google, YouTube's parent company, censored Senator Rand Paul.[178] YouTube banned a video in which the Kentucky senator used the name Eric Ciaramella. Anonymous, unelected Google employees flushed thoughtful commentary by an influential U.S. senator down the memory hole. That's power.

Facebook took its most Orwellian steps to date by removing legitimate and accurate news reports simply for mentioning the alleged "whistleblower's" name. Facebook censored LaCorte News, a news organization founded by former Fox News executive Ken LaCorte, to protect Ciaramella. LaCorte's page was erased despite having built up 3.4 million followers.[179]

Facebook also removed individual Breitbart posts naming Ciaramella.

As outrageous as this seems in a country that prides itself on "freedom of speech," Washington did nothing. Even though Ciaramella was a semipublic figure (he had served on the National Security Council) and was believed by many to be engaging in a public effort to significantly undermine the legally elected American president, merely uttering his name was a thought crime punishable by cancellation.

This was a preview of things to come.

The impeachment was still doomed in the Senate. Article one on abuse of power failed 52 to 48. All Republicans other than Mitt Romney voted to acquit President Trump. Article two failed 53 to 47 purely along partisan lines.

CNN had reported, "A somber Pelosi wields her impeachment power in 'sadness,'" but the Democrat Media Complex celebrated throughout the impeachment process. On January 15, 2020, a "solemn" Pelosi sent the articles of impeachment to the Senate, but not without a signing ceremony replete with commemorative pens.[180]

Though impeachment supposedly centered on Trump's alleged corruption, it became clear as the saga wore on that he was being held to a different set of rules as veterans of the Washington swamp. Even if you disagree with me and believe that Trump's Zelensky phone call was corrupt, Trump was engaging in a type of behavior that appears to be commonplace in our nation's capital. I believe the establishment media bears significant responsibility for this reality. For example, the press devoted little coverage to Burisma while Joe Biden was vice president. Searches show that the *New York Times* and *Washington Post* published only three articles mentioning Burisma prior to 2019.[181] (Recall that Hunter joined the board in 2014 and Schweizer's *Secret Empires* was published in March 2018.)

In fact, James Risen, who in 2015 wrote the first article that appeared in the *New York Times* about Hunter, Joe, Burisma, and Ukraine, penned an essay for the *Intercept* in 2019, wagging his finger at conservatives' preoccupation with the story, saying it had been "lost in a swamp of right-wing opposition research, White House lies, and bizarre follow-up stories."[182] It does not appear that Risen wrote about Burisma between that 2015 article and when Trump had landed himself in the impeachment soup. Where was his follow-up in all those years in between?

And why was it that Trump's supposed quid pro quo was worthy of attention but not Biden's? Joe's conflict of interest appeared to be at least as overt. After all, Joe apparently knew that his son was working for Burisma. (The *New Yorker* reported that Hunter discussed Burisma with Joe: "Dad said, 'I hope you know what you are doing,' and I said, 'I do.'")[183]

Several Obama administration officials raised concerns about Burisma, but it appears that Joe was not receptive.[184] Biden reportedly told one State Department official that he didn't have the "bandwidth" to deal with concerns about Hunter and Ukraine.[185] Later, on the campaign trail, a member of the public asked Joe about Burisma; Joe called him "fat," "a damn liar," and challenged him to a push-up contest.[186] (Biden flack Symone Sanders absurdly said that Biden was saying the word "facts," not calling the overweight man "fat.")

The *Atlantic*'s Sarah Chayes summed up the shady influence-peddling culture that has subsumed Washington, D.C., in a September 27, 2019, article titled "Hunter Biden's Perfectly Legal, Socially Acceptable Corruption": "The renewed focus on Ukraine raises jangling questions: How did dealing in influence to burnish the fortunes of repugnant world leaders for large payoffs become a business model? How could America's leading lights convince themselves—and us—that this is acceptable?"

While Chayes believes that Trump did commit an impeachable offense—she described it as "shockingly corrupt" and "a danger to American democracy"—she laments that the ethical standards for businessman-politicians is too often whatever is legal. "All too often, the scandal isn't that the conduct in question is forbidden by federal law, but rather, how much scandalous conduct is perfectly legal—and broadly accepted," she writes.[187]

The media's collective hypocrisy of acting like Trump engaged in anything worse than D.C. business as usual is too much to bear.

Actually, maybe the biggest surprise of the whole impeachment ordeal was that for once in Trump's Washington, things actually were "business as usual."

Though, in Trump's Washington, I suppose nothing was ever "business as usual."

It is believed that on the exact day Speaker Pelosi sent the article of impeachment to the Senate, the first person with the Wuhan coronavirus arrived in the United States from China. The first COVID-19 case was confirmed in Washington State six days later. While America focused almost exclusively on the Senate impeachment trial, the Chinese virus began wreaking havoc. Donald Trump was acquitted on both impeachment articles on February 5, the same day the House Democrats finally took up coronavirus.

The Democrats had always believed that impeachment was a win-win. Best-case scenario, they get lucky and actually throw Trump out of office. Worst-case scenario, they tar a president they loathe, make his life miserable, and stall his agenda.

What happened in actuality was that they had distracted the entire country during the crucial first few weeks of what would become the biggest epidemic in a hundred years.[188]

Impeachment scholars can differ on whether impeachment is a "political act." If you were undecided on this issue, I believe you now have your answer.

This particular time-consuming and ultimately insignificant impeachment was nothing more than a political tactic by Pencil Neck and the Resistance. (Could be the name of an eighties cover band.) And it wasn't a particularly effective one at that. Just a few months later, the Democrats held their virtual Democratic National Convention and didn't use the "I" word at all.[189] In fact, the key players in the impeachment, most notably Adam Schiff, were not given prominence during the convention.[190]

Ultimately, impeachment was all just for show, and to give Trump a hard time.

Nothing more.

CHAPTER 2

MEET THE PRESS

Before I get into a few deep-dive examinations of three of the most dangerous purveyors of weaponized fake news in the American media landscape (the *New York Times*, MSNBC, and Bloomberg News), I believe it's important to focus on a few individuals who control the American news landscape, to one degree or another. These are the people who fund, publish, edit, report, or anchor the news broadcasts you and your fellow citizens consume on a daily basis. They are not neutral automatons or merely "liberal-leaning." No, these individuals brazenly advance the agenda of the corporate media apparatuses and the Democrat Party, and meeting a few of them will give you a sense of how they make decisions that benefit already powerful establishment insiders and disenfranchise the individual and the outsider.

There are many examples that are well known. The fact that George Stephanopoulos, who hosts ABC's *Good Morning America,* was Bill Clinton's White House communications director is so often repeated in articles and books on media bias that it is a running joke in the Breitbart newsroom.

It's also fairly well known that CNN's Jake Tapper is married to a former Planned Parenthood field organizer.[1]

CNN's Jim Sciutto joined the network from a gig in the Barack Obama administration.[2]

CNN's Chris Cuomo, or as he is known at Breitbart News, "Fredo," is the younger brother of Democrat New York governor Andrew Cuomo and the son of former Democrat New York governor Mario Cuomo.

"Fredo" is a reference to the dumb brother in the Godfather movies who ended up in a media job. I credit Breitbart writer, and my actual godfather, John Nolte with popularizing the nickname. CNN's Fredo was humiliated in August 2019 when he melted down at a heckler who called him "Fredo" to his face in New York City; Fredo responded by saying the word "Fredo" is the equivalent of the N-word, but for Italians. (It isn't.)[3]

CNN head Jeff Zucker chose Fredo to anchor the prime-time 9 p.m. hour over Tapper.[4] Since then, Fredo has made a fool of himself on a number of occasions. He has defended the radicals of Antifa multiple times, calling the group a "good cause"; he once compared the violent far-leftists to Allied troops storming the beaches of Normandy, France, in World War II.[5] Cuomo has said Black Lives Matter protests need not be peaceful (which directly contradicts the language of the First Amendment of the U.S. Constitution).[6] "Now too many see the protests as the problem," he opined on his CNN show, referring to the violent uprisings after George Floyd's death in the summer of 2020. "No, the problem is what forced your fellow citizens to take to the streets: persistent, poisonous inequities and injustice." So, the Black Lives Matter looters were victims of the system and were not actually part of the problem. Cuomo also had a hoax "quarantine" after being diagnosed with coronavirus (more on this later) and was busted in blatant mask hypocrisy, ignoring the advice he had given to his television audience—and the threats from his more powerful brother.[7] Technically, the elder Cuomo should have fined his younger brother.[8]

CNN seemingly doesn't care about conflicts of interest.[9] After all, network president Jeff Zucker let his then-fifteen-year-old son Andrew join Democrat senator Cory Booker's Internet start-up as a "millennial adviser." The Zucker spawn was even given stock. It was a stupid move by Zucker, especially since the teenage son of a media mogul didn't need the money. Jeff famously threw young Andrew a lavish bar mitzvah just two years prior at the Four Seasons hotel featuring superstar rapper Drake. Drake's fee for the evening was reportedly $250,000 (Zucker purportedly cheapo-ed out when Kanye West, Andrew's first choice, asked for a cool million for one night's work, according to *Elle* magazine).[10]

The list goes on.

Behind-the-scenes decision makers at outlets like CNN are also literally in bed with the Biden/Democrat establishment. Take CNN senior vice president of newsgathering Virginia Moseley, for example.[11] Her husband, Tom Nides, served as deputy secretary of state under Hillary Clinton. He is currently managing director and vice chairman of the super-national investment bank Morgan Stanley. Nides was a top bundler for Biden's 2020 campaign and is on the advisory board of the Biden Institute at the University of Delaware.[12] It appears as though Nides and Moseley shamelessly feed each other information: WikiLeaks released an email showing Nides tipping off Hillary Clinton campaign manager John Podesta to a favorable CNN poll that was soon to be released. Biden secretary of state Tony Blinken was a CNN analyst.[13]

Karine Jean-Pierre, Biden's deputy press secretary, is married to CNN anchor Suzanne Malveaux.[14]

Big business cash. Democrat politics. Corporate media influence. These are the ingredients that create a culture of corruption among America's ruling class.

While the revolving door of CNN employees and Democrat Party power players spins in a seemingly endless loop, other media companies are just as bad.

(Though several Breitbart employees joined the Trump administration, we openly state our biases.)

Over at MSNBC, presidential historian Jon Meacham, legal analyst Barbara McQuade, political analyst Richard Stengel, and health expert Ezekiel Emanuel all ditched the peacock network for Biden World.[15]

As with CNN, MSNBC's less-public influencers are dedicated establishment Democrats. NBCUniversal CEO Jeff Shell was a major bundler for the Obama campaign.[16] In 2013, President Obama appointed him chairman of the Broadcasting Board of Governors, which oversees Voice of America and Radio Free Europe/Asia. Shell's wife, Laura, was a heavyweight bundler for Biden.[17] His sister is Dana Shell Smith, whom Barack Obama appointed ambassador to Qatar; she was held over into the early months of the Trump administration, only leaving after she had trashed the American president while she was overseas.[18]

Jeff Shell is one of the most powerful people at NBCUniversal, and his family is passionately dedicated to the Democrat political establishment, yet we're expected to believe they will preside over responsible news coverage. This isn't mere bias; this is potential corruption.

One of the more shameless stars of NBC News is none other than

Chuck Todd. Todd's wife, Kristian Denny, is a major Democratic campaign consultant.[19] According to OpenSecrets, Denny's firm, Maverick Strategies, was paid over $900,000 by the Bernie Sanders campaign in 2020 and over $1.5 million from Sanders in 2016, among many examples.[20]

In 2008, soon after she had become a U.S. senator, Amy Klobuchar and her husband, John Bessler, began renting a house in Arlington, Virginia, from Todd. She and her husband paid the Todds $3,200 a month.[21] This relationship went undisclosed for years in interviews and debates, even when Todd was the moderator.

Print media has the same incestuousness issues as TV news.

New York Times media correspondent and former BuzzFeed editor in chief Ben Smith has maintained his stock in BuzzFeed, an outlet he is tasked with covering. He claimed that he intended to sell his shares—as of March 2021, this hasn't happened yet (more on Smith later). NBCUniversal is one of BuzzFeed's largest shareholders and is a "strategic partner." Smith seems to have an especially close relationship with NBC; NBC media correspondent Dylan Byers was given the scoop that Smith was moving over to the *Times*.[22] Smith also famously (and embarrassingly) defended NBC and attacked Ronan Farrow after NBC had passed on Farrow's Pulitzer-winning #MeToo reporting.[23] NBC has pumped in $400 million to BuzzFeed; observers have speculated in the past that NBC will one day take over BuzzFeed outright.[24]

But maybe this is all just coincidental and not at all evidence that the media elite are easily capable of widespread corruption and are on a collective mission to maintain the status quo.

"Suckers and Losers": A Fake News Instant Classic

The single fakest fake news story of the 2020 election news cycle—and there was a lot of competition—was a report published in the *Atlantic* by editor in chief Jeffery Goldberg.[25] On September 3, 2020, Goldberg posted an article with the bombshell headline "Trump: Americans Who Died in War Are 'Losers' and 'Suckers.'" Notice there are no caveats or legalese in this headline. There is no wiggle room. The way this is written, Goldberg knows Trump said these horrible things. The subheadline was equally emphatic: "The president has repeatedly disparaged the intelligence of service members, and asked that wounded veterans be kept out of military parades, multiple sources tell The Atlantic."

Explosive, if true. Appalling, really. No one should vote for Donald Trump if he actually said these things and meant them. And the EIC of the *Atlantic* was gambling his name on the headline being accurate.

And the timing of this story was literally too good to be true. These accounts of a saga that played out in 2018 somehow surfaced mere weeks before the 2020 presidential election.

And not just that. The story was released (coincidentally, so we're to believe) right as terrific jobs data was released and promising news was breaking in the Middle East, where relations between Israel and the Muslim world were normalizing by the day. In other words, it interrupted a precious favorable news moment for President Trump.[26] All of this was placed on the back burner, while we dealt with yet another anti-Trump hysteria du jour.

A summary of the *Atlantic*'s story: Goldberg reported that Trump canceled an appearance at a commemoration ceremony for fallen American Marines at the Aisne-Marne American Cemetery outside of Paris in 2018. Why did he bail on the visit? Because he allegedly "feared his hair would become disheveled in the rain," according to this super-serious news report. "Why should I go to that cemetery? It's filled with losers," Trump allegedly said. Trump then reportedly referred to 1,800+ Marines who perished at Belleau Wood as "suckers."

The story exploded across international media. It was everywhere. You couldn't avoid it. It was the perfect Rorschach test. If you were on the left, you're thinking that with exactly two months to go until election day, the vaunted *Atlantic* had finally gotten the Bad Orange Man dead to rights. And they had four(!) sources backing up their headline. But, if you were a Trump backer, every word of the article read like satire, a left-wing fantasy, or maybe one of Adam Schiff's stupid dramatizations.

In a massive yet entirely predictable breach of journalistic ethics, it's also possible that the *Atlantic* coordinated the article launch with the Biden campaign. The piece ran on a Thursday evening, and by the following morning a left-wing group called VoteVets already had cut an anti-Trump ad around it, which aired on MSNBC's *Morning Joe*. The rapid nature of this timeline is suspicious.

That morning, the Biden campaign held a press call featuring Democrat senator and Purple Heart recipient Tammy Duckworth (IL), Democrat congressman and Marine Conor Lamb (PA), and Gold Star dad and 2016 DNC star Khizr Khan.[27] The duration of the call was spent explaining that Donald Trump is a particularly horrible person.

Joe Biden held a press conference later that day.[28] He opened with a statement in which he invoked his late son, Beau, who was a veteran, in order to trash Trump as unfit for office. "When my son volunteered and joined the United States military, and went to Iraq for a year, won the Bronze Star and other commendations, he was not a sucker," he said, treating the *Atlantic*'s bogus story as if it were a papal bull.[29]

The first question at the presser went to a reporter from—brace yourself for shocking information—the *Atlantic*! The question, asked by reporter Edward-Isaac Dovere,[30] was what you would have expected, only more absurd: "When you hear these remarks—'suckers,' 'losers,' recoiling from amputees—what does it tell you about President Trump's soul, and the life he leads?"

What does a fake news smear tell you about President Trump's soul!? This was a preview of the type of questions I'm sure we'll see asked of Joe Biden throughout his administration.

Other media moved quickly to boost the *Atlantic*'s Trump attack.

Even the tech platforms seemed to be all in on hyping the story. It soared across the social web without any of the notes of caution or fact-checks that became increasingly commonplace throughout 2020.

NBC News White House correspondent Peter Alexander did his part to try to legitimize the story by asking President Trump if he needed to apologize.[31]

Even some Fox News personalities got in on the fake news bonanza. Reporter Jennifer Griffin claimed that she had confirmed some of the details of the *Atlantic* story, citing two—brace yourself for shocking information—unnamed "senior" administration officials.[32]

Were they the same "sources"? How would we ever know? Everyone is anonymous. And what makes them "senior" anyway? Does anyone really know? But it didn't matter, so long as the story harmed Trump.

President Trump called for Griffin to be fired, at which point several of her Fox colleagues jumped in to defend her.

There was one glaring hole in the *Atlantic*'s reporting, though: all four sources were anonymous. There wasn't a single on-record witness cited who backed up the article's central claims.

Trump World maintained that the president couldn't make the helicopter trip to the cemetery that day due to inclement weather around Paris; FOIA'd documents suggest weather was indeed the reason for the cancellation.[33]

A flood of on-record sources who were on the trip with President Trump denied Goldberg's anonymous accounts. The U.S. ambassador to France and Monaco, Jaime McCourt, threw heavy shade at the *Atlantic*, telling Breitbart exclusively, "I never spoke to the *Atlantic*, and I can't imagine who would." "POTUS has NEVER denigrated any member of the U.S. military or anyone in service to our country," she continued.[34]

More and more on-record witnesses weighed in:

Former White House press secretary Sarah Sanders called the story "total BS."

Actual senior adviser Stephen Miller called it a "despicable lie."

Presidential counselor Johnny DeStefano said the story "is not true. Period."

Deputy White House press secretary Hogan Gidley said the piece contained "disgusting, grotesque, reprehensible lies."

The president's former body man Jordan Karem said, "This is not even close to being factually accurate. Plain and simple, it just never happened." "Again," he tweeted, "this is 100 percent false."[35]

And finally, the pièces de résistance, anti-Trump forces with firsthand knowledge of the trip and the conversations in question began disputing the *Atlantic* and Jeffrey Goldberg. Trump's former national security adviser John Bolton, who had turned on Trump in highly dramatic and public fashion, flat out denied both the Goldberg report and the Jen Griffin report during an interview on Fox News. "That was false and I recounted that in my book, *Room Where It Happened*," said Bolton. Here's what he said occurred:

> The people I recall being there were John Kelly, one of his aides, Mike Pompeo, myself, Jamie McCourt, our ambassador to France. We had this discussion, it was mostly John Kelly presenting the logistical reasons why the trip couldn't take place and the president assented to the recommendations that he not go. He didn't protest that he really needed to go. He just sort of took the facts as they were, a very straight weather call.[36]

This account is devastating to the *Atlantic's* credibility because not only did Jeffrey Goldberg allege that Trump said horrible things about dead troops, but Trump also allegedly refused to commemorate them because it would have messed up his coif. Bolton, a Trump hater, says he can't confirm the former charge and flat out rejects the latter.

Former deputy White House chief of staff Zach Fuentes put the final dagger in the *Atlantic's* report via an exclusive comment to Breitbart News.

Remember, all roads lead to Breitbart.

Fuentes, a close ally of then–White House chief of staff John Kelly, had briefed President Trump on the weather that day. Here's what he told our Washington political editor Matthew Boyle:

> You can put me on record denying that I spoke with *The Atlantic*. I don't know who the sources are. I did not hear POTUS call anyone losers when I told him about the weather. Honestly, do you think General Kelly would have stood by and let ANYONE call fallen Marines losers?

The last point is critical, and something that the *Atlantic* probably didn't consider. John Kelly might have had a strained relationship with President Trump, both while serving as chief of staff and afterward, but he is a four-star general and Gold Star father.[37] His son Robert M. Kelly was killed on November 9, 2010, by an improvised explosive device in Afghanistan while serving his nation as a Marine.[38] The *Atlantic's* report implies that General Kelly stood idly by as Donald Trump trashed dead troops, like his own son.

This was unthinkable, if not impossible.

The fake news story had officially collapsed.

If you think that this would be a setback for Jeffrey Goldberg or the *Atlantic*, you're misunderstanding what is important in establishment American media circles. Credibility, integrity, accuracy, even breaking big stories are no longer what is rewarded by our media. Weaponizing your platform to attack Donald Trump and his supporters on behalf of the corporate establishment is the apotheosis of journalism in these modern times.

Yes, Goldberg and the *Atlantic* had served their purpose. What would have been a terrific news cycle for President Trump was wiped off the front pages for a few days while the media debated this hoax.

The *Atlantic* reportedly saw a big influx in subscriptions after the fake news article grabbed international media attention. (The *Atlantic* never retracted the story, and editor Goldberg says he stands by his reporting.) Instead of condemning the *Atlantic* for their shoddy and clearly partisan journalism, the media was in a congratulatory mood.[39] "The Atlantic gained 20,000 subscribers after Trump dismissed it as a 'dying' magazine," CNN enthusiastically reported.[40]

Weeks later, long after the *Atlantic* story had been debunked, Barack Obama repeated the "suckers" and "losers" lie while on the stump for Joe Biden. Said Obama, "I can tell you this, Joe Biden would never call the men and women of our military 'suckers or losers.' Who does that?"[41]

As Orwell warned, "Who controls the past controls the future. Who controls the present controls the past." The truth isn't necessarily the *truth*. The *truth* is what the fake news media and the Democrat establishment decide is the *truth*. If the *Atlantic* and Joe Biden and MSNBC all agree to push an obvious lie, does that lie over time become the *truth*?

I shudder to think how history will remember this event.

The *Atlantic* and Laurene Powell Jobs

As a news outlet, the *Atlantic* is abominable. They once had to massively overhaul an anti-science article that claimed fetal heartbeats are "imaginary"; the author was lamenting that advances in sonograms and other technologies used to monitor pregnancies (and save lives) were leading to fewer abortions.[42] The magazine routinely uses solo anonymous sources to trash Donald Trump and his allies.[43] They attempted to hire a single conservative columnist, a Never Trump troll from the *National Review* named Kevin Williamson, who made it exactly one column before getting fired, canceled by the woke mob. The essence of his one column for the *Atlantic* was—you guessed it—criticizing others in the conservative movement, including the venerable Victor Davis Hanson, also of *National Review*. It must have been incredibly awkward when Williamson slinked back to *NR* after trashing his colleague.

The *Atlanatic* ran a major piece legitimizing more censorship by Big Tech oligarchs and praised China's Internet authoritarianism.[44] From an article by Jack Goldsmith, a Harvard Law School professor, and Andrew Keane Woods, a professor of law at the University of Arizona:

In the great debate of the past two decades about freedom versus control of the network, China was largely right and the United States was largely wrong. Significant monitoring and speech control are inevitable components of a mature and flourishing internet, and governments must play a large role in these practices to ensure that the internet is compatible with a society's norms and values.

According to Freedom House, China ranks among the worst countries on earth when it comes to Internet freedom.[45]

Horrible journalists, often horrible people. But they do all these horrible things with the patina of sophistication. The magazine is very old and very glossy and lots of important people used to write there and some still do. That means something to certain people.

But it really only needs to mean something to *one* person. And that person is Laurene Powell Jobs. Jobs, whom Vox describes as "one of the world's most important philanthropists," is the widow of Apple founder and billionaire computer guru Steve Jobs. She has become a secret superpower behind a vast network of left-wing media outlets, organizations, and politicians.

Laurene Powell Jobs topped Business Insider's list of world's richest women in tech in 2019, even though she's not really "in tech."[46] She's in the philanthropy/being an heiress business. What Jobs does is leverage her incredible wealth, infinite Rolodex, and relatively secretive public persona to wield unfathomable amounts of influence on the American culture. If there's a well-known persona comparable to Laurene Powell Jobs, it's Hungarian billionaire George Soros. Soros is known for his philanthropy, but also for being a one-man piggy bank for the far left. (Recently, Soros-connected groups have spent big pushing the Green New Deal, taxpayer-funded health care for illegal aliens, and the expansion of mail-in voting.)[47]

A good share of Laurene Powell Jobs's power is through the Emerson Collective (EC), which she founded; she currently serves as its president.[48] The Emerson Collective, according to *Forbes*, is "a hybrid philanthropic and investing limited liability company." That's a pretty murky description (which is probably the point), but it seems like the EC has devised a clever and convenient structure where they can claim they are "investing" when the business has a chance to succeed and they are doing "philanthropy" when they fund entities for purely ideological reasons with little or no hope of making money. I'm not sure which of the two categories it falls under, but the Emerson Collective owns the *Atlantic*.[49]

Obama's education secretary Arne Duncan and general services administrator Dan Tangherlini are part of EC.[50] Emerson Collective employees give almost exclusively to Democrats.[51]

The Emerson Collective funds Democratic causes that most nonprofits wouldn't be able to touch. For example, in 2016, EC gave $2.5 million to DNC super-PAC Priorities Action USA. Nonprofits are normally restricted from engaging in overt political activity, but EC's unique structure has thus far kept them legally protected. EC also hosted a dozen DNC-aligned voter registration groups for a fund-raiser in 2020.

Forbes lists Jobs as one of the ten richest women on earth, with a net worth of around $16 billion, mostly from her family stakes in two of the world's biggest companies: Apple and Disney.[52] The revenue from a print magazine with a mediocre digital presence like the *Atlantic* in a given year probably isn't enough to pay for the crew and annual maintenance on her yacht. So why does EC invest in this brand? It's possibly because Laurene Powell Jobs has an agenda and sees sleekly packaged fake news as a way to advance it.

In a *New York Times* puff piece on Jobs and the Emerson Collective, EC managing director of media and former *New York Times* reporter Peter Lattman (again, the media is incestuous) said that "we invest in and support super high-quality journalism."[53]

Who doesn't love "super high-quality journalism"?

So, which outlets are supplying this journalism?

The EC funds the *Atlantic* and Axios, both prestige brands. They also fund *Mother Jones,* which is far left but does get some good scoops. ProPublica, which is part of the activist left but also does solid reporting, is also EC funded.[54] The Emerson Collective has also partnered with NowThis, a hyperpartisan left-wing viral news video operation targeted at millennials; NowThis champions woke causes and makes heroes out of Democrat politicians and leftist celebrities. Axios broke the news of the partnership (again, so incestuous!) between the Emerson Collective and NowThis.[55]

(Axios routinely breaks news about businesses that share the same investors; I found well over a dozen examples of this while researching this book. Of the examples I encountered, Axios only disclosed the business relationships about half the time.)

The synergy between Jobs's media empire and her political agenda is not exactly subtle. The Emerson Collective has partnered with Stacey Abrams's Fair Fight voting effort, which has been touted at Emerson Collective outlets, including Axios, the *Atlantic*, and NowThis.[56]

Laurene Powell Jobs and the Emerson Collective's business model is simple, fairly genius, ethically suspect, and potentially corrupt. Fund the activists, organizations, and politicians that share her ideology, and fund the media outlets that are supposed to cover them neutrally. This not only ensures a degree of positive coverage, it makes it far less likely any nosey journalists will snoop around—after all, many of them are literally on the payroll. The EC media outlets are providing incalculable amounts of what is the equivalent of soft money contributions to their favorite causes and candidates.

Jobs is more than just a major Democrat donor; she is said to have a "tight" personal relationship with Kamala Harris, who was a California senator before becoming vice president.[57] Naturally, the *Atlantic* has lavished praise on Harris, barely stopping short of endorsing her during the 2019–20 Democrat primaries.[58] Here is how the *Atlantic* described the scene when Kamala ordered a pulled pork sandwich at a humble South Carolina barbecue joint: "[T]he patrons are dazzled by Harris, whose star quality drew 20,000 people to her kickoff rally in Oakland. The dynamism she displayed there made the event feel like a cause, or a concert—Kamalapalooza—and gave her campaign significant momentum."

Evan Ryan, who previously worked as an aide to Hillary Clinton, Joe Biden, and John Kerry, was tapped as Joe Biden's White House cabinet secretary.[59] In 2016, she was recruited by Axios in what *Vanity Fair* called an "unconventional hire."[60] She helped spearhead the Washington-insider website's marketing and branding. She stepped down in May 2020, exercising over $350,000 in stock options, before joining Team Biden.[61] Her husband, Tony Blinken, is the U.S. secretary of state.

This is a massive network of Washington insiders, all conveniently placed throughout Laurene Powell Jobs's empire.

Some of Jobs's political efforts are much more brazen. She has funded ACRONYM, a Democratic technology venture, which has "invested" $25 million into Courier Newsroom.[62] Courier Newsroom claims to fund independent local newsrooms across the country. In actuality, Courier has avoided restrictions on online political advertising by couching pro-DNC content as news. For example, Courier produces laudatory pieces and videos on Democrat causes and candidates with factory-like regularity.

Bloomberg's Joshua Green described Courier as "the Left's plan to slip vote-swaying news into facebook" under the guise of "hypertargeted hometown news."[63] Left-of-center media watchdog NewsGuard was even more cynical: "Courier and Acronym are exploiting the widespread loss of local journalism to create and disseminate something we really don't need: hyperlocal partisan propaganda."[64]

This is all dirty. Perhaps this doesn't violate the letter of the law, but it appears to me that it violates the spirit of it. It's certainly unethical not to disclose these clandestine partnerships—it's arguably fraudulent not to. The Federal Election Commission (FEC) should be all over this; they are aware of what ACRONYM is doing.[65] And Laurene Powell Jobs is the connective tissue for all of these causes and outlets.

Interestingly, ACRONYM also launched Shadow Inc., the software developer behind the app that bungled the reporting of the results of the 2020 Iowa caucuses.[66]

According to an auditor commissioned by the Iowa Democratic Party,[67] the DNC's efforts to meddle with Shadow's software led to massive delays in reporting the caucus's results. "Without the DNC's intervention in that process, the IDP may have reported results in real-time as it intended," according to the report.

After app failures caused massive delays in the reporting of the results, Shadow Inc. came under fire for ties to the Democrat establishment. David Plouffe, President Obama's campaign architect, is on ACRONYM's board, and several top Shadow Inc. execs worked for Hillary Clinton.[68] Shadow's website also is far from transparent in terms of who owns it and runs it.

FEC records revealed that Pete Buttigieg's campaign paid at least $21,250 to Shadow for "software rights and subscriptions." When Buttigieg, the thirty-eight-year-old small-town mayor from Indiana, arguably won the caucuses, #MayorCheat trended on social media.[69] I guess Pete wasn't Twitter's preferred candidate!

Laurene Powell Jobs is a leviathan and her tentacles are seemingly everywhere in America's liberal landscape. She funds the prestigious, supposedly neutral liberal press; she funds the muckraker left-wing press. She funds Democrat candidates; she funds Democrat activists. She is well connected with the Democrat establishment and with the biggest international businesses. All of these entities work together, and Jobs is often the most important person in the various hierarchies. Yet she remains mysterious and far from a household name. Perhaps that's why Inside Philanthropy named her 2019's "Least Transparent Mega-giver." (Inside Philanthropy isn't exactly a right-wing group; they named George Soros "Philanthropist of the Year" that year.)

Much of her philanthropy is shielded from public view, and much of it isn't clearly philanthropic. Emerson Collective is billed as a "social change organization" (emersoncollective.com/social-justice/ is a festival of woke). But EC functions primarily as a private business owned by Jobs's personal trust. This shields it from IRS disclosure rules and allows it to more freely engage in political activity.

It's sly and devious, but considering how many media outlets are aligned with Jobs either financially or ideologically, it's no surprise that little reporting has been done on what appears to be a shadowy influence operation.

After all, if you're in media, she might be your boss one day. Maybe she already is.

Laurene Powell Jobs went to the Wharton School of Finance at the University of Pennsylvania and Stanford, she worked for Merrill Lynch and Goldman Sachs, she married well and inherited a lot of money, and her wealth is tied up in some of world's biggest companies. She *is* the establishment.

Her most prestigious publication, the *Atlantic*, was founded by Emerson Collective namesake Ralph Waldo Emerson; it had the founding motto "of no party or clique." That sentiment is laughable today under Jobs's leadership. It is one of the corporate Democrat establishment's favorite weapons. The Emerson Collective office features a mural inspired by Malcolm X's famed "Ballot or the Bullet" speech; the speech, largely about civil rights and black nationalism, is highly critical of the Democrat Party and powerful whites. What would these men think of a plutocrat tech heiress appropriating their names and legacies as part of a tenebrous political power play?

No one knows, and Laurene Powell Jobs certainly doesn't care.

CHAPTER 3

MOB RULE MEDIA

The *New York Times* in the Age of Woke

Adolph Ochs, the son of German-Jewish immigrants who came of age in Tennessee, purchased the *New York Times* (*NYT*) out of bankruptcy in 1896. Since then, members of the Ochs-Sulzberger family have continuously presided over the "newspaper of record." In 2017, Arthur Gregg (A.G.) Sulzberger took over as publisher, making him the fifth generation of Ochs-Sulzbergers to helm the *Times*.[1] His father, Arthur "Pinch" Sulzberger Jr., served as publisher from 1992 to 2017 and remained the company's chairman through the end of 2020.[2]

Over the years, the *NYT*'s leadership has come to represent a who's who of power players in elite progressive social circles. The New York Times Company board currently includes executives from AIG, Facebook, GoDaddy, Verizon, and more.[3]

(We are supposed to assume that the Gray Lady's coverage of these businesses and their respective industries is perfectly neutral and unbiased, without fail.)

In April 2018, John W. Rogers Jr. was elected to a board seat. A childhood friend of Craig Robinson, Michelle Obama's older brother, Rogers is a close associate of the Obamas.[4] He became an early supporter of Barack Obama's political career and has been an insider ever since, even allowing Obama's transition team to use the offices of his firm, Ariel Investments.[5] Following their tenure in government, Valerie Jarrett and Arne Duncan, both members of the Obamas' inner circle, joined Ariel. In 2019, the *New York Times* published a glowing profile of Mellody Hobson, Ariel's co-

CEO (with Rogers).[6] The *Times* did not disclose any of these relationships to their readers.

To put it more succinctly, the *New York Times* is a family business run in concert with powerful figures from Wall Street, Silicon Valley, and the Democrat Party.

If the establishment had an establishment—and it does—it is the *New York Times*. And it is crystal clear to honest observers of the *Times* that their editorial decisions reflect the people in their leadership.

The *New York Times* has been able to rely on a deep bench of supporters to steer it through crisis. In 2007 and 2008, during the financial crisis, New York City hedge fund Harbinger Capital Partners bought 20 percent of the *NYT* before mostly selling it by 2010.[7] Harbinger made it big betting against the housing market during the 2008 financial crisis, but was later fined $18 million by the SEC over an improper loan the company made to its chief executive, Philip Falcone.[8] Falcone used $113 million of his clients' funds to pay his personal taxes; he admitted to wrongdoing and agreed to a five-year ban from trading by the SEC in 2013.[9]

Mexican billionaire Carlos Slim Helú loaned the New York Times Company $250 million in 2009.[10] Slim doubled his stake to 16.8 percent in 2015, making him the company's largest shareholder. In 2017, he reduced his stake back to 8 percent.[11]

Why would Slim, a telecommunications magnate and one of the world's richest men (*Forbes* said he was in fact *the* richest person alive from 2010 to 2013), get involved in the *New York Times*? The *Times* was worth about $1 billion at the time, or roughly one-fiftieth Carlos Slim's wealth.[12] Is it because he wanted to beef up the copy desk and felt the need to ensure the metro editor got a raise? Or was it, perhaps, to gain influence via what was arguably the world's most important newspaper?

Slim has been a fierce advocate for America to grant amnesty to illegal aliens.[13] The *Times* has consistently pushed for amnesty since Slim's arrival.[14] In August 2014, he personally launched a campaign to advance this agenda.[15]

A month later, in September 2014, when Facebook was worth a mere $200 billion (it's worth about three-quarters of a trillion dollars today), founder and CEO Mark Zuckerberg went to Mexico City to deliver a speech at a charity event hosted by Carlos Slim, where he discussed, according to *Forbes*, reforming the U.S. immigration system.[16]

Rebecca van Dyck, then Facebook's marketing chief, joined the NYT Company board the following year.[17]

Connections like these are endless at the *Times* and an investigative team could spend years turning over every stone, each one revealing potential for corruption.

All of this is to say that the paper known for the motto "All the news that's fit to print" is run in a manner less focused on comprehensiveness and accuracy and appears to be more focused on advancing agendas and vested interests. The *New York Times* is often used as a weapon for and against causes, usually political or cultural; those interests typically align with the globalist and liberal establishment figures who make up their personnel.

The *New York Times* is, essentially, a weapon. And that weapon is quite powerful.

Media Tricks to Fix the News

Reading the *New York Times*, as well as any other establishment media publication, requires something like a secret decoder ring; what is written on the page (or spoken in a broadcast) is not always literal and can only be fully understood if you know how to break the code.

Here are some other examples of hacks to better understand the establishment media. Feel free to take a photograph of this cheat sheet and save it for reference!

- Anything that can be politicized, will be politicized.
  Reportage on things that cannot be politicized (an increasingly smaller percentage of the paper) is typically far more credible.

- Good news on a preferred narrative typically appears on the front page.

- Bad news about a preferred narrative appears deep within the paper, or not at all.

- Good news on an undesirable narrative appears deep within the paper, or not at all.

• Bad news about an undesirable narrative is to be treated the same as good news for a preferred narrative.

• Within a given article, information that confirms the paper's preferred narrative is to be featured at the top of the article, ideally in the first sentence.

• Within a given article, information that rebuts a preferred narrative or confirms an undesirable narrative is to appear deep in the article, or not at all.

• An article's "hero" should be anyone who advances the causes of globalism, wokeness, skepticism of America and its values, and/or political leftism.
  ○ Additional unofficial "hero points" are added or subtracted based on the hero's race, sex, sexual orientation, and/or socioeconomic status.

• An article's "villain" is typically anyone in the article who advances the causes of nationalism, conservatism, or traditional American values.
  ○ A villain can also be someone who is insufficiently outraged at those who do not embrace modern woke leftism.
  ○ When someone is a villain, their race, sex, sexual orientation, and/or socioeconomic status are mostly irrelevant unless they can be used to portray the villain in an even more unfavorable light.

• Heroes need not be actual heroes; they can simply be victims.

• Heroes get glamorous "hero shot" photographs when possible.

• Villains get unflattering photographs, or none at all.

• Errors are acceptable, so long as they do not hurt the cause of globalism or modern woke leftism.
  ○ Errors that portray a preferred narrative negatively or an unfavorable narrative positively are never to be made. Ever.
  ○ Corrections are to be published discreetly, deep within the paper, if at all.

• Publicly acknowledging updates and corrections made to published stories is a business decision, not an ethical one. Meaning, do not draw attention to a mistake unless the attention will likely benefit the publication.

  ○ If posting an update or correction mitigates further reputational damage from the mistake or it enhances the paper's brand, acknowledge the update.

• If a villain is mentioned, a thumbnail biography of their worst moments and negative attributes must be included in the article, even if it does not furnish a fair representation of their life and works.

  ○ Any perceived sexism, racism, bigotry, or corruption in their past, even if previously discredited, must be mentioned.

  ○ Positive attributes are not to be included unless in the context of a "fall from grace" story arc.

• If a hero is mentioned, a thumbnail biography of their best moments and positive attributes must be included in the article, even if it does not furnish a fair representation of their life and works.

  ○ Any past instances of sexism, racism, bigotry, or corruption need not be mentioned.

  ○ Negative attributes are not to be included unless in the context of a triumphant story arc.

This list could go on and on. Try to add some more rules on your own!

Since the Trump era, the *Times'* favored narratives typically have centered on the villainy of President Trump and his allies, who are regarded as illegitimate, corrupt, and even dangerous. I've already mentioned a number of these examples in the Fake News Hall of Shame section.

Some mistakes have relatively low stakes but are highly revealing of the minds of the people who run the "newspaper of record." For example, in May 2018, the *Times* underestimated the crowd size at a Nashville rally for President Trump—by about 550 percent (they said about 1,000 people attended; fire marshals suggested it was around 5,500).[18] It's unthinkable that this mistake could have happened with a Democrat president.

Occasionally, the target of their fake news fights back. In June 2017, the *Times* published an editorial that blamed Sarah Palin for the shooting of then-congresswoman Gabby Giffords in Tucson in 2011.[19] Palin sued the *Times*, which corrected the story.[20] In August 2020, a judge said the lawsuit could continue (it is ongoing at the time this book is being written).[21] In this case, the fake news cost the *NYT* more than just credibility.

The *Times* often makes "mistakes" that make ideological adversaries seem racist or conspiratorial. For example, in November 2016, the *New York Times* falsely smeared Breitbart as a "birther" website, stating that we have "fed the lie that Mr. Obama is a Kenyan-born Muslim."[22] Breitbart has never published a single piece of content that advances that viewpoint, but in 2012 we were first to report what is likely the origin of the "birther" conspiracy: a pamphlet put out by Obama's literary agency (the now defunct Acton & Dystel) that claims the man who would become the forty-fourth president of the United States was "born in Kenya and raised in Indonesia and Hawaii."[23] However, we included a five-paragraph-long(!) note from senior management at the top of the article when it was first published, stating emphatically that we believe he was born in Honolulu, despite what his agency might have wanted us to think at the time.

(In 2015, the *Washington Post* reported on a leaked internal Clinton-world memo confirming that top Hillary Clinton staffers had been the impetus of the "birther" movement. They had planned to portray Barack Obama as not having American roots during the 2007–2008 Democrat primary.)[24]

Other fake news items made the *Times* itself seem like the ones trafficking in the conspiracy theories.[25] On April 6, 2020, four reporters, including superstar White House correspondent Maggie Haberman and chief White House correspondent Peter Baker, wrote that Trump potentially stood to profit if the controversial antimalaria drug Plaquenil (the brand name of hydroxychloroquine [HcQ]) became a widespread treatment for the coronavirus COVID-19. The president had a small but indirect financial stake in Sanofi, a French company that makes the drugs.

They appear to be entertaining the possibility that Trump isn't pushing HcQ because he genuinely believes it could be a safe way to help people, but he was hyping it to make money off the people who would listen to his advice and acquire the drug. Thus, since he has a vested interest (beyond trying to avoid more Americans dying on his watch), his opinion on the matter should be discounted, so the *Times* would have liked you to believe.

The *Times'* not-so-subtle suggestion that Trump's HcQ promotion was also presidential graft bounded across American media, and even made the massive British paper the *Guardian*.[26]

But even leftist fact-check outlet Snopes rated the claim "mostly false," stating "Trump's financial stake in these companies is virtually negligible—contained indirectly via mutual funds—and administered through three family trusts he does not control. As a generic drug, hydroxychloroquine is unlikely to provide any one company with significant profits compared to other proprietary drugs."[27]

Financial website MarketWatch noted that Trump's stake in Sanofi could be as small as $99.[28] The implication is that the *New York Times* was suggesting that a billionaire with golf courses on multiple continents and five-star hotels across the world might have been trying to bilk the American public on HcQ so that he could make a few bucks.

None of these essential facts appear in the *Times'* article. (Remember: information that rebuts a preferred narrative is to appear deep in the article, or not at all.)

It would be easy to brush this off as typical left-wing anti-Trump fake news, but if HcQ had turned out to be a miracle cure, the *Times'* article would have certainly gotten innocent people killed.

The Habermans

Maggie Haberman, the marquee name of the four authors on the HcQ piece and also a CNN contributor, was certainly the most powerful reporter on Trump World during his presidency (unless you count the tweeter in chief Trump himself). Trump officials, especially the president, continued to feed her information throughout his term. Trump craves attention from the *New York Times* and always has; multiple people close to the former president have explained this wildly self-destructive instinct to me, always repeating the mantra "it's his hometown paper." Haberman was the top White House reporter of the former New Yorker's hometown paper, so she got the access. Simple as that. She was even dubbed the "Trump Whisperer" by media-establishment colleagues.[29]

(Despite claims to the contrary, Trump continuously tried to win over the media establishment. This is perhaps why he did ten hours of interviews with Bob Woodward, which turned into the mega-bestselling book *Fear*.)

In December 2016, the Intercept's Glenn Greenwald and Lee Fang published a document reportedly from hacker "Guccifer 2.0" that confirmed[30] the suspected coziness between the Hillary Clinton campaign and the establishment media. Haberman, who was then at *Politico*, was referred to as a "friendly journalist" who "never disappointed" if you placed a story with her. (Haberman was among the group of journalists who humiliated themselves in 2015 when they allowed the Clinton campaign to corral them with a literal rope during an event in New Hampshire.[31])

In 2018, when President Trump clearly referred to brutal MS-13 gang members as "animals," the media falsely insisted he was talking about all illegal immigrants.[32] Haberman amplified that fake news, appearing to suggest that context doesn't necessarily matter because of Trump's past "dehumanizing" comments about "immigrants of color."[33]

In the Trump era, this type of journalism not only gets you on page A1 of the country's biggest paper, it wins you awards.

To get a sense of the conspiratorial minds Haberman and her colleague Baker possess, look no further than when in October 2020 they published a bizarre story that Trump had delivered a speech in front of "digital backdrop" and not from the South Lawn of the White House as it had appeared on his Twitter feed.[34]

The *Times* published the baseless (and, frankly, absurd) conspiracy theory and then quietly deleted it at around 3 a.m. the following day.[35] They never acknowledged that the article was updated, nor did they post a correction.

(Remember: Errors are acceptable, so long as they do not hurt the cause of modern woke leftism. It is not necessary to acknowledge to readers that an article has been updated since its original publication.)

The consequences for pushing such blatant fake news were, as far as I can tell, nonexistent for Haberman. First of all, her mistakes almost always made Trump look worse than he deserves, which is acceptable at the *Times*. But perhaps more important, it was as if Trump couldn't help himself from giving her scoop after scoop.

For these reasons, not only is Haberman able to get away with inaccurate reporting, but she got to cash in on the access with a CNN contributorship. Haberman is not particularly well spoken nor is she telegenic, but she had access to the then-POTUS, which is all you need.

In 2018, for example, she referred to the resignation of General James Mattis from his post as secretary of defense as an "astonishing rebuke of Trumpism."[36] The president's base despised Mattis and believe him to be an archetypal globalist. The general even reportedly said that Joe Biden must eliminate "America First" from U.S. foreign policy.[37] Whether you like "Trumpism" or not (disclosure: I consider President Trump's foreign policy to have been an overwhelming success), it is difficult to disagree with the assessment that Mattis leaving the Trump cabinet only made "Trumpism" stronger.

Haberman also delivers via CNN low-impact punditry, like declaring that Trump's one-on-one meeting with Vladimir Putin in Helsinki in the summer of 2018 marked the worst week of his presidency.[38] As it turned out, the meeting ultimately appeared to hold little significance in Trump's presidency, positive or negative.

Haberman seems to test-drive her news theories, perhaps compulsively, on her Twitter page. In September 2019, she speculated that based on his tweets, President Trump might have received national employment data prior to the standard set day and time they are released each month.[39] She also suggested that he was spinning the jobs numbers (which he would have obtained unethically, or maybe even illegally) on Twitter. This would have been, in her words, a "deeply questionable action by a President." More likely, as Twitter users pointed out, the president was tweeting about the payroll processor ADP's data that is typically released just prior to the official national data. After being called out online, she let the tweet stand, and lightly blamed Trump for her faux pas, noting the president "could attempt to be clear in what he's referring to."

Incredible journalisming.

Haberman even egged on verified Twitter users who were suggesting that the Marine Corps Band played "Edelweiss" at a White House event as an homage to the Nazis, tweeting "Does . . . anyone at that White House understand the significance of that song?"[40] Of course, the president of the United States was certainly not sending a secret white power message via the Marine Corp Band. As media writer and film critic John Nolte wrote at Breitbart News, "Edelweiss is a brilliantly subversive anti-Nazi tune penned by two German Jews, Richard Rodgers and Oscar Hammerstein II, for their 1959 Broadway smash 'The Sound of Music.'"[41]

Haberman was also among the unscrupulous establishment media figures to push the Covington Catholic hoax, documented in detail earlier in this book. She was eventually named as a defendant in a lawsuit brought by lawyers representing the students.[42]

Maggie Haberman is also part of a complex web of familial, media, and corporate ties. Her brother, Zach, is an NBC News politics editor.[43] Her husband, Dareh Gregorian, is an NBC News politics reporter.[44] Her father, Clyde, worked for the *New York Times* for years. Her father-in-law is Vartan Gregorian, president of the Carnegie Corporation.[45]

In 2016, Vartan Gregorian founded the Aurora Prize for Awakening Humanity with fellow Armenians Ruben Vardanyan and Noubar Afeyan.[46] Afeyan and Vardanyan were John Podesta's business partners at Joule Unlimited, a now-defunct Putin-connected energy company that saw massive investment from the Kremlin during Podesta's tenure.[47] Joule was sponsored by a Russian state-controlled investment fund that had Putin's backing. Podesta is a longtime Clinton insider and ran Hillary's failed 2016 campaign.

Former Hillary spokesman Nick Merrill said of Haberman in 2015: "We have a very good relationship with Maggie Haberman of Politico over the last year. We have had her tee up stories for us before and have never been disappointed."[48]

No surprise there.

Haberman's mother, Nancy, is executive vice president of Rubenstein & Associates, a powerhouse New York PR "fixer" firm.[49] They have serviced all sorts of famous and infamous clients, from Donald Trump and Rupert Murdoch, to Leona Helmsley and Al Sharpton, to the Museum of Modern Art and the Metropolitan Opera. According to *Elle*, Nancy has represented several Trump projects.[50] Nonetheless, Maggie Haberman has made a career covering Rubenstein clients such as Trump and Rudy Giuliani. Nancy Haberman's clients include a partnership between the Hult International Business School and Clinton Global Initiative (she organized an event for CGI featuring Bill Clinton himself).[51]

Perhaps all of these deep family and corporate conflicts of interest played no role in any of the Habermans' work. Maybe Maggie's connections to Clinton World, including her reporting that earned praise from

Hillary's team, are all just happenstance. More likely, though, is that the Habermans are humans, and like other humans, their work product is influenced by who they are and their personal environment. And the Habermans are the New York establishment. When you evaluate their reporting, particularly on people who threaten to disrupt the current social and political conditions, you should keep that in mind.

Racism Is the New Russia

After the Russia hoax hysteria (mostly) ended with the whimper of the Mueller report, the *New York Times* refocused its newsroom around race in America. I'm not sure it was necessary to formalize this—it seemed like every media report in 2020 addressed race at one level or another—but that was the decision made from on high by executive editor Dean Baquet.[52]

So, the *Times* and their staff, who constantly seem to fan the flames of racial division, anointed themselves the authorities on America's most sensitive subject. The *Times'* use of the terms "racist," "racism," "white people," "whiteness," and "white supremacy" have skyrocketed in recent years. *Tablet* magazine crunched the numbers. From 2011 to 2019, the *Times'* use of the terms racist/racists/racism went from 0.0027 percent of all words to about 0.02 percent, or a 700 percent increase. The word "whiteness," for example, had a usage rate near 0.0001 percent in 2015, according to *Tablet*. Since then, it makes up typically between 0.0005 percent and 0.0007 percent of words, a jump of approximately 500 to 700 percent. Use of terms like "white privilege" and "racial privilege" leapt about 1,200 percent between 2013 and 2019.[53] During this time, America's perception of race relations in the United States backtracked.[54] The *Economist* reported in September 2020 that Americans' views of black/white race relations were at a twenty-year low.[55] According to a chart provide by *Tablet*, over 80 percent of white liberals considered racism in the United States a big problem in the year 2020, which is more than double what it was in 2010.[56]

Though the *Times* strove to be more authoritative on the issue of race, they consistently employ people who are racial bigots, or at least have done bigoted things in their pasts.

Here are some examples:

• Jazmine Hughes, an associate editor of the *New York Times Magazine,* unabashedly disparaged whites and Jews on her Twitter feed. From a seemingly endless list of examples: In 2015 she tweeted, "no new white friends 2k15." Also in 2015: "Hi, my name is Jazmine Hughes, and my self-care regimen is

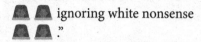 ignoring white nonsense ."

In 2016 she tweeted: "good morning everyone except for white women." From 2017: "Jews are inDEED good with money"; she emphasized the word "deed" with capital letters.[57]

• *New York Times* political editor Tom Wright-Persanti, a senior staff editor, mocked Jews and minorities on Twitter. Breitbart News broke this story in a 2019 exposé. From 2010: "I was going to say 'Crappy Jew Year,' but one of my resolutions is to be less anti-Semitic. So . . . HAPPY Jew Year. You Jews." In 2009, he tweeted "Who called the Jew-police?" Wright-Persanti also tweeted a number of anti-Indian tweets in 2008 and 2009, including: "Mohawked Indian Guess employee, to @snitkin: 'Yo, you like these watches? I sell 'em under the table, if you know what I mean.'" Wright-Persanti apologized for the offending tweets.

Wright-Persanti had also trashed the *New York Times* on Twitter, often with colorful language. "What the NYTimes does is take your story, spice it up with a dash of *douche zest* and then a million people read it," he tweeted in October 2010, according to the *New York Post*. (Breitbart News asked *Times* spokeswomen if they agreed the paper used a dash of "douche zest" in their articles. They did not reply to our inquiry.)[58]

• The *Times* added tech writer Sarah Jeong to the editorial board in 2018. Jeong has what can be seen as a lengthy history of racist comments about white people. Some examples from her Twitter feed:

　○ "Are white people genetically predisposed to burn faster in the sun, thus logically being only fit to live underground like groveling goblins" o "Dumbass fucking white people marking up the internet with their opinions like dogs pissing on fire hydrants"

   o #CancelWhitePeople[59]

After these tweets and many more surfaced online, she played the victim card and cited examples of racist tweets she had received.[60]

The classic "two wrongs make a right" excuse! Or the answer to racism—is more racism!

The *Times* seemed to concur with Jeong's illogic as well, releasing a statement standing by her. "Her journalism and the fact that she is a young Asian woman have made her a subject of frequent online harassment," a spox for the Gray Lady said. "For a period of time she responded to that harassment by imitating the rhetoric of her harassers. She sees now that this approach only served to feed the vitriol that we too often see on social media."

Jeong stayed on the *Times* editorial board for about a year until quietly resigning for unexplained reasons.[61]

• Gina Cherelus, *Times* fact-checker, has spent much of the last decade tweeting derogatory comments about whites, Asians, and homosexuals, whom she refers to as "dykes" and "faggots."[62]

• In April 2019, the *New York Times* ended the publication of political cartoons in its international print edition after it published two seemingly anti-Semitic cartoons in the same week. In the April 25 international edition, the *Times* published a depiction of Israeli prime minister Benjamin Netanyahu as a dachshund, wearing the Star of David, while being walked on a leash by Donald Trump, who wears a yarmulke. The *Times* retracted the cartoon and acknowledged the anti-Semitic tropes within, stating that it was "an error of judgement to publish it," but did not apologize.[63] They apologized a day later, stating "we are deeply sorry," but only after heavy social media pressure.[64]

• Just a few days later, another anti-Jewish cartoon appeared in the international edition of the paper. In this image, Prime Minister Netanyahu is descending a mountain, clad in a robe, his eyes blacked out, and he's holding a stone tablet above his head with the Star of David on it. The Israeli prime minister appears to snap a picture of himself with a selfie-stick attached to a smartphone.

The *Times* put out yet another statement, this time denying the cartoon was anti-Semitic. More interesting, though, they announced a rather extreme change in editorial policy: "we've decided to suspend the future publication of syndicated cartoons," the *Times* stated.[65]

While some of the people associated with the bad decision making eventually left the company, rarely does the *Times* publicly oust a writer or editor for their bigotry. Additionally, the *Times* was rarely transparent about how the responsible parties were hired, how they developed such horrible judgment, or what consequences befell them after they were exposed and public outcry ensued. There was little or no credibility in every instance. For example, those who made the decisions that led to the publication of the seemingly anti-Semitic cartoons remain a mystery to this day, despite the fact that they are responsible for the cessation of all syndicated political cartoons from the *Times'* international edition.[66]

Personally, I remain genuinely negative on "cancel culture" and have not called for any *Times* writers to be fired for the aforementioned bigotry, or for any other reason. However, it would be nice if the Gray Lady would look in the mirror before publishing insane headlines like "Exit Polls Point to the Power of White Patriarchy" by Charles Blow, which they ran on November 4, 2020.[67] I could also do without *Times* exposés on how lawns—yes, lawns—are a symbol of racism (and global warming), or explainers on how air-conditioning is sexist.[68]

After all, Michael Goodwin of the *New York Post* reported in 2020 that the Ochs family, as in the Ochs-Sulzbergers who own the *New York Times*, owned slaves themselves.[69]

The 1619 Project and the Insistence America Is a Horrible Place

In August 2019, the *New York Times Magazine* unveiled the 1619 Project, an ambitious series attempting to "reframe" American history with slavery as the foundation upon which our nation was based.[70] The "1619" vision of America is diametrically opposed to Americans' most fundamental collective beliefs about our origin and purpose. With the 1619

Project, 1619, the date the first slave ship arrived in what would become Virginia, was America's true founding and its defining moment. "In God We Trust," *E Pluribus Unum*, and Life, Liberty, and the Pursuit of Happiness had all been overemphasized by educators over the last four hundred years, and slavery had been underestimated.

This wasn't just a vanity project for the *Times*. The Pulitzer Center quickly unveiled school curriculum based on the 1619 Project.[71]

It may have been widely celebrated by the woke left, but 1619 was widely criticized by experts. Shortly after the project was published, a group of decorated historians wrote a letter to the *Times* critiquing it. The main objection to the content of 1619 was that it contained numerous falsehoods and had an opaque fact-checking process, but the tone of the letter suggested perhaps some deeper outrage. From the letter (emphasis mine):[72]

> [E]rrors, which concern major events, cannot be described as interpretation or "framing." They are matters of verifiable fact, which are the foundation of both honest scholarship and honest journalism. *They suggest a displacement of historical understanding by ideology. Dismissal of objections on racial grounds—that they are the objections of only "white historians"—has affirmed that displacement.*

Yes, that is correct: the 1619 Project creator, Nikole Hannah-Jones, has dismissed critics specifically because they are "old, white male historians." Back to the letter:"[73]

> *On the American Revolution, pivotal to any account of our history, the project asserts that the founders declared the colonies' independence of Britain "in order to ensure slavery would continue." This is not true. If supportable, the allegation would be astounding—yet every statement offered by the project to validate it is false.* Some of the other material in the project is distorted, including the claim that "for the most part," black Americans have fought their freedom struggles "alone."

The contention that America was founded not in the name of freedom but to preserve slavery is perhaps the most-often cited falsehood in critiques of the 1619 Project, and for good reason. If true, this would have been the historical bombshell of my lifetime. Luckily for all of us, it is fake history.

The original text of the original 1619 Project essay contained the following passage: "Conveniently left out of our founding mythology is the fact that one of the primary reasons the colonists decided to declare their independence from Britain was because they wanted to protect the institution of slavery."[74]

Since publication, the words "some of" were added before the words "the colonists." The *Times* noted the update with an "Editor's Note," insisting this massively significant correction was not in fact a "correction."

1619 won a Pulitzer[75] anyway and the 1619 Project was named a "Top Work of Journalism of the Decade" by New York University's journalism school.[76]

Until this point in America, as Cambridge American history teacher Nicholas Guyatt put it, "Liberals and conservatives alike have imagined the story of the United States as a gradual unfolding of freedom." If the claim that America was actually created to preserve slavery is true, as the 1619 Project argued, our country's founding premise was pure evil and virtually every citizen for hundred years had been fed a lie to cover it up. It would be, literally, the greatest hoax in the history of the country.

More from the historians' letter:

> Instead, the project asserts that the United States was founded on racial slavery, an argument rejected by a majority of abolitionists and proclaimed by champions of slavery like John C. Calhoun.

This point is particularly relevant in the midst of our modern-day "cancel culture," where human beings are canceled, as opposed to just their bad ideas: the 1619 Project's central premise—that America was founded on racism, not freedom—was held by slavery's biggest defenders and rejected by Lincoln and the abolitionists.

Leslie M. Harris, a professor of history and African American studies at Northwestern University who helped fact-check 1619, claimed that her objections went unheard at the *Times*. Harris wrote at *Politico* that the *Times* refused to remove or qualify a claim that the colonists wanted independence from Britain specifically to protect the institution of slavery, despite her insistence that it was inaccurate.[77]

Another falsehood that fit the *Times*' preferred narrative roundly refuted: that America has always been racist to its core.

(Remember: Within a given article, information that rebuts a preferred narrative or confirms an undesirable narrative is to appear deep in the article, or not at all.)

The 1619 Project also contained simple fundamental errors, like falsely stating the Declaration of Independence was signed on July 4, 1776; most signatories signed on August 2. (Sure, this one seems relatively minor, but 1619 was supposed to be a definitive historical text. Wasn't it?)

The essay contains the line "anti-black racism runs in the very DNA of this country." If Nikole Hannah-Jones truly believes this is true of America, then is it really a surprise she'd be willing to stretch and strain the truth to try to discredit the notion that we were founded in glory?

Hannah-Jones was hardly secretive about her agenda. In July 2020, she tweeted, "I've always said that the 1619 Project is not a history. It is a work of journalism that explicitly seeks to challenge the national narrative and, therefore, the national memory. The project has always been as much about the present as it is the past."[78]

She ultimately deleted the tweet, perhaps because it threw under the bus everyone who had defended her journalism.

Jake Silverstein, the *New York Times Magazine* editor, brazenly wrote in the *Times* that he rejected historians' requests for corrections to the piece.[79] Baquet continued to laud the 1619 Project even a year later, stating, "1619 is one of the most important pieces of journalism *The Times* has produced under my tenure as executive editor. It changed the way the country talked about race and our history."[80]

Sadly, this latter part of his statement is accurate, just not in a good way.

In June 2020, Black Lives Matter rioting had spread across the United States. Lives had been lost, businesses had been destroyed, and an epic flight from American cities had just begun.[81] On June 20, the center-right *New York Post* published an article by Claremont Institute Senior Fellow Charles Kesler titled "Call them the 1619 riots." The paper's official Twitter account tweeted the link to the op-ed with an image of a toppled statue and stone pedestal with the words "SLAVE OWNER" and "GEORGE FLOYD" crudely spray-painted on it. Hannah-Jones tweeted the link with her blessing: "It would be an honor. Thank you."[82]

Nikole Hannah-Jones, who suggests her vision is in keeping with pacifist Rev. Dr. Martin Luther King Jr.,[83] has defended looting as "a symbolic taking"; she said this on CNN.[84] She also told CBS that "destroying property, which can be replaced, is not violence."[85]

A few days later, the Federalist unearthed a public letter she had written in 1995 where she stated "the white race is the biggest murderer, rapist, pillager, and thief of the modern world."[86] She savaged Christopher Columbus and many groups of white people with intense language and imagery. She saved some of her toughest language for European settlers. Perhaps this was when the 1619 Project was first conceived.

She even pushed an unproven conspiracy about how Africans had arrived in the Americas before Columbus and deserve credit for Aztec temples.[87]

That is who I believe Nikole Hannah-Jones is: a racist conspiracy theorist with a victim complex who embraces violence, publishes glaring falsehoods, and hates America. She directs all this passion toward pushing her narratives with semi-fictional "journalism."

And she is exactly who the New York Times and the Pulitzer Board yearn to celebrate.

The purpose of the 1619 Project was clear: to frame 1619 as America's true founding in order to further guilt Americans for our country's horrible legacy of slavery. How do we know this was the point? Because the Times said so. Silverstein wrote that 1619 "aims to reframe the country's history, understanding 1619 as our true founding."[88] Nikole Hannah-Jones tweeted in August 2019, "I argue 1619 is our true founding," before deleting it.[89] But by September 2020, Hannah-Jones was arguing the exact opposite: "The #1619Project does not argue that 1619 is our true founding. We know this nation marks its founding at 1776," she tweeted.[90]

That same month on CNN, Hannah-Jones stated emphatically that the 1619 Project "does not argue that 1776 was not the founding of the country, but what it does argue for is that we have largely treated slavery as an asterisk to the American story."[91] Both parts of that statement seem equally dishonest.

The banner display on Hannah-Jones's Twitter feed is literally an image of the date "July 4, 1776" crossed out and replaced with "August 20, 1619."[92]

From my vantage point, she's either crazy, or she thinks everyone else is.

She continued to push her agenda with a lengthy, highly aggressive case for slavery reparations for the *Times* in the summer of 2020—the peak season of the "1619 riots."[93]

She simply is not credible on the issue of race, yet she is held up as a singular authority on the issue. The *Times* is not credible on the topic, either, and they will continue to publish her. Both will continue to garner awards.

This is the *Times'* business model. Objectivity is not their objective. Their objective is to "teach our readers to think" more like the *Times* on race. Dean Baquet said as much himself: "I mean, one reason we all signed off on the 1619 Project and made it so ambitious and expansive was to teach our readers to think a little bit more like that."

And in some parts of America, they seem to have succeeded.

It is tempting but foolish to put the 1619 Project fiasco squarely at the feet of Nikole Hannah-Jones: she's privileged, angry, can't stop tweeting idiotic stuff, and even dyes her hair red for reasons that remain a mystery. She's unique, yet she is still representative of the growing preoccupation with race hysteria.

Baquet made it clear that race relations are the focal point of the *Times'* journalism. In a staff meeting in 2019, he indicated that the newsroom would be shifting coverage from the Russia, Russia, Russia narrative to Trump's supposed racism. In a leaked transcript of the meeting, Baquet is quoted as saying the newsroom's primary focus would be on "what it means to be an American in 2019," which "requires imaginative use of all our muscles to write about race and class in a deeper way than we have in years," he said. Baquet went on:

> Race in the next year—and I think this is, to be frank, what I would hope you come away from this discussion with—race in the next year is going to be a huge part of the American story. And I mean, race in terms of not only African Americans and their relationship with Donald Trump, but Latinos and immigration.[84]

In 2020, the *NYT* triumphantly announced it would start capitalizing the "B" in "black": "It seems like such a minor change, black versus Black," the *Times'* national editor, Marc Lacey, told the *Times*. "But for many people the capitalization of that one letter is the difference between a color and a culture."[95]

The *Times* has chosen, as of now, not to capitalize the word "White." (I'm capitalizing it here, just this once.) Their explanation? "White doesn't represent a shared culture and history in the way Black does, and also has long been capitalized by hate groups."

I would be inclined to agree with this assertion, but I read the 1619 Project and learned that our nation is rooted in white supremacy, and critiques of 1619 by white historians were rejected *specifically* because of the critics' race.

It appears as though the *New York Times* regards whiteness as a "shared culture and history" when they wish to attack white people without getting blowback.

Canceling Cotton

Arguably, the *New York Times'* most high-profile article in recent memory was not the 1619 Project, but a simple op-ed written by popular Arkansas senator Tom Cotton.

Senator Cotton's credentials are impeccable. He has multiple degrees from Harvard; after graduating from Harvard Law, he enrolled in the army, became a combat veteran, served in Iraq and Afghanistan, and was awarded the Bronze Star; he kept watch over Arlington National Cemetery as part of the army's legendary and notoriously rigorous 3rd U.S. Infantry Regimen, aka the "Old Guard."[96] He's also a rare Republican who has a sterling reputation with both the establishment and populist wings of the GOP, leading on a number of issues from China to immigration to what to do about censorship by Big Tech.

Senator Cotton is a frequent guest on my morning radio show, *Breitbart News Daily,* where he speaks clearly and boldly, but is not above delivering the occasional jokey sound bite; he freely mocks the Left yet never loses his temper.

If you're a staffer at the *New York Times,* he certainly gives you a lot to hate.

When the *Times* published an op-ed by Cotton in June 2020 arguing for a crackdown on rampant BLM protests, all hell broke loose in the newsroom.

What did Cotton suggest that was so unsayable in the summer of 2020? That a "show of force" was the best way to stop the rioting that was decimating America's cities. From the piece:

> One thing above all else will restore order to our streets: an over-whelming show of force to disperse, detain and ultimately deter lawbreakers. But local law enforcement in some cities desperately needs backup, while delusional politicians in other cities refuse to do what's necessary to uphold the rule of law.[97]

Despite people losing their lives and countless businesses being destroyed, even dedicating a single column to considering if military force would be a legal and effective solution had the wokesters hopping mad. Tack on a needlessly incendiary headline (literally "Send in the Troops"), and the left-wing staff was about ready for a full-on revolt. (The *Times* would own up to writing the headline themselves, not Senator Cotton.)

It was game on. Various far-left snowflakes, including numerous *Times* employees, took to social media to repeat the charge that publishing the piece "puts Black @NYTimes staff in danger."[98] The minorities who were killed in the riots, or those who lost their businesses, were apparently not a priority for the enraged journalists.[99]

The News Guild of New York, which represents journalists across the greater New York area, scolded the *Times* in a statement: "Invoking state violence disproportionately hurts Black and brown people," it read. The guild even went as far as saying that the piece "jeopardizes our journalists' ability to work in the field safely and effectively."[100]

Then–editorial page editor James Bennet explained the op-ed page's disobedience: "Times Opinion owes it to our readers to show them counter-arguments, particularly those made by people in a position to set policy."[101]

He even offered a sop to the snowflake-left by stating that "we under-stand that many readers find Senator Cotton's argument painful, even dangerous."

Two days after the op-ed was published online, the *Times* added a five-paragraph-long, 317-word editor's note to the top of the article. The mini-essay was half explanation, half mea culpa. Though Cotton's piece was not taken offline or retracted, the editors took the stunning half measure of publicly stating "the essay fell short of our standards and should not have been published." Specifically, the piece "[fell] short of the thoughtful approach that advances useful debate."

These statements were immediately met with mockery and derision online, especially because the *Times* has published Russian president Vladimir Putin, Venezuelan dictator Nicolás Maduro, Turkish president Recep Tayyip Erdoğan, and earlier in 2020, Sirajuddin Haqqani, the deputy leader of the Taliban.[102]

Radicals and dictators often have a safe space at the *New York Times*, but Harvard-educated combat veterans currently in the U.S. Senate do not.

The *Times* wasn't done submitting to the woke mob. The paper stated that they would be adding additional layers of editing going forward, "including expanding our fact checking operation and reducing the number of Op-Eds we publish."[103]

Additional fact-checking is a non sequitur; most of the outrage at the piece was over Cotton's opinion, not facts.

The pledge to run fewer op-eds is tantamount to censorship and will inevitably lead to more ideological orthodoxy in the paper. This is a massive victory for the Left.

Bennet took the fall for the *Times*, resigning just a few days after the Cotton essay was published. Publisher Arthur Gregg Sulzberger took the side of the left-wing cyberbullies, and it appeared that he threw Bennet under the bus: "Last week we saw a significant breakdown in our editing processes, not the first we've experienced in recent years," he told his newsroom. Sulzberger continued: "James would not be able to lead the team through the next leg of change that is required."

(Bennett did admit that he had not read the essay before it was published. As editor-in-chief of Breitbart, I've had a long-standing rule where I must review all opinion pieces.)[104]

And just like that, a conservative Bronze Star winner and a liberal Manhattan newspaper editor were canceled.

All for not conforming to the *New York Times'* newsroom consensus.

The Caliphate Calamity

At the *New York Times*, sloppy or outright misleading journalism isn't reserved only for political articles. Sometimes it appears in other sections of the enterprise. Take, for example, the "Caliphate" nonfiction podcast project from 2018.

A *New York Times* press release called it the "most ambitious form of audio storytelling to date."[105] "Caliphate" prominently featured the story of Shehroze Chaudhry (aka Abu Huzaifa), a Canadian man who claimed to have been a member of ISIS. Chaudhry's story was full of vivid details. He talked of his time as an executioner for the Islamic State; in one instance he described how blood "sprayed everywhere" after he beheaded and crucified an accused drug dealer. "I had to stab him multiple times. And then we put him up on a cross. And I had to leave the dagger in his heart," he said.[106] Intense stuff, even for those who have grown somewhat numb to Islamic State atrocities.

The project was helmed by Rukmini Callimachi, a star reporter for the *Times*. She was hired in 2014 to cover the Islamic extremism beat. She's been a Pulitzer finalist, and in 2016 she won the International Center for Journalists' Integrity in Journalism award.[107] "Caliphate" itself was a smash hit and a major critical success, taking home a Peabody in 2018.[108] It even spawned debate in Canada's parliament about how a killer such as Chaudhry was allowed to walk the streets of Canada.[109]

There was only one problem: many of the key facts of the story are unconfirmed.

I reached out to Rukmini Callimachi for comment or clarification on Caliphate-gate; she declined.

In September 2020, Chaudhry was arrested by the Royal Canadian Mounted Police for "hoax-terrorist activity."[110] An RCMP spokesperson confirmed that "[t]he charge stems from numerous media interviews where the accused . . . claimed he travelled to Syria in 2016 to join the terrorist group ISIS and committed acts of terrorism," and that Chaudhry was the same man who represented himself as Abu Huzaifa on "Caliphate."[111]

Callimachi attempted to limit the damage by breaking the news herself on Twitter. All of a sudden, Chaudhry's questionable credibility was the source of the podcast's "narrative tension," she claimed on Twitter.[112]

At Breitbart News, we call this "BenSmithing," a term coined by Breit-bart senior writer John Nolte and named after *New York Times* media col-umnist Ben Smith, who perfected it (Smith was formerly the BuzzFeed editor-in-chief).[113] To "BenSmith" something is to ensure that news that is unfavorable to the media's preferred narrative is broken in a way that dismisses the revelations as unimportant. You can "BenSmith" your own bad news or you can feed it to a friendly colleague who will frame it for you in a favorable way.

In this instance, Ben Smith himself, who had recently been anointed the *Times'* top media writer, wrote extensively about Callimachi and "Caliphate," praising her for, among other things, turning "distant con-flicts" into "accessible journalism."[114]

Smith can praise Callimachi all he wants, but that doesn't negate the fact that "Caliphate" came under considerable fire for inaccuracies.

In an attempt to salvage the podcast, the *NYT,* according to Smith, solicited freelance journalists in Syria to track down any signs Chaudhry had been a member of ISIS; instead they learned Islamic State defectors had never heard of him.

"Caliphate" was on the verge of being shelved until two sources within the U.S. intelligence community confirmed to the *Times* that they believed Chaudhry to be a member of the Islamic State. Just like that, "Caliphate" was back on track.

While that may have been sufficient confirmation for the *Times*, the *Wall Street Journal* had decided to pass on the story because they didn't trust a key source.

As *Washington Post* media critic and occasional contrarian Erik Wemple has pointed out, Callimachi was no stranger to controversy. In 2018, for example, she arranged for the *New York Times* to purchase foot-age of a terrorist attack on U.S. soldiers in Niger. The subsequent story was affixed with the following note:

> Helmet-camera footage from Sgt. Jeremiah Johnson was appar-ently seized by the militants after his death. It was later pro-vided to a news agency in Mauritania, the Agence Nouakchott d'Information, or A.N.I. The New York Times, seeking details that would help explain how the attack occurred, bought rights to the video from the news agency last month.[115]

ANI has a known track record of being in contact with several branches of al Qaeda.

And the *Times* apparently bought footage from them.

Some of Callimachi's colleagues objected to this decision, wrote Wemple, citing ethics rules against purchasing information. He also wrote that they were concerned about lack of objectivity on the part of ANI. (Multiple journalists I spoke to on background defended ANI as a credible outlet.)[116]

According to Wemple, Callimachi drew scorn from scholars and Iraqi officials alike for removing records from Iraq that were recovered from the Islamic State.[117] This also drew her into conflict with Margaret Coker, who was then the *Times*' Iraq bureau chief, which led to Coker's abrupt resignation.

The drama continued to swirl around Callimachi. In October 2019, she detailed alleged payments by the Islamic State to a rival group, Hurras al-Din (HaD). An independent researcher later alleged that the documents at the heart of the story were forged. Some of them, the researcher claimed, even seemed to predate HaD's founding. Another expert cited in the story recanted after learning he had only reviewed a portion of the documents, ultimately determining that they were not genuine. The *Times* appended the story with a disclaimer disclosing that "questions were raised" about its source documents. In December 2020, the *Times* tacked on an audio correction to the beginning of all twelve parts of the podcast. Baquet described the fiasco as "an institutional failing."[118]

(Remember: If posting an update or correction mitigates further reputational damage from the mistake or it enhances the paper's brand, acknowledge the update.)

While Rukmini Callimachi remains a correspondent for the *New York Times*, Andy Mills, who was co-host and a producer of the podcast, resigned, but not necessarily over Caliphate. (Mills admitted to other "unprofessional behavior" in a public resignation letter.)[119]

The *New York Times* ultimately did have a public reckoning when it came to the "Caliphate" chaos. This is a striking contrast to the "1619 Project," which was gutted after core claims made within were drastically scaled back or retracted. "1619" is praised and defended by the *New York Times* and is part of school curricula. I will venture a guess as to why this discrepancy exists: the woke Twitter mob that now runs the *New York*

Times. As inaccurate and dishonest as it is about our country, "1619" is simply uncancelable at this time. The values are simply too righteous.

Right around the time Mills resigned, the *Times* was also canceling Donald McNeil Jr., a forty-five-year *New York Times* veteran who had recently been one of the top reporters in the world on COVID-19.[120] It came out in January 2021 that in 2019 while on a $5,500 per student *Times* "Student Journey" trip in Peru, McNeil had used the word "n***er," supposedly in the context of a bizarre teaching moment. Dean Baquet investigated the matter soon after the incident and determined that McNeil deserved to be disciplined but not terminated because his intentions were not "hateful or malicious." Enraged *Times* staffers fired off a letter to publisher A. G. Sulzberger blasting the paper for their stance on McNeil.[121]

Days later, McNeil resigned.

This is mob rule. The editor in chief made a decision ostensibly based on an investigation, the rank-and-file objected via emotional letter, and the decision was overturned, or at least that's how it appears. This series of events renders the *Times* just a little more chaotic—and a little more woke.

Also remarkable about the McNeil cancellation is that we don't know exactly what it is that he said. Contrast that with Sarah Jeong, who stayed in her job even though her scandalous comments were made publicly.

Staff columnist Bret Stephens wanted to take issue with the *Times* in a piece for their opinion section, but it was allegedly spiked.[122] (Newsrooms often do not report on themselves, but the *Times* is a notable exception to that rule.) The column appeared in the *New York Post* instead.

I don't know Donald McNeil, I don't know anything about his behavioral history, and I certainly don't have any insight into what his wild explanation was for using that word in a conversation with young people on a learning trip. But I do know that if the leader of an organization as prestigious as the *New York Times* makes a decision and the woke mob can get it reversed more than a year later with a pressure campaign, we are officially in a not-so-brave new world in American life.

Canceling in the Name of Inclusion

In 2017, the *New York Times* published a glowing profile of the Sleeping Giants, a group of far-left activists who lead advertising boycotts against conservative outlets and personalities it deems problematic. (Much more on them later.) Sleeping Giants are purely partisan—they target center-right media and center-right media alone—but they claim that they are "brand safety" advocates who are trying to protect businesses. This is, naturally, a giant hoax. Their mission, as far as I can tell, is to starve their ideological foes of resources by convincing businesses to withhold advertising dollars from them. While the *New York Times* is clearly on the political left, it was still a surprise in the Breitbart newsroom when they published an opinion article supportive of the Sleeping Giants' censorship campaign called "How to Destroy the Business Model of Breitbart and Fake News."

(Labeling Breitbart News as "fake news" is another disingenuous tactic used to silence us. I've long argued that Breitbart is held to a higher journalistic standard than the establishment press. Any factual mistake we make is immediately pounced on by any number of establishment media-backed fact-checkers, and the offending story or headline instantly becomes viral across the social web and liberal media. We're instantly held accountable for any error or oversight.)

The article, written by the Dickensian-named Pagan Kennedy, is shocking not so much in that it attacks Breitbart, but in that it is a direct call for censorship of a competitor. Kennedy solicits *Times* readers into the culture war, recruiting activists to help her harm allegedly dangerous, evil Breitbart. Her rationale? "This struggle is about much more than ads on Breitbart News—it's about using corporations as shields to protect vulnerable people from bullying and hate crimes," she wrote. Apparently, the *New York Times* in concert with well-funded leftists singling out Breitbart News for cancellation is not "bullying," it's anti-bullying, or something.

In fact, the *Times* routinely uses "bullying" as a tactic (though I prefer the terms "intimidation," "threats," "pressure campaigns," or "weaponized fake news"). For example, in June 2020, blogger and psychiatrist Scott Alexander (his pseudonym) took down his popular blog, Slate Star Codex. He claimed the *New York Times* planned to publish his real identity, threatening the separation between his online commentary and his professional life as well as his personal safety. "Some people want to kill me or ruin my life, and I would prefer not to make it too easy," he wrote.[123]

The following month, Tucker Carlson accused the *Times* of planning to dox him by publishing his home address. He described the situation in a powerful monologue on his popular Fox News show *Tucker Carlson Tonight*:

Last week, *The New York Times* began working on a story about where my family and I live. As a matter of journalism, there is no conceivable justification for a story like that. The paper is not alleging we've done anything wrong, and we haven't. We pay our taxes. We like our neighbors. We've never had a dispute with anyone. So why is *The New York Times* doing a story on the location of my family's house? Well, you know why. To hurt us, to injure my wife and kids so that I will shut up and stop disagreeing with them.[124]

A *Times* spokesman denied the allegation.

Tucker had good reason to be concerned about doxing. Less than two years earlier, a left-wing mob of protesters showed up at his house and reportedly vandalized his home.[125] Carlson said his wife was forced to hide in the kitchen pantry, thinking it was a home invasion.[126]

A police report said that an anarchist symbol—commonly associated with Antifa—was spray-painted across Carlson's driveway.[127]

The *Times* is well aware that threats to media figures are commonplace in the USA at this time. Even writers for the *New York Times* are threatened—especially the ones who hold nonconformist opinions.

In April 2017, the *Times* hired Pulitzer Prize–winning conservative opinion writer Bret Stephens.[128] Stephens was a star at the *Wall Street Journal*, where he wrote on foreign affairs. Hardly a radical, Stephens is a "Never Trump" stalwart: he's occasionally a villain on the Breitbart.com front page.

But, he's not left enough for the snowflakes at the *New York Times*, so outrage ensued when he was allowed inside their bubble.

James Bennet, then editorial page editor, enthusiastically proclaimed Stephens's arrival as a boon for the paper's intellectual diversity bona fides. Stephens wasted no time hitting a third rail. His first column for the *Times* was a defense of climate change skepticism.[129] Some of his new colleagues immediately set their sights on the heretic. Journalism publication Poynter aggregated about a dozen examples of *Times* employees who voiced public disapproval of the column (most of these social media posts have since been deleted). Community editor Bassey Etim even advised Twitter users to "yell" at Stephens using the paper's comments section.[130]

During the ordeal, Stephens observed that "perhaps" the Left is worse than the Right when it comes to haranguing and bullying. Ya think?

Two days after Stephens was hired by the *Times*, the Gray Lady added his *Wall Street Journal* colleague Bari Weiss to their ranks of opinion writers.[131] Weiss is strongly pro-Israel and seems to hate Donald Trump. Glenn Greenwald called her a "carbon-copy" of Stephens.[132] Weiss has smeared Breitbart News unfairly, using the hackneyed and debunked attack vector that we are anti-Semitic and have a "poisonous ideology."[133] Nonetheless, she wasn't nearly woke enough for the *New York Times*.

From her new perch, Weiss criticized the excesses of modern feminism, including the Women's March embrace of radicals.[134] She wrote about how #MeToo sexual assault allegations against comedian and actor Aziz Ansari were way overblown and hurt the cause of female empowerment.[135] She was also among the first mainstream writers to cover the rise of anti-woke thought leaders gaining popularity using alternative platforms like podcasts and YouTube channels; collectively, these individuals were given the somewhat silly name "intellectual dark web."[136] The "IDW," as it became known, are not necessarily right-wing and many harbor animosity to Donald Trump, but they all eschew the political correctness and closed-mindedness that dominate mainstream culture in this woke moment.

All of her aforementioned pieces were met with strong opposition and even outrage.[137] And, like Stephens, Weiss was attacked publicly by some *Times* staffers. But unlike her new colleague, she felt the situation was unsustainable and she resigned in dramatic fashion. Weiss published a resignation letter where she (accurately) attacked the *Times* for caving to the social media hordes.

"Twitter is not on the masthead of *The New York Times*. But Twitter has become its ultimate editor," Weiss wrote on her website. "As the ethics and mores of that platform have become those of the paper, the paper itself has increasingly become a kind of performance space. Stories are chosen and told in a way to satisfy the narrowest of audiences, rather than to allow a curious public to read about the world and then draw their own conclusions."

Weiss was being literal here. In August 2019, the *New York Times* changed the main A1 headline on a completed edition of the newspaper after public outcry from the woke left. "TRUMP URGES UNITY VS. RACISM" led the *Times* August 6, 2019, edition, until it didn't. Trump had in fact urged unity against racism after a weekend that saw two mass shooting, but the media establishment insisted on making the story about guns that day. Left-wing Twitter mobbed the *Times* over the original headline, which they changed to "Assailing Hate But Not Guns."

One section in Weiss's publicly posted resignation letter suggests the culture at the *New York Times* is exactly as bad as we outsiders suspect it is, if not worse:

> My work and my character are openly demeaned on company-wide Slack channels [Slack is an app used for inter-company communication] where masthead editors regularly weigh in. There, some coworkers insist I need to be rooted out if this company is to be a truly "inclusive" one, while others post ax emojis next to my name. Still other *New York Times* employees publicly smear me as a liar and a bigot on Twitter with no fear that harassing me will be met with appropriate action. They never are.[138]

At the *New York Times*, if you do not conform, you will endure unrelenting pressure until you are disappeared. All of this in the name of "inclusivity."

All the Propaganda That's Fit to Print

As previously noted, the *New York Times* can occasionally be "inclusive" of ideas outside of mainstream American thought, so long as those ideas come from the radical left or authoritarians.

By October 2020, with Weiss pushed off the pages of the *Times,* the Gray Lady had even more room for op-eds like "Hong Kong Is China, Like It or Not," written by a pro-Beijing politician defending China's brutal crackdown on pro-democracy protesters in Hong Kong. The article followed the Chinese Communist Party's imposition of a "national security" law on Hong Kong that stripped the island of what remained of its autonomy from mainland China. The piece, written by Hong Kong pol Regina Ip, echoes CCP talking points that Hong Kong assimilation is both inevitable and necessary:

> The West tends to glorify these people as defenders of Hong Kong's freedoms, but they have done great harm to the city by

going against its constitutional order and stirring up chaos and disaffection toward our motherland.[139]

Pure Beijing propaganda, published in toto in America's most popular paper.

While this piece was revealing, it shouldn't have been a shock to perceptive readers. After all, the *Times* did publish an opinion piece on the positives of communism as recently as 2017.[140] "For all its flaws, the Communist revolution taught Chinese women to dream big," wrote *Times* contributor Helen Gao.[141]

Also in 2017, Pulitzer-winning *Times* columnist Nicholas Kristof echoed North Korean propaganda in a public relations coup for the brutal communist regime. "North Koreans like to have fun, too," he tweeted. Kristof, perhaps the *Times*' most famous columnist on international affairs, took to Instagram to post pictures of a pizza lunch in Pyongyang as he was serenaded by the locals.[142] Dictatorships can be super charming.

Sometimes, the *New York Times* would actually get paid to publish Chinese propaganda "advertorials" on its website. The *Washington Free Beacon* reported that in 2018, the *New York Times* took $50,000 from the state-owned *China Daily*. The *Times* had run more than two hundred news article–like advertisements (i.e., pieces of propaganda) over the last decade, according to the *Free Beacon*, articles that downplay Chinese atrocities and promote tourism for the communist country.[143] The *Times* eventually removed them without much fanfare.

In this case, the *New York Times* was far from the worst offender. According to disclosures, the *Washington Post* and the *Wall Street Journal* were paid millions by the Chinese to publish similar content.[144] Freedom House notes that in the case of the *Washington Post*, the *China Daily* advertisements also appeared online. In fact, disclosures indicate that the *Los Angeles Times*, *Seattle Times*, *Chicago Tribune*, *Foreign Policy*, *Houston Chronicle*, *Boston Globe*, and others all took the communist cash to publish communist content via advertising supplements. The scheme was apparently international, as London's *Daily Telegraph* chose to stop publishing Chinese propaganda last year as well.[145]

So, many of America's biggest newspapers got paid off to betray our country by printing propaganda from our nation's top geopolitical foe.

This must have been a major scandal, right? Wrong. These revelations came and went from the news cycle in a brief moment and the story was relegated mostly to conservative media.

After all, it's not like the *Times* had done something really scandalous, like publishing the opinion of Senator Tom Cotton.

The Deep State Times

For years the *Times* had insisted the "deep state" doesn't exist.[146] The "deep state" is a catch-all for a corrupt class of permanent bureaucrats, mostly anonymous, who make their careers in the various government agencies in and around Washington, D.C. The "deep state" fights to preserve the status quo of big-government globalism popularized by all recent presidents not named Donald Trump. All of a sudden, the *Times* opinion page not only began to acknowledge that the "deep state" is real, but it started openly praising it. Editorial board member Michelle Cottle opined in October 2019, "They Are Not the Resistance. They Are Not a Cabal. They Are Public Servants." The piece begins "President Trump is right: The deep state is alive and well."[147]

This admission was long overdue, considering the *Times* had already published the quintessential piece of evidence that the "deep state" did exist and was trying to shut down the Trump agenda.[148] In 2018, the *Times* ran an essay by an anonymous "senior official in the Trump administration" who said that there were many within the bureaucracy working against the agenda of the "impetuous, adversarial, petty and ineffective" president.

It was a surprise that the *Times* would publish an anonymous piece at all, especially from an alleged public servant who was admittedly working clandestinely to undermine a duly elected American presidency.

They appended a dramatic note explaining why they were making an exception to basic journalist norms (this, conveniently for the *Times*, added to the hype): "The *Times* is taking the rare step of publishing an anonymous Op-Ed essay. We have done so at the request of the author, a senior official in the Trump administration whose identity is known to us and whose job would be jeopardized by its disclosure."

The news cycle was explosive. It seemed like all of American media became momentarily fixated on the nameless essay. Major publications speculated that it could have been authored by Defense Secretary James Mattis, UN ambassador Nikki Haley, or even Vice President Mike Pence![149] It could have been anyone!

Based on the protections afforded the author and the grandiose introduction, it is clear that is what the *Times* wanted you to think. The author must have been someone with a lot of power and a strong reputation, a household name, a highly credible brand.

"Anonymous" went on to author a book called *A Warning*, which naturally became a number one *New York Times* bestseller.

After all that, it was quite a surprise when the world finally learned the actual identity of "Anonymous." Just prior to the 2020 election, it was revealed that "Anonymous" was hardly a "senior official" at all, and he wasn't on staff at the White House. He was a young Department of Homeland Security chief of staff named Miles Taylor. In other words, "Anonymous" would have had limited access to President Trump and not a lot of institutional power. "Senior official" is an honorific typically reserved for cabinet secretaries and actual senior White House advisers, but the term had lost much of its significance during the Trump era as newsrooms became increasingly comfortable publishing anonymous sources who would feed them Trump administration gossip.

Soon after, Taylor left the administration for jobs at Google and CNN.[150] He endorsed Joe Biden for president. While on CNN before the big reveal, Taylor was asked point-blank by Anderson Cooper in August 2020 if he was in fact "Anonymous," and Taylor lied about it, obnoxiously: "I wear a mask for two things, Anderson: Halloweens and pandemics. So no."

Simply put, for the *Times* to hold up this ordinary bureaucrat as a "senior official" seemed to be nothing short of a hoax designed to harm President Trump.

The Miles Taylor "Anonymous" saga is emblematic of the mind-set at the *New York Times* during the Trump era. Journalistic first principles do not matter, so long as the end result is a bad news cycle for President Trump or his allies.

That is weaponized fake news.

This is what the *New York Times* does best.

CHAPTER 4

NBC "NEWS" AND THE CORPORATIZATION OF MASS MEDIA

If you fact-checked the expression "it takes money to make money," you'd have to rate it a "mostly true" statement. Sure, it's possible to make money from little or nothing, but it's certainly easier to have a little seed cash to get you going.

The same can be said about power. It takes power to get power, or at least it's easier to get more power once you have a little. Ask Laurene Powell Jobs. It's much easier to cut deals, leverage relationships, buy competitors, and claim territory when you already have clout to tout. Perhaps this explains why, despite independent media's incredible growth over the past decade, it seems like Americans have never been so inundated with big corporate media brands.

NBCUniversal is a potent example of this. When you think "NBCUniversal," your mind probably goes first to the NBC network and their rainbow peacock logo, their various news divisions, and Universal Pictures movies. Yet those brands only represent a portion of corporate assets associated with NBC.

For starters, NBCUniversal isn't even at the top of the corporate hierarchy. That honor goes to the Comcast Corporation, which acquired NBCUniversal in 2011.

Comcast assets also include Xfinity cable provider, sports and entertainment venues, the massive British media brand Sky, and many others.

Under the NBCUniversal banner, you'll find the National Broadcasting Company and NBC Studios, E!, Syfy, USA, Bravo, Telemundo, DreamWorks, dozens of local television stations, Golf Channel, MLB

Network, the Fandango ticketing company (now a streaming service!), the Universal theme parks, and seemingly countless other properties.

Many of these brands house other brands. For example, Universal Pictures owns the family-friendly Illumination animation studio and has a first-look deal with genre movie factory Blumhouse.

Comcast NBCUniversal's reach is seemingly limitless and thus, its potential for conflicts of interest when it comes to news reportage is endless as well.

For example, why would NBC News do a big exposé on Chinese concentration camps when there is a Universal Studios in Beijing? Or why would NBC make it clear to their readers and viewers that China is the world's worst human rights abuser on earth when, say, the new James Bond is set to open and Universal is handling the international distribution?

A Philadelphia 76ers fan claimed in 2019 that he and his wife were kicked out of a preseason game against the Chinese Guangzhou Loong Lions *in Philadelphia* (a city that is allegedly not communist) for holding up signs and chanting slogans in support of anti-Beijing Hong Kong protests.[1] If this sounds like fake news to you, consider the following facts: (1) The 76ers play in the Wells Fargo Center, which is owned by Comcast Spectacor (a sports entertainment brand under the Comcast umbrella). And (2) Comcast—which owns all of those Universal properties that make money in China—is based in Philadelphia.

So, it is perfectly logical—and anti-American—that a fan said he was kicked out by the 76ers for showing support for the Hong Kongers. Maybe this was a decision by a low-level stadium employee; or maybe it was a business decision by a multinational media conglomerate with a lot of interests to protect.

(Earlier in the week, many of the NBA's Chinese partners began severing their ties with the league after Houston Rockets general manager Daryl Morey tweeted in support of pro-democracy protesters in Hong Kong.[2] In response, the NBA officially apologized to any "offended" Chinese fans.)[3]

As a publicly traded company, Comcast NBCUniversal's main responsibility is to their shareholders, not to a moral imperative to report fairly and honestly, nor to God or country or American values like liberty.

You might find that fact depressing, but that doesn't make it less true.

When it comes to issues of sports, entertainment, business, and international affairs, NBC's news programming is not fully trustworthy due to an infinite number of potential conflicts of interest.

But Comcast NBCUniversal is not alone in this regard.

CBS is actually ViacomCBS Inc. It controls sporting networks, news divisions, Paramount Pictures, and entertainment channels MTV, Nickelodeon, the CW, BET, and Pluto TV. Other ViacomCBS subsidiaries touch additional parts of life such as mixed martial arts, event promotion, conferences, intellectual property management, and numerous international brands. At the time I'm writing this, it also owns the publisher of this book, Simon & Schuster, which it sold last year to Penguin Random House. Penguin Random House is owned by the German media conglomerate Bertelsmann, one of the largest media companies in the world. Bertelsmann has many other business interests on multiple continents, from education and information technology to logistics and much, much more.

ABC is owned by the Walt Disney Company, which has dominion over Pixar, Marvel Studios, Lucasfilm, ESPN, National Geographic, A&E, the Hulu streaming network (NBC is also an equity stakeholder of Hulu), and numerous worldwide travel-related endeavors including theme parks, hotels, and cruises.

News Corporation, which owns Fox News Channel and the Fox Business Network, also owns HarperCollins Publishers, Dow Jones & Company, the *Wall Street Journal*, realtor.com, and dozens of international sports and news brands, among others.

CNN is owned by WarnerMedia, which also controls HBO, dozens of Warner Bros. brands, DC Films, Castlerock Entertainment, TBS, TNT, advertising giant Xandr, as well as various sports channels. AT&T—which owns WarnerMedia—is the world's largest telecoms company and mobile phone service provider, and it also controls DirecTV as well as buildings and sports/concert venues around the world.

Every connection is another conflict of interest and reason for the news properties under their respective multi-multibillion–dollar umbrellas to think twice before reporting the truth. Or even reporting at all.

While I don't assume any of these conglomerates formally have hard-and-fast rules that prevent reporting on their other assets, you can rest assured that good news within the corporate family tends to be amplified and negative news is downplayed.

It's just good business.

So, if you're a news brand like NBC News that represents merely a branch or two on the giant tree that is the global powerhouse Comcast NBCUniversal, what do you do to establish a clear identity?

In this case, you become the megaphone for America's activist left.

Chopper Under Fire: The Andy Lack Story

In April 2020, NBC News chairman Andy Lack published an op-ed defending the integrity of the press.

No, it was not written satirically.

Why Lack, who had presided over the far-left news network while it aired what I believe to be some of the biggest fake news hoaxes ever pushed on the American public (I document many of them in this chapter), believed his words would make a difference is beyond me, but he tried nonetheless.

In the piece, published at nbcnews.com/*think* (irony is not his strong suit), Lack complained about how the proliferation of news outlets, the ubiquity of social media, and flagging digital advertising rates had put the media establishment in jeopardy. He whined that accountability was dead, yet some journalists were doing the best work he'd seen in his decades in media. And all of this could be traced to one orange, manly thing: Donald Trump. From the letter:

> In the last decade, the ugliest and most cunning threat to journalism comes from leaders in different parts of the world increasingly questioning not just the veracity of what is being reported, which isn't new, but the integrity of those who report it, which is. Some leaders have gone further and egged on their supporters to target and harass anyone they don't approve of in the media.[4]
>
> President Donald Trump came into office railing against many of the foundations of our democratic institutions, including a free press.[5]

In actuality, Donald Trump did remarkably little to infringe on a free press. While Trump has *complained* about the press ad infinitum (complaining about the press is protected under the First Amendment—you're even allowed to say the "the fake news" is the "enemy of the people"), he has done almost nothing to encroach upon press freedom.

I would say Trump has done *literally* nothing to encroach upon media freedom, but he did suspend CNN White House correspondent Jim Acosta's "hard" press pass for twelve days in November 2018.[6]

It was yet another utterly forgettable moment that was wildly overblown by the establishment media. Here's the scintillating story: During a combative exchange with President Trump at a press briefing, Acosta appeared to push away a young female White House intern who was trying to take the microphone from him. The White House retaliated by suspending his "hard pass," which allows the highest access level to the White House. (The White House released what Kellyanne Conway called a "sped up" video of the skirmish, which arguably made the exchange seem more dramatic than it was.)

"Hard passes" are tough to come by. For example, Breitbart News currently has a grand total of one "hard pass" for the White House, despite the fact that we consistently rank among the top five pure news websites in America according to Amazon-owned alexa.com. Establishment media outlets often have far more than that.

Considering the state of free press elsewhere on earth, this is as mild as a rebuke can get. Mexico, for example, saw a dozen journalists murdered in 2019 alone.[7] Press freedom organizations documented hundreds of acts of aggression toward Mexican media members that year.[8]

According to the Committee to Protect Journalists (CPJ), China is arguably the country most hostile to a free press. (If this fact shocks you, it's because America's establishment press never told you about it!) In its annual report, the CPJ found that China imprisoned reporters for things as simple as reporting on the Hong Kong pro-democracy protests without being sufficiently critical of them. The CCP marched reporters into concentration camps along with groups such as the Uyghur Muslims. Any journalist who could be accused of "picking quarrels and provoking trouble" is liable to be incarcerated.[9]

For two years running, China has been the world's top jailer of journalists.[10]

Saudi Arabia has also cracked down on journalists critical of Crown Prince Mohammed bin Salman (MBS); the CPJ reported MBS's authorities imprison reporters without due process and often torture them. Even "beating, burning, and starving political prisoners" is reportedly not uncommon in the Kingdom.

In Turkey and Egypt, journalists are regularly accused of terrorism or threatening governmental stability.

Russia, Vietnam, Turkmenistan, and Iran are all particularly hostile to a free press, according to CPJ.

There is almost no data at all on North Korea; as John Hayward, one of Breitbart's top reporters on international news, wrote in 2019, "The pragmatic view of this discrepancy is that reliable information about the treatment of opposition journalists is extremely difficult to obtain from secretive North Korea. The cynical view is that troublesome reporters in North Korea are more likely to be killed than imprisoned." [11]

But, back in the comparative utopia known as the United States of America, Jim Acosta got bumped down a notch in the pecking order for twelve days.

It's a relief our republic is still here today.

Unfortunately, it's clear that the typical American media executive appears to consider a mild inconvenience endured by a low-rated TV personality as significantly more alarming than when people are murdered or put into concentration camps in communist countries.

There was more media hand-wringing about press passes in 2019 and 2020, but it never again caused the same level of alarm as those twelve harrowing days in November of 2018. [12]

In actuality, Donald Trump helped the American media in some ways, sparking more interest in the news, thus elevating readership and viewership. CNBC (perhaps NBC's lone somewhat-credible news brand) reported in 2018 that "Trump's 'fake news' fight has helped media ratings and readership." [13] The evidence backs it up. Fox News, MSNBC, and CNN all saw increased numbers since the 2016 election. [14]

According to Axios, the *New York Times* and the *Washington Post* both tripled their subscriptions from 2016 to November 2020; the *Times* went from just over 2 million to just over 6 million subscribers while the *Post* went from about 1 million subscribers to 3 million. [15] The Gray Lady's website is apparently accessed by at least half of the adults in the United States in any given month. [16] The *Wall Street Journal* also recently reported a rise in subscribers to record levels. [17]

Political and news podcasts are always among the most downloaded, and many of them are from the likes of big establishment brands like NPR, *New York Times*, *Washington Post*, and yes, even NBC.[18]

If you track the most viral stories on the Internet based on Facebook engagements, you'll see some new media outlets like Breitbart and the Daily Wire at the top of the heap, but we are typically joined by Fox News, CNN, NBC News, and the *Washington Post*.[19]

The evidence is overwhelming. Trump only made Big Journalism bigger.

Trump and other members of his senior staff regularly passed over conservative new media for scoops and fed the establishment media beast. The *New York Times*, Axios, and even the London-based mega-newswire Reuters regularly got the hottest exclusives from Trump World. White House press briefings, when they happened, appeared to be dominated by outlets like CNN, CBS, PBS, and ABC.

There is a point to be made that many local outlets and digital-only platforms have struggled mightily during this time.[20] But the struggles aren't necessarily due to lack of readers; they're due to a rapid decline in the advertising market. Digital ads aren't nearly as valuable as they once were, and the establishment media largely have themselves to blame for this (I will explain in the chapter on the far-left activist group Sleeping Giants).

Back to Andy Lack and his absurd column.

As the chairman of NBC News and MSNBC, Lack himself has hardly been a steward of reputable journalism. In fact, in a field of low-integrity individuals, he has somehow managed to distinguish himself.

When Andy Lack joined NBC News, it was in the midst of a scandal. *NBC Nightly News* anchor Brian Williams was found to have repeatedly lied about his experiences covering the Iraq War. Williams, then anchor of the network's flagship evening newscast, admitted that he had reported a false story about being in a Chinook helicopter in Iraq that was forced down by RPG fire during America's invasion of the country in 2003.[21]

Williams was exposed in 2015 when military newspaper *Stars and Stripes* was told by crew members of the 159th Aviation Regiment that even though a helicopter was hit by two rockets and small arms fire that day, it wasn't anywhere in the vicinity of Williams. He still repeated the claim that it was his chopper under fire.[22] Williams ultimately apologized, admitting that he said he "was traveling in an aircraft that was hit by [rocket-propelled grenade] fire. I was instead in a following aircraft."

Lack suspended Williams but didn't fire him. Today, Williams anchors a nightly show on MSNBC.

Andy Lack, the self-styled arbiter of media ethics, had made his first move as chairman of NBC: save the job of a guy who had been caught stealing war valor for more than a decade.

This proved to be a harbinger.

Joy Reid, the Most Ironically Named Pundit

Throughout his tenure at NBC, Andy Lack consistently defended and promoted Joy Reid. Throughout her career, Reid seems to embody the term "failing upwards." She had an MSNBC show called *The Reid Report* that ran from February 2014 to February 2015. The show was canceled due to abysmally low ratings.[23]

But in 2016, after Lack had assumed the helm, Reid was given a week-end morning show ironically called *AM Joy*. It is not particularly upbeat. It's a typical cable news punditry program featuring left-wing talking heads haranguing about what they believe are horrible elements of American society, especially racism, bigotry, and Trump.

In 2017, a Twitter user who goes by the handle @Jamie_Maz unearthed *Reid Report* blog posts that featured blatant bigotry toward then–Florida governor Charlie Crist. There appears to have been an effort to "out" him as a homosexual on multiple occasions. He was referred to as "Miss Charlie."[24]

Reid apologized for the posts, but later blamed a hacker.[25] (Why would any sane person apologize if they were a victim of a hacking? I doubt they would.)

According to the archived posts, the blog also promoted 9/11 conspiracy theories on multiple occasions.[26] On one occasion, a "truther" documentary that alleged that the U.S. government was behind the attacks on the World Trade Center was recommended to readers.[27]

Reid eventually denied writing these anti-American sentiments.[28]

As this saga played out in the press, Reid took the schizophrenic approach of minimizing or denying the things she had done while simultaneously apologizing profusely for them.

She was never able to prove that she had been hacked. A cybersecurity expert was never able to find convincing evidence of infiltration, either.[29]

The FBI even opened an investigation, wasting taxpayer dollars; to this day, no major findings from the investigation have been widely reported.[30]

The alleged hacking remains a mystery. Reid eventually gave up her noble quest for the truth. She lost her *Daily Beast* column and an LGBTQ group rescinded an award that they intended to give her, but MSNBC gave her a pass.[31] They put out a statement standing by their anchor while dropping the fallacious "hackers" narrative, replacing it with a new angle that she had simply "evolved."

In July 2020 she was given a new show called *The ReidOut,* which would air nightly at 7 p.m. ET, the slot formally occupied by legendary political commentator Chris Matthews.

BLMSNBC

Reid, like many of her colleagues, had a big blind spot for conspiracies that absolved the Left and vilified the Right, often with no evidence at all. In August 2020, amid the BLM riot season, Reid unleashed a tweet storm about the violence in Kenosha, Wisconsin, that was so flagrantly dishonest, it's a wonder she wasn't immediately promoted to head of the network. Here it is, edited slightly for clarity:

> [President Trump is] going to Kenosha to whip up more violence.
>
> Violence and mayhem, perpetrated by people who support HIM, unleashed at night and let's just be clear: by white nationalist mobs . . . in cities with few Black people, IS HIS RE-ELECTION STRATEGY. Period.[32]
>
> The "riots" are not Black Lives Matter marches gone wrong. Armed white nationalists are mobbing these cities to take advantage of protests and scare fellow white people into quietly siding with them. It's an old, tried and true strategy: using fear & anti-blackness for politics.

Reid's main evidence that the violence was actually due to far-right extremists appears to be that many of the perpetrators were white. Not only is the assertion genuinely racist, but it is also pretty dumb. Breitbart News often publishes police mug shots of Antifa leftists, and the most often represented group are young whites.

Interestingly, Reid's acknowledgment that there were mobs in our cities contradicts the media's insistence that the riots were mostly peaceful.

Perhaps Reid didn't get that memo.

Polling data in September 2020 showed that the vast majority of Republicans and about half of Democrats were concerned that the protests/riots had overwhelmed American cities.[33] After that, there were noticeably fewer demonstrations across the county. According to the *USA Today*/Ipsos poll, Americans said seemingly every institution made the protests more dangerous, from BLM and Antifa to conservative media and President Trump himself, but the largest share of the blame fell on the mainstream media.[34]

#MeToo

In October 2017, NBC reporter and former anchor Ronan Farrow published a bombshell report about Harvey Weinstein's sexual misconduct, not at one of NBC's affiliated networks, but in the *New Yorker*. It was arguably the signature piece of journalism of the #MeToo era. And according to Farrow, NBC had passed on it.[35]

Farrow's former producer at NBC, Rich McHugh, who had recently left NBC News, said that "the very highest levels of NBC" had stood in the way of the story in what he called "a massive breach of journalistic integrity."[36]

Noah Oppenheim, the president of the network, denied the claim, stating that the reporting did not meet their standard for publication.

Farrow won a Pulitzer for his journalism on #MeToo for the *New Yorker*.[37]

There seemed to be a bad fact-pattern developing for Oppenheim and Andy Lack: McHugh's claim fit the narrative that NBC turned a blind eye toward predatory men.

Weeks after Farrow's Weinstein exposé was published, NBC anchor Matt Lauer was abruptly fired following a sexual harassment complaint by a female coworker.[38] Rumors had circulated about Lauer's conduct with women for years, but the network claimed it only became aware of his behavior recently.[39]

According to a report in *Variety* featuring complaints from multiple women, Lauer's 30 Rockefeller Center office was a secluded place where he could make inappropriate sexual advances toward women. The lede of the article set the tone for the explosive report: "As the co-host of NBC's 'Today,' Matt Lauer once gave a colleague a sex toy as a present. It included an explicit note about how he wanted to use it on her, which left her mortified." [40]

Lauer's desk allegedly had a button underneath it so that he could close and lock the door without having to leave his chair. (*Architectural Digest* notes that Lauer's wasn't the only office at NBC with such a button; he's just the only one who got caught allegedly using it this way.) [41]

The *Variety* story portrays Lauer as obsessed with sex, having affairs within the office, quizzing colleagues on their sex lives, and making them play "Fuck, Marry, Kill," a game where people confess with whom they'd like to have sex. [42] (Lauer has emphatically denied the allegations against him and has heartily criticized Ronan Farrow's journalism.)

It had been a long-running punch line that Lauer is a dirty dog. His former boss and now CNN head honcho Jeff Zucker joked at a 2008 Friar's Club roast of Lauer that he is "the only guy I know who uses Purell both before and after he masturbates." [43]

Martha Stewart said at the same event, "I hear NBC executives call Matt the 'Cock of the Rock,'" in reference to Rockefeller Center, where the *Today* show is typically recorded.

Lauer seemed to own his reputation as a pervert that night; he appeared to have joked that he'd had anal sex with Katie Couric and that his co-anchor Ann Curry knows he has a "big dick." [44] Couric later joked about Lauer performing oral sex on Curry. [45]

Sure, these are jokes at a roast. But I've never heard of another journalist who has been roasted in exactly this way.

So, it appeared that bigwigs at NBC and the current president of CNN appear to have known about the real Matt Lauer—but did nothing. "The morning news show was No. 1 in the ratings, and executives were eager to keep him happy," *Variety*'s Ramin Setoodeh and Elizabeth Wagmeister reported, perhaps explaining the executives' seeming indifference. [46]

In his book *Catch and Kill*, Farrow published the account of Brooke Nevils, an NBC producer who alleged Lauer anally raped her without lubricant in his hotel room while covering the 2014 Winter Olympics in Sochi, Russia. [47] (Lauer was never charged and called the allegations "false and salacious.")

But much of Farrow's ire wasn't directed just at alleged rapists: he documented what the *Hollywood Reporter* described as a "cover-up culture" at NBC emanating from the executive suite, particularly Andy Lack himself. Farrow also details how Lack and NBC News president Noah Oppenheim helped kill stories about Weinstein's behavior toward women.[48]

After the exposé ran in the *Hollywood Reporter*, Lack penned a memo to his staff denying Farrow's account of events, saying the young journalist "uses a variety of tactics to paint a fundamentally untrue picture."[49] In the memo, Lack attempted to shame Farrow by saying he was not willing to accept NBC's standards and suggested that his big Weinstein story had already broken at the *New York Times*.

Oppenheim later seemingly took a swing at Farrow in a memo sent to NBC staff: "Farrow's effort to defame NBC News is clearly motivated not by a pursuit of truth, but an ax to grind," he wrote. "It is built on a series of distortions, confused timelines and outright inaccuracies."[50]

As they so often do, the establishment media circled the wagons to defend the oligarchs at NBC News. In May 2020, *New York Times* media reporter Ben Smith published an article on the saga critical of—wait for it—Ronan Farrow. From the article titled "Is Ronan Farrow Too Good to Be True?":[51]

> Two other NBC journalists, neither of whom would speak for the record, expressed a different view, which is shared by network executives: That Mr. Farrow was a talented young reporter with big ambitions but little experience, who didn't realize how high the standards of proof were, particularly at slow-moving, super-cautious news networks. A normal clash between a young reporter and experienced editors turned toxic.

So Farrow was a reckless amateur and the town elders, ever benevolent, just simply couldn't get through to him.

It's noteworthy that Smith was editor-in-chief of BuzzFeed, a far-left clickbait blog with a small, fledgling news division.[52] The largest shareholder of BuzzFeed is—wait for it—NBCUniversal. Coincidentally—I'm serious, this is purely coincidental—Ben Smith retained stock in BuzzFeed at the time the Farrow piece was published. Also—and this is for sure coincidental, too—NBC News added Smith to a new online media division composed of an "all-star group" of journalists, all of whom appear to be on the political left.

Besides, it is the height of irony for Smith, who was the editor who first published the bogus Trump/Russia "pee pee" dossier, to lecture anyone on unethical journalisming.

Smith didn't disclose his ties to NBC, but he did include the following disclosure in his *New York Times* column: "Disclosure: I don't cover BuzzFeed extensively in this column because I retain stock options in the company, which I left in February. I've agreed to divest those options by the end of the year."[53]

If I were the media reporter for the *Times*, or anywhere else, I'd submit that this is not an adequate description of the vested interest the author (Smith) has in his subject (NBC). Ironically, while the *New York Times* often reports on itself, their top media correspondent doesn't "extensively" cover another major media outlet because of said columnist's conflict of interests. But, apparently, he is all clear to report on a third media outlet to which he's also connected.

I reached out to Smith in March of 2021 and asked if he had in fact sold his stock as promised. He directed me to a *Times* column he wrote in January 2021, which featured yet another disclosure: "I don't cover BuzzFeed extensively in this column, beyond leaning on what I learned during my time there, and The Times has required that I not do so until I divest my stock options in the company."[54] I asked him why he delayed selling off his shares; he didn't offer a response and suggested I reach out the *Times*' corporate communications for more information. I did. They did not respond.

I also asked Smith what became of the NBC team of "all-star" journalists. He told me the initial announcement "was the extent of it, amusingly, I believe—it had no compensation and no responsibilities."

I can't imagine why the term "fake news" became so popular.

#MeToo, Part Too

The pattern at NBC was clear: go to great lengths to protect powerful men accused of misconduct during #MeToo. In 2018, for example, Two former colleagues, including Linda Vester, accused Brokaw of sexual misconduct.[55] So what did NBC do? According to Emily Smith of the *New York Post,* executives pressured female employees to sign a letter in support of

Brokaw.[56] (Brokaw denied the allegations in a blistering statement attacking Vester's credibility. He was never charged.)

NBC has consistently refused to conduct an independent investigation of its handling of sexual assault allegations. Even Fox News, arguably the only major network caught up in more #MeToo scandal drama than the peacock network, has consistently hired outside investigators to handle alleged misconduct.[57] As journalist Megyn Kelly pointed out (Kelly worked at both networks), "There needs to be an outside investigation into [NBC].[58] They investigated themselves. That doesn't work. Fox News had an outside investigator. CBS News had an outside investigator. NPR, the NFL. This is how it's done."

That's how it should be done, but that was never going to happen at NBC with the leadership team of Andy Lack, (then–MSNBC president) Phil Griffin, and Noah Oppenheim.

When NBC had hired Lack, he arguably had a track record of not responding appropriately to sexual assault claims made against his colleagues and subordinates. This dates back to at least 2004, when he was CEO of Sony BMG Music and learned that a former top Sony executive named Charlie Walk had allegedly sent graphic sexual content to female employees via company email, according to a *Rolling Stone* report.[59] Lack never disciplined Walk; a spokesperson told the press he wasn't even aware of Walk's alleged bad behavior. Walk has since been the subject of media reports that allege he has abused women over decades.[60]

Lack of action became Andy Lack's pattern, and finally, the chickens came home to roost.

In May 2020, Lack resigned as NBC News chairman amid news that the New York attorney general's office was investigating the network's handling of sexual assault claims.[61]

As NPR's longtime media correspondent David Folkenflik wrote at the time, "The surprise wasn't in the announcement of Lack's departure, but that it had taken so long."[62]

Andy Lack had fallen so far even government-funded media was wondering why he hadn't been terminated yet. That's a level of disgrace few establishment execs will ever experience.

The Madness of Maddow

As has been documented so far in this book, NBC seemed to have had a hand in shaping every single major fake news event in the Trump era. From the Kavanaugh hoax, to the Jussie Smollett phony hate crime, to RussiaGate. If there is a major news story where the Left has a vested interest, it appears as though NBC's newsroom rarely lets the facts get in the way of their preferred narrative.

And for a while, it worked. At least as far as business is concerned. Rachel Maddow, MSNBC's most popular pundit, at one point had the highest ratings in all of cable news while in the throes of the Russia collusion news cycle. She brought in a huge readership of "MSNBC Moms," the type of liberal who might have always been on the left, but it was not yet a crucial part of their identity.[63] That is, until the Bad Orange Man cheated his way into power thanks to Putin.

She was, quite simply, the media face of the Russia collusion hoax. Between Trump's election and May 2019 (the month after the report from Robert Mueller's special counsel investigation was released), Maddow spread too many conspiracy theories to list here, but here are a few lowlights compiled by journalist Aaron Maté, who himself is on the left:[64]

- She speculated that Putin could have *kompromat* (the Russian word for resources collected to blackmail a target) on Trump that he would use to manipulate the American president.[65]

- Maddow, who had hyped that Putin could have tapes of Trump with prostitutes, falsely claimed to her audience that she had never let herself even "think about" that those tapes existed.

- She fear-mongered that Russia could "kill the power" in the Midwest, which would cause Americans to freeze to death.

- She walked her audience through a hypothetical scenario where Trump takes orders directly from Putin.

- In a particularly conspiratorial dot-connecting rant, she suggested that a $50,000 bill Michael Cohen sent Trump for "tech services" could have actually been to pay off Russian hackers. Her logic relied on the discredited Steele "pee pee" dossier.

• She said that thanks to Russia, the FBI is "starting to bleed out." Nothing in the Mueller report suggested that is the case.

• She speculated that Rex Tillerson got the secretary of state job after a recommendation from Putin. She later floated that Tillerson had "hollowed out, disappeared, and muted" parts of the State Department not favorable to Putin.[66]

• She stated that the White House edited out a crucial portion of a joint Trump/Putin press conference. (This was demonstrably false.)

• She suggested that the NRA might have been used by the Russian government for an "illegal intelligence operation."

• She recommended that we "start preparing for what the consequences are going to be if it proves to be true" that "the presidency is a Russian op."

• Maddow suggested the social media hashtag #Kids4Trump was part of a Russian op "to destroy American democracy."

• She said that Paul Manafort was the "obvious choice" to be Donald Trump's campaign manager—"from the Russian perspective."

This is merely a partial list of the conspiracy theories pushed on her MSNBC prime-time show. Individually, each one of these examples of unjustifiable speculation represents irresponsible journalism. But collectively, they provide a compelling case that the most watched anchor on MSNBC's signature show is a full-blown kook.

And she was obsessed.

Rachel Maddow stretched to make Russia the center of every story. In April 2017, she and colleague Lawrence O'Donnell indulged in a conspiracy that Trump had coordinated a missile attack on Syria with Putin. From the Intercept:

It's "impossible," fellow anchor Lawrence O'Donnell told Maddow on April 7, to rule out that "Vladimir Putin orchestrated what happened in Syria this week—so that his friend in the

White House could have a big night with missiles and all of the praise he's picked up over the past 24 hours."

Maddow concurred, suggesting that only the FBI's ongoing probe into Trump's alleged collusion with Russian electoral interference will determine the truth. "Maybe eventually we'll get an answer to that from [FBI director] Jim Comey," Maddow said.[67]

She had gone even too far for the *Washington Post*'s Erik Wemple, who was no friend to the Trump administration. Wemple noted that she dedicated remarkable amounts of time to the "pee pee" dossier: "She seemed to be rooting for the document," he noted. "And when large bits of news arose against the dossier, Maddow found other topics more compelling."[68]

Wemple was right. Maddow, like so many others in our establishment press, appeared to be rooting that the president of the United States was a Russian asset.

Maddow's lost about half a million viewers, or a sixth of her audience, after the Russia hoax was debunked, but they would eventually return, searching for the next hysteria about the Bad Orange Man.[69] She smashed records in her January 16, 2020, interview with Rudy Giuliani associate and accused fraudster Lev Parnas (will we get Trump this time?!) and again in July 2020 with her Mary Trump interview (we'll definitely get Trump this time!!), pulling in a remarkable 5.2 million viewers.[70] After all, Trump paranoia was a part of her audience's identity now.

Though Maddow's credibility will never be the same, the off-the-wall anti-Trump conspiracies packed and presented in a calm, Rhodes-Scholarly way remain deeply satisfying to many Americans in the era where opinion journalism has been subsumed by *emotion* journalism.

Others on the network with lower ratings do not share Maddow's unruffled and studious demeanor, but they do share her often deluded and conspiratorial mind. Some examples:

• May 2019: Host Chris Hayes suggested that "regular people" conspired to suppress the economy under Obama because they wanted him to fail. The economy roared during the beginning of Donald Trump's first term not because of tax cuts and deregulation but perhaps because people "didn't want full employment, they didn't want wage growth and empowered workers and they certainly didn't want that happening under a Democratic president," according to Hayes.[71]

• August 2019: MSNBC's *The Last Word with Lawrence O'Donnell* used a chyron that said "TRUMP-INSPIRED TERRORISM" after the mass shooting in an El Paso Walmart.[72] In the segment, O'Donnell interviewed a *Guardian* writer and author of a piece titled, "We must call the El Paso shooting what it is: Trump-inspired terrorism."[73] At no point during the exchange did either man note that the shooter had claimed he had held radical racist views before Trump became a politician.[74]

• August 2019: On MSNBC with Rachel Maddow, Lawrence O'Donnell teased that Russian oligarchs close to Putin possibly cosigned loans Donald Trump got from Deutsche Bank. O'Donnell tweeted the same report.[75] An attorney for Donald Trump immediately denied the claim, calling the MSNBC reportage "false and defamatory."[76] But the story already had exploded online. In a midnight tweet, director Rob Reiner, who is often a guest on MSNBC, accepted the report as true and demanded the president's indictment over the story.[77] O'Donnell apologized the following day, acknowledging he had no idea if the story was true or not.[78] Even after the on-air retraction, O'Donnell left the fake news tweet live online for hours, though he would eventually delete it.[79]

• August 2019 (this was a crazy month at MSNBC): Appearing on Brian Williams's show *The 11th Hour,* Frank Figliuzzi, a former high-level FBI bureaucrat and MSNBC national security contributor with black eyes, suggested on-air that Trump could be sending a secret message to Nazis. Trump ordered flags flown at half-mast after deadly shootings in Dayton, Ohio, and El Paso, Texas, but planned to raise them on August 8. Figliuzzi suggested this was an homage to Hitler and a dog whistle to white supremacists. His explanation:

> The president said that we will fly our flags at half-mast until August 8th. That's 8/8.
>
> [...]

The numbers 88 are very significant in neo-Nazi and white supremacist movement. Why? Because the letter H is the eighth letter of the alphabet and to them, the numbers 88 together stand for "Heil Hitler."

• May 2020: MSNBC's Ali Velshi reported live from the BLM riots in Minneapolis, stating, "I want to be clear on how I characterize this. This is mostly a protest. It is not, generally speaking, unruly." Behind Velshi in the frame as he delivered this report, the viewers could see a building engulfed in flames while demonstrators gathered round.[80] That same day, the *Today* show anchor tweeted network guidance on covering the riots in Minneapolis, stating that "it is most accurate at this time to describe what is happening there as 'protests'—not 'riots.'"[81]

• September 2020: Figliuzzi (yes, he was not let go for his insane Nazi conspiracy theory) told host Nicolle Wallace the "notion of Antifa, as being some kind of organized group, is laughable."[82] Antifa is a violent, radical left activist group that most certainly has organized elements. Attorney General Bill Barr referred to them as a "group."[83] The Department of Homeland Security called Antifa-linked violence in Portland "organized."[84] Texas officials said that looting that took place in Austin in the summer of 2020 was "organized by an Antifa web page." Antifa has organized riots on Facebook.[85] Even CNN's leftist anchor Don Lemon has referred to Antifa as an "organization."[86]

• October 2020: MSNBC prime-time anchor Chris Hayes promoted a zany conspiracy theory that the Republicans traded 100,000 American lives to assure that Justice Amy Coney Barrett would get confirmed to the Supreme Court. His logic on how he got to the incredibly scary and incredibly round "100,000" number is not remotely clear. Joy Reid had her colleague's back and accepted it at face value. Reid tweeted that Republicans would have traded a million lives to get Barrett seated on the court.[87]

MSNBC lives to inflame, not inform. This isn't merely reckless journalism, it's weaponized lunacy.

Weaponizing Fake News to Crush the Competition

Sometimes NBC's activism gets a little more overt. In June 2020, NBC News reporter Adele-Momoko Fraser reported that ZeroHedge, a popular financial news blog with a libertarian political bent, and the Federalist, a moderate conservative opinion website that features pro-Trump content, would no longer be able to generate revenue from Google Ads.[88] Fraser worked at the time for something called the "NBC News Verification Center" (even Orwell might have said that name is too on-the-nose). Google Ads is one of the biggest ad platforms in the world and makes up the bulk of Google's annual revenue.[89] NBC News tweeted at the time, "Two far-right sites, ZeroHedge and The Federalist, will no longer be able to generate revenue from any advertisements served by Google Ads."[90]

NBC's definition of "far-right" is apparently anything more conservative than the DNC's party platform.

The reason for the alleged ban? What else could be the reason in the summer of 2020? "Racist articles."

Or maybe not. As it turns out, the story wasn't accurate. ZeroHedge told Breitbart News that they had been banned over their comment section.[91] ZeroHedge removed the offending comments and was reinstated a few weeks later.[92] The Federalist was never banned at all; they had merely been given a warning. NBC updated their story after Google refuted key claims in it.[93]

The most stunning part of this saga wasn't that a big establishment outlet had exaggerated claims in a negative story about smaller right-of-center outlets; it was that the reporter thanked far-left activists for "collaborating" on it. Fraser tweeted upon publication of the mostly fake news article, "Thanks to @SFFakeNews and @CCDHate for their hard work and collaboration!" @SFFakeNews is the handle for a project called Stop Funding Fake News (ironic!) by the Center for Countering Digital Hate (@CCDHate). Stop Funding Fake News is a card-carrying member of the conspiratorial far left. For example, they've suggested that brands like Ford and Microsoft "fund racism."[94] Stop Funding Fake News, a British advocacy group, smears Breitbart on its website and openly advocates that we should be "defunded."[95]

CCDH's chairman is Simon Clark, a fellow at the far-left Center for American Progress, which is funded by leftist billionaire George Soros.

Clark, Oxford educated and incredibly white, considers "combating violent white supremacy" among his top life goals. CCDH's leadership appears to be deeply tied to the United Kingdom's left-wing political parties.

Fraser eventually walked back her boast about working with a shadowy foreign entity to blacklist American journalists.[96]

Even though she had been caught—publicly—weaponizing a mostly fake story in an effort to deplatform conservatives, she retained her job at NBC.

It does appear, however, that the "Verification Center" did not survive the ordeal. @NBC_VC hasn't tweeted since the day Fraser's article published.[97]

NBC also puts significant money and effort into spreading their version of weaponized "journalism" and attacking those who report information unfavorable to the Democratic Party. Since 2016, they have hyped boycotts of Breitbart News that have been led by far-left "brand safety" hoaxsters called "Sleeping Giants."[98] In what amounts to light corporate warfare, they've enthusiastically plugged boycott campaigns against Fox News hosts Sean Hannity, Bill O'Reilly, Tucker Carlson, and Laura Ingraham.[99]

And in an era where corporations are increasingly "woke," they can do so with relative confidence that there will not be a reciprocal boycott of NBC.

NBC invested big into Vox, BuzzFeed, and Axios—all aimed at expanding a new online advertising business. In fact, NBC invested a staggering $400 million in BuzzFeed, the viral millennial-focused website that is known for listicles of cats, 1990s nostalgia, and the occasional video of their employees drinking their own urine.[100] Just like any highly reputable news source, BuzzFeed has their own line of "sexual wellness" products, including a vibrator.[101] "The NBCUniversal and BuzzFeed partnership offers marketers innovative, holistic solutions," NBCUniversal proclaimed.[102] "Holistic solutions"? The pomposity is breathtaking. But then again, who wouldn't be proud to team up with the geniuses behind the exposé "24 Bizarre Pogs That Will Leave You Scratching Your Head" and the critically acclaimed "Can We Guess What Your Pubes Look Like Based on Some of Your Lifestyle Choices?"[102]

The NBC/BuzzFeed relationship was to "shape the future of storytelling," according to NBC. In retrospect, that claim was overly grandiose as well. BuzzFeed has since gone through massive high-profile layoffs, including gutting their news desk.[104]

In 2016, NBCUniversal launched Concert, an online ad platform, in conjunction with left-wing Vox Media. Their stated goal is to create the world's "largest premium advertising marketplace online."[105] In 2018, they added additional leftist media brands to their roster, including *Rolling Stone*, Funny or Die, *New York* magazine, and more.

Concert's promotional material repeatedly touts "safety" for brands, which is the same language used by left-wing activists when calling for boycotts of conservative media.[106]

It's fitting that NBCUniversal, a massive international brand known for the ideological leftism of its properties, would both encourage advertising boycotts at the same time they built a massive digital advertising arm focused on left-wing brands.

Meacham Hits the Third Rail

With all of the corruption, impropriety, and fake news happening, it raises the question: Is it even possible to cross the line at Comcast NBCUniversal? We know of at least one person who found himself across it: historian and failed magazine editor Jon Meacham.[107]

Meacham is a Pulitzer Prize–winning presidential biographer also known for being the editor of *Newsweek* during its precipitous decline from 2006 until his high-profile ouster in 2010.[108] Meacham's television persona is that of the old-timey school rector; he calmly, yet pompously, delivers hard truths in trying times to young whippersnappers who simply don't know the ways of the world. He's the type of man who wears his reading glasses so far down the tip of nose, you marvel at how they don't just slide right off. In other words, he seems like an asshole. He speaks lyrically (if I'm being charitable), but the content is always essentially the same: Trump bad, Democrats good. Thus he fits in perfectly with MSNBC's cast of characters.

In November 2020, just after the election, Meacham went on MSNBC as a paid contributor and authority on the presidency to praise a speech by Joe Biden—a speech Meacham himself had helped write. Meacham didn't disclose on-air that he was touting the magnificence of his own ideas. He even brazenly cited specific moments in Biden's address he thought were particularly strong. You almost have to admire his shamelessness.

This dishonesty was too much for NBC, apparently, and Meacham was dropped as a paid contributor when they found out—which is particularly remarkable considering that Joy Reid and Brian Williams remain employed by the network to this day.

But collectively, the media, both establishment and new media alike, yawned at all this. After all, within a week of election day, several MSNBC contributors had cut ties with the network to formally join the Biden apparatus.[109] (MSNBC was not alone in this regard; CNN contributor Jen Psaki immediately quit her commentator job, was hired by Team Joe and Kamala, and promptly went back on CNN for an interview in her new role. She later became White House press secretary.)[110]

Though Meacham was formally out at MSNBC, he'll still be welcomed on the network as an unpaid guest, according to the *New York Times*.[111]

This gives me great confidence. Everyone has learned their lessons and now takes journalistic integrity very, very seriously.

After years of media handwringing about overlap between the Trump administration and Fox News and even Breitbart News, Meacham's actions are particularly humorous. Everyone was in on the joke that MSNBC is *figuratively* the Biden operation; maybe MSNBC is *literally* the Biden operation after all. They couldn't even wait until all the votes were counted before embarrassing themselves this profoundly.

"Bias," Evolved

It's clear that one of MSNBC's primary functions is to advance the Democratic Party. I don't think any honest person disputes this, at least on a broad level. However, if you look at what the MSNBC brass truly considers *thought crimes*, a pattern reveals itself that only mistakes that threaten the broader business interests of the multinational conglomerate Comcast NBCUniversal are truly unacceptable.

They also have savaged anti-establishment voices who are on the left. For example, NBC News published a report stating that populist liberal Tulsi Gabbard, a former congresswoman and Democratic presidential candidate, "has become a favorite of the sites Moscow used when it interfered in 2016." Take journalist Glenn Greenwald, for example. Greenwald's politics are overwhelmingly situated on the left, yet he does not unquestionably toe the Democrat Party line, so MSNBC talking head Malcolm Nance smeared him as an "agent of Trump & Moscow." [112]

As Greenwald wrote at the time, "MSNBC does not merely permit fabrications against democratic party critics. It encourages and rewards them." [113]

This is an evolution in media "bias."

(Aside: I sparred with Nance during the "Overtime" portion of *Real Time with Bill Maher* in the summer of 2017. Breitbart had previously written about a tweet he sent stating that Trump Tower Istanbul "is my nominee for the first ISIS suicide bombing of a Trump property."

Nance confronted me on the article, demanding I apologize because we had, according to Nance, smeared him. He also suggested that Breitbart was responsible for dozens of death threats made against him. I told him I was unfamiliar with the article and that if his account was accurate, I'd be happy to apologize. As it turns out, he was mistaken or being dishonest. The Breitbart report was entirely accurate, so I never apologized. Nance eventually deleted the tweet about bombing TrumpTower.)

Conservatives have long pointed out that our journalist class tends to come from the same backgrounds, attend the same colleges, and live in the same cities, etc. They're bubbled. We get it. That's why they all seem to compete with each other to see who can be most woke and most outraged at America. But another bubble that is less often discussed but arguably more disturbing is how the vast majority of journalists are inculcated in similar corporate cultures.

Typically, those cultures follow a few principles: political correctness should be your default, brand safety is priority number one, globalism is better than nationalism, the collective is more important than the individual, and China's massive, economically ascendant population is a gold mine for American media conglomerates. The list goes on. The familiar is better than the new, and those who are in "the club" never have to apologize for anything aside from things that hurt "the club."

Corporations are amoral; their loyalties are to their boards of directors, their shareholders, and to future business prospects. That's why NBC's news brands can routinely embarrass themselves publicly without consistent consequences. Integrity and accuracy simply aren't priorities.

Most of the mistakes by their journalists documented in this chapter do significant reputational damage to the NBC brands with some sections of the population, but they do not significantly threaten their global business prospects. At least not in the eyes of the Comcast NBCUniversal brass. And so long as the vast majority of our news content is controlled by an oligarchy of a few conglomerates that have essentially the same agenda, not much will threaten those business prospects in the near term.

Independent media is the only antidote to this.

That is, until a major corporation buys them out.

CHAPTER 5

BEIJING BLOOMBERG

In late November 2019, billionaire businessman Michael Bloomberg, then seventy-seven years old, joined the Democrat primary race. Bloomberg, an unpopular former three-term mayor of New York, entered the race when it was already well under way. Kamala Harris, for example, had announced her candidacy ten months prior.[1]

It was already too late to contest in the first four momentum-building states—Iowa, New Hampshire, Nevada, and South Carolina. At the moment he joined the fray, the nomination was down to a geriatric socialist (Bernie Sanders) and a geriatric establishment Democrat with declining mental function (Joe Biden). At that point, according to the Bloomberg campaign, Trump was on a "path to victory."[2] So, the pint-sized (and also geriatric) New York pol decided to give it a go.

It became one of the most intense—and ultimately short-lived—news cycles of the election season.

Bloomberg was well known to the Breitbart audience prior to his presidential run for how he spent much of his public life after serving as mayor.

Bloomberg had founded the "Everytown for Gun Safety" anti-firearms group. The group has pushed for numerous gun controls, including universal background checks, red flag laws, "assault weapons" bans, high-capacity magazine bans, and more. They've opposed arming teachers as well as campus carry.[3]

Bloomberg himself, an oligarch billionaire, is protected by the near-constant presence of armed guards.[4]

While the Left claimed Trump harbored dictator-like tendencies and might give himself an extra term or three, Bloomberg himself had controversially managed to repeal New York City's term limit to give himself four more years as mayor.[5]

(The Big Apple voters immediately reinstated the two-term limit after Bloomberg won.)[6]

Yet, Michael Bloomberg turned out to be a deeply flawed presidential candidate who was particularly easy to define: he was an old, short, out of touch, gun-grabbing, Big Gulp–banning, panda-hugging egomaniac. In other words, he was a perfect character for the Breitbart.com front page.

But two things had me genuinely concerned at the outset of his campaign: he was one of the most powerful people in global news media and that he seemed more than willing to take a knee for Communist China.

Bloomberg made his billions mostly from being the founder of Bloomberg LP; he owns about 90 percent of the companies' shares. Bloomberg LP is best known for its famed financial services product, the "Bloomberg Terminal," a software system that provides real-time financial news and data. Bloomberg's namesake business also happens to be one of the world's biggest employers of journalists. The company consists of websites, a television network, radio stations, a news wire, and *Bloomberg Businessweek* magazine, among other divisions.[7]

In short, Bloomberg is one of the biggest news organizations on earth. Thus, anyone working in media is either a past, present, or potential future employee of Michael Bloomberg.

And should Bloomberg ever become president, he would have thousands of journalists around the world "reporting" for an outlet that bears his name. The president of the United States' name would literally be on their paychecks.

In this scenario, at least mild corruption is inevitable. Arguably, it's a legitimate threat to democracy.[8] Bloomberg News could be the closest thing to state-run media we've ever had in America.

The only problem for Michael Bloomberg (and a blessing for the rest of us) is that he turned out to be a lousy candidate.

The Bloomberg campaign got off to an inauspicious start. Early polling showed "Mini Mike," as President Trump nicknamed him, at a mere 3 percent within the Democratic Party.[9] The biggest challenge facing his campaign out of the gate were the legitimate attacks on Bloomberg for his record as New York mayor, as well as his past political positions.

Bloomberg was instantly criticized for the controversial "stop-and-frisk" policing policy that was operational during his tenure in Gotham. Under the policy, the New York Police Department could detain, interrogate, and even search civilians on the street who were considered reasonably suspicious. Critics of the policy noted that demographics most often subject to "stop and frisk" were blacks and Latinos, that is, it's racist. Others made the case the policy was not constitutional.[10] (Proponents of "stop and frisk" have asserted that it tends to benefit black and brown Americans because it drove down crimes in their communities, particularly murder.)[11]

The far-left *New Republic* magazine included it among a list of grievances in an article titled "Michael Bloomberg's Polite Authoritarianism."[12] And Bloomberg wasn't exactly polite about it. In 2015, he gave a speech to upper-crust and incredibly white attendees at the Aspen Institute where he spoke at length about "stop and frisk" in the context of murders committed by young male minorities.[13] The comments surfaced while he was on the campaign trail in February 2020. A fairly shocking passage:

> [W]e put all the cops in minority neighborhoods. Yes, that's true. Why do we do it? Because that's where all the crime is. And the way you get the guns out of the kids' hands is to throw them up against the wall and frisk them.

That sounds a little cold. What's more, it's seemingly an admission that under Bloomberg's leadership, New York City applied stop and frisk specifically to people because of their race. Even the pro-Democrat media couldn't pass up this one up, and Bloomberg was pilloried for it. NPR, *Slate*, the *Chicago Tribune*, *Newsweek*, the *Washington Post*, and many others covered the quote; virtually all the stories on the quote were negative.

"Stop and frisk" was such a political loser for Mini Mike that he apologized for it just prior to announcing his candidacy.[14] Interestingly, he did note in his mea culpa that the policy did in fact drive down crime.

Kissing the Communist Ring

This wasn't the only angle of attack that stuck to Bloomberg. The nationalist right pounced on one of the first interviews Bloomberg gave on the campaign trail, on PBS's *Firing Line* with Margaret Hoover. In the interview, Bloomberg praised China's handling of environmental issues and defended their authoritarian system of government. Some lowlights from the interview:

- Bloomberg said that "China is doing a lot" to curb greenhouse gas emissions, even though he acknowledged they continue to build coal-fired power plants.

- He said the Chinese Communist Party (CCP) "listen[s] to the public." (The CCP is under no obligation to listen to the people; they are only accountable to the Politburo.)

- He said that "Xi Jinping is not a dictator." (He most certainly is. He even made himself "president for life.") [15]

- He said "[Xi] has to satisfy his constituents, or he's not going to survive." (Answering to a few CCP elites who he can easily muscle around is not a "constituency.")

- He said "no government survives without the will of the majority of its people." (This is historically illiterate. If there is no democracy and a ruler has loyalty from major institutions, including the military, he doesn't need a majority of the people.)

This interview was so mind-bogglingly out of touch that even the left-wing media dinged Bloomberg for it; *New York* magazine's Eric Levitz wrote in a scathing piece that Bloomberg's *Firing Line* interview "signaled that he intends to run in the 'unrepentant Stalinist' lane of the Democratic primary." [16]

This wasn't the first time Bloomberg praised China's rulers in public. In 2018, Bloomberg held its first Bloomberg New Economy Forum in Singapore. [17] According to a press release, the forum "enables global leaders from East and West to come together to forge common ground, establish deep personal connections, and chart the course toward a new economy with a sustainable, inclusive future." Sounds noble.

At the event, however, Mike Bloomberg introduced Chinese vice president Wang Qishan by lavishing praise on him:[18]

Today, he is the most influential political figure in China and in the world and he has played a key role in Chinese finance and politics for more than 30 years, helping to lead that country to a period of extraordinary growth, navigate challenges along the way, including the financial crisis of 2008.

Wang had previously been Xi's "anti-corruption chief"—that is, until he had been accused of corruption himself.[19] Wang, commonly known as Xi's "firefighter" lieutenant, would later play a key role in China's suppression of Hong Kong political protests in 2019.[20]

It's notable that Bloomberg not only praised this man, but he described him as the most influential political figure "in the world." I suppose if you're a billionaire international businessman with an authoritarian streak, that might be the exact type of guy who has an ass you'd like to kiss.

Apparently, Wang regarded Bloomberg's obsequiousness as excessive. In his speech, he referred to Bloomberg's words of praise as "peng sha"— a rough English translation is "blowing smoke."

A pattern is emerging. Michael Bloomberg really seems to like the most powerful people in the CCP. Perhaps this is out of genuine affection (though that would be disturbing), but more likely he's flattering them because he has vested business interest in being seen as friendly toward Xi Jinping and his associates.

Michael Bloomberg is in the information business: Bloomberg LP collects and distributes financial information to clients around the world. Naturally, this includes China. Clients access this information through the company's main product, the Bloomberg Terminal (or just "Bloomberg," as it is often called), at a cost of around $24,000 per year, per terminal. (This cost is estimated; they don't publicize their pricing.)

All business that is done in China is done at the blessing of the Communist Party. Bloomberg's access to data from the Chinese market— which is the world's second largest and fastest-growing market—depends on the approval of Beijing.

Foreign distributors of financial data—of which Bloomberg is one of the largest—are forced to seek licensure from the State Council Information Office (SCIO), which is an agency under the auspices of China's State Council. In other words, his ability to do business in China is subject to the will of what is effectively China's executive branch.

According to China's Provisions on Administration of Provision of Financial Information Services in China by Foreign Institutions (translated):[21]

> Foreign institutions providing financial information services in China must be approved by the State Council Information Office. Foreign institutions without the approval of the State Council Information Office may not provide financial information services in China.

Since the Bloomberg license is renewed every two years, the pressure is always on. This could explain the ass kissing.

But it isn't just ass kissing. China also can bar Bloomberg (and any foreign institution) from providing all sorts of financial information services in China. So, not only is Bloomberg's access to the Chinese market subject to review and cancellation by the Communist Party every twenty-four months, the CCP can (and will) restrict any content it believes undermines the national interest.

Bloomberg LP's license has since been renewed by China's Cyberspace Administration, the agency responsible for online censorship and control of the Internet.[22]

Michael Bloomberg himself as well as his top executives have met regularly with Chinese Thought Police throughout recent years, according to government records:

- On August 19, 2015: Michael Bloomberg met with Jiang Jianguo, director of the State Council Information Office (SCIO) and deputy director of the Publicity Department of the Communist Party of China; the latter office is the CCP's department, which makes Jianguo the vice minister of propaganda. According to the Chinese government, they discussed "international exchange and cooperation in the field of media."[23]

• December 21, 2015: Bloomberg LP global executive vice president Kevin Sheekey met with Jiang as well as Zhang Fuhai and Zhang Hongbin, respectively the director general and deputy director general of the SCIO Internet Affairs Bureau. They run an arm of the Chinese regime that deals with Internet censorship.[24]

• On July 13, 2016, Bloomberg executives reportedly met in Beijing with Chinese propaganda minister Jiang,[25] this time to discuss "Belt and Road" strategic cooperation and the South China Sea. The Belt and Road Initiative (BRI) is China's global project to gain economic dominance throughout the world via a massive network of infrastructure projects bankrolled by Beijing. BRI deeply intertwines China to other countries, particularly developing nations, via a network of investments.[26] China skeptics consider the ambitious project essentially a "debt trap" scheme where nations ultimately default on loans extended to them, which allows the CCP to gain economic and political control over them.[27] Often the Chinese are able to use their new economic leverage to expand their military capabilities in a given region.[28] Beijing has staked a claim to much of the South China Sea, despite the fact that much of that territory is legally sovereign to Taiwan, Brunei, Malaysia, Vietnam, and the Philippines.[29] China has little regard for the fact that the United States considers this behavior illegal; in fact, America's position makes China furious.[30] Beijing is engaging in similar behavior in the East China Sea, where they illegally claim territory that belongs to Japan, among other nations. Ecuador, Chile, and Argentina are among several other countries that have asserted China has violated their sovereign waters.[31] Details of the conversation between Bloomberg brass and the CCP aren't public.

• June 7, 2017: Kevin Sheekey, who was then vice president of government relations at Bloomberg LP and went on to become Michael Bloomberg's campaign manager, again met with communist propaganda minister Jiang. According to the Chinese government, "they talked about China-U.S. media exchanges and cooperation, the introduction of Chinese stories to the world, and efforts to promote healthy and stable relations between the two countries."[32]

• July 11, 2018: Otis Bilodeau, senior executive editor of Bloomberg Asia Pacific, met with the vice minister of the SCIO, Guo Weimin, one of the top Communist Party spokesmen.[33]

• April 13, 2018: John Micklethwait, editor in chief of Bloomberg News, met with the vice minister of the SCIO. From a Beijing readout: "The two sides held discussions on strengthening media cooperation between China and the U.S., enhancing understanding between Chinese and Western citizens, presenting China to the world, as well as China-U.S. relations."[34] In other words, the CCP claims that Bloomberg's top editor advised a top communist official on how to "present China to the world."

• May 9, 2018: Jiang Jianguo, the deputy propaganda minister, met again with Sheekey in Beijing. This time they discussed, according to Beijing, "expanding communication and cooperation between the media of China and the U.S., promoting understandings between Chinese and western citizens, as well as China-U.S. relations."[35]

Translation: the future campaign manager for Michael Bloomberg's presidential run met yet again with one of the CCP's top propagandists, and according to Beijing, they repeatedly discussed cooperation between the two nations and their media establishments.

This goes far beyond "cozying up to China." Bloomberg executives have flown to China to meet with top Communist Party members, including propagandists, in order to forge deep partnerships on all manner of issues.

Public details of these conversations between Bloomberg brass and the CCP are extremely limited.

Though this section of Breaking the News focuses on Bloomberg because they appear to be the most deferential to the CCP, they are not the only western news organization subject to Chinese regulatory pressure. Thomson Reuters, Dow Jones, and the Economist have all received licenses to distribute financial information in China.[36]

In December 2019, Reuters reporters revealed that Refinitiv, the financial information service co-owned at the time by Reuters' parent company, had blocked more than two hundred stories about the ongoing Hong Kong protests.[37] (To its credit, Reuters reported this; they also have since sold its remaining stake in Refinitiv.) Reuters editor in chief Stephen Adler (not to be confused with Steven Adler, the drummer for Guns N' Roses) condemned the censorship. But, just days earlier, he met with SCIO vice-minister Guo Weimin.[38]

Adler has met multiple times with Chinese regulators to discuss matters including "ways to comprehensively and accurately present China in the media" and "views on deepening cooperative relations," according to the SCIO. Perhaps concerningly, he also sits on the board of the Committee to Protect Journalists. Additionally, Adler is the Chairman of the Columbia Journalism Review and is the Chairman of the Reporters Committee for Freedom of the Press.

Dow Jones, which publishes the *Wall Street Journal*, chose not to renew the contract of its CEO, William Lewis, shortly after three journalists were expelled from China over harsh coverage.[39]

Covering for the Corrupt

Bloomberg's newsroom consistently protects the CCP in their reporting. There is no clearer example of this than when Bloomberg News spiked what would have been a blockbuster story that would supposedly have exposed corrupt financial ties of Xi Jinping's family, among other rich and powerful Chinese. The investigation reportedly took nearly a year to complete.[40]

In 2012, a team of Bloomberg reporters published a major report focusing on the accumulation of wealth of the most powerful people in China, especially the family of Xi Jinping, who at the time was set to become the general secretary of the Chinese Communist Party.[41] The report led to death threats, and at least one reporter removed his family from Hong Kong because they believed it to be unsafe.[42] Bloomberg's website was blocked in mainland China, which the company's head of corporate communications believed to be a direct reaction to the story.[43]

Soon after, the journalist on the story who had to flee Hong Kong due to threats, Mike Forsythe, got to work on a similar investigation on a different subject: Wang Jianlin, China's richest man. Only this time, Bloomberg had no intention of running the story.

The *Columbia Journalism Review* described it in dramatic fashion at the time:

> The reported spike came after an extensively footnoted version of the story had been fact-checked and pored over by company lawyers, and after members of the reporting team had been praised internally for yet more stellar work. The Times reported that [longtime editor in chief of Bloomberg News Matthew] Winkler, in a conference call with reporters, defended the decision not to publish the story by likening the situation to the need for self-censorship by foreign bureaus in Nazi Germany to preserve their ability to continue reporting there.[44]

NPR published a transcript of the aforementioned conference call with reporters and Winkler, who was also a Bloomberg News cofounder. The key section of NPR's report, emphasis mine:

> "The inference *is going to be interpreted by the government there as we are judging them,*" Winkler said. "And they will probably kick us out of the country. They'll probably shut us down, is my guess."[45]
>
> Winkler suggested reporters could find a uniquely "Bloomberg" way to cover the wealth of Chinese ruling elites. But he added a caution about covering the regime.
>
> "It has to be done with a strategic framework and a tactical method that is . . . smart enough *to allow us to continue and not run afoul of the Nazis* who are in front of us and behind us everywhere," Winkler said, according to the audio reviewed by NPR and verified by others. "*And that's who they are. And we should have no illusions about it.*"

To recap: Bloomberg's top editor says unequivocally that the Chinese ruling class is composed of Nazis, but their reporting should not make the Nazis feel "judged." Because if they do, the Nazis will kick them out, which would be bad.

(When this story broke in April 2020, it was not lost on us in the Breitbart newsroom that Bloomberg had dedicated significant resources to portraying President Trump and his supporters as Nazis and racists.[46] Some examples: "Trump's New Slogan Has Old Baggage from Nazi Era," "Stung by Criticism, White House Says Trump Abhors Neo-Nazis," and "Trump's Racism Infests the Republican Party."[47] Bloomberg Law reporter Benjamin Penn once falsely reported that a Trump official made anti-Semitic comments on Facebook; while the story was retracted, Penn still kept his job at Bloomberg, which he still held as of early 2021.[48] In 2020, Michael Bloomberg himself compared Trump's border security measures to Nazi Germany—in a speech delivered on Holocaust Remembrance Day.)[49]

Yet, as repulsive as it is, Winkler's statement that Bloomberg will continue do business with "Nazis"—but will cover said Nazis with extreme judiciousness—actually has a logical basis. If Bloomberg continues to report on the financial dealings of China's top officials, the entire enterprise is likely to lose access to the world's second-biggest financial market. If Bloomberg News is banned from China, you can guarantee that some, if not all, of the other divisions of Bloomberg LP would be banned, too.

The *New York Times*, among other publications, got details of the Bloomberg editor's new philosophy. "[Winkler] said, 'If we run the story, we'll be kicked out of China,'" one employee said, according to the *Times*.[50]

So, they chose to self-censor, literally selling out to the Chinese communist regime.

Bloomberg News suspended Forsythe, one of the lead reporters on the spiked articles (he was accused of leaking details of the fiasco to the *Times*). Forsythe's wife, Leta Hong Fincher, an academic and journalist who covers China, wrote years later that Bloomberg attempted to intimidate her into signing a nondisclosure agreement (NDA) barring her from discussing the controversy—even though she has never been an employee of Bloomberg.

Unsurprisingly, Fincher attributed the alleged forcefulness of the Bloomberg brass to the profit motive: "Bloomberg's company, Bloomberg LP, is so dependent on the vast China market for its business that its lawyers threatened to devastate my family financially if I didn't sign an NDA silencing me about how Bloomberg News killed a story critical of Chinese Communist Party leaders," Fincher wrote in the Intercept in 2020. "It was only when I hired Edward Snowden's lawyers in Hong Kong that Bloomberg LP eventually called off their hounds after many attempts to intimidate me."[51]

Michael Bloomberg at the time was recused from the company while serving his twelfth and final year as New York City mayor. But even he felt compelled to deny that his news service squelched the reporting: "No one thinks that we are wusses and not willing to stand up and write stories that are of interest to the public and that are factually correct," he said in a November 2013 news conference.

While this humiliation certainly made Bloomberg LP look both weak and corrupt in the American media, it also took a toll on Bloomberg's business within China. The *New York Times* reported in November 2013 that financial terminal sales to state-owned enterprises slowed and that new Bloomberg journalists were denied residencies by the Communist Party.[52] The *Times* also reported that employees believed the organization was even less likely to publish negative stories on Xi Jinping or wealthy and powerful Chinese families thereafter.

Yet, Bloomberg's even softer approach to China in the years since has apparently served its central purpose: Bloomberg still does a lot more business in China than its competitors. In March 2020, China made good on its 2013 threat and decided to not renew the visas of American journalists from a number of major publications, including the *New York Times, Washington Post,* and *Wall Street Journal.* Bloomberg News was not among those blacklisted.[53]

Covering Your Boss: A Soft Money Story

During his brief run for president in 2019 and 2020, Michael Bloomberg not only indicated he'd be a "Panda Hugger" (a derogatory expression for overly pro-China policy makers), he actually seemed to borrow from China's unfree-press playbook. In November 2019, Bloomberg News editor-in-chief John Micklethwait instructed the newsroom to limit coverage of Mike Bloomberg and his rivals in the Democratic primary.

"We will continue our tradition of not investigating Mike (and his family and foundation) and we will extend the same policy to his rivals in the Democratic primaries. We cannot treat Mike's Democratic competitors differently from him," Micklethwait told the Bloomberg newsroom in a memo sent to editorial and research staff.[54]

In the surprisingly candid communiqué, Micklethwait noted that the investigations into Trump, Mike Bloomberg's ultimate would-be rival, would proceed anyway. He said what was seemingly a de facto soft money contribution to the Democrat Party was justified because the Trump administration is "the government of the day." In other words, Micklethwait admitted in a memorandum to his staff that they would continue to investigate the leaders of one political party and not the other.

As previously noted, Kevin Sheekey, Bloomberg LP's global head of communications and one of the company's frequent ambassadors to China, would become Mike's campaign manager.

Many others would follow suit and leave the Bloomberg business for the Bloomberg campaign. This includes executive editor Tim O'Brien, a man who was sued by Trump after publishing a book called *TrumpNation* over a decade earlier. O'Brien had made the claim that President Trump, who was then a New York businessman, was not in fact a billionaire. The case was dismissed.[55]

Senior executive editor David Shipley also joined the campaign, as did opinion editors Zara Kessler, Mark Whitehouse, and Jessica Karl. At least a half-dozen others from the newsroom joined Team Mini Mike as well.[56]

This inequity was quickly recognized by the Trump campaign, which revoked press credentials for Bloomberg News reporters covering the president's rallies and campaign events.[57] On at least one occasion, the president's reelection campaign expelled a Bloomberg reporter from an event.[58]

Other journalists reacted negatively toward the way Bloomberg, *The Business* was handling Bloomberg, *The Candidate,* according to a report from the *Columbia Journalism Review.* Megan Murphy, the former editor of *Bloomberg Businessweek,* tweeted, "This is not journalism." BuzzFeed's Ryan Mac predicted a "chilling effect on the rest of the news room." Then–*Daily Mail* White House correspondent David Martosko forecast Trump would use the conflict of interest to bludgeon Bloomberg, *The Candidate*—as well as Bloomberg journalists.

The *New York Times'* Jim Rutenberg suggested that Bloomberg would be better off simply letting the press be free, tweeting "let journalists do journalism, endorse idea that those seeking to lead the democracy need to live with a press free+strong."[59] But perhaps Mr. Rutenberg was not familiar with Michael Bloomberg: the man who banned Big Gulps, instituted "stop and frisk," pushed draconian gun control, abolished term limits, and repeatedly kowtowed to the Chinese communists.[60] In his pint-sized heart, Michael Bloomberg is as much of an authoritarian as you'll find in mainstream American politics.

Mini Mike's Epic Fail

The rest of the Bloomberg campaign did not go much better than the campaign launch.

In December 2019, the Intercept broke the story that some members of "Team Mike" were actually inmates making far below the minimum wage.[61] Yes, billionaire Bloomberg's campaign used prison labor to make campaign calls. Though technically the deal was made through a third-party contractor (the campaign pleaded ignorance when the Intercept reached out to them for comment), Bloomberg did in fact exploit a ProCom call center that operates out of an Oklahoma prison.

It should go without saying that Bloomberg didn't utilize the prison call center because he has a passion for providing opportunity for the incarcerated. It was almost certainly chosen because it's incredibly cheap. John Scallan, a ProCom founder, told the Intercept the Oklahoma Department of Corrections is paid $7.25 an hour and the incarcerated people get between $20 and $28 a month to work the phones.

Still, prisoners are often willing to do the job at these rates because there is little other opportunity for them while they are doing time.

A man worth perhaps $50 billion putting desperate Americans to work for slave wages was not good optics for a would-be-president—or any human being.

Bloomberg fired the contractor who got him into the deal and disavowed the exploitation.[62]

Bloomberg's ability to embarrass himself while wasting his own money only seemed to increase throughout the campaign. Throughout February, Bloomberg pushed an astroturf campaign to buy social media influence. On February 13, 2020, it was revealed that Bloomberg was paying Instagram stars to promote his candidacy using memes (witty Internet postings designed for social media virality).[63] A few days later, it came out that Bloomberg was paying up to $2,500 per month to people who would simply praise him online or even in private text messages.[64]

On February 22, Twitter decided the campaign had officially gone too far and accused the accounts responsible for pro-Bloomberg content of "platform manipulation."[65] Dozens of Bloomberg-connected accounts had been caught posting identical content, which violates Twitter's "platform manipulation" rules, leading to widespread suspensions.

Bloomberg dropped out of the race on March 4, only about three and a half months after he launched it. When it was all said and done, he had spent $900 million to win a mere 58 delegates (1,991 delegates are required to secure the nomination).[66] That's a staggering $15.5 million per delegate! He didn't carry a single state and his lone "victory" came in America Samoa.

Even when Bloomberg was out of the race, his influence was still felt throughout the rest of the campaign. Just after dropping out of the Democrat primary, he transferred $18 million to the Democratic National Committee, stating how important it is that the DNC is well funded. Naturally, this delighted DNC chair Tom Perez, who said at the time, "Mayor Bloomberg and his team are making good on their commitment to beating Donald Trump."[67]

In late summer of 2020, Bloomberg pledged at least $100 million to help Biden win the crucial swing state of Florida (the man really can't help but waste money).[68] Bloomberg owns property in Wellington, an enclave of Palm Beach County known as "the winter equestrian capital of the world."[69] He also committed to giving at least $60 million to help Democrat House candidates.[70]

Bloomberg set a plan in place in the fall of 2020 that would pay off fines on tens of thousands of convicted criminals in Florida so that their right to vote would be restored. This follows a Florida state amendment passed in 2019 that reinstated the right to vote for certain felons, provided that they were all paid up on any fees owed.

The amendment, known as Amendment 4, seemingly makes it possible for billionaires to essentially buy votes. The American Civil Liberties Union (ACLU) and the Brennan Center for Justice were consultants on the amendment; both organizations are heavily funded by left-wing billionaire activist George Soros.[71]

Once Bloomberg's plan was reported, it was immediately panned as pure racism.[72] Florida's governor and attorney general called for an investigation shortly thereafter.[73] (It is unclear whether an investigation was ever started.)

It's unlikely Michael Bloomberg will stop spending his money to wield political influence. He's likely to direct his news outlet to pursue narratives that are favorable to him and not his political opponents. He'll continue to compromise basic American principles in order to gain access to the Chinese market, despite human rights abuses by the Communist Party. He'll continue to attempt to use his bottomless coffers to influence voters across the country—perhaps for himself and definitely for Democrats with simpatico worldviews.

Even though his 2020 presidential candidacy turned into a colossal joke, crushing his reputation across the political spectrum, he has already seized some power by getting reappointed as United Nations climate envoy.[74] How a China apologist who flies in private planes could hold this title is yet another illustration of how the global influence game is played.[75]

But the most important thing to acknowledge about Bloomberg is that he won't be the last mega-rich newsman to vie for the highest office in the land. And while his 2020 presidential run could one day be a historical footnote, or even a cosmic joke, it could also prove to be the beginning of an era where our media elite, our business elite, and our political elite aren't just theoretically on the same side; they are literally one and the same.

CHAPTER 6

SLEEPING GIANTS AND THE CANCELLATION OF MAGA

To many on the left, the election of Donald Trump in 2016 was a call to arms. It was clear that arrogance was among the key reasons the Democrats had lost that presidential election. They thought Hillary Clinton, the politician probably most familiar to Americans other than Barack Obama, would beat out Donald Trump, a man who had only been a Republican for a few years and a politician for a few months. And why wouldn't they feel that way? The entire establishment media told them the election was all but a guarantee. At the start of election day, *Huffington Post* declared that there was a greater than 98 percent chance that Clinton would win, the *New York Times* had Trump's chances at 15 percent, and betting markets gave the former reality TV star about 18 percent.[1] Nate Silver's FiveThirtyEight website gave Trump a 29 percent chance to get the most Electoral College votes; Silver would later congratulate himself for being the least wrong of the forecaster class.[2]

If you didn't read websites like Breitbart, listen to talk radio, or watch a few particular shows on Fox News, you would have been blindsided by the results as well.

It quickly became clear to those Democrats who at least partially accepted the 2016 results (how many have fully accepted them is still not clear) that they needed to *immediately* get ready for the 2020 race to make sure they didn't repeat the same mistakes. New activist groups sprang up quickly. The Women's March began on January 21, 2017. Get-out-the-vote efforts began almost instantly. Anti-Trump protesting became the new

Sunday brunch for young liberals; their social time became activism time because not a moment could be wasted.[3] The Bad Orange Man must be defeated.

The Left was fired up.

They knew their best shot to guarantee a victory in the 2020 election was to crush conservatives' reach across the web. Facebook, Twitter, Google, and YouTube all would do their parts to try to limit our reach. Many in the Democrat Party establishment who chose to acknowledge the results of the 2016 election knew that it was via these massive tech platforms that independent conservative media was able compete with—if not beat outright—the establishment press. Clinton campaign press secretary Brian Fallon understood the phenomenon; he said as much at an event at Yale University:

> One of the realities that I don't think was truly appreciated by our campaign was just how profound the Breitbart effect was in cultivating a standalone ecosystem in conservative media that very aggressively and successfully promoted certain stories and narratives we had a blind-spot for during the campaign.[4]

Barack Obama echoed the sentiment when he said, "Breitbart did something pretty interesting. Now, they didn't create a whole new platform, but they did shift the entire media narrative in a different direction—in a powerful direction."[5]

David Brock, founder of the far-left watchdog group Media Matters, ripped the Left's online media strategy. "We had a strategy that was just out of date," he said. "Breitbart and the others just kicked our butts."[6] He went on to create Shareblue, which he described as the "Breitbart of the left."[7]

But one group of radical leftists attempted to delegitimize the 2016 election and secure the 2020 campaign by destroying the conservative news industry itself. They devised a plan to try to alter the business models of prominent right-wing news outlets and opinion makers. For well over a year, they focused solely on Breitbart News before expanding to a few other targets like Tucker Carlson. The objective was simple: try to cut off our advertising dollars. They would accomplish this by waging a campaign to pester businesses on social media to make sure their advertisements won't appear programmatically (that is, via computer algorithm, not manual placement) against conservative news content.

The original group behind this tactic is known as Sleeping Giants (the name is a nod to the power angry left-wing activists can have over business), and it was founded by advertising industry veteran Matt Rivitz and tech marketer Nandini Jammi.

I view Rivitz and Jammi as the OG champions of the cancel culture.

Their plan would backfire in a colossal way. Breitbart News, Tucker Carlson, and their other targets are still standing and arguably bigger than ever, but the ad industry that had previously funded online journalism has been severely diminished.

Yes, Matt Rivitz, Nandini Jammi, and Sleeping Giants didn't take out Breitbart, but they did severe damage to the online news business.

Additionally, their efforts to purge pro-Trump content from the Internet would drastically escalate the cancel culture that has made America more divided than at any time since the Civil War.

The Origins of "Fake News"

It began with ISIS videos. In 2015, YouTube scrambled to appease advertisers amid reports of their ads appearing online before extremist and other indefensible content. "YouTube has clear policies prohibiting content intended to incite violence, and we remove videos violating these policies when flagged by our users," a YouTube spokesperson said.[8]

But soon, as is so often the case in our current media landscape, "extremist" content morphed into any content that harmed the Left or benefited Donald Trump in any way.

By 2016, The Donald was The Boogeyman, not ISIS or anyone else who advocates literal violence. And the ad industry turned out to be far more scared of Trump than they ever were of radical Islamic terror. In January 2017, just after Trump's election, the Interactive Advertising Bureau (IAB), an industry trade group representing six hundred ad-related companies including Google and Facebook, called for the industry to address the growing fake news crisis. Companies needed to "take responsibility" for fake news online. IAB president and chief executive Randall Rothenberg said it was a "moral failure" and a "crisis" that fake news was allowed to "flourish."

"Get yourself out of the fake anything business," Rothenberg said, according to the *Wall Street Journal*. He made this proclamation to a room full of media, advertising, and tech industry executives.[9]

"Any company sitting in this room has the ability to police itself and to actively banish fakery, fraudulence, criminality, and hatred from its midst—and it is your obligation to do so," he said.[10]

The IAB added "fake news" to its short list of categories of content that must be avoided by advertising brands—a list that includes death, terrorism, drugs, and war.

At that point, the term "fake news" was beginning to have its media moment.

Breitbart began running stories on "fake news" in mid-November 2016, just after Tech Crunch (in an article literally called "Rigged") accused Facebook of allowing "fake news" to proliferate on its platform.[11] When we dove into the details of the story, we learned that the Left's beef was not so much with false information, but with accurate news that didn't favor Hillary Clinton and their agenda. So, it was no surprise when we learned that Assistant Professor of Communication Melissa Zimdars of Merrimack College in Massachusetts published a list of "fake news" websites that included Breitbart.com.

On November 15, 2016, we ran an article with the headline "It Begins: College Professor Lists Breitbart as 'Fake News' Site."[12] "It Begins" is a common refrain we use at Breitbart News, usually tongue-in-cheek, when a new narrative reveals itself. This time it was no joke. We knew what was coming next: a battle for ownership of the term "fake news."

I knew what the political and media establishments were going to do: they would try to portray information that didn't fit their preferred narratives as "fake news" so they could kill the messenger in lieu of being forced to cover the legitimate information conservative platforms report.

This would be the dawn of a new witch hunt culture where self-appointed censors—through harassment and blatant manipulation—would impose speech controls on those who did not align with the status quo consensus.

The ultimate goal: use the term "fake news" to demonetize the online Right, starving it of resources.[13]

So I, along with my colleagues, began to serialize stories at Breitbart co-opting the term "fake news." "Fake News: New York Times Falsely

Claims Breitbart 'Birther' Site," ran a headline from Breitbart's Joel Pollak on November 21, 2016.[14] Another from the same day by Pollak: "More Fake News: New York Times Calls Bannon 'White Nationalist.'"[15] The next day, John Hayward published "12 Fake News Stories from the Mainstream Media"; in this article he listed mainstream media whoppers from Rathergate to the Jayson Blair scandal at the *New York Times* to the phony campus rape exposé by *Rolling Stone*.[16]

(In November 2014, *Rolling Stone* magazine published a lengthy—and now infamous—article called "A Rape on Campus," written by author Sabrina Erdely, that purported to document a gang rape by University of Virginia frat boys. The story was discredited, and *Rolling Stone* paid the UVa fraternity $1.65 million after settling a defamation suit. In fact, the Columbia Graduate School of Journalism concluded that *Rolling Stone* failed to engage in "basic, even routine journalistic practice."[17] The article was eventually retracted. However, in a tweet that has not been retracted, journalist Sarah Jeong, mentioned earlier in this book, an eventual member of the *New York Times* editorial board, expressed support for the fake rape victim.[18] This is a nominee for "Fake News Hall of Shame.")

On November 25, my friend Ann Coulter and I spent an hour on radio together, where we dedicated time to explaining the new speech controls that were coming to America in the wake of Trump's election.[19]

The idea took hold across conservative media and politics: take the term "fake news" from the Left.

By December 8, 2016, "fake news" would permanently assert itself in America's consciousness. After she had lost the election but long before she would ever come to grips with what happened (let's be honest, she never fully did), Hillary Clinton delivered a speech at the retirement ceremony for Nevada Democrat senator Harry Reid. From the speech (emphasis mine):

> Let me just mention briefly one threat in particular that should concern all Americans—Democrats, Republicans, and independents alike, especially those who serve in our Congress: the epidemic of malicious *fake news* and false propaganda that flooded social media over the past year. It's now clear that so-called *fake news* can have real-world consequences. This isn't about politics or partisanship. Lives are at risk—lives of ordinary people just trying to go about their days, to do their jobs, contribute to their

communities. It's a danger that must be addressed and addressed quickly. Bipartisan legislation is making its way through Congress to boost its response to foreign propaganda, and Silicon Valley is starting to grapple with the challenge and threat of *fake news*. It's imperative that leaders in both the private sector and the public sector step up to protect our democracy and innocent lives.[20]

In just that brief section of what was largely a bitter, selfish speech, she used the term "fake news" three times. At this point, the bogus Russia collusion narrative was in full flight, and that was surely on her mind. Perhaps she was thinking of the deranged and discredited anti-Clinton Pizzagate conspiracy theory, which had been in the news that week. (Pizzagaters believe that Clinton campaign manager John Podesta was running a pedophile ring at a Washington, D.C., pizzeria and hid it through coded emails. As previously noted, we never promoted the story at Breitbart.) But more likely, in my opinion, she was thinking about the rise of legitimate conservative media outlets that got information detrimental to Hillary Clinton into the hearts and minds of American voters.

Perhaps she wanted to brand those outlets as "fake news" to further the narrative that the election was stolen from her by "the Deplorables" she so loathed.

And as editor-in-chief of Breitbart News at the time, I took this personally.

As we often do at Breitbart, we used mockery and ridicule to pick apart the narrative.

8 Times Hillary Clinton Pushed Fake News[21]

Fake Newsman Brian Williams Slams Fake News[22]

10 Ways the CIA "Russian Hacking" Story Is Left-Wing "Fake News."[23]

Those are just a few of the "fake news"–themed stories we ran at Breitbart over the next couple of weeks.

On January 11, 2017, Donald Trump first weaponized the term that would become a signature catchphrase: on that day, he told CNN's Jim Acosta that he wouldn't take a question from him at a press conference because "you are fake news."[24]

It wasn't the first time Trump had used the expression, but it was the first time he had used it as a devastating dunk on the establishment media.

The rest, as they say, is history. The term "fake news" was owned by Trump and his movement. The Left had failed.

But America's "cancel culture" was just getting started.

The "Brand Safety" Hoax

It was this environment that spawned the Sleeping Giants, a network of far-left ad industry workers who waged what I regard as a partisan pressure campaign to bankrupt Breitbart. The Sleeping Giants, who often stayed entirely anonymous, are left-wing activists who wage social media warfare against conservative media. Their go-to tactic to try to cancel us with a "brand safety" hoax; they use relentless social media pressure to convince companies that advertising on content the Sleeping Giants don't like is jeopardizing their business.[25]

Jammi admitted that the operation functions in a deceptive way, explaining that they utilized a "vagueness" that "helped us look like a mysterious group bigger than we were." In other words, there weren't nearly as many people tweeting at advertisers to drop Breitbart as Sleeping Giants would have liked you to believe.[26]

What content does Sleeping Giants not like? Just one kind: conservative content, typically produced by Breitbart News.

They have called Breitbart News and our staff every name under the sun, repeating many of the common smears against us covered in the first chapter of this book.

They believe we are "anti-Semitic," even though Breitbart is owned and edited by Jews.[27] Breitbart is also 100 percent pro-Israel, the lone Jewish state on earth, and has a bureau in Jerusalem. The concept for Breitbart News originated in Israel, where Andrew Breitbart and Larry Solov, two Jews, decided to try to build a media empire and change the world. Slandering us in this way should have instantly discredited them and revealed their intensions as partisan hacks.

They call us racists and bigots, despite the fact that even the *New York Times Magazine* has acknowledged we have a record of hiring and promoting minorities and women better than mainstream newsrooms.[28]

We're also "super racist," because all of the blacks, Jews, and Latinos who work at Breitbart are actually more racist than your average racist, or something.[29]

And we're "funded by white supremacists." Calling this claim "baseless" would be a gross understatement.[30]

All of these were lies to try to toxify Breitbart.

Sleeping Giants sent a signal to advertisers that if you do business with Breitbart, you are enabling racists and thus you are pretty much a racist, too. You are funding hate speech. And just like that, some advertisers began efforts to pull their ads from our website. In a few cases, ad networks (third-party intermediaries that function like an algorithmic auction that bid on ad space) put in place blacklists that included Breitbart.

It soon became obvious the Sleeping Giants were not motivated by opposing hate groups; they were trying to silence people for partisan political reasons. One of Sleeping Giants' leaders told the *New York Times* that he was struck by Breitbart's racism "after his first visit to the site in November 2016."[31]

So, these incredibly engaged pretend nonpartisans had never once been to Breitbart before the 2016 election, but upon a quick visit or two, assessed that we're racist and must be destroyed, and immediately launched a massive boycott campaign against us. Or at least that's what they say.

As conservative writer Mark Hemingway pointed out in RealClearPolitics, Sleeping Giants overlook left-wing bigots. They worked with the organizers of the Women's March despite their ties to Louis Farrakhan, whom the ADL describes as the nation's most popular anti-Semite.[32] They have promoted Linda Sarsour, who has advocated against Zionism and praised Sharia law.[33] They targeted Fox News over widespread allegations of sexual harassment, but they conveniently sidestepped similar controversies at NBC and CBS.[34]

Sleeping Giants has never even attempted to operate aboveboard. While they tried to destroy those whom they blame for the rise of Trump, they have gone to incredible lengths to conceal their identities. Yahoo Finance even noted that they correspond via generic email addresses and a blocked phone number.[35] As marketing professionals, the Sleeping Giants claimed that they needed to stay anonymous due to conflicts of interest. In this case, the Sleeping Giants are correct; this is a legitimate concern and one that should have been a red flag for journalists. Britton Taylor, for example, one of the few known Sleeping Giants, works for Wieden + Kennedy. Several W+K clients, including Coca-Cola and Nike, were targeted by Sleeping Giants' pressure campaign.[36]

"The conflict of interest" provided the excuse the Sleeping Giants, especially the cowardly Rivitz, used to stay in the shadows. Once their names were out there, they knew they would be accused of McCarthyism, reported on at length, and attacked online. The cowards preferred to smear their targets anonymously with minimal blowback.

As Sleeping Giants often points out, pulling ads from a specific website isn't quite so simple. Most online ads appear "programmatically," meaning that they tend to show up on your device based off third-party algorithms that assign ads to you based on information like your browsing habits and interests. For example, the vast majority of ads that appear on Breitbart are not a result of, say, Toyota sending us $1 million and then we post a bunch of Prius banners. Typically, the advertisements you see at Breitbart.com are controlled by a middleman, often Google, which displays ads that their algorithm thinks will be effective on a given consumer.

Until Sleeping Giants came along, most companies that advertise via online banners were not aware of exactly where their ads were being displayed. Sleeping Giants made them aware, so long as those ads showed up at Breitbart.com. (Mind you, if the ads were not successful for the advertising companies and third-party networks, they were not likely to appear on Breitbart.) If they did, Sleeping Giants minions would tweet at the company until they figured out a way to make sure their brand was never seen on a Breitbart story again.

This worked, to a degree. Some businesses did pull their ads, though many others didn't. But those companies determined to disenfranchise their own potential customers who were Breitbart readers had to put in a lot of effort. Disentangling your ad dollars from the networks that deliver the ads to news websites was often no small task, and it was a potentially expensive one. If that effort was undertaken, it was done specifically at the behest of the woke social media mob.

In November 2016, a man named Brian O'Kelley, the CEO of AppNexus, said that he had decided to ban Breitbart from what was one of the biggest digital ad networks. He attributed the blacklisting to a sharpening of the "hate speech" policies and a desire to control "brand safety," but it seems to me that it was a subjective decision about politics.[37] Less than two years later, AppNexus would get bought out by AT&T, and less than a year after that, Breitbart would be back on the network (now known as Xandr). How did we get back on? "Breitbart inquired how it could return to our platform, satisfied our requirements, and is reinstated," a Xandr spokesperson said. An AT&T representative noted that they gave us a thorough review and we "complied with their content guidelines."[38]

How could a hate speech website also comply with publicly traded megacorporation AT&T's guidelines? Maybe because we aren't a hate speech website. And maybe we were really banned the first time for being insufficiently woke. Our millions of readers buy a lot of products from companies that advertise online, and Xandr seemed more interested in making money off our audience than caving to a handful of Twitter trolls. So, we were back on.

Sleeping Giants' ultimate goal was to change the way online advertising works. Sites like Breitbart made perfect boogeymen to pressure advertisers into reducing or eliminating entirely their purchases from programmatic ad distributors.

The establishment had already grown angry at digital advertising distributors because they gave the opportunity for small, independent media to flourish, ending the dominance previously enjoyed by major newspaper publishers. *New York Times* media writer Jim Rutenberg summed up the phenomenon in 2017:

> [Google and Facebook] are gaining increasing control over digital distribution, so newspapers that once delivered their journalism with their own trucks increasingly have to rely on these big online platforms to get their articles in front of people, fighting for attention alongside fake news, websites that lift their content, and cat videos.[39]

So, the advertising industry vets at Sleeping Giants weren't just sticking it to the Right, but also to Big Tech for allowing alternative media to thrive. (The Sleeping Giants' "white whale" has always been Amazon. The far-left blacklisters have gone to extreme lengths to convince the online retail giant to drop ads from Breitbart, thus far to no avail.)[40]

The establishment media, who have been getting their pockets picked by Big Tech, loved what the Sleeping Giants were doing (Pew reported in July 2020 that Google and Facebook were gobbling up about half of digital display advertising revenue in the United States), so they gave them a lot of hype.[41] Recall the opinion piece by Pagan Kennedy discussed in the prior chapter on the *New York Times,* "How to Destroy the Business Model of Breitbart and Fake News"; the centerpiece of the plan to cancel Breitbart was by using the Sleeping Giants.[42] NBC has repeatedly hyped Sleeping Giants–led boycott efforts against Breitbart News, among other outlets.[43] After Matt Rivitz's name was first reported by the *Daily Caller*, the *New York Times* immediately swooped in and published a puff piece profile on him and Jammi, replete with hero-shot photographs.[44] (Remember: Heroes get glamorous "hero shot" photographs when possible.)

Adweek produced a steady drumbeat of positive stories on Sleeping Giants.[45] *Fast Company* praised them.[46] Vox's Recode pumped them up.[47]

Virtually all of the mainstream coverage the Sleeping Giants got was positive, even though these outlets were falling for a trap that would cost their companies millions.

What Hath Sleeping Giants Wrought

While Sleeping Giants failed in their efforts to stop Breitbart—in fact, all of their top targets are still in business—the deplatforming tactic they pioneered has contributed to rapid upheaval in the journalism industry. As *Wired* put it, Sleeping Giants helped wreck the news business: their "boycotts scared brands away from journalism."[48]

Once Sleeping Giants reset advertisers to thinking it was a *choice* whether to advertise against certain news content, the advertisers quickly decided it wasn't only right-of-center news that needed to go on their blacklist. What about terrorism or violence? What about content on hot-button issues like race? And more apropos, what about news on a devastating pandemic? Now that Sleeping Giants forced them to think about it, many advertisers decided it was inappropriate to sell product on stories about a deadly plague.

Even the word "Trump" in an article or video could trigger an advertiser blacklisting, according to the *Wall Street Journal.*[49]

The BBC wrote in May 2020, "Not only have sales slumped . . . but advertising revenue has as well. Not least because many firms don't want to put their ads next to stories about the pandemic—rather difficult when that is the biggest story around."[50]

Thus, as most newsrooms dedicated all possible resources to covering the Chinese coronavirus, it became even harder to monetize their journalism on it. Software designed to promote "brand safety" began blacklisting any site that mentioned COVID-19.[51] "Coronavirus Ad Blocking Is Starving Some News Sites of Revenue," blared a BuzzFeed headline.[52]

Thanks, Sleeping Giants!

From the *Wired* story:

> [Sleeping Giants co-founder] Jammi watched the news business go into a financial tailspin. Even as traffic to coronavirus coverage soared, advertisers slashed their marketing budgets, starving publications of revenue. Hundreds of publishing-industry layoffs, furloughs, and pay cuts soon followed.
>
> [. . .]
>
> When the pandemic hit, terms like "coronavirus" and "Covid-19" found their way onto block lists. The results were disastrous. A leaked spreadsheet from one major advertiser showed that software was blocking more than half of the company's ads from appearing on the sites of dozens of reputable publications, including the Boston Globe, CBS News, and Vox. . . . Many brands were skipping block lists and pulling their ads out of news publications entirely. The news media was getting a smaller slice of a shrinking pie.

Brutal.

Jammi saw this slow-motion train wreck coming and even Ben-Smithed it in her marketing newsletter, pleading with advertisers to return to news outlets. In her own words:

> Hey folks, Nandini here. As keyword blacklisting "coronavirus" continues to decimate the news industry, I have had the sinking feeling that Sleeping Giants (a campaign which I co-run) has something to do with it.
>
> When Sleeping Giants started tweeting at companies asking

them to take their ads off Breitbart, we thought we made it pretty clear why: Breitbart was a media outlet promoting hate speech and bigotry, and advertisers' dollars were funding it.

What we never imagined was that brands would turn off the tap on all "NEWS & CURRENT EVENTS" too.

What?! The Breitbart blacklist backfired!? This must be news to people who only read that they were heroes in the *New York Times* or watched a fawning package on Sleeping Giants on CNN.[53]

The advertising industry reckoning that the Sleeping Giants so desperately wanted against conservative outlets soon had morphed into blacklisting thousands of keywords, most of them nonpolitical and often uncontroversial.[54] Pages containing words as simple as "climate change," "immigrant," "fat," and "Asian" could mean no revenue for the publisher. Once the coronavirus pandemic hit, online news outlets were in big trouble.[55]

"Coronavirus: When using the c-word gets you blacklisted," German outlet *Deutsche Welle* wrote.[56]

"Publishers complain about media buyers blacklisting coronavirus content," read an *Ad Age* headline.[57]

"Advertisers shun coronavirus coverage, hastening news media battle for survival," reported Reuters.[58]

It's ironic, sad, and darkly delicious, but it is true: the Sleeping Giants revolutionized the ad industry, and it cost many journalists their jobs. Not to mention hundreds of millions of dollars, if not more, were withheld from the news publishing industry thanks to these blacklists.[59] In fact, cybersecurity firm Cheq estimated billions of dollars in ad revenue were lost in 2019 alone for "incorrect blocking of safe content on premium news sites."[60]

And people who lost jobs or missed opportunities or didn't get a raise might want to thank Matt Rivitz and Nandini Jammi.

Breitbart, on the other hand, has never had even a single round of layoffs in our company's history.

Jammi went on to suggest that advertising on hard-hitting news is a great idea, but the horse was out of the barn. She was simply trying to soothe herself after watching her Frankenstein's Monster devour her friends.

The digital advertising industry was changed forever. The Sleeping Giants had hobbled it in their failed attempt to crush Breitbart.

Canceling the Cancelers

Matt Rivitz got his comeuppance when he and the Sleeping Giants got partially canceled in July 2020, when Nandini Jammi publicly denounced her fellow cofounder for allegedly mistreating her. "It was clear that even though I was doing the same level of work as Matt, he did not consider me an equal," Jammi, a woman of color, told BuzzFeed News.[61]

Jammi posted a lengthy article on Medium where she—wait for it—claimed she was a victim of Rivitz's alleged bigotry. "My white male cofounder gaslighted me out of the movement we built together," Jammi jammed in a dramatic Medium post. "Was I just here performing free labor in service of a white man's personal brand?" she asked.[62]

Rivitz posted a groveling apology on social media, where he whines about personal struggles, including facing a potential lawsuit from Breitbart. "Women, particularly women of color, often are not heard in our society and she deserves to be listened to," the Sleeping Giants cofounder preached.[63]

It was poetic justice to see Rivitz get targeted for cancellation.

But the "brand safety" hoax show must go on. Rivitz is now working with Nobl, a company that wants to automate Sleeping Giants' work. (Yes, these fascists literally call themselves "Nobl"; if Orwell were alive, I'm sure he'd be impressed.) Nobl "uses language detection to identify patterns around conspiracy theories and hate content and funnel programmatic money that would be spent on it to more quality outlets."[64] So, robots will do the blacklisting on behalf of the woke mob. What could go wrong?

Nandini Jammi is now working as a "brand safety" consultant.

Maybe, in the end, Sleeping Giants wasn't about Breitbart at all. Maybe it was just a cynical business play for a couple of ad execs who saw where their industry—as well as the country—was headed: toward a more deeply partisan place where corporations that were once politically neutral are now agents of the Left. If that happened, then maybe, just maybe, they'd get rich off our nation's division.

The Cancellation Industry

Unfortunately, but entirely predictably, the Sleeping Giants are not the only entity currently engaged in censorship efforts. Major left-aligned players in the media are building censorship tools that could be used to filter content.

The Poynter Institute, for example, which receives funding from the left-wing Knight Foundation and George Soros's Open Society Foundations, established the International Fact Checking Network (IFCN), which Facebook integrated into its own services in 2016.[65] The following year, Google began tagging search results with fact-check tags developed with IFCN.[66]

However, no blacklisting effort by the media and corporate establishments against smaller upstarts is more transparently biased and offensively on the nose than Microsoft's Newsguard.

Newsguard, launched in 2018, is a browser extension that rates the wholesale trustworthiness of news outlets. With backing from the Knight Foundation and Publicis, a prominent advertising conglomerate, Newsguard offers "credibility" rankings for news articles.[67] Newsguard's biggest corporate partner is Microsoft, which features it automatically on its Edge Internet browser.[68]

The premise of Newsguard is straightforward and idiotic: it is a web browser plug-in that brands all links from a given outlet as either trustworthy (marked with a green shield) or untrustworthy (marked with a red shield). That's it. So, Breitbart typically has a red shield, and CNN always gets a green shield, as do other fake news outlets featured in this book, like BuzzFeed, the *New York Times*, NPR, the *Washington Post*, and even the *Huffington Post* and *Rolling Stone*.[69]

That means that hoax articles like those surrounding RussiaGate will get a green shield, even if they are entirely false, so long as they get published by an outlet that Newsguard deems credible.[70] Likewise, legit, 100 percent factual, indisputable truths from websites Newsguard declares are not credible get branded with a red shield.

If you search for Breitbart content in Google and you have the Newsguard plug-in installed, you could get as many as twenty-nine red shields on a single page.[71] It's not exactly subtle.

If two outlets publish the same exact content, say, a transcript of a press event or a syndicated news wire, one could get a green shield, one could get red. Breitbart, for example, syndicates the Associated Press. The identical article from the AP could appear elsewhere, like at *U.S. News & World Report*, and get green, but at Breitbart.com, it will be red.[72]

If the establishment media gets a story wrong, they still get green shields. If Breitbart fact-checks the story, we get a red shield. Again, one can't help but think of Orwell, who wrote in *1984* that "whatever the Party holds to be the truth, is truth." And 2 + 2 can sometimes = 5. That is Newsguard.

If that isn't absurd enough, Newsguard brands the Breitbart.com store as fake news. Yes, links to our merch get labeled as not credible.[73]

How do we get to green? We haven't been able to figure that out, despite our best efforts. Through considerable energy expenditure, Breitbart was able to maintain a green rating for about two years, and despite (because of?) noticeable improvements in our journalism, they decided to turn us to red in September 2020, just in time for the heat of election season. I personally wasted weeks trying to work with them in good faith (I know, don't laugh) and I couldn't crack their code. And just like that, hundreds of thousands of pieces of factual content get labeled as not credible.

Breitbart's experience shows that the effect of Newsguard's actions isn't to improve journalism but to cancel it. Any outlet that challenges the establishment media status quo is most likely to be "red" or on the brink of "red." Until they conform, of course.

Who are these self-appointed hall monitors of all online journalism? You'll be shocked to know they're mostly veteran establishment journalists and D.C. power players. Their advisory board includes Tom Ridge, the first United States secretary of homeland security, appointed by George W. Bush; Don Baer, Burson-Marsteller CEO, chairman of the board of PBS, and former White House communications director under Bill Clinton; Elise Jordan, NBC News political analyst, *Time* magazine contributor, and former speechwriter for Never Trumper Condoleezza Rice; and John Battelle, cofounder of *Wired*, among others.[74]

Some of them have even pushed fake news on their own.[75] Richard Stengel, who is currently an analyst for MSNBC and was previously an Obama administration undersecretary, has been previously criticized for numerous factual errors in a *Time* magazine piece he wrote about the U.S. Constitution.[76] Retired general Michael Hayden relentlessly hyped the bogus Russian collusion narrative in national media, even the absurd "pee pee" dossier.[77] Hayden also compared the Trump administration border detention policies to the Holocaust.

Any conservatives on their board are neocons; there are no populists to be found, as far as I could tell. At Newsguard, Bush, Clinton, and Obama alumni abound.

The core objective of Newsguard is obvious to me, and it has nothing to do with journalistic integrity: it operates to blacklist alternative media, causing them to lose credibility, advertising, or both. It's a win-win: either upstart media will conform and behave more like the establishment, which has the same effect of enshrining more power in the hands of big corporations, or they get canceled. It's the Microsoft way!

Newsguard even admits its intention to form a financial blacklist—right on their website! (Did I mention they're not particularly bright?)

From a section called "brand safety" (there's that phrase again!):

> By licensing the NewsGuard ratings, advertisers limit their advertising, including programmatic advertising, to sites that meet the NewsGuard criteria. Advertisers use this data and related information about sites to craft efficient—and safe—ad campaigns.[78]

And with the help of Newsguard, advertisers can cancel anyone that doesn't get the Microsoft/Obama/Clinton/Bush seal of approval.

Next up for the Masters of the Universe at Microsoft/Newsguard? "ElectionGuard!" This is an election safety system that will "modernize" elections.

This fusion of leftist anti-freedom radicalism and corporate profit-seeking has become the new normal; America's biggest media and tech companies are colluding in plain sight to make life difficult for those who threaten the status quo.

If this is reminding you a little of Chinese-style censorship, it's because that's precisely what it is.

Improper thought cannot be tolerated—brand safety depends on it.

These types of efforts normalized the cancellation of mainstream conservative thought and set the stage for the massive social media purge of January 2021, when President Trump and other conservatives were removed from various social media platforms. Once Trump was at his weakest point in five years, the corporate totalitarians dealt a ruthless blow to the former president and his movement.

They had been preparing for this moment for years.

CHAPTER 7

MOSTLY PEACEFUL RIOTS

The Story of Black Lives Matter

While in the process of being arrested for suspicion of using a coun-terfeit twenty-dollar bill, George Floyd was handcuffed and pinned to the ground when police officer Derek Chauvin kneeled on his neck for several minutes while three other officers looked on and did nothing. Floyd eventually died, which set off days of protesting and, yes, riot-ing. Much of the establishment media insisted the protests were mostly peaceful, and whatever violence was occurring was done by white nationalists.

On May 28, MSNBC's Ali Velshi stated, while reporting from Minne-apolis, Minnesota, that "this is mostly a protest, it is not generally speak-ing unruly"—while viewers watched buildings burn behind him.[1]

A couple of days later, MSNBC correspondent Garrett Haake referred to riots near the White House as "peaceful protesters trying to come out here and express their anger," using the word "peaceful" multiple times in the segment.[2] While this was going on, the network showed footage of a blaze at iconic St. John's Episcopal Church. It is said that every president since Madison has prayed at St. John's.

On June 1, 2020, President Trump took a short walk from the White House across Lafayette Square to the church, which also became a brief media obsession. In order to clear a path for the president and a select few members of his administration, the police took relatively extreme measures to disperse a group of protesters so that POTUS and his coterie could pass. (Lafayette Square is a common location for political protests and gatherings and has become a main rallying point for Black Lives

Matter activism in D.C. A few days later, Mayor Muriel Bowser would create Black Lives Matter Plaza just north of the square.) The Democrat Media Complex, as they so often do, wildly exaggerated the law enforcement response, stating that they had used tear gas on peaceful protesters. Jake Tapper's CNN show featured a chyron at the bottom of the screen that said "Peaceful Protesters Tear Gassed for Trump Church Photo-Op."[3]

Some other examples of how the events were described by prominent media and Democrat figures:

Elizabeth Warren: "The President of the United States tear-gassed peaceful protestors"

Joe Biden: "He's using the American military against the American people"

Hillary Clinton: "Tonight the President of the United States used the American military to shoot peaceful protestors with rubber bullets & tear gas them"

CNN's Oliver Darcy: ". . . [P]eaceful protesters just had rubber bullets and teargas shot at them so the President could have that photo op"

Podcast host and Obama bro Jon Favreau: "The President had peaceful protesters shot with tear gas and rubber bullets so he could get his picture taken"

Kamala Harris: "Donald Trump just tear-gassed peaceful protesters for a photo op."

The list is endless.

Now, I don't think the president was wise to make this jaunt to the famed house of worship at that particular moment, and I said so on my radio show *Breitbart News Daily* at the time. The president had just given a tight and persuasive speech on the need for law and order and he distracted from his own narrative. But clearing out a couple of protesters was hardly *gassing* his own people.

Still, former president Obama even repeated the tear gas lie at the funeral for congressman and civil rights icon John Lewis.[4]

Not one of these statements was retracted when Washington, D.C.–based WTOP reported that the Park Police said they deployed smoke canisters, not tear gas.[5] They also said the protesters, who were warned multiple times to disperse, hurled water bottles at cops.[6] When a curfew took effect a few minutes later, many of these same protesters ignored it.

From a statement put out by the USPP:

> As many of the protestors became more combative, continued to throw projectiles, and attempted to grab officers' weapons, officers then employed the use of smoke canisters and pepper balls. No tear gas was used by USPP officers or other assisting law enforcement partners to close the area at Lafayette Park.[7]

So not only was there no tear gas used, but the smoke wasn't used until the protesters had become violent and attempted to grab officers' weapons.

Even Nancy Pelosi ultimately acknowledged perhaps it might not have been tear gas after all. She said to MSNBC's *Morning Joe*, "Maybe they didn't have tear gas, I don't know. But they had the elements of it."[8] Whatever that means.

Actress Mia Farrow tweeted, without irony, that the president should have stopped and listened to the unruly mob outside the White House on his way to St. John's.[9] As silly as this sentiment is, it's also dangerous.

All of this lying was to suggest that violence was carried out on Trump's behalf.

As the expression goes, the boy was crying "wolf."

Soon after the president's controversial walk across Lafayette Square, new eight-foot-tall barriers were placed along the White House perimeter. Violent "protesters" tried and failed to take them down.[10]

The media insisted throughout the BLM riot season that the protests were generally peaceful:

> "A peaceful protest, then looting, on Van Nuys Boulevard," wrote the *Los Angles Times*.[11]

> "Third night of looting follows third night of mostly peaceful protest," reported the *Wisconsin State Journal*, unironically.[12]

Some other headlines from around this time:

New York Times: "Police in Washington Use Tear Gas on Protesters"[13]

NBC's *Today*: "Peaceful Protests of George Floyd's Death Take Place Across the World"[14]

LA's ABC: "Peaceful protests seen across Los Angeles, OC, over George Floyd's death"[15]

LA's KTLA 5: "Peaceful protests in L.A. County overshadowed by violence"[16]

NBCLA: "Peaceful Protests Turn Violent in Fairfax District"[17]

CBS Evening News: "Peaceful California protests overshadowed by violence and looting"[18]

ABC News: "Police use tear gas, push back peaceful protesters for Trump church visit"[19]

As the days of violence and destruction wore on, some in the media must have seen the "mostly peaceful" narrative was wearing thin. It's easy to see why when the NYPD commissioner Dermot Shea explained that bricks were being strategically placed throughout the city and distributed to "peaceful" protesters, presumably to hurl at windows or law enforcement personnel.[20] Not to mention, Commissioner Shea said that Molotov cocktails and cement-filled water bottles were used to attack officers.

CNN's prime-time rageaholic Chris Cuomo, who regularly defends Antifa, asked his audience, rhetorically, to "please, show me where it says protesters are supposed to be polite and peaceful."[21] Here is what the First Amendment actually states:

Congress shall make no law respecting an establishment of religion, or prohibiting the free exercise thereof; or abridging the freedom of speech, or of the press; or the right of the people peaceably to assemble, and to petition the Government for a redress of grievances.

"*The right of the people peaceably to assemble.*" Moments like these are why he'll always be known as "Fredo." The remark by Cuomo also revealed that he knows the protests weren't so peaceful after all, and he appeared to be okay with that. In fact, the prime-time CNN anchor and brother of New York's governor arguably encouraged more violence with this sentiment. Frightening.

Also on CNN, national correspondent Sara Sidner gave out a rationale for violence:[22]

> You don't listen to us when we speak, so you listen to us now, don't you? So, acting out gets attention and they know that. Because the other way hasn't gotten them the attention. It hasn't done anything. It hasn't changed anything, so they're hoping this will.

I can only gather from this rant that Sidner is not satisfied with the amount of notice the Black Lives Matter movement has received over the years and believes that rioting is justified to rectify this inequity.

In a poll conducted by Monmouth University, over half of college-educated young Americans said the riots were at least partially justified.[23] If you've spent any time on a college campus over the last sixty years . . . or know someone who has . . . or even read about someone who has, this poll probably doesn't shock you.

Again, this is not bias, this is weaponized media, quite literally.

The other narrative that was briefly tested surrounding the riots in the aftermath of George Floyd's death was that white supremacists were in fact the ones instigating the unrest.

Reza Aslan, formerly with CNN, tweeted, "White Supremacists= Trump Supporters. These are Trump supporters burning and looting." Alexandria Ocasio-Cortez published protest guidelines that included a warning to be aware of "white supremacist infiltration."[24] MSNBC host Joy Reid said unequivocally that the "anarchy and infiltration" came from "white nationalist groups."[25] Minnesota lieutenant governor Peggy Flanagan accused "white supremacists" of being behind the rioting and looting while the state's governor, Tim Walz, also a Democrat, said that he suspected the same.[26]

None of that is true, at least not to a substantial degree. The far-left Southern Poverty Law Center eventually stepped in and did their best to make sure the Democrats didn't continue to embarrass themselves. Howard Graves, an SPLC research analyst who tracks white supremacists, told the *New York Times* that "I have not seen any clear evidence that white supremacists or militiamen are masking up and going out to burn and loot." [27]

The SPLC admitted it's not white supremacists. Case closed, right?

After the death of George Floyd, demonstrators burned the precinct in Minneapolis. [28] Rioters in Kenosha, Wisconsin, did $50 million in damages. [29] In New York City, 450 businesses were damaged. [30] Yet the media, as previously documented in this book, declared the riots "mostly peaceful." About 93 percent of the protests this summer were peaceful, according to a report from the Armed Conflict Location & Event Data Project. [31] First of all, this doesn't sound accurate. And second of all, the report still noted that 220 "protests" became violent! Hundreds of episodes of political violence!

CNN comically declared demonstrations in Kenosha as "'fiery but mostly peaceful." [32] The *Atlantic* commanded you to not "fall for the 'chaos' theory of the protests." [33]

Crime due to Black Lives Matter even went beyond the demonstrations themselves. There was concern nationwide of a "Ferguson effect," or as left-wing Wikipedia defines it, "an increase in violent crime rates in a community caused by reduced proactive policing due to the community's distrust and hostility towards police." [34] The theory, which came into prominence after the high-profile police shooting of Michael Brown in Ferguson, Missouri, in 2014 is that increased scrutiny on police would lead to more lax policing, which would lead to a rise in crime in many major cities. The concept is eminently reasonable and logical.

In June 2020, in the heat of the BLM news cycle, the NYPD reassigned six hundred plainclothes officers from anti-crime teams to more community-oriented approaches. What does that mean? No one knows, exactly, but it's certainly good news for the bad guys. This was branded as "21st century policing." [35]

Police retirements surged. In Chicago, officers called it a career at twice the normal rate. In New York City, retirements went up by 75 percent. [36]

But left-wing "explainer" website Vox suggested that the Ferguson effect really does not exist, even though they acknowledged a surging homicide rate in most U.S. cities. [37] The *New York Times* not only cast doubt that the Ferguson effect is real, but even if it does exist, the Gray

Lady mused, "The idea that the police have retreated under siege will not go away. But even if it's true, is it necessarily bad?"[38]

But in the aftermath of the George Floyd protests, crime *did* spike in cities that enacted policies that weakened police. An actual headline that appeared in the *New York Times* in September 2020: "A Violent August in N.Y.C.: Shootings Double, and Murder Is Up by 50%."[39] Homicides increased 50 percent in Minneapolis; officers left the force en masse.[40] Seattle, home of the hilarious yet horrifying CHOP (Capitol Hill Occupied Protest zone, an actual rogue state within the middle of the city limits), saw a 525 percent increase in crime compared to the previous year.[41]

In the meantime, the media continued to excuse the rioting as "peaceful." ABC News tweeted on July 26, 2020, about racial justice riots in Oakland: "Protesters in California set fire to a courthouse, damaged a police station and assaulted officers after a peaceful demonstration intensified."[42] This type of framing was common.

Even though Antifa riots in Portland, Oregon, continued into 2021, journalist Andy Ngo reports that more than 90 percent of the one-thousand-plus cases had been dropped.[43] This can be seen as a tacit invitation to continue the lawlessness. "Mostly peaceful" left-wing rioters sure have it good.

Anti-Semitism among the BLM rioters was largely glossed over by our press (and the Black Lives Matter leaders), even when Jews were specifically targeted during that chaotic moment.[44] In June 2020, a synagogue in Los Angeles was vandalized with anti-Semitic slogans like "fuck Israel" as Black Lives Matter protested nearby.[45] The *Times of Israel* reported at the time, "Synagogues, schools and Jewish memorials vandalized with anti-Semitic, anti-Israel slogans, Jewish-owned businesses battered, particularly in Fairfax district." In August, Kenosha, Wisconsin, rioters vandalized a synagogue.[46] And in October 2020, rioters in Philadelphia, Pennsylvania, violently targeted Jews who wore traditional head coverings while yelling "Synagogue of Satan," among other verbal attacks.[47]

BLM also has ties to a former communist organizer connected to far-left extremism. Susan Rosenberg is the vice chair of Thousand Currents, which, until summer 2020, managed BLM's fundraising.[48] Rosenberg was a central figure in the all-female terror group May 19th Communist Organization (aka M19).[49] She was convicted of explosives possession and sentenced to fifty-eight years in prison. She also had ties to the Weather

Underground and the Black Panthers. Her sentence was commuted by Bill Clinton.

Yet, much of corporate America was on board to fund the radical group. Amazon, for example, gave directly to Black Lives Matter, as did Microsoft.[50] (Amazon would eventually blacklist social media network Parler from their servers because they posed a "risk to public safety."[51] From their vantage point, it is actually the Right that is the violent threat in America today.)

Democrats themselves have either called for or supported violence or used overtly violent images to describe how their conservative political opponents ought to be treated:

- In July 2020, Democrats blocked a bill condemning mob violence.[52]

- Kamala Harris promoted the Minnesota Freedom Fund, which paid bail fees for Minneapolis rioters and urged the defunding of the police. She urged her followers to "chip in."[53]

- According to *Politico*, Alexandria Ocasio-Cortez and youth protesters "stormed" Nancy Pelosi's office to push for a climate plan.[54]

- Anti–Brett Kavanaugh protesters stormed the Capitol and cornered then-senator Jeff Flake in an elevator.[55]

- Nancy Pelosi: "You have to be ready to throw a punch."[56]

- Eric Holder: "When they go low, we go high. No. No. When they go low, we kick them."[57]

- Hillary Clinton: "You cannot be civil with a political party that wants to destroy what you stand for."[58]

- Congresswoman Maxine Waters (D-CA) urged her supporters to go up and harass Trump administration officials at gas stations in an unhinged rant: "I want to tell you, these members of his cabinet who remain and try to defend him, they won't be able to go to a restaurant, they won't be able to stop at a gas station, they're not going to be able to shop at a department store. The people are going to turn on them. They're going to protest. They're going to absolutely harass them until they decide that they're going to tell the president, 'No, I can't hang with you.' This is wrong. This is unconscionable. We can't keep doing this to children." [59]

• 1619 Project writer Nikole Hannah-Jones: "Destroying property, which can be replaced, is not violence." [60]

• CNN's Don Lemon compared BLM rioting to the Boston Tea Party. [61]

• *GQ* magazine published an article titled "Why Violent Protests Work." [62]

• Vox.com: "Riots are destructive, dangerous, and scary—but can lead to serious social reform." [63]

Like many of the other lists in this book, this one can go on and on and on.

A Tool of the Establishment

Black Lives Matter became the ultimate 2020 Rorschach test. Major media, left-wing politicians, and corporations treated it like the most significant protest movement in a decade or more. Visionary, virtuous, pure. Conservatives saw the exact opposite. We saw BLM as violent, partisan, and hypocritical. It was even unclear what demands we were being asked to meet in order to satisfy them and get them to stop destroying American cities.

Still, the establishment got on the bandwagon instantly.

Black Lives Matter was co-opted by athletes, big business pandered to it, and even centrist Republicans like Mitt Romney embraced it. Meanwhile, the protesters and rioters flouted coronavirus restrictions and looted businesses that had already suffered through the lockdowns.

Yet BLM had a couple of clever tricks that insulated it from some criticism. First, the name "Black Lives Matter" established the premise that if you don't support the movement, you don't believe black lives matter in the literal sense. This is absurd, of course. Everyone other than truly evil racists agrees that black lives matter, even if they think Black Lives Matter is damaging the country. Second, while BLM has known leaders, the movement as a whole is diffuse. Its amorphousness made it more difficult to attack.

These devices along with the undeniably heinous nature of the George Floyd protests allowed for the violent movement to gain momentum before anyone could push back against it.

In addition, President Trump was put in a difficult position. He had to choose between putting down the riots—and being framed as a racist lashing out at black protesters—or letting our metropolises burn, hindering his ability to claim that he was the law-and-order candidate.

Essentially, he chose the latter.

Thus, America suffered through our most violent and chaotic summer in recent memory, and it didn't appear as though anyone was doing anything about it.

With the benefit of hindsight, we now know the chaos didn't help Donald Trump.

CHAPTER 8

CHEAT BY MAIL AND THE TRUE STORY OF THE 2020 ELECTION

On February 4, 2021, *Time* published an article by Molly Ball titled "The Secret History of the Shadow Campaign That Saved the 2020 Election." In the piece, Ball suggests there was a vast effort, a literal "conspiracy," by a network of partisan political operatives, union leaders, and business titans who harnessed the "energy from the summer's racial-justice protests" and created a mail ballot "revolution in how people vote" that led to Trump's ouster. The article is incredibly long—it's more like a chapter of a book— but it makes it clear that it wasn't voting machine tampering that was the key to the Democrats' victory; it was incredibly intense, incredibly well-funded activism. Some of the objectives of the "galactic center for a constellation of operatives across the left" (her words) were to wage a relentless effort to emphasize mail voting (that is, push for more relaxed rules and then encourage voters to use them) and recruit Big Tech leaders to a war on disinformation (we now know that turned into a war on facts that were harmful to Joe Biden or helpful to Donald Trump). The cabal also sought to recruit anti-Trump Republicans and conservatives to their side, or at least induce them not to support Trump if he challenged the results.[1]

The article was written in a self-congratulatory way ("Democracy won in the end. The will of the people prevailed."), so Ball isn't exactly a reliable narrator, but her points are well taken. She was offering a glimpse at a playbook that was used to beat Donald Trump.

Donald Trump has been a generational political sensation. The amount of passion and emotion he inspires in his supporters is practically unfathomable. Only Barack Obama is even close in the Western world at this time. Trump rallies were like rock concerts; people would wait in line for days to see one live. When Trump said that "I could stand in the middle of 5th Avenue and shoot somebody and I wouldn't lose voters," I don't believe he was exaggerating all that much.[2] His polarizing personality certainly inspired more people to vote against him than a generic Republican (according to an NBC News/*Wall Street Journal* poll, 46 percent of voters had already decided to vote for Trump's opponent in the general election by the end of October 2019).[3] But for tens of millions of Americans, Donald Trump can do no wrong.

Despite the media's insistence that America was heading in a terrible direction, before the coronavirus pandemic drastically altered our way of life, Donald Trump looked unstoppable. Employment and economic numbers were at historic levels (the unemployment rate hit a fifty-year low in 2019).[4] Black workers saw wages rising after a "decade of stagnation," and that's according to the left-of-center *New York Times* (surprisingly throwing some shade at Obama).[5] There had been substantial progress toward Middle East peace for the first time in decades. ISIS's caliphate had been defeated.[6] Trump was getting judges confirmed at a rapid rate.[7] And these were good judges; one might even say, the *best* judges. NAFTA had been replaced. After three years of almost no progress on his signature issue, he was finally restoring integrity to America's southern border. Though he hadn't gotten too far in his goals of taking on a rising China and eroding the power of the Big Tech oligarchy, he certainly posed a much greater threat to these leviathans than most other would-be presidents, especially Democrats.

Finally, my personal favorite Donald Trump success story: until the spring of 2020, Donald Trump had convinced countless Americans that our national media was a disgrace.

In December 2020, Gallup released a poll showing Donald Trump was the man Americans admired most.[8] He supplanted Barack Obama, who had topped the list for twelve consecutive years. Joe Biden ranked a distant third, well behind Obama, who was second. Trump had triple the first-place votes of the man who had beaten him just a few weeks before.

So how did Donald Trump lose?

Sometimes, the former president cost himself dearly. He was also, at times, a victim of a corrupt system and the target of the unfortunate pandemic news cycle.

The media played their part as well.

Seemingly every single day throughout 2020, multiple times a day, Americans were peppered with polling data suggesting that Joe Biden was winning the race in a landslide, much of it obviously inaccurate.[9] On October 28, for example, an ABC/*Washington Post* poll showed Biden up on Trump 17 points in Wisconsin, a state Trump had carried in 2016.[10] Biden won Wisconsin in 2020, but by a mere 0.7 percent.[11] That's not merely a big whiff. You might even say that is a bit suspicious. This seemingly fake poll was weaponized against Trump.

Of course, a big section of conservative America was not talking to pollsters because of fear of being canceled.[12] Being a Trump supporter was a *thought crime* in many circles; you ran the risk of being called a racist, fired, and in extreme circumstances, seeing your family harassed just because you supported the president. Breitbart has documented hundreds of examples of this over the years.[13] A few recent lowlights:

- February 2020: A woman allegedly punched a former NYPD officer in a Nashville bar for wearing a MAGA-style red hat that said "Make Fifty Great Again."[14]

- February 2020: A man threatened to cut the throats of pro-Trump Arizona State University students.[15]

- January 2020: A man with antigovernment beliefs fatally stabbed his Trump-supporting boss and draped an American flag over him, according to deputies.[16]

- December 2019: Five students were charged with battery after a fourteen-year-old who wore a MAGA hat was beaten.[17]

- August 2020: Protesters swarmed Rand Paul after his 2020 RNC speech. Paul tweeted at the time: "Just got attacked by an angry mob of over 100, one block away from the White House. Thank you to @DCPoliceDept for literally saving our lives from a crazed mob."[18]

- Humboldt County, California, Republican headquarters was vandalized six times in two years.[19]

This could explain why the final RealClearPolitics average of national polls undersampled Trump voters by about 2.7 percent in relation to the final results.[20]

But the national vote doesn't matter all that much. The Electoral College is how we decide elections in the United States, and President Trump maintained multiple paths to 270 electoral votes throughout the race. Yet every time one of these horrible polls came out, especially national polls (as opposed to battleground state polls, which made Trump's chances seem slightly higher), the media would remind everyone yet again that Trump is destined to be a loser.

While there has always been a certain level of fraud in American elections, history shows that if you're going to stop it on a large scale, it must be done prophylactically, that is, before election day. How many times have you heard of the results of an American election getting overturned for any reason, especially widespread vote fraud? Though it's not necessarily impossible, it simply hasn't happened with any regularity, if it has even happened at all. Donald Trump and his allies filed dozens of legal challenges, many of which were brought by capable lawyers and presented to the public by seasoned spokespeople, but they never showed proof in court that the election was stolen by illegal means. Even if there was illegal tampering with the election that took place, it wasn't proven in a court of law, which was the only standard that ultimately mattered.

I still don't believe the 2020 election met the standard for integrity that Americans deserve and should expect. I have spoken about this extensively on radio and in media appearances, and my team at Breitbart ran dozens of articles on this subject matter in the run-up to November 3. But the crucial point I want to emphasize is that I am quite confident that if not for the combination of two factors, Donald Trump would have been elected to a second term: first, the coronavirus pandemic and subsequent changes to our voting rules; and second, the manipulation of information and voters by the Silicon Valley Masters of the Universe. These were the two major factors that destroyed the president's hopes of winning reelection. I cover the former here, and the latter in a subsequent chapter.

Losing an Election, and Then the Narrative

Many America-first nationalists were led to believe that it was hacking and cheating judges that swung the election, and if they merely fought hard enough, Trump would remain president. They were badly misled. At one point, they were even told to believe that Vice President Mike Pence could undo the entire election with the stroke of a pen. The former president advanced this sentiment himself, tweeting, "The Vice President has the power to reject fraudulently chosen electors."[21]

(Think of how absurd that sounds. Does that mean Kamala Harris can single-handedly overturn the next election? And if that really is the rule, why has no other vice president ever exercised it?)

In a pivotal moment for our nation's history, we lost sight of the manipulation that was taking place in plain sight by political activists, our media, and the tech establishment.

This is where we must focus if we want to restore the integrity of our elections.

Trump supporters spent much of the two months between election day 2020 and inauguration day, January 20, 2021, trying to flesh out all the ways that election integrity was compromised. Some theories were pretty far-fetched. Like, for example, voting systems developed by Hugo Chavez in Venezuela used an algorithm to flip votes to the exact number needed to change the outcome of the election.[22] Or that Communist China had bought the Dominion Voting Systems and used it to flip votes.[23] Or that U.S. voting servers are in Germany. None of these appear to have merit.

Another popular talking point in some right-of-center circles was that "live computerized fraud" was shown in real time on CNN because of a CIA supercomputer called "Hammer" and a software program called "Scorecard." However, the viral clip that circulated widely on YouTube and social media was actually from the 2019 Kentucky gubernatorial race.[24] In the video, CNN displays graphics of vote totals for the same race in two different places, one in the top right of the screen and one in the bottom scroll. The two graphics showed different vote counts for the same race, which reasonably caused concern. However, that race was determined not to be compromised due to fraud.

Or, at least this is what we've been told by the establishment fact-checkers and what the U.S. Cybersecurity & Infrastructure Security Agency tells us. In this case, I'm inclined to believe them. The viral clip was deleted across the Internet for violating disinformation rules.

Still, many claims of fraud deserve legitimate scrutiny. These are often simple things that are difficult to guard against, especially when ballots are mailed out across the country, voter rolls are not routinely cleaned up, and voter ID laws are not in place. Sometimes the dead vote, sometimes people vote twice, sometimes people illegally fill out ballots for others. In an Electoral College system where a few thousand votes in a few key states can swing the whole direction of the country, these irregularities must be taken seriously. An anonymous (alleged) top Democrat operative explained in detail how he "fixed" mail-in votes to change the results of elections for decades in an explosive exposé in the *New York Post* published just before the election.[25] He describes allegedly distributing fake mail-in ballots, paying homeless people to vote, and even throwing away mail-in ballots in Republican strongholds, among other tactics. How many more people like him are out there?

"Curing ballots" was also a massive concern for those focused on fraud. "Curing" is when a voter will have the opportunity to fix a problem with their already-submitted mail-in ballot or envelope before their vote is discarded. Several states allow for voters to make actual changes to their absentee ballots after they have turned them in. Georgia Democrats went *door-to-door after the election* to help voters "fix" mistakes on their ballots to make sure they would count.[26]

Rudy Giuliani led efforts by the Trump Team to challenge the results.[27] He noted that in certain states, "curing" of ballots was allowed in parts of the state that were more heavily Democratic, but not allowed in parts of the state that were more Republican. Pennsylvania, he said, examined ballots in parts of the state, but hundreds of thousands of ballots in other parts of the state were not examined at all.

All of these possibilities raise serious red flags about election integrity. Taken together, many in the conservative movement are never going to accept that Joe Biden won fair and square.

Statistical anomalies certainly suggest the election might have been less than legitimate. Some examples, with a hat tip to Patrick Basham of the *American Spectator*:[28]

- President Trump received more votes in 2020 than any incumbent president in the history of the country.

- Trump received more than 11 million more votes than he did against Hillary Clinton in 2016. By contrast, Barack Obama received significantly fewer votes in 2012 when he ran for reelection than he did in 2008 when he ran for president the first time.

• President Trump's support among black and Hispanic voters rose significantly despite the fact that he was demonized as a racist for five straight years.

• Though Trump overachieved *overall* in 2020 with minority voters, a massive outpouring of black votes *for Biden* in big cities in Michigan, Pennsylvania, Wisconsin, and Georgia likely delivered Biden victories in all of those states. (Conveniently for Democrats, this also complicated legal challenges by the Trump Team because any questioning of the vote count in these cities was branded as racism, voter suppression, and disenfranchisement.)[29]

• Trump won Iowa, Ohio, and Florida, all by much larger margins than the polls predicted. As Basham notes, "only Richard Nixon has lost the Electoral College after winning this trio, and that 1960 defeat to John F. Kennedy is still the subject of great suspicion." Some scholars and historians have suggested that organized crime, which favored Kennedy, swung that election.

• Biden won the most votes in the history of American elections—by a long shot. He received approximately 11 million more than Barack Obama received when he made history in 2008 by becoming the first black POTUS. That is a lot of votes for a man who spent most of the campaign in his basement.

• All this is particularly shocking considering literally no one showed up to at least one Biden/Harris event that took place in Arizona, a state the Democrat ticket carried.[30]

• Biden won a record-low 17 percent of America's counties.[31]

Some of these implausible numbers are no doubt attributable to the widespread use of vote-by-mail due to the coronavirus crisis. Widespread mail voting surged in the 2020 race. According to Pew, for the thirty-seven states (and the District of Columbia) where data is available, mail-in ballots accounted for over half of all primary votes cast.[32] This number surged ostensibly so that people would stay safe from COVID, but this also put Democrats at a massive advantage.

ABC counted at least thirty states (plus D.C.) that made at least one change to their electoral system amid the pandemic.[33] Ballotpedia thinks about forty states made changes for the 2020 general election.[34]

That is chaos, and it greatly benefits Democrats.

Prior to the 2020 election, Democrats wanted widespread mail-in voting; not so coincidentally, this would help them community-organize the vote. Here is the process, as laid out by Breitbart writers Rebecca Mansour and James Pinkerton in a prescient column from September 2020 (with slight edits by me):[35]

- Use the pandemic to push for nationwide vote-by-mail.

- Enlist all the messengers at your disposal (Hollywood, corporate media, Big Tech, pro sports) to push vote-by-mail.

- Get millions of questionable mail-in ballots turned in.

- Send Democratic lawyers into key districts to fight for every challenged ballot. Use the courts and progressive election officials to keep the count going as long as possible with as little verification as possible.

- Set expectations that the election will not be decided on November 3. Plan for mass protests in the streets. Scare people into believing that Trump won't leave office.

- Challenge the results in court with the help of election officials and district attorneys who had risen to power with George Soros's piggybank.[36]

- Let the Supreme Court pick the next president. Or let Nancy Pelosi do it.

This is almost exactly as it played out. (Though I don't believe the Supreme Court "picked" the president, its decision to not take up any of the challenges brought by pro-Trump lawyers was the final nail in the coffin for MAGA's chances of retaining the White House.)

People went to bed early morning on Wednesday, November 4, thinking Trump was favored to win, only to wake up to see a clearer path emerging for Biden. When all the counting was done, Biden hadn't just won, he had shellacked Trump in the popular vote and won handily in the Electoral College.

Ballot Harvesting

It is much easier to turn in a less-than-legal ballot than it is to overturn one.

With new voting "drop boxes" in place (more on those later), the Democrats were practically invited to "ballot harvest." Ballot harvesting is when a third party (read: political operatives) is allowed to handle your vote (read: collect your ballot) and turn it in for you. This comes with a number of major pitfalls. With mail-in voting there is, naturally, no onsite monitoring. This means the intimidation, coercion, forgeries, or even bribery can take place without anyone ever knowing about it. This is a massive threat to the integrity of the system.

Politically speaking, widespread ballot harvesting is more likely to favor Democrats, who have vast, well-funded networks of community organizers who can get more ballots turned in. As a 2018 Pew poll noted, "Democrats [are] more politically active than Republicans." This explains why the Soros-funded Brennan Center lauds legal and legitimate assistance to voters casting their absentee ballots, though they consider the term "ballot harvesting" a pejorative.[37] The Brennan Center for Justice, which is located at New York University School of Law, is allegedly non-partisan but is heavily funded by Soros's Open Society Foundations.[38] Soros has been described by the left-leaning *Atlantic* as "the left's most prominent benefactor."[39]

The conservative Heritage Foundation has taken a strong (and I believe impeccably reasoned) line against ballot harvesting. Election expert Hans von Spakovsky concludes: "Election fraud of any sort, by any perpetrator, is an affront to America's republican values. Giving third parties who have a stake in the outcome of an election access to voters and their absentee ballots in an unsupervised setting is not wise and is a proven threat to the integrity of the election process."[40]

A cynical view of ballot harvesting, which is the one I hold, is that it has the potential for intentional and literal fraud. In an obvious example, people can fill out ballots on behalf of those who wouldn't otherwise vote. Or ballots can be switched before being turned in. Even in places with "signature matching" (comparing a signature on the ballot to a signature logged by the registrar), it's not fail-safe. Do all of your signatures look alike?

A less cynical take on ballot harvesting—but one that is nonetheless devastating to conservatives—is that it will mean that community organizers will approach low-civic-engagement voters, convince them to vote for Democrats, and then turn in their ballots for them. While this is low integrity, it is legal in many parts of the country.

Ballot harvesting laws vary from state to state; the practice is often legal with some restrictions. It has also been employed in voter fraud schemes that have led to arrests.[41] Logically, the more people who handle your mail-in ballot, the more likely there is to be vote tampering. As von Spakovsky notes, everyone has a vested interest in your vote! The more people between the voter receiving the ballot and the voter turning it in, the more confusion, the harder to verify, and the easier it is to cheat. You can see why Democrats tend to love it.

Legendary California Democrat Willie Brown wrote in August 2020 that "Democrats own the GOP in mail voting." I certainly agree with him.[42]

Allegedly due to COVID, a Michigan judge ruled that postmarked mail-in ballots can be accepted for two weeks after election day. North Carolina accepted ballots for nine days past November 3. Wisconsin was allowed an extra six days to stuff letter boxes with ballots and then count the vote.

When Pennsylvania's Supreme Court said that mail-in ballots could be counted for three days after the election, I began to inform loved ones that I was of the opinion that Trump was probably going to the lose the election.[43]

Cheat-by-mail was going to be the difference.

Most states have different rules about postmarks and signatures, making the fog of war intense around election day. Wisconsin doesn't even appear to require a postmark at all! (Then why do they need six extra days?!) Pennsylvania's new voting rules also didn't require evidence the ballot was postmarked on time.[44]

The burden of proof is already incredibly high to overturn even a single state on challenged ballots. You can see why, considering the nature of the rules. In the aftermath of the 2020 election, Trump supporters repeated the mantra "Stop the Steal" on a loop. If the "steal" was going to be "stopped," it needed to be done long before this current slate of cheat-by-mail rules were set in stone.

Other 2020 election peculiarities include:

- Windows were blocked, sometimes with pizza boxes, as observers attempted to monitor the counting of ballots.[45]

- In several cases, results were delayed by unusual circumstances surrounding the 2020 election. Nevada, which sent mail-in ballots to every voter, afforded every ballot postmarked on election day a week to be received by an election office.[46] As a result, counties had until November 12 to finish counting votes. Other states saw more unexpected delays.[47] Counting in several Atlanta-area counties was held up due to software glitches with their new voting equipment. In Philadelphia, counting was delayed after Democrats appealed a judge's ruling that allowed Republicans to more closely observe canvassing.[48]

- Absentee ballots were rejected at a historically low rate.[49] Rejected absentee/mail-in ballots as a percentage of total absentee/mail-in ballots returned dropped in most states where data is readily available.[50] This is especially true of Georgia, which had one of the nation's highest rejection rates in 2016 (6.42 percent) and one of the lowest in 2020 (0.35 percent), according to Ballotpedia.[51] (I explain this discrepancy later.)

- Arcane laws in several states that delay the counting of mail-in votes until election day in several key states gave the impression that Joe Biden votes were constantly trickling in for days after the election. The delayed vote count on mail-in ballots is likely why betting markets saw President Trump's chances of victory rising steadily throughout election night, only to crash days later.[52]

The Case Trump Could Have Made

Elections are never perfect; there are always violations of election laws and procedures. In the case of the 2020 presidential election, it is possible widespread violations possibly even effected the outcomes in certain states. But, to be clear, I am not talking about conspiracies involving cyber-ninjas, Venezuela, Frankfurt, voting machines, and software. Though I am not an attorney, I spoke to multiple lawyers who were among the hundreds of volunteers who helped the Trump campaign and RNC early in the election legal effort in the days after election day. They asked that I not use their names in this book, out of fear of cancellation.

(Yes, cancel culture is in the legal profession as well. Lawyers are getting the signal that to represent conservatives and Republicans could cost you your job, even if your client would be the president of the United States and your argument would be a constitutional argument that is accepted by a large part of the legal profession and has a decent chance of winning before the U.S. Supreme Court. Some lawyers who held prestigious legal positions in the Trump administration that would normally be their golden ticket with law firms are instead finding it hard to find jobs.)

Occam's razor generally holds: the simplest explanation in a situation is the most likely. And the most likely explanation is that a perfect storm of several factors is what cost Trump reelection. The part of that storm involving voter fraud appears for the most part to be old-fashioned, run-of-the-mill violations of election laws, albeit violations on what might have been an unprecedented scale.

The reason for these massive election-law violations, and in some ways the biggest difference between 2000 and 2020, is mail-in balloting. (The 2000 election turned on a difference of 537 votes in Florida, and was ultimately decided by the Supreme Court in *Bush v. Gore*.) But that's a difference in degree, not in kind. Mail-in ballots are subject to all sorts of problems that you don't find with in-person voting in front of election officials on election day. That's why the Carter-Baker Commission Report, which is the 2005 bipartisan commission report conducted after the 2000 election to rebuild voter confidence, concluded that mail-in balloting is inherently vulnerable to all sorts of fraud and abuse. In fact, the report said mail-in ballots are "the largest source of potential voter fraud." [53] Until this past election cycle the Carter-Baker Report was considered the gold standard for election integrity, as seen by its being cited authoritatively by the Supreme Court, [54] though it has been ignored in recent years by Democrats since they began pushing mail-in voting.

Mail-in ballots were almost nonexistent in 2000, so a difference of several hundred votes in one state determined the presidency. Tens of millions of mail-in ballots were cast in 2020, and could have made a difference of tens of thousands of votes in several states, which could have potentially decided the presidency. That doesn't necessarily mean that without it Trump would certainly have prevailed in 2020, but at bare minimum it means that some voters will lack confidence in the outcome of the election, and that kind of serious doubt about the legitimacy of an election result is poisonous to a free and democratic form of government like ours.

Take a look at three states that people talk about.

GEORGIA: Trump never got his day in court in Georgia. Trump's lawyers filed his lawsuit on December 4, 2020. The margin between the candidates was less than 12,000.[55] After weeks of research, Trump's lawyers argued that there were at least 60,000 illegal ballots cast.[56] This included 2,600 ballots cast by felons, 15,700 by voters who moved out of state (of which 5,000 registered in their new state before election day), over 40,000 who moved from one place in Georgia to another but did not reregister at their new residence, 1,000 who listed a PO box as their residence, another 4,000 who listed no home at all, over 8,000 ballots cast by voters who died before election day, and up to 66,000 who may have been underage, according to the lawyers. Under Georgia law, if a court finds that the number of illegal ballots is bigger than the margin between the winner and the runner-up, the court must throw out the election result and order a new election, they argued. But the court here—in Fulton County, the Democrat stronghold where the state capital of Atlanta is located—never held a trial, or even a hearing on the case. It wasn't until January 4, 2021, that another court took the case and assigned a trial date of January 8—two days after Congress was supposed to meet. After the January 6 riots, that case was withdrawn. Georgia's courts never ruled on who actually won the November 2020 election for president in that state.

What's more, in Georgia, if someone votes by mailing an absentee ballot, the signature on the ballot envelope supposedly must be verified against both the signature on the application for a ballot and also the signature on that voter's registration file. In recent elections, between 2.9 and 3.5 percent of absentee ballots got rejected during this verification process. But in 2020, one of the groups led by Stacey Abrams sued, and Georgia secretary of state Brad Raffensperger entered into a consent decree (an agreement to settle a dispute) that required only that the absentee ballot signature be checked against the application *or* the file, not both. As a result, only 0.34 percent of absentee ballots were rejected, according to Trump's legal team.[57]

Just like that, evidence of mass mail-vote irregularities virtually vanished. At least legally speaking.

Thanks, Brad.

From the huge number of mail-in ballots that were cast, under the normal rejection rate, Biden would have gotten at least 30,000 fewer votes, according to court filings by candidate Trump, which would have tipped the state to the former president by about 20,000 votes.

This raises the issue of the Article II Electors Clause in the U.S. Constitution ("Congress may determine the time of choosing the electors, and the day on which they shall give their votes; which day shall be the same throughout the United States"). The way some pro-Trump lawyers explain it is that the Georgia General Assembly passed an election law that required all three signatures to match, and someone who was not a legislator—Raffensperger—entered into an agreement that rewrote the law to change an "and" to an "or."[58] Without that arguably illegal consent decree, an election challenge in Georgia would not have even been necessary. Also without that decree, it is likely that David Perdue would have won his Senate seat on November 3; there would not have been a runoff for that seat, Republicans would still hold the Senate, and this country would be in a much different place regardless of the White House.

WISCONSIN: Biden's margin of victory was about 20,000 votes, which was 0.6 percent of the statewide vote. Trump's lawyers filed suit, arguing that 220,000 ballots—that's 11 times the margin—were illegal.[59] Wisconsin law forbids absentee ballots unless a voter requests one. That request needs to specify an approved reason, because Wisconsin law doesn't allow no-excuse mail-in voting. If someone helps a voter fill out a ballot, that person needs to include their name, relationship, etc., because state law generally forbids someone else being involved with the ballot unless it's someone like a spouse or adult child (to prevent fraud or voter intimidation). Wisconsin also requires voter ID, and requires that absentee ballots must be directly delivered to an approved government location (that is, no drop boxes).

Trump's lawyers sued, arguing that one or more of these Wisconsin laws were violated for those 220,000 votes, and that these illegal ballots went heavily for Biden. The Wisconsin election was certified on November 30, and on December 1 the lawyers filed suit in the Wisconsin Supreme Court. But a 4–3 liberal majority rejected the idea of conducting an initial hearing in the state's highest court, and remanded the case back down to county court for a trial.[60] A liberal trial judge ruled in favor of Biden, then the case went back up to the Wisconsin Supreme Court. On December 14, the Wisconsin justices by the same 4–3 split declined to rule on the merits of the lawsuit.[61] They said it was filed too late in the game, over the dissenting conservative justices, who argued that many of the challenged ballots did in fact violate Wisconsin law.[62] Trump's lawyers then appealed to the U.S. Supreme Court, but those justices put off voting until February 2021 on whether to hear the case, essentially killing it, since the presidential inauguration happens on January 20.

PENNSYLVANIA: Of the 6.8 million votes counted, Biden took 50 percent, and Trump took 48.8. But there were a host of lawsuits, more than we fully cover in this chapter. In September 2020, Democrat secretary of state Kathy Boockvar gave counties guidance that state law does not require that they must verify signatures on mail-in ballots.[63] The state does not have a voter ID requirement unless you're a first-time voter.[64] The Pennsylvania Supreme Court—which has a majority of liberal Democrats—set aside the law enacted by the Pennsylvania legislature allowing people to challenge mail-in ballots. In another suit the court rewrote the legislature's statute requiring mail-in ballots to be received by 8 p.m. on election day, ruling that instead voters needed to have them in by 5 p.m. on Friday—three days later.

Another Pennsylvania law allows each candidate and party to have representatives in the room when absentee ballots are being counted.[65] Although that law had always been regarded as allowing those representatives to be physically alongside election officials so they could see the envelopes and ballots, in the two biggest Democrat strongholds, Philadelphia County and Allegheny County (where Pittsburgh is located), observers were kept at a distance of twenty feet or more, ostensibly because of COVID. In Philadelphia, dozens of tables were set up in a convention hall where some of the tables were over one hundred feet away. Liberal county judges ruled against the Trump campaign's demands to be close enough to see if the ballots were fraudulent, but a couple of days later the intermediate court (called the Commonwealth Court) ruled in favor of Trump, saying that the statute would make no sense whatsoever if the observers were kept so far away that they could not observe anything.[66] But again, the Pennsylvania Supreme Court reversed.[67] In Philadelphia County alone there were over 340,000 mail-in ballots, of which Biden won over 270,000. In other words, that violation of Pennsylvania law in one county by itself conceivably gave Biden a margin of 200,000, more than twice his margin of victory in the state. Trump's lawsuits argued that in total, over 800,000 ballots statewide were illegal because they violated state election laws as enacted by the Pennsylvania legislature, and under the Electors Clause of the U.S. Constitution should not have been counted.

One of these cases petitioned for U.S. Supreme Court review during the time that there were eight justices on the Court after the death of Justice Ruth Bader Ginsburg. On October 19, the Court tied 4–4 on whether to stay the Pennsylvania Supreme Court, meaning that even moderate-leaning Brett Kavanaugh voted to block what the Pennsylvania court did. But for some reason unbeknownst to me or the attorneys I consulted with when researching *Breaking the News*, those lawyers did not try again for a stay after Justice Amy Coney Barrett was confirmed, which could have been the tie-breaking vote in favor of following the plain meaning of the Pennsylvania statute.

Several days later, when lawyers tried a different tack that the Supreme Court didn't have time to finish before election day, Justice Samuel Alito (joined by Justices Clarence Thomas and Neil Gorsuch), wrote, "The constitutionality of the [Pennsylvania] Supreme Court's decision . . . has national importance, and there is a strong likelihood that the State Supreme Court decision violates the Federal Constitution."[68]

These weren't the only battleground states with problems. Other lawsuits raised claims of problems in Nevada, Arizona, and Michigan. Lawsuits claimed there were noncitizens who voted, out-of-state people who voted, and so on. Mail-in ballots are every bit the disaster that the bipartisan Carter-Baker Report predicted they would be, and delivered Biden so many votes that America will probably never know if Trump would have won those battleground states under normal rules; that is, the rules that were in place pre-pandemic. If Trump had won just three of those six states, he would have been taking the oath of office on January 20, 2021, instead of Biden.

So how did the media deal with all this? First, and most sadly of all, they didn't have to deal with most of it. There were simply too many cases and too many distractions in too short of a time frame for these legitimate concerns to get a fair public hearing. Shiny objects like whether vote-counting technology companies literally changed reported results dominated the conversation on the right (I have seen no proof this happened on a wide scale), and the Left portrayed anyone who questioned the results as traitors to democracy. It was as if they hadn't lived through the last four years of Democrats claiming the 2016 election was illegitimate.

Second, lawyers supporting Trump, his campaign, the RNC, state Republican parties, or other candidates filed more than sixty lawsuits, which was like throwing spaghetti against the wall. Lawyers tell me most of these suits were idiotic, many brought by B-list or even C-list attorneys, and got thrown out of court on technicalities or because they were suing the wrong people or asked for the wrong things. But each of these generated another headline along the lines of: "Trump loses again!" Democrat mega-lawyer Marc Elias regularly tweeted updates mocking Trump's court challenge record. This type of tweet was common: "🚨BREAKING: Trump and his allies have now lost an astounding SIXTY-ONE post-election lawsuits. Overall, they are 1-61."[69] (Elias blamed faulty voting machines for the Democrat losing a tightly contested congressional race in New York's 22nd District. Does that make him a traitor?)[70]

Third, Trump amped up some of the bad cases way too much, putting his own official credibility behind those suits. It became like the boy who cried wolf, because when those flawed lawsuits were thrown out, it gave the media ammunition to say that Trump's claims were "baseless" or had been "rejected by the courts."

Fourth, it gave the courts cover not to uphold the law, such as the Georgia county court that refused to hold a hearing on the campaign's big lawsuit, which the lawyers I talked to said should have been a major victory for Trump. It could have potentially led to a new election in Georgia, or opened the door for the Georgia legislature to weigh in at statehouses where Republicans had control.

All Hell Breaks Loose

Then the ultimate tragedy came on January 6 itself. Top constitutional lawyers who serve in Congress, like Senator Ted Cruz and Senator Josh Hawley—joined by a dozen other senators and over 140 House members—were ready to raise issues like these as objections to the states I've mentioned above. Some of them knew these facts and legal problems and were going to put many, if not all of them, on the record. This plan got derailed, however, as pro-Trump protests turned violent with the storming of the U.S. Capitol.

Thousands of supporters had gathered by the White House to protest the certification of Joe Biden's victory in the November election and to hear speeches from Rudy Giuliani, President Trump, and others. In Trump's speech, he called on supporters to "fight like hell" and urged Republicans to "take back our country" (he also said his supporters would be marching "peacefully"). It's difficult to quantify how many people stormed the Capitol that day, but acting U.S. Capitol Police Chief Yogananda Pittman testified that around eight hundred people entered the building.[71] Protesters then marched to the Capitol and, along with other agitators, breached the complex and clashed with police.[72] Things turned riotous. Windows were smashed, significant property damage was inflicted, and ultimately hundreds were arrested.[73] Five people died during the fracas, which lasted several hours. Lawmakers were evacuated and congressional business was shut down.

Many in attendance were simply frustrated idiots who didn't hurt anyone or anything, but they should have had the common sense to know that rushing a restricted federal building without proper authorization is not the best way to support Donald Trump.

Perhaps if the Capitol riot hadn't taken place that day, the foundation for future elections and challenges could have been presented on the Senate floor with the world looking on.

Those who were involved with these post-election challenges for Trump explained to me how they thought it could work going forward.

First, just like in *Bush v. Gore*, the U.S. Supreme Court could have granted review in each of the serious election challenges from the battleground states. Instead, the justices let those challenges creep into February and March of the following year, when they couldn't do any good. Second, state legislatures—faced with the facts presented in the lawsuits—could have weighed in. The Electors Clause of Article II of the Constitution says that state legislatures appoint electors to the Electoral College to vote for president. Although every state does so in modern times through taking part in the November election day, another federal law—3 U.S.C. § 2—says that if a state participating in the national election fails to appoint electors through that process, then the state legislature can determine on a later date how to appoint the electors for the state so they can have a say in who would be the nation's next president.

Every state legislature does this through passing additional statutes to make a system for post–election day challenges and recounts. But the lawyers tell me that it means more—that it's Congress acknowledging that if a state's election system fails to produce a clear winner, if the system breaks down or the courts are deadlocked or delay past the drop-dead date (like what happened in 2020), Article II of the Constitution gives state legislatures the authority to hold hearings, consider evidence, identify fraud and irregularities, or take issue with election administrators or judges who failed to follow the state election laws as the legislature enacted them, and determine who the lawful winner of the state's elections is.

As a layman, the latter option sounds far-fetched to me, but it would have been interesting to hear it presented and debated (if the country is even capable of debate on an issue like that at this point). It would have been an aggressive move and the media surely would have joined Biden and the Democrats in screaming that the sky was falling, but some people thought it might have worked, or at least opened up a compelling constitutional discussion with future implications. Instead, we spent January 6 and a few days thereafter getting updates on body counts from the riot and seeing photos of demonstrators wearing Viking helmets and beaver pelts.

One observation that I came to while conversing with people on these potential election improprieties is this: there appear to have been real problems in the elections in those battleground states, the sort of problems that would normally generate serious lawsuits. However, instead of Trump deciding to focus the public's attention on the kind of meat-and-potatoes election problems mentioned above, problems on a massive scale that might have tipped the balance in a very close state, he was increasingly surrounded by people who wanted to assert those claims of international conspiracies that many establishment Republican lawmakers and party leaders found too tough to accept or sell to the public. And as mentioned above, people supporting the president filed dozens of bad lawsuits with poor arguments and second-class lawsuits, giving a hostile media ammunition and the ability to frame all these legal challenges as a big joke, or worse. As that happened, although some Republican lawmakers continued to press the argument that Trump had carried their state, enough GOP lawmakers put distance between themselves and the fight that the numbers in the statehouses were clearly less than the majority that would be required to pass joint resolutions supporting Trump electors. I don't think it's likely Trump would ever have mustered majority support with the conventional arguments, but, to put it kindly, the spy-thriller movie arguments that some of the people around him were pushing certainly didn't work either.

What Comes Next

As is their custom, the media focused almost entirely on angles that made Trump and his supporters look bad in the aftermath of the election. Meanwhile, the problems with mail-in balloting are still with us. So what is to be done now? Republicans and conservatives are launching campaigns in 2021 and 2022 to restore safeguards to the ballot box. Let's hope they are robust and effective. One lawyer I interviewed emphasized the word "restore" instead of "reform," because most of the GOP's goals are simply to put back in place safeguards that previously existed that Democrats have systematically erased. Republicans ought to restore laws governing what happens before, on, and after election day; hopefully that process is well under way.

Before and on election day, the key is voter-ID laws that include a picture and signature. State driver licenses should clearly say if the driver is a citizen. There should be no automatic registration for signing up for welfare benefits. And if anyone called for jury duty is dismissed because they are not a citizen, or if anyone is convicted of a felony, that name should be removed from the voter rolls.

On election day, laws should encourage each voter to show up at their precinct polling location. Absentee voting should be only for special circumstances, only for a short period before election day, and only with safeguards to ensure the identity of the voter and that the vote is cast free from undue influence. And no absentee or mail-in ballots should be allowed after election day (with the exception of military ballots coming from overseas, as long as they are postmarked by election day). Absentee ballots need to include features like bar codes that make each one unique and impossible to forge, and counting the ballots needs to be done in a secure manner so each ballot is accounted for.

After election day, laws should specify streamlined court procedures to make sure that what happened in Georgia never happens again, and so that all legal challenges are heard with time for appeals before the Electoral College meets in mid-December to cast ballots for president.

Republican voters should demand all this. And they should demand competent, tough, and levelheaded attorneys to make the case to the public. And I bet most Americans would support all these ideas as common-sense safeguards to protect their votes.

CHAPTER 9

THE TRUMP VIRUS

The Chinese coronavirus pandemic news cycle was the one the media had prepared for (prayed for?) throughout the Trump era. It was the opportunity of a lifetime: a chance to massively expand government power, an opportunity to elevate the world's biggest corporations while crushing the individual and small businesses, and most important, an opening to convince Americans that our country had become a horrible, almost uninhabitable hellscape because of the Bad Orange President. Jane Fonda wasn't being ironic when she said COVID-19 is "God's gift to the Left." Of course it is.[1] Government hadn't grabbed such a foothold on the way Americans live their lives in generations, maybe ever. The freedom to operate a small business, send your children to school, dine at a restaurant (even in their parking lots), and the ability to legally exercise alone outdoors without covering your face were taken from us.

These rights went away quickly, sometimes overnight. And when the science made clear that most of the new mandates were an ineffectual overreaction, government kept their boot on the citizenry.

And many Americans were pretty much fine with all that. Or at least they weren't upset enough to do anything about it. Huge sections of the public actually seemed to love the sudden erosion of rights; a November 2020 YouGov poll suggested 64 percent of Americans would support a temporary lockdown in their state, and a December Vox.com poll showed that just over half of voters would support a one-month lockdown.[2]

After all, Donald Trump had done this to us, and we were all his victims. And the victimhood was exquisite. It just felt so good.

Many Americans even chastised those who didn't relish their new restraints. A May 2020 viral video of a woman getting hounded out of a Staten Island grocery store by other customers for not wearing a mask heralded months of COVID shaming that would intrude on all of our lives.[3]

The next day, MSNBC mask-shamed Wisconsinites in a live segment where anchor Katy Tur asked reporter Cal Perry if Lake Geneva, Wisconsin, residents were "not worried about their personal safety?" "I haven't met anybody who is," the reporter responded. "You can see here, nobody's wearing [masks]."[4] It was at this moment that a bare-faced citizen passing by on the street chimed in, "Including the cameraman." Perry agreed with him, humiliated. "Including the cameraman," he parroted back. The hero citizen continued, now off camera: "Half your crew isn't wearing 'em."[5] It was pure television bliss, but also enraging hypocrisy.

Tom Hanks went on an unhinged mask-shaming rant: "Wear a mask, social distance, wash our hands," he said. "Those things are so simple, so easy, if anybody cannot find it in themselves to practice those three very basic things—I just think shame on you. Don't be a pussy, get on with it, do your part."[6]

The *New York Times* mask-shamed: "Trump May Have Covid, but Many of His Supporters Still Scoff at Masks," they reported, without citing evidence that more face-diaper usage would have prevented Trump from getting the virus.[7]

An anonymous Instagram account published photos of University of North Carolina students who were not following protocol.[8]

The message was clear: conform or get publicly targeted for harassment.

So, most of us obeyed. It's less hassle.

Additionally, all of the Left's *favorites* thrived during the pandemic.[9] Democrat politicians and unelected career bureaucrats became the heroes of the coronavirus narrative. The world's billionaires, most of whom are globalists and advance the agenda of the establishment wing of the Democrat Party, saw their wealth expand at a record rate. No sector saw their wealth and power increase more than mega-corporations.

The country's biggest businesses, such as Target, Walmart, and especially online retailers like Amazon were deemed essential while their smaller competitors were not.

Houses of worship were deemed superspreaders while liquor stores and pot shops thrived. As of November 2020, beer, wine, and liquor sales were up 18 percent, 24 percent, and 31 percent especially due to the pandemic and online sales were growing at a rate over 500 percent at one point, according to Nielsen.[10] Legal marijuana also hit record numbers.[11]

China made out like bandits.[12] Despite the virus originating in Wuhan, the communist regime was able to sell unfathomable amounts of protective equipment and work-from-home essentials.[13] From a December 2020 *Fortune* magazine report:

> Demand for pandemic-related products fueled the exports responsible for much of China's economic uptick this year. Medical device exports soared 46% in the first six months of 2020, textile exports—including face masks—jumped 32%, and notebook computer exports grew 9.1% in the same period, reflecting a global shift to work from home and remote schooling.[14]

The pandemic also revealed America's dependence on generic drugs made in China.[15] China produces about 97 percent of all antibiotics in the United States and 80 percent of the active pharmaceutical ingredients (APIs) that are used to make drugs in the U.S., according to the Council on Foreign Relations.[16] For example, the United States imports about 95 percent of our ibuprofen (the drug found in Advil and other common brands) and 70 percent of our acetaminophen (the active ingredient in Tylenol) from China, according to Rosemary Gibson, an editor at the peer-reviewed medical journal the *Journal of the American Medical Association (JAMA)*.[17]

China also has a dominant share when it comes to medical supplies. For example, Beijing's Ministry of Foreign Affairs claimed to produce over 70 billion masks in just the months of March through May 2020 (for comparison, all the countries on earth produced about 20 billion masks total in 2019).[18] A functional monopoly when it comes to personal protective equipment, China sometimes demands public praise in order to get access to the PPE they make. Elizabeth C. Economy (yes, that is actually her name), a Hoover Institution fellow and the director for China studies at the Council on Foreign Relations, said she was struck by "the extent to which the Chinese government appears to be demanding public displays of gratitude from other countries; this is certainly not in the tradition of the best humanitarian relief efforts." "It seems strange to expect signed declarations of thanks from other countries in the midst of the crisis," she continued.[19]

Desperate industries and nations needed to do even more business with the communist regime than before the Chinese virus broke out in order to keep capital flowing. Struggling companies prioritized their own bottom lines over holding China accountable. Most businesses behave this way in boom times; the pandemic only exacerbated this behavior. It is no coincidence that the United States' trade deficit with China surged in 2020 to a fourteen-year high, despite the fact that the communist country was responsible for the plague.[20]

In fact, China was the only major economy to grow during 2020.[21] They grew by 2.3 percent that year, which is much lower than the 6.1 percent growth rate they achieved in 2019,[22] but it's still remarkable considering the United States, Europe, and Japan all contracted.

Beijing's massive global infrastructure initiative, "Belt and Road," fared surprisingly well during the pandemic.[23] China saw a big manufacturing sector expansion during this time.[24] While America's entertainment industry was crippled for months, China surpassed the United States as the world's biggest film market.[25]

The Chinese virus seemed to be benefiting, of all places, China, at least economically. And considering that China has limited press freedom, the world largely accepted their propaganda that they were also vanquishing the virus. As of February 2021, China had only reported a total 4,829 COVID-19 deaths, or less than 1 percent of the deaths America had reported at that time. So either China beat the virus almost instantly, or they simply stopped counting. I think any intellectually honest person assumes it's the latter. Multiple reports from March 2020 suggested that the death toll in Wuhan was ten times the communist nation's official numbers.[26]

Many establishment outlets, to their (mild) credit, acknowledge on occasion that China's numbers are understated, but the outrage is insufficient. Some in the corporate press even have praised China for their handling of the virus. In September 2020, *Newsweek* ran the headline "How China Beat Coronavirus Over the Last Six Months."[27] In October 2020, the *Wall Street Journal* reported that "China Beat Back Covid-19."[28] The

Washington Post used the exact same expression in December: "China beat back covid-19 in 2020."[29] How could they possibly know that China had "beaten" it? As far as I can tell, only through Beijing propaganda.

The *New York Times* put out a piece in February 2021 that rivals any propaganda printed by the CCP itself in their story "Power, Patriotism and 1.4 Billion People: How China Beat the Virus and Roared Back."[30] From the article:

> With equal measures of coercion and persuasion, it has mobilized its vast Communist Party apparatus to reach deep into the private sector and the broader population, in what the country's leader, Xi Jinping, has called a "people's war" against the pandemic—and won.[31]

It's as if Xi Jinping wrote the sentence himself.

CNN's Fareed Zakaria said on New Year's Day 2021 that China "essentially vanquished the virus without a vaccine."[32] At the very moment Beijing was in "emergency mode," dealing with an outbreak of the virus, according to the *South China Morning Post*, a Beijing mouthpiece.[33] Seemingly, Zakaria and CNN were going even farther than the CCP propagandists to praise China.

Disturbing. But anything to make America look bad in the eyes of the people.

Lockdowns and Face-Diaper Mandates

It began in mid-March 2020, with President Trump's "15 days to slow the spread."[34] The objective was pretty clear and most all Americans were on board: everyone shut down as much as humanly possible for a couple weeks so that we can "flatten the curve." "Flatten the curve" was the catch-all for collectively doing whatever we could in the short term to make sure our hospital system didn't get overwhelmed with sickly and dying Americans. The objective wasn't likely to eradicate the virus in that brief time frame, but it would potentially buy time for the nation's medical facilities to catch up on knowledge, PPE, medicines, ventilators, and hospital beds.

Then the guidelines were extended an additional thirty days.[35] As I said on my national radio show at the time, when the goalposts are moved once, there is no guarantee they won't be moved again. And again. And again. Potentially for infinity.

Trump and the coronavirus task force led by Vice President Mike Pence, to their credit, began phasing out this first set of national guidelines thirty days later, but much of the nation, especially in states with Democrat governors, embraced a lockdown culture where the new normal became government mandates restricting privileges we had taken for granted.

In many of these states, lockdowns were imposed on a one-size-fits-all basis. This meant that even if there was no outbreak and hospitals were not overwhelmed (that is, the curve was flat), lockdowns and slowdowns often remained in place.

Next came the mask mandates. It seemed to dawn on the establishment media and Democrat Party overnight that covering your mouth and nose with pretty much anything was the key to beating the virus. Dr. Anthony Fauci, who had been the lead doctor on President Trump's coronavirus task force, told *60 Minutes* in early March, "Right now, in the United States, people should not be walking around with masks."[36] He continued: "Wearing a mask might make people feel a little bit better and it might even block a droplet, but it's not providing the perfect protection that people think that it is. And often, there are unintended consequences; people keep fiddling with the mask and they keep touching their face."[37]

"It might even block a droplet"? It was clear he didn't believe at this time that the science suggested that masks would save us all. It sounds like he thought masks were a symbol of public health conscientiousness. (In May 2020, he literally said masks are "a symbol for people to see that that's the kind of thing you should be doing.")[38]

But all of a sudden in April 2020, when the virus had been in the United States for over two months, the Centers for Disease Control and Prevention (CDC) began recommending voluntarily wearing cloth face coverings in public.[39] Little was done to educate the public on how to keep a mask clean and sterile (if that's even possible), how often masks should be replaced, the functional difference between cloth masks, surgical masks, and the N95 respirator masks (among other options), or if there are any health issues that should preclude someone from wearing a mask. We all were simply told to mask up! And don't ask too many questions.

What's more, a paper published in a CDC journal suggested that cloth masks "may give users a false sense of protection against coronavirus."[40] That doesn't sound good!

A close family member who is a doctor and treated patients on the coronavirus "front lines" went through an elaborate fitting process to match her with the perfect N95 for her specific face shape. Yet we normal civilians were told, essentially, that if we all wore a piece of fabric we got at the Gap or a paper made-in-China face diaper handed to us before we enter Whole Foods, we would drastically alter the course of the virus. Maybe that's the case, but would someone please show us the data? Would someone please explain *the science*?

Though governments and establishment media took a strong pro-lockdown and pro-mask-mandate line, it is not obvious that states that impose the strictest rules fare generally better when it comes to death rate than states with more lax rules. If there is clear empirical data to support the suggestion that lockdowns and masks are the key to vanquishing COVID-19, the media and the Democrats certainly don't do a very good job elucidating it to the public.

Instead, what we heard were appeals to patriotism. (And I remember when Trump was mocked for jingoism.)[41] On July 4, 2020, Andrew Cuomo said "real patriots wear masks."[42] On August 13, 2020, California governor Gavin Newsom tweeted, "Be a patriot, wear a mask."[43] Joe Biden himself offered this sentiment throughout the campaign; on Halloween 2020, he posted a video to social media stating emphatically, "Be a patriot. Wear a mask."[44] No, he wasn't talking about a Michael Myers or scary clown mask. Though I suppose those wouldn't hurt.

If the evidence is on their side (and maybe it is), why not just cite it? Why do we have to take their word for it? Can't these Democrats trust the public with the truth? Or are they being disingenuous with us? Or did they really mean that "patriots" are only those who obey Democrats, unquestioningly?

Americans largely obey their government overlords despite their egregious hypocrisy. Democrat stars like Speaker of the House Nancy Pelosi (caught maskless at a hair salon in August), Dr. Fauci (spotted with his mask under his chin at a Washington Nationals game in July), and New York governor Andrew Cuomo (caught bare-faced at a presser in October) all got busted not practicing what they preached when it comes to masks.[45] Anti-Trump CNN journos Kaitlan Collins and Chris "Fredo" Cuomo let their masks slip, literally. Collins was caught removing her mask while in the White House press briefing room near other journalists moments after the TV cameras stopped rolling.[46] Tucker Carlson reportedly obtained a letter from the management of Fredo's New York City apartment building stating he was failing to abide by the building's mask protocols; the governor's baby bro has been known to say "wear a damn mask" on television.

Yet, as of the beginning of 2021, Americans were still being told by the government to cover up their faces in dehumanizing masks, sometimes even while alone in open spaces. When will this end? No one knows. Perhaps years. One British professor finally said what many of us secretly fear: we might wear masks *forever*.[47] Elected leaders certainly aren't putting a timetable on things. The citizenry and media haven't demanded the authorities commit to benchmarks that could be met that could trigger an end to the face-diaper ordinances.

There is practically no discussion of mask sterility protocols. Admit it, your favorite mask is filthy. How do you properly sneeze while wearing your mask? Where do you place them when you take them off? On a filthy tabletop or in your pocket? How and how often should you wash your visage diapey?

All of these are basic questions that go without answers in our press.

Why is that? Why wouldn't the media want to distinguish between the masks that might keep us safe and the ones that probably won't? Why wouldn't they want us to have the necessary information to keep our countenance nappies as fresh and sterile as possible? Do they even care about our health at all?

Ahhh. Maybe the media is not interested in these questions because for most of them, masks are not about public safety as much as they are about power. The control over people's lives dictated from our ruling class appears to be their true objective.

California governor Gavin Newsom, who famously directed his subjects to pull their masks up *in between bites* even while eating dinner out *with their own families*, was caught violating a number of his own ordinances.[48] In November 2020, he attended a dinner birthday party at the ultra-posh French Laundry restaurant in California wine country. He was there to celebrate the birthday of well-known lobbyist Jason Kinney. The French Laundry may be the single most opulent restaurant in the United States. The price of a meal can easily exceed $1,000 per person, especially if you order the truffle or wagyu supplements off the chef's tasting menu. And if you really want to indulge, why not try the sommelier's recommended wine pairings, too? Newsom is a wine industry veteran. The total number of guests at the event seemed to exceed Newsom's own state guidelines. The governor's pals went maskless. The dinner appeared to take place inside (Newsom lied by saying it was outside, during a pseudo-"apology").[49]

Pretty appalling, even for a bubbled plutocrat in a single-party state like California. While this hypocrisy might not be overly surprising, it revealed an important point about our modern-day political elite: they don't actually believe their own bullshit.

And why would they? On January 9, 2021, Reuters published the following headline: "ICUs clogged on the way in, morgues on the way out in California's COVID crisis."[50]

That's because keeping America safe was always a secondary objective; keeping the citizens under control was mission critical.

And they were succeeding at that, spectacularly.

The Xenophobia Virus

"Hong Kong Expands Power to Isolate Individuals to Fight Chinese 'Mystery Pneumonia.'"[51] This was the headline of the first story on the Wuhan coronavirus we posted to Breitbart News way back on January 7, 2020. "The Chinese Communist Party has documented 59 cases of pneumonia in the city of Wuhan in the past two weeks," wrote our world editor, Frances Martel. The number of cases would soon be in the tens of millions. The communist regime was able to rule out that the mysterious plague was a recurrence of SARS or MERS, but it was clear early on that a coronavirus was suspected.

Hong Kong, which was being reabsorbed by the communist mainland controlled by Beijing, was concerned that the massive prodemocracy protests that had flooded its streets could lead to devastating health consequences. (Western media was not nearly as concerned that protests could be superspreader events when Black Lives Matter protested and rioted throughout the United States and beyond in the summer of 2020.)

Two weeks later, on January 22, senator and China hawk Tom Cotton would call for a travel ban from China, a scoop broken at Breitbart News.[52] On January 31, President Trump took his advice and banned travel from China, which possibly slowed the spread and saved lives.[53]

Joe Biden, ever the leader, suggested that Trump's plan was rooted in "hysterical xenophobia."[54]

The Democrat Media Complex took Biden's lead. The global pandemic that started in Wuhan, China, and would devastate quality of life all over the globe was originally viewed as a racial issue. People concerned about the outbreak were bigots. Our media wasn't afraid of the virus; they were afraid that China would get in big trouble, and, more important, Trump would have been right.

So, they suggested we were all racists.

On January 24, 2020, NPR posted the headline "Wuhan Coronavirus 101: What We Do—And Don't—Know About the Outbreak Of COVID-19." They've since revised the article to remove "Wuhan" from the headline, but the rest of the article remains unchanged.[55] On March 3, NPR posted a story titled "When Xenophobia Spreads Like a Virus."[56]

On January 29, left-wing tech mag *Wired* posted this story: "We Should Deescalate the War on the Coronavirus," which included this passive: "Fear, finger-pointing, and militaristic action against the virus are unproductive. We may be better off adjusting to a new normal of periodic outbreaks."[57]

On January 31, CNN wrote, "As the coronavirus spreads, fear is fueling racism and xenophobia." This article is a bit schizophrenic because it simultaneously shows that CNN is wound up about bigotry but still refers to the virus as "Wuhan coronavirus outbreak."[58]

On January 29, *New York Times* writer Farhad Manjoo published a column with the title "Coronavirus is scary. How we respond to it may be worse." Some choice quotes:

> So far, the Wuhan coronavirus is not much more frightening than the outbreaks of other recent coronaviruses like SARS in 2003 or MERS in 2012, each of which killed fewer than a thousand people around the world. The new virus's death toll has just

exceeded 130; for context, according to the CDC, about 15 million Americans have been sickened by the seasonal flu so far in the 2019–2020 flu season, and 8,200 have died from it.[59]

Manjoo also explained that his real fear, seemingly, was—racism!

It might be used to justify unnecessarily severe limits on movement and on civil liberties, especially of racial and religious minorities around the world.

Considering that this column aged like a banana, Manjoo recanted much of his original position a few weeks later. Though, he tried to save face by saying his analysis was mostly "on point."[60]

In February, Vox lamented the paranoia that was causing people to wear masks and stop shaking hands, even in low-risk areas. "The coronavirus exposes the history of racism and 'cleanliness.'"[61]

The *Daily Beast* was concerned that Italians are super-duper racist for not going to Chinese restaurants. From a February article: "Italians refused to go to Chinese restaurants and shops when the virus first emerged. Now they are being shunned worldwide. The stigma is spreading faster than the virus itself." "The reality is that the real problem is not fear of catching the virus, but fear of getting caught up in the global reaction to it," the *Beast* declared.[62] Italy went on to have one of the highest death tolls from COVID in all of Europe.[63]

Donald Trump continued to sound the alarm on the Chinese virus in his 2020 State of the Union address, way back on February 4. Nancy Pelosi famously—and obnoxiously—ripped up the speech during a House floor tantrum. On February 24, Pelosi unequivocally promoted tourism in San Francisco's Chinatown: "We think it's very safe to be in Chinatown and hope that others will come. It's lovely here. The food is delicious, the shops are prospering, the parade was great. . . . Please come and visit and enjoy Chinatown."[64]

By late April, Pelosi was criticizing President Trump's travel ban for not going far enough.[65]

As they always do, the media allowed her to skate on this. (Fox News's Chris Wallace pressed her on whether she "underplayed the threat" of the issue in April; she responded by saying that she was "offsetting" what Trump was saying at the time, which had made Asian Pacific Americans "a target of violence across the country.")[66]

In July, the House Speaker declared on Joy Reid's always-credible MSNBC program that "the Trump virus" was rolling like "a freight train" and "this president has been the biggest failure" in U.S. history.[67]

Pelosi wasn't alone in being a reverse xenophobe. New York mayor Bill de Blasio said on February 14 that the virus "should not stop you from going about your life, should not stop you from going to Chinatown and going out to eat. I'm going to do that today myself."[68]

Blame Trump!

When it became clear that the coronavirus was here to stay (at least for a while) and it was not a racist conspiracy by the Deplorables, the Democrat Media Complex had to change their approach. (They had to have seen this coming; major media had called the virus the "Chinese" or "Wuhan" virus literally dozens of times themselves.)[69] The narrative they settled on was that the virus was Trump and conservative America's fault. They hyped this narrative aggressively in order to push past criticisms that the Democrats were waging a pro forma impeachment fight as the virus initially spread throughout the United States.

Trump was shamed for a reported shortage of testing. While testing is necessary, it also quickly accelerated the scary infection and death toll numbers that were used to bludgeon Trump.

He was (reportedly) desperately slow to address the alleged ventilator shortage. Yet, months later, tens of thousands of emergency ventilators hadn't been used.[70]

He was also potentially killing people by recommending hydroxy-chloroquine.[71] Headlines like this one from the BBC, "Trump drug hydroxychloroquine raises death risk in Covid patients, study says," were rampant across the Internet in May 2020 after the vaunted medical journal *Lancet* published a bombshell report.[72] Two weeks—and countless articles dunking on the Bad Orange Man later—the study was retracted.[73] The media even tried to blame Trump for a guy in Arizona who died from drinking fish tank cleaner that contained chloroquine. The lede sentence from an NPR report dated March 24, 2020: "An Arizona man is dead and his wife was hospitalized after the couple ingested a form of chloroquine, a chemical that has been hailed recently by President Trump as a possible 'game changer' in the fight against the novel coronavirus, according to the Phoenix hospital that treated the couple."[74]

(Remember the rules: Within a given article, information that confirms the paper's preferred narrative is to be featured at the top of the article, ideally in the headline and or the first [lede] sentence.)

No, Donald Trump never suggested drinking fish tank cleaner. If he did, trust me, far more people would have tried it.

Why Trump didn't defund taxpayer-funded fake news like NPR, I'll never know.

Maybe HcQ wasn't the miracle cure Trump World had hoped, but the antimalaria drug was long ago approved by the Food and Drug Administration and you theoretically need a prescription to get it. Of all the threats facing our country, HcQ wasn't in the top thousand. Yet, for a few crucial weeks in the middle of a pandemic, the media seemed obsessed with taking it down. Neil Cavuto of Fox News might have been the most hysterical of them all, proclaiming on television after Trump announced he was taking the drug that (in the case of certain vulnerable people) "it will kill you. I cannot stress that enough. This will kill you."[75]

All of these narratives came, were used to bludgeon Trump, and went.

By mid-March, the fake news trial balloons were constant:

Never Trump commentator Max Boot wrote in the *Washington Post* that the "[c]oronavirus wouldn't have happened if Hillary Clinton had won."[76] Actually, Clinton did not show much leadership during the early stages of the pandemic. Her public proclamations were generally simplistic and banal. She accused Trump of "racist rhetoric" and demanded more testing.[77] This is not exactly bold or visionary, nor does it offer the public any clear sense of where her coronavirus plan would have meaningfully differed from Trump's.[78]

They couldn't believe that Trump told the states to find their own ventilators! Actually, he said *try* to find ventilators but the federal government will help, too.[79]

Horrible Trump dissolved the CDC's pandemic preparedness division! Actually, the *Washington Post* framed it as a "reorganization" and said that critics have "misconstrued or intentionally, misrepresented."[80]

Trump called the virus a hoax! Actually, Trump thought the Democrats weaponizing the virus against him was a "hoax"; even establishment fact-checkers acknowledged that.[81]

Trump is muzzling Dr. Fauci! Actually, Dr. Fauci was on video so often during 2020 that I'm pretty sure I saw him in a few of my home movies. Fauci even said relatively early in the crisis on MSNBC that "I'm not being muzzled." (Though you should take that with a grain of salt, because Fauci contradicted himself on a number of occasions, most notably with regard to masks.)[82]

Check out this chaotic footage of an overcrowded New York hospital! Actually, that's Italy, a country with socialized medicine.[83]

Check out this chaotic hospital footage of an overcrowded Philadelphia facility! Actually, that's also Italy.[84]

Well, Sean Hannity killed a guy by convincing him to go on a cruise! That was fake news from *the New York Times*.[85] Actually, the man had disembarked more than a week before Hannity made the remarks that allegedly convinced him to go on the trip. They couldn't even prove that the deceased contracted the virus on the trip. The *Times* quietly updated the article to include the exculpatory evidence that clears Hannity from any direct responsibility.[86]

Well, we know the evangelicals are the superspreaders. Actually, some people believe keeping houses of worship closed while Walmarts are open is a violation of the First Amendment.[87]

And the South is the worst! Worse than New York and New Jersey? Do you understand math? Also, I thought Cuomo was the victim-hero of Trump and his horrible policies. Why is a surge in New York Trump's fault, but a surge in the Sun Belt is the South's fault? Oh yeah, Southern governors are mostly Republicans.[88]

And the hospitals will be overrun! Actually, the American Hospital Association estimates that hospitals lost over $200 billion in revenue between March 1 and June 30.[89] This didn't only hurt hospitals, it also damaged the broader economy: "approximately half of the annualized 4.8% U.S. GDP decline in the first quarter of 2020 is attributed to health care services, especially delayed elective procedures," the *Harvard Business Review* reported.[90] This led to mass layoffs.[91] When restrictions eased, doctors were met with a massive backlog of patients.[92] That means people were suffering with other ailments.

But that's just because hospitals postponed or limited elective surgeries. Exactly, but we're not talking about (only) boob jobs and rhino-plasties. Many states' stay-at-home orders applied to medical procedures deemed "non-essential," but what does that mean?[93] *According to Harvard Business Review*: "most elective surgical cases fall somewhere between vital preventative measures (e.g., screening colonoscopy) and essential surgery (e.g., cataract removal). Ample literature across surgical special-ties demonstrates worse patient outcomes and higher costs when these treatments are delayed."[94]

China's numbers are far better than the United States. They really know what they're doing. Actually, China's data is so cooked that the Brit-ish government refuses to recognize it.[95]

All of the above stories were fake, most were repeated over and over, and few were ever "fact-checked." I have witnessed Facebook's fact-checking hypocrisy firsthand at Breitbart News. We consistently have to fend off what we regard as erroneous fact-checks while we have docu-mented left-wing, establishment, and Chinese media outlets that have gotten away with reporting what appear to be falsehoods.[96] This ensures the fake news continues. Consistently—and uncritically—the establish-ment parroted figures put out by the communist regime in China, that is, CCP propaganda.[97]

CNN was particularly disgraceful throughout 2020, shamelessly bran-dishing coronavirus cases and death toll numbers. Touting the number of "cases" does not have much purpose at all beyond making Americans feel upset and fearful about the virus; public health officials are primarily con-cerned with hospitalizations and deaths. A "positive test" when someone shows no symptoms is essentially meaningless to anyone other than the postive person who is supposed to quarantine for a couple of weeks so as not to infect others.

While the coronavirus death toll is a big, scary number, it is dispalyed on CNN and elsewhere without any context whatsoever. For example, some areas around the country group those who died *with* COVID and those who died *of* COVID as the same. In other words, if someone tested positive and was asymptomatic but died of cancer or a car accident or a spelunking mishap, they might go up on CNN's board. The way COVID deaths are counted isn't always clear or consistent. How many regular CNN viewers know the numbers are much more complicated than the data that appears on screen?[98]

How big is the number who died *with* COVID but not *of* COVID? Maybe it's one-in-twenty, but maybe it's closer to one-in-three, as one group of Oxford researchers reported.[99]

Heart disease accounts for about 650,000 deaths in America every year.[100] Cancer causes another 600,000.[101] Smoking-related conditions kill about 480,000 annually, according to the CDC.[102] Now consider that many on CNN's board are in the dubious "died *with* coronavirus" group. I say this not to minimize the Chinese virus; I say this because there is no CNN ticker for those conditions, nor should there be.

On CNN, every COVID death is portrayed as another healthy and prosperous American cut down in their prime due to Trump's virus and Trump's virus alone. Data paints a much more nuanced picture. As of September 2020, here was the CDC's data on COVID-19 survival rates: 0–19 years old, 99.997 percent; 20–49 years old, 99.98 percent; 50–69 years, 99.5 percent; and 70+ years old or older, 94.6 percent.[103] Long story short, the virus hits the elderly much harder than other demographics. Also according to the CDC, 94 percent of COVID-19 deaths involved underlying medical conditions.[104]

Yet, on shamelessly partisan CNN, the corona ticker constantly took up about a third of the on-screen real estate on every show throughout much of the last year of Trump's presidency. Once Biden took office, the data display was limited drastically, only returning for segments on the coronavirus.[105]

Shameless, yet hardly surprising.

But changing television programming doesn't necessarily change the course of a virus. Whether CNN likes it or not, daily deaths were constantly at near-record levels throughout the early days of Biden's presidency. For example, the COVID-19 body count in Biden's first three week was over 73,000 Americans, which is more than all Americans who lost their lives in the Vietnam War. That meant more Americans were dying each day of the Chinese virus on average than died in the 9/11 terrorist attacks. Yet CNN decided that now was the time to limit the death toll display.

It looks to me like this is virtually an admission that the point of the graphic was just to make Trump look like a killer.

Yet young, healthy Americans were forced to forgo athletic seasons and school semesters. They were told that if they played sports, they would get the virus and maybe be fine but *probably* infect their family and *maybe* kill them. One Breitbart reader told me his college *javelin* season was canceled due to coronavirus. Javelin! What activity is more socially distanced than throwing spears?

Why would anyone trust CNN on the virus anyway after anchor Fredo Cuomo's hoax quarantine back in April 2020? Fredo, who contracted the virus, claimed he was quarantining in his basement over Easter weekend, but that strains credulity. The *New York Post* reported that Cuomo was spotted outdoors and was confronted by a sixty-five-year-old East Hampton resident who reportedly said, "Is that Chris Cuomo? Isn't he supposed to be quarantined?"[106]

It was. And he was.

He was busted. So, Cuomo attempted to BenSmith the news himself on his SiriusXM radio show, ranting that he was a victim of "some jackass, loser, fat tire biker" who got in his face. Breitbart and other outlets featured the radio clip prominently. The BenSmithing plan was backfiring, but it didn't stop Cuomo from fake-emerging from his basement during his CNN show as if he had been trapped in quarantine for two weeks, like a good little subject of his brother, Emperor Governor Cuomo.

It's almost impossible to be more dishonest than this unless you're a pathological liar. But it is the Cuomos we're talking about, so who really knows.

If there was any doubt the crazies had taken over the proverbial asylum, it was eliminated in May 2020 when CNN featured teen green activist Greta Thunberg on a live town-hall panel on the virus.[107]

In the midst of a once-in-a-century pandemic, who does Jeff Zucker tap for his panel? The Climate Change Kid.

It became clear that the establishment media was avoiding any coronavirus discussion that could make the plague seem even a touch less horrifying.

But in fact, a broader national discussion about public health is probably warranted at this point. Obesity, for example, is at epidemic levels in the United States, but is rarely discussed unless in the context of "body positivity." Not only is obesity a problem in its own right, but it makes many other health-related issues even worse. Obesity vastly increases a person's risk of developing hypertension and/or diabetes, which can be a deadly cocktail when mixed with COVID-19.[108]

But instead of doing anything actually helpful, like leading a frank discussion about behavioral changes Americans can make to save lives (and if you want to be honest, trillions of dollars on health care costs), we get *Cosmopolitan* magazine printing multiple covers of obese women with the caption "This Is Healthy."[109]

No, this is Orwellian.

Suicides, opioid usage, alcohol abuse, depression, missed vaccinations, canceled chemotherapy; the health problems other than coronavirus we largely ignored during the 2020–21 pandemic were myriad.[110] There is a deep concern that mask mandates will affect a child's emotional and intellectual development.[111] Even NBC sounded the alarm on the coronavirus's effect on children:[112]

> It means higher rates of suicide. Higher rates of depression, addiction, mental illness and physical disability, particularly for young children who are growing and developing right now. They'll face more developmental delays leading to deficits in their education as they grow.

It will probably take years to determine exactly how much health and psychological damage was done by the reaction to the coronavirus pandemic. I, for one, dread what we will learn.

Divorces spiked (up 34 percent from March through June 2020, year over year), separations spiked, even domestic violence got much worse (over 61 percent of women living with their abusers in the United Kingdom reported worsening abuse during lockdown, according to advocacy group Women's Aid) during the pandemic.[113] At least one Massachusetts hospital found "a significant year-over-year jump in intimate partner violence cases who sought emergency care." Abuse hotlines rang off the hook. Yet all of this was rarely of interest to our national media.[114]

After all, if the media did consider some of these horrifying facts, maybe we might decide to reopen the country and take back control of our own lives. But that would involve not using the coronavirus to beat up on Trump, and the media certainly wouldn't have that.

Obviously the psychosocial distresses of the pandemic are a far greater burden on children than the virus itself.[115] Yet, as is often the case, the children are disenfranchised by our establishment media. The teachers' unions made sure kids stayed home despite the consensus that the children were likely safer in the classroom than elsewhere.[116] The doctors knew this, but the politicians favored the unions over the science.

In July, MSNBC host Craig Melvin was stunned when an NBC News/MSNBC segment featuring pediatricians unanimously agreed they would send their kids back to school in the fall.[117]

By November, CDC director Robert Redfield and Dr. Anthony Fauci said the science was decidedly on the side of keeping schools open.[118] But this didn't carry sway in some parts of the country. Right around that time, Bill de Blasio enacted more school closures in New York.[119] Chicago Teachers Union (CTU) tweeted that "the push to reopen schools was rooted in sexism, racism and misogyny." (They deleted it later.)[120] A CTU leader who identifies as "socialist" emphatically asserted that schools were "unsafe"—from a sunny vacation in Puerto Rico.[121] Los Angeles had some of the most intense school closures in the country at the time, even as they saw the nation's worst virus outbreak, suggesting the lockdowns weren't having much of an effect, if any.[122]

In single-party Democratic cities like Los Angeles, New York, or Chicago, the real coronavirus authorities aren't doctors or even the politicians; they're the teachers' unions, and our children are just their political cannon fodder in their battle to get paid to not work.

Our establishment media carried water for the Democrats and the unions while our children suffered.

Biden repeated the mantra "science over fiction" throughout the 2020 campaign, but once sworn in, he started to defy the recommendations of his own handpicked scientists, including his own CDC director, Dr. Rochelle Walensky, a Johns Hopkins–trained physician with a master's of public health from Harvard. Walensky told reporters, "There is increasing data to suggest that schools can safely reopen and that safe reopening does not suggest that teachers need to be vaccinated."[123] "Current data from schools, from summer camps and whatnot also suggested that the children not only have decreased rates of symptoms, but have decreased rates of transmissibility," she said.[124] White House spokeswoman Jen Psaki dismissed the scientific recommendation by Biden's handpicked actual scientist by saying Dr. Walensky "spoke to this in her personal capacity."[125]

This is a stunning rebuke considering that the media had peppered us with headlines that it was Trump who had put too much political pressure on the CDC. "Trump officials interfered with CDC reports on Covid-19," wrote *Politico* in September 2020.[126] From CNN in August 2020: "CDC was pressured 'from the top down' to change coronavirus testing guidance, official says."[127] And from the *New York Times* in September 2020: "Behind the White House Effort to Pressure the C.D.C. on School Openings."[128] All of these articles advanced the narrative that Trump chose politics over science and we must keep our children home.

Now Biden is in office, and his CDC director was openly defied if not outright disparaged from the White House briefing room.

After President Trump lost reelection, some more frank discussion about the secondary effects of the virus all of a sudden started to appear in the establishment press. Some notable examples:

- *New York Times*, January 24, 2021: "Surge of Student Suicides Pushes Las Vegas Schools to Reopen"[129]

- *New York Times*, February 14, 2021: "'What's the Point?' Young People's Despair Deepens as Covid-19 Crisis Drags On"[130]

- *Wired*, January 10, 2021: "It's Not Just You: Everyone's Mental Health Is Suffering"[131]

- CNBC, February 10, 2021: "Nearly half of U.S. workers suffer from mental health issues since Covid-19 pandemic hit, report finds"[132]

- *Nature*, February 3, 2021: "COVID's mental-health toll: how scientists are tracking a surge in depression"[133]

- WebMD, February 10, 2021: "Child Suicides Rising During Lockdown"[134]

- *U.S. News & World Report*, January 29, 2021: "Children's Hospitals Battle COVID-19, Surging Mental Health Needs"[135]

- ABC News, February 20, 2021: "Pandemic-fueled drinking causes wave of alcohol-related liver disease and hospitalizations, report says"[136]

- NBC News, February 9, 2021: "Covid crisis is exacerbating LGBTQ alcohol abuse, studies find"[137]

With teen suicides regularly in the news, MTV announced the release of a documentary about depressed and suicidal young people.[138] That's nice, but what would really help is if people with major platforms simply took a bold stand to reopen the schools—and the rest of the country.

Other victims of the lockdowns deserve consideration, yet get almost zero. Women, particularly working mothers, were forced out of the workforce during the pandemic. Workforce participation declined for both sexes during this time, but mothers dropped out at nearly three times the rate of fathers.[139]

Black families were hit perhaps the hardest of any during the pandemic.[140] First of all, black Americans suffered significantly from the Chinese virus itself, mostly due to the fact that they are more likely to have more than two medical comorbidities, according to *JAMA* (*JAMA* also noted that when controlling for age, sex, and comorbidities, black Americans' survival outcome is at least as good as whites').[141] Black Americans were nearly three times as likely to be hospitalized and nearly twice as likely to die with COVID-19 than whites.[142] Black families were considerably more likely to have fully remote learning than higher-income white families. Blacks were 19 percent less likely than whites to choose to return to school, which the media attributed to skepticism of the system.[143] Considering that the media had spent much of the last five years convincing American citizens that we're a racist country, this isn't exactly a surprise. Black families on average have fewer recourses and more single-parent households; this again favors the children of affluent whites.

So many Americans were ignored by our press as they pursued their narrative of blaming the virus on Trump. The damage it caused to the public health, both mental and physical, will never fully be known.

A Tale of Two Governors

A teachable media moment amid the pandemic chaos was the contrast between the way the press portrayed New York governor Andrew Cuomo and Florida governor Ron DeSantis.

When it came to the China virus, New York fared the worst of any state in the union, by far. There is virtually nothing good that can be said about the way the Empire State handled itself. It had some of the most deaths on earth, arguably the greatest level of economic devastation in America, and long, recurring lockdowns.

President Trump even sent the USNS *Comfort*, a 1,000-bed hospital ship, to New York Harbor; it had only twenty patients on it before being sent back to its home port in Virginia.[144] The *Comfort* was supposed to be used for non-coronavirus patients, but with the lockdowns, there were far fewer car accidents, construction accidents, gunshot wounds, and many other injuries that would precipitate an emergency room visit. The *New York Times* reported, "Guidelines disseminated to hospitals included a list of 49 medical conditions that would exclude a patient from admittance to the ship." Furthermore, Americans avoided medical care for much of the year due to fear of the virus and running up medical bills during the economic crisis.[145]

Still, Democrat governor Andrew Cuomo enjoyed one of the highest approval ratings in the country.[146]

The New York governor messaged to the press like the situation was well under control, or at least on the way to being under control. "Everybody is doing exactly what we need to do," Cuomo said during a March 2 news conference with New York City mayor Bill de Blasio. "We have been ahead of this from Day 1," Fredo's big bro said.[147] He directly contradicted himself during a March 30 press conference, stating, "I am tired of being behind this virus. We've been behind this virus from day one."[148] About six weeks later, New York State would cross one thousand coronavirus deaths in a single day.

Cuomo said in April 2020 that "data suggests we are flattening the curve so far." If that was the case, why did it take until February 2021 for indoor dining to return to New York City?

Cuomo brazenly published a book on pandemic-era leadership on October 13, 2020. On that day, New York recorded 1,391 new coronavirus cases. New York then experienced a massive coronavirus surge, hitting 19,560 new cases on January 8, 2021, fourteen times more than the day Cuomo's book was released. All the while, the statewide lockdowns crushed countless businesses and even entire industries. Unemployment for the state hit 14.7 percent in April, the highest rate since the great depression.[149] By September, Yelp reported that over 11,000 New York City businesses had closed. Most closures—63 percent—were expected to be permanent. The Partnership for New York City estimated that perhaps 80,000(!) of the city's small businesses would not outlive the pandemic.[150]

But beyond the economic devastation in New York, Cuomo was responsible for the single most devastating public policy decision of the entire pandemic: cramming sick patients into nursing homes, essentially sentencing many other patients to their deaths. The number of New York nursing home coronavirus fatalities is still unknown, but the number is believed to be about 15,000 as of February 2021.[151] Cuomo attempted to blame federal guidelines for this policy, that is, Trump's coronavirus task force; the task force told me Cuomo wildly misinterpreted their recommendations.[152] Centers for Medicare and Medicaid Services (CMS) administrator Seema Verma laid it out in an interview on *Breitbart News Daily*:

> The governor continues to be confused about the policy. . . . And he keeps saying that it was federal guidelines that allowed him to create the policy that he had, and I just want to be very clear with your listeners and the public, because it's important to protect our most vulnerable citizens. Our guidelines very clearly say that a nursing home can accept somebody that's COVID-positive, as long as the facility can follow the CDC guidelines around isolation. But it also says—and I'm reading this—it says, "If a nursing home cannot, then it must wait until these precautions can be discontinued." So the guidance couldn't be any clearer.

Cuomo's rhetoric only escalated as the virus wore on. "Donald Trump caused the COVID outbreak in New York," he said on September 8.[153] In October, he told the ladies of *The View* that he's holding Trump "responsible for every" coronavirus death in the United States.

Pretty absurd, especially considering the virus originated in China and that parts of Europe struggled with it at least as badly as the United States (it's impossible to truly know how nations with dictatorships and closed press fared with the virus).

Yet this level of Trump derangement wasn't even the most over-the-top in the establishment media. Government-funded PBS host Alexander Heffner told Al Sharpton on Sharpton's MSNBC show that Trump's coronavirus response was "genocidal" and "mass murder."[154] This type of talk wasn't atypical.

Florida, meanwhile, kept its economy mostly open and still fared relatively well with the virus. A candidate for line of the year came in a failed attempt by PolitiFact to ding Governor DeSantis for exaggerating his success against the virus: "Only about half of the 10 most stringently regulated states saw rates of cases, deaths and hospitalizations that were twice as high as Florida's—DeSantis' benchmark."[155] This is a gobbledygook argument, but I think the point they are making is that only five out of the ten states they looked at were twice as bad as Florida. Take that, Ron! But the "fact-check" does admit that "Broadly speaking, we found that Florida's record, at least as of the beginning of December, compared favorably with most states across the country, including those with tighter restrictions."

Florida has the largest population of over-sixty-five-year-olds in the United States other than California; they have about a million more seniors than does New York. Seniors make up over 20 percent of Florida's population, compared to New York's 16 percent. Yet, as of March 2021, according to *New York Times* data, Florida's death rate is less than two-thirds of New York State's and nearly identical to New York City's. Also as of March 2021, 247 New Yorkers and 355 New York City residents out of every 100,000 died of COVID-19, respectively,[156] compared to 149 out of every 100,000 Floridians.[157]

Data changes, and the virus is still with us, but it paints a clear picture that Florida's coronavirus strategy was superior to New York's.

The chickens began to come home for Governor Fredo's Brother in late January 2021. Democrat New York attorney general Letitia James found that New York had been drastically undercounting the COVID-related deaths in the state's nursing homes.[158] "The state's acknowledgment increased the overall death toll related to those facilities by more than 40 percent. Ms. James's report had suggested that the state's previous tally could be off by as much as 50 percent," the *New York Times* wrote when James's report was released in January 2021. This revelation meant that the New York nursing home death count surged by at least 3,800.

The *New York Post* reported that Melissa DeRosa, New York's secretary to the governor, said that the data was covered up specifically to avoid a potential investigation from the Trump Justice Department.[159]

All this information came out, conveniently, just a few weeks after Joe Biden had been sworn in as president.

This devastating information about Cuomo's failures was probably surprising to people who only get news from the establishment media. CNN anchor Chris Cuomo ignored the story when it broke, choosing neither to criticize nor defend his governor brother at his darkest moment. As the scandal grew, Chris Cuomo acknowledged it on air but said "obviously I cannot cover it because he is my brother."[160] Perhaps the rationale for this editorial decision was that it's a conflict of interest (it is), but the network didn't appear at all concerned when Fredo did coronavirus prop comedy while on-air with his brother Andrew, teasing him back in May with multiple oversized nasal swabs, joking about the coronavirus test.[161]

More women came forward.

Eventually, in March of 2021, left-leaning journalism non-profit Poynter wrote that "CNN has a Cuomo problem." (I think it's safe to say at this point the May Q-tip segment was inappropriate.)

Right around the time the Cuomo bros were playing games on CNN while New York's elderly died en masse, Florida governor Ron DeSantis was beating expectations. Even left-wing *Politico* wrote in May 2020—the sentiment still holds true—"let's just come out and say it: DeSantis looks more right than those who criticized the Sunshine State's coronavirus response."[162] Stunningly, the beltway-centric publication noted that the media was biased against DeSantis, despite the numbers:

> Yes, there's media bias, too. Cuomo also has something else DeSantis doesn't: a press that defers to him, one that preferred to cover "Florida Morons" at the beach (where it's relatively hard to get infected) over New Yorkers riding cramped subway cars (where it's easy to get infected).

The "Florida Morons" remark was a reference to media like the New York *Daily News* attacking DeSantis for opening beaches in April.[163] The quote also obliquely mentions an MIT study that raised concern that the filthy and still fully operational New York subway system was leading to a surge in the virus.[164]

Despite their large elderly population, Florida continues to outperform other states, even with relatively mild shutdowns and mask rules. DeSantis continues to be vindicated despite the media's insistence that he had put the entire state in jeopardy. Here is a smattering of headlines when Disney World reopened (at limited capacity and with various safety precautions in place) in July 2020:

- NBC: "Disney Reopens Despite Worsening Virus Outbreak in Florida, Faces Backlash"[165]

- Vox: "Disney World has reopened, despite the threat of coronavirus"[166]

People: "Disney World Opens Despite Coronavirus in Florida"[167]

NPR: "Disney World Orlando to Reopen Despite COVID-19 Surge in Florida"[168]

Washington Post: "Disney World set to reopen despite severe outbreak unfolding in Florida"[169]

More NBC: "Disney World reopens even as coronavirus cases soar in Florida and across U.S."[170]

Guardian: "Disney World set to reopen at weekend despite coronavirus surge in Florida"[171]

CNN: "Disney World reopens as coronavirus cases spike in Florida"[172]

- *New York Times*: "Disney World Opens Its Gates, with Virus Numbers Rising"[173]

It seemed as though every single establishment media outlet took the exact same angle. Though technically accurate, it's clear that the objective was to frame Florida's Republican government as reckless, putting us all in jeopardy. After all, DeSantis and Company shouldn't be trusted because virus cases were on the rise at the time.

(Recall the media rules: Within a given article, information that confirms the paper's preferred narrative is to be featured at the top of the article, ideally in the headline and or the first [lede] sentence.)

Few of these outlets doubled back and noted that hysteria over Disney World's opening was entirely misplaced. Florida cases went down after the reopening and no outbreaks were traced to the theme park. The *New York Times*, to their credit, is an exception, though they waited several months to report the good news. They reported in October 2020, "At Disney World, 'Worst Fears' About Virus Have Not Come True."[174]

Governor Gavin Newsom did not get the memo out in California. Disneyland in Anaheim, California, would remain closed for roughly a year, most of that time after Disney World in Florida had successfully reopened.[175] Disney parks were open all over the world, including in China. The decision for the California parks to remain locked down had devastating economic consequences. Despite many reopenings, Disney hemorrhaged over $2 billion in operating income from their parks in the first quarter of fiscal year 2021.[176] They had to lay off tens of thousands of workers. Even local businesses were crushed by the lack of economic activity in the area. According to the *Wall Street Journal*, Dara Maleki, who owns pizza restaurants near both Disneyland and Disney World, saw sales dip 90 percent at his SoCal location but only 30 percent in Florida.

DeSantis continued to ignore the establishment media haters.[177] He lifted major restrictions in late September 2020, including shutdowns and mask mandates, which did not lead to any outbreaks.[178]

The DeSantis "hero" profiles from the establishment press were nonexistent. But while he isn't being rewarded by our broken media, he is being rewarded in other ways. In February 2021, the *New York Post* ran the headline "New Yorkers are fleeing to Palm Beach—and NYC businesses are following." "New York City is alive and well—in Palm Beach, Florida," the *Post* wrote.[179]

Fox Orlando reported in February 2021 that Disney was considering moving some operations from California to Florida.[180]

It's not difficult to imagine why.

In a moment that the most genius satirists could never have dreamt up, Andrew Cuomo won an International Emmy award for "masterful use of TV to inform & calm people around the world" in November 2020.[181] Like President Trump, Cuomo held regular press briefings but with a decidedly more tranquil atmosphere. How many people did Cuomo lull into a stupor as the virus raged on? How many journalists who attended these episodes of daytime reality television were missing the biggest stories of the moment, such as the bodies piling up (but not being accurately counted) in our nursing homes?

We'll never know the full extent of the damage caused to New York by Andrew Cuomo's failures. But we do know that the media and entertainment class found him simply dazzling.

Going Viral

Of all the narratives covered in this book, the coronavirus is perhaps the most difficult to write about, especially as someone without a medical education. (Thankfully, I'm blessed to have a number of doctors in my family, even a "frontline" doctor who treated coronavirus patients, who helped me immeasurably to frame issues responsibly.) First of all, this is a *novel* virus. The facts are constantly changing. The COVID-19 landscape is certainly going to be different the day you read this book than when I wrote this chapter. At Breitbart News, we were among the first American outlets to express concern about the virus, and among the first to frame the lockdowns and crackdowns as seemingly ineffective against the virus and devastating to many Americans' finances and our collective psyche. All of these things can be true at the same time! The virus has in fact been a menace, especially to the elderly and the infirm. (To be clear: I have never been in the camp of people who thought the coronavirus was "just the flu.") Yet the discussion about the virus on a national level was controlled by an agenda-obsessed establishment press who looked to take advantage of the pandemic to frame Donald Trump as unfit for office.

Trump hurt himself with endless daily press conferences where only national reporters from the establishment media were allowed to ask him questions. There was never a panel of doctors assembled. Local news and new media were mostly excluded. What's more, as social distancing became the norm, many outlets on the periphery of the White House press pool, like Breitbart News, had less of a chance to get into briefings to ask questions due to limited space. He handed the narrative to the worst group of people imaginable: the permanent White House press pool. This was one of the few colossal blunders of his administration.

Trump correctly warned about one thing, though: "the cure" could become "worse than the disease." We were at first unprepared for the pandemic, then we wildly overreacted to it. Instead of learning lessons along the way, we appeared to get increasingly irrational. Shutdowns and mask mandates are apparently not panaceas, but any suggestion they are not is batted down instantly by armchair fact-checkers. Few if any of them are doctors and rarely do they offer empirical evidence for their ardent claims, and they are all too keen to advance infringement on freedoms.

In January 2021, Dr. Fauci said that "there's no data that indicates" double masking would work. Days later, the CDC updated their coronavirus guidance to recommend wearing multiple face diapers at the same time in certain cases. So, which is it? And if double masks really were the answer, why did no one think of this nine months ago? Confusion like this from our medical community creates a sense of societal chaos. And it has been constant since the virus crossed into our country.

The notion of personal responsibility was rarely considered throughout the pandemic news cycle; trusting Americans to manage their own risk was taken off the table immediately in many states. Who took that discussion off the table? Politicians and corporate media elite who favor a bigger state and a diminished citizenry. As noted multiple times throughout this book, no group benefited from the pandemic more than the world's biggest companies.

As is often the case, the establishment media's coronavirus coverage was counterproductive for Americans. We were constantly told to remain locked down, masked up, and bummed out. Any digression from this was met with public condemnation, unless of course you were Nancy Pelosi maskless in a salon, or Anthony Fauci maskless at a ballgame, or Governor Newsom maskless at a dinner party, or . . . We could have been collectively examining states and countries that performed better than others and made adjustments accordingly. But we didn't do that. The Democrats and their allies in the media saw red. Or actually blue. They knew that the worse the virus seemed, the more likely they could use it to oust Donald Trump in November.

Science was irrelevant, unless it could help them achieve their ends.

Consider the surreal juxtaposition of the media and Democrats openly encouraging the Black Lives Matter protests, which were obsessively described as "mostly peaceful" but often devolved into full-blown rioting. Los Angeles mayor Eric Garcetti, for example, enacted some of the most stringent and longest-lasting lockdowns in the country; LA children were forbidden from attending school well into 2021. Yet Garcetti appeared maskless at a massive Black Lives Matter rally in June (he was not socially distanced). Coronavirus data showed a big spike in cases in the city after the rally.[182]

Kamala Harris encouraged her Twitter followers to pay for bail for protesters via the Minnesota Freedom Fund. The MFF, an organization that has advocated for "defunding" of police, also raked in cash from Hollywood stars like Justin Timberlake, Steve Carell, and Seth Rogen. These funds can go to releasing violent criminals, including those who have been charged or convicted of rape and murder.[183] Not only did the then-senator rubber-stamp horrific violence, but this also is a de facto endorsement of the superspreader protest events.

The goal was never to stop the spread. The goal was to oust the Bad Orange Man.

In time, the Democrat Media Complex would use the "Trump virus" to make the aforementioned fundamental changes to the voting process. I believe these changes were an essential factor in Joe Biden's victory.

CHAPTER 10

THE MASTERS OF THE UNIVERSE

Breitbart News refers to the leaders of the high-tech industry as "the Masters of the Universe." Former attorney general Jeff Sessions used the moniker in 2014, likely as an homage to Tom Wolfe, who characterized the Wall Street titans of the 1980s as "the Masters of the Universe."[1] Either that, or the former attorney general is really into He-Man.

The sobriquet for the Big Tech elite stuck because it fits: never in world history have so few anonymous, unelected people had so much power. The Masters of the Universe have the ability to control and manipulate the vast majority of information flow that takes place in the United States. If "knowledge is power," then what is it if you have near-total control over what knowledge people acquire?

Silicon Valley is also, unfortunately, a hostile place if you're not on the left. Famed tech investor Peter Thiel—cofounder of PayPal and a Facebook board member—has said that "Silicon Valley is a one-party state."[2] You can guess what party he was referring to. I don't know of anyone who would refute him.

So, what does it look like when all of our technologies are controlled by people with the same ideology, particularly if it's an ideology that's susceptible to woke hysteria and inclined to engage in censorship? Well, you get a lot of hysteria and censorship.

Since I've been on national radio, I've asked nearly every elected official I've had on my show about the threat Big Tech companies and their inordinate control over American minds poses to democracy.

Every one of the politicians has expressed at least some level of concern about this fact, but none have been able to successfully curtail their power. Donald Trump didn't make any progress in this department (he exasperatingly referred to Microsoft, Apple, Google, and Amazon as "MAGA" in 2020).[3] The tech elite boomed during the Trump years, dragging the stock market skyward with them. This appeared to make the former president personally proud. He lavished praise on the Silicon Valley super elite as he took credit for the bull market that preceded the pandemic.

Silicon Valley spreads millions of dollars on politicians and thought leaders every year, lining the pockets of Democrats and media figures alike. Even conservatives were quickly bought off. *National Review*, for example, is a subsidiary of the National Review Institute, which received money from Google[4] (CEO Sundar Pichai confirmed this when asked by the House Judiciary Committee).[5] *National Review* editor-in-chief Rich Lowry wrote an article for *Politico* literally titled "Don't Break Up Big Tech"; nowhere in the article does he disclose that his organization had received money from Google. Unconscionable, but not uncommon.[6]

While our elected officials have stood by and let Big Tech get bigger than any industry ever in the history of the world, the Silicon Valley elite were gradually ramping up crackdowns on conservative content. Here are a few lowlights, delineated by platform, all of which predate the massive purge of conservatives from the Internet in January 2021 just after the Democrats took control of the Senate and just prior to Biden's inauguration (I'll address that later):

Twitter:

• Twitter has used the tactic of shadowbanning, particularly against conservatives since 2016.[7] (CEO Jack Dorsey has admitted to Congress that Twitter was "unfairly filtering" hundreds of thousands of accounts, but also maintains that Twitter does not "shadowban anyone based on political ideology." "Shadowbanning" is the expression used when a blacklisted poster's content does not appear in the feeds of their followers unbeknownst to the poster and/or the follower. The tactic was thought to be used primarily to marginalize spammers, but it was turned against conservatives. Leftist outlet Vice reported that Twitter had shadowbanned multiple top conservatives.[8]

• Twitter has banned other prominent figures, most of whom are conservative. The highest-profiles bannings were of Alex Jones and InfoWars and former Breitbart writer Milo Yiannopoulos.[9] Most of these were rooted in accusations of hate speech, a category apparently so broad that it includes the statement that "men are not women," for which Twitter banned feminist writer Meghan Murphy in 2018.[10]

• In March 2019, Twitter suspended a contributor to the conservative *Washington Examiner* for tweeting "learn to code," a phrase frequently used to mock many journalists' advice to unemployed blue-collar workers, during a debate about tech-related unemployment.[11]

• In July 2020, Twitter blocked Breitbart out of our account for four days after we posted live-video footage of anti-establishment doctors discussing the coronavirus and lockdowns.[12] Breitbart had aired footage of a group of physicians called America's Frontline Doctors who held a rally in Washington, D.C., where they raised questions about the medical community's response to the pandemic. Though there was hours of content on a range of issues, most controversially, several doctors enthusiastically endorsed hydroxychloroquine as a treatment for COVID-19. One even (inaccurately) called it a "cure." Breitbart never endorsed any of the content discussed by the frontline doctors; we merely aired the footage and transcribed parts of it. Twitter locked us out until we deleted the content.

• Also in July 2020, Twitter came under fire for blocking a tweet from President Trump, but not tweets from Iranian supreme leader Ayatollah Khamenei that called for Israel's destruction.[13] Khamenei often calls for "the elimination of the Zionist regime" and uses highly aggressive language about Israel and the Jewish people. By contrast, in June 2020, Twitter had labeled a straightforward tweet from the president as a violation of their "[r]ules about abusive behavior . . . specifically, the presence of a threat of harm against an identifiable group." Here's the tweet: "There will never be an 'Autonomous Zone' in Washington, D.C., as long as I'm your President. If they try they will be met with serious force!" As of early 2021, many of Khamenei's tweets were still online while Trump has been banned for life.

Facebook:

• In the run-up to the 2018 midterm elections, Facebook banned 251 anti-establishment accounts and removed 559 more pages, accusing them of "coordinated inauthentic behavior."[14] They've done similar purges before other elections worldwide.

• Facebook keeps a "hate agents" list of content producers who are on the verge of getting banned. As of May 2019, the list was heavily weighted with conservatives, including Candace Owens.[15]

• In 2019, Project Veritas reported that Facebook routinely suppressed conservative pages—a tactic they called "deboosting."[16] According to a whistleblower, Facebook "deboosted" several prominent conservative pages, but targeted relatively few aligned with the Left.[17] According to a whistleblower, Facebook tagged pages for deboosting without notifying their owners, effectively leaving them with no knowledge or recourse.

• Facebook began testing a "news" section in fall 2019, after its previous iteration was accused of spreading fake news.[18] Through the new feature, Facebook funneled millions of dollars to establishment media outlets to license their content, again to the detriment of independent news.[19]

• In 2020, Facebook built an "Oversight Board" to oversee content bans (the idea was hatched by anti-Trump Harvard law professor Noah Feldman), and packed it with leftists including a member of George Soros's Open Society project.[20] There are apparently no conservatives on the "Facebook Supreme Court."

• Extreme far-left content, including calls for violence, are common on Facebook. One such group, dubbed "The Base," remains active despite calls for "militancy to intensify."[21]

Google:

• According to internal chats obtained by the *Daily Caller,* Google employees discussed suppressing search results for conservative sites like Breitbart and the *Daily Caller* immediately following the 2016 election.[22]

• In audio leaked to Breitbart News, Google discussed "steering" the conservative movement "away from the more sort of nationalistic incendiary comments, nativist comments" following the 2018 Conservative Political Action Conference (CPAC).[23]

• Weeks later, Google circulated a memo titled "The Good Censor," arguing that tech platforms needed to move away from the "American tradition" of free speech to a more European model that encourages "safety and civility."[24] The document, leaked in its entirety to Breitbart News, explicitly cited the 2016 election as well as recent elections in Germany as reasons for the shift. The internal report also showed that government requests to censor content on Google's platforms were increasing. The blacklisting business was booming.

• In January 2019, Breitbart News revealed that YouTube, which is owned by Google, has deliberately suppressed search results for videos containing controversial terms, including "abortion," on its platform.[25] Google CEO Sundar Pichai had recently told Congress that the company did not "manually intervene" on particular search terms.

• A Google insider later told Project Veritas that YouTube suppresses content from conservative PragerU and independent videographers Dave Rubin and Tim Pool.[26]

• Project Veritas reported in July 2019 that one thousand Google employees signed a petition to blacklist Breitbart from Google's ad service.[27] Their sentiments echo the goals of left-wing activists such as Sleeping Giants, who target the advertising revenue of right-wing news sites and personalities.

• According to a 2019 audit of Google search results conducted by researchers at Northwestern University, Google's search results overwhelmingly favor left-leaning, mainstream media outlets.[28] Of the twenty news sites most commonly featured in Google's "top stories" section, only one was somewhat conservative (Fox News). Google is one of the most influential drivers of traffic to online news sites.

The other tech giants who have less direct control over the news you consume aren't much better:

• An analysis of Wikipedia highlighted by a former Wikipedia-editor-turned-whistleblower revealed that the Internet encyclopedia's articles on American politicians relied on mostly leftist media.[29] Not only is Wikipedia one of the most trafficked information websites in the world, but inaccurate information posted there appears in "knowledge panels," which are blocks of general information on a person or topic that appear prominently at the top of Google searches and on Facebook.[30]

• In 2017, Apple banned conservative social media brand Gab (during the purge of conservatives form the Internet following the January 6 riot at the Capitol; it also banned Parler) from its App Store, claiming they did not adequately suppress "objectionable content." According to a statement posted to Medium, Apple's App Store Review Team "found references to religion, race, gender, sexual orientation, or other targeted groups that could be offensive to many users."[31] Yet Apple is also one of the most tolerant of China's human rights abuses. It was listed in a study that concluded it relies on Uyghur slave labor.[32] Apple has been criticized for sending user data to the Chinese.[33]

• Though Amazon thus far has resisted the urging of the Sleeping Giants to blacklist Breitbart, they did remove conservative journalist Mike Cernovich's media-bias documentary *Hoaxed* from the Prime Video page.[34] (They also blacklisted Parler from their cloud servers in what was one of the more shocking developments in the 2021 purge.)[35]

Examples of pro-establishment, anti-conservative bias are endless. Yet whenever a tech platform does not expand their blacklists, they are treated as though they are evil right-wingers. The best example of this: when Facebook listed Breitbart as one of two hundred sources eligible for their Facebook News feature, establishment journalists were apoplectic.[36] No one on the right threw a tantrum because CNN was included, though maybe we should have.

Big Tech had developed all sorts of weapons in the aftermath of 2016, and they would be brought to bear on the 2020 election. Everyone should have seen this coming. As reported exclusively by Breitbart News and our top tech reporter, Allum Bokhari, Google vice president Kent Walker stated in a tearful all-hands company meeting just after the 2016 election that the company intended to make populism and nationalism a "blip" or a "hiccup" in the march toward "progress."[37]

When people on the left make declarations like this—and they actually have the power to make their vision a reality—I tend to take them seriously. And Google did have that kind of power, especially if the other tech powerhouses were simpatico. Search engine expert (and Hillary Clinton and Joe Biden voter) Dr. Robert Epstein, the senior research psychologist at the American Institute for Behavioral Research and Technology, said that he believed Google shifted a full 6 million votes or more in the 2020 election toward Joe Biden. The real number might be closer to 15 million, he says.[38] "Based on the data that we're collecting, I would say that if what we're seeing is present nationwide they are probably shifting this year in this election about 15 million votes without anyone's awareness, except for what I'm doing, without leaving a paper trail for authorities to trace," Epstein told Tucker Carlson back in October. The researcher claimed that he and a team of about six hundred field agents had analyzed about 1.5 million searches and said that "we're finding very substantial pro-liberal bias in all ten or at least nine out of ten search results on the first page of Google search results, not on Bing or Yahoo though." Epstein had told me in a 2018 interview that Google "could shift ten percent of the voting population of America with no one knowing that they had done this, and without leaving a paper trail for authorities to track."[39]

One method, Epstein emphasizes, is that Google's autocomplete suggestions when you begin typing a term into their search bar appear to have been manually altered to protect Democrats from negative searches.[40]

Epstein found other shocking tactics used by Google. "We also found what seems to be a smoking gun," Epstein told Tucker Carlson.[41] "We found a period of days when the vote reminder on Google's homepage was being sent only to liberals—not one of our conservative field agents received a vote reminder during those days." Epstein had hundreds of field agents deployed across battleground states collecting hundreds of thousands of data points.

We at Breitbart experienced Google's apparent manipulation first-hand. Google began purging Breitbart's content since the 2016 election. Our search visibility in July 2020 versus 2016 was down 99.7 percent (that means the likelihood that you find a Breitbart article when doing a routine Google search was almost zero). Google emphatically denies that there is political bias in their search engines.

On April 4, 2016, Breitbart ranked in the top ten search positions (the first page of Google search results) for 355 key terms. By July 20, 2020, that number was down to one search term. We had nearly 17,000 terms in the top 100; that number dropped to around 50 by summer of 2020.[42] All of this happened despite Breitbart working diligently with industry experts to optimize our position in search engines.

Overall, our Google traffic was down about two-thirds over that time period. We believe most of the remaining third of the traffic was due to searches with the term "Breitbart" in it. If you didn't use the term "Breitbart," it was unlikely you'd see any Breitbart results, even if we were one of the Internet's subject area authorities (think issues like immigration, Donald Trump, and media bias, to name a few).

On May 5, 2020, Google killed all of Breitbart's traffic on stories about Joe Biden.[43] We went from tens of thousands of impressions on searches for "Joe Biden" to literally zero. Google had flipped a switch and turned off the traffic.

To reiterate: if you want to search for "Joe Biden" or "Biden," the chances of you getting a Breitbart article are virtually nil unless you add the word "Breitbart."

This appeared to be a concerted effort by the Masters of the Universe to ensure that Breitbart's content was not accessed by Google users, thus protecting Joe Biden before the general election.

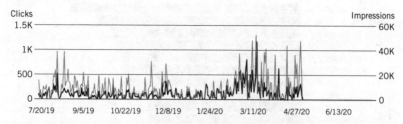

Google search traffic to Breitbart News from the search term "Joe Biden" from July 2019 to July 2020. Gray = clicks. Black = impressions. *(Image credit: Breitbart News)*

A search engine expert with decades of experience in the industry told us in a July 2020 interview that he's never seen anything like this:[44]

> I've never experienced such a wholesale removal of rank and visibility on specific concepts on a site as I have seen being applied to Breitbart. Removal is the key, not dropping in rank, which would be an organic devaluing. These ranks are just simply gone, overnight, while other topics have been untouched.
>
> The sheer fact that there are thousands of pages of Breitbart content that reference Biden that were ranking before May 6, that now have no rank or impressions on search is a sign of manipulation, not algorithmic devaluing.

No kidding.

According to DOJ, Google controls a staggering 88 percent of the U.S. search market.[45] That's what you call a monopoly. And this monopoly is seemingly working hard to suppress Breitbart's reach.

These aren't the only data points that suggest manual suppression. The percentage of traffic to Breitbart from Google is 9 percent; other leading publishers see an average of 30–50 percent of their traffic from search. And it's not just Breitbart that is squeezed like this. Publicly available data on search traffic from Amazon-owned Alexa.com reveals that conservative news outlets get a far, far lower percentage of their traffic from Google than establishment and left-wing outlets.

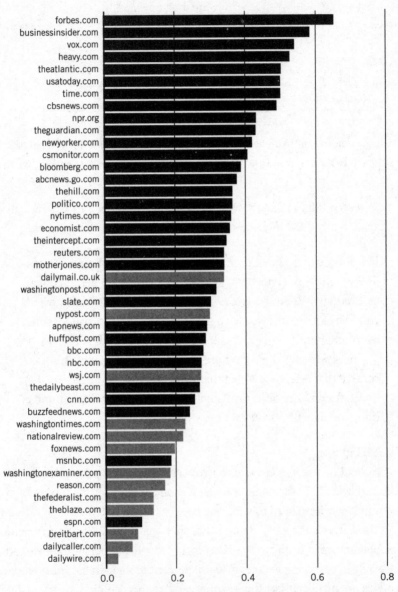

Percentages of website traffic from Google, via Alexa web rankings. Gray = media sources with conservative or libertarian-leaning editorial stances. Data is a six-month average as of July 7, 2020. (Image credit: Breitbart News)

In fact, they literally prioritize sites that plagiarize Breitbart ahead of our own content. Even scoops and exclusive interviews are hidden deep within Google's results while clickbait copy/paste sites are promoted above us in search results.[46]

If you search for a Breitbart headline verbatim, you still might not ever see a Breitbart story appear in your results.[47] Breitbart News reporter Allum Bokhari described the phenomenon on November 2, 2020, the first time we covered it at Breitbart:

> Even when the exact headline of a Breitbart News article is typed into Google, search results will frequently return results to obscure websites instead of Breitbart itself—sometimes websites that scraped Breitbart's content without permission.
>
> For example, we conducted a Google search for the following Breitbart News original article: "Joe Biden Touts 'Most Extensive & Inclusive Voter Fraud Organization in History of American Politics,'" by Kyle Olsen.[48] The top search result is from a website called Geopolitics News, which plagiarizes both the headline and the full content of the article—complete with Olson's bio.[49]
>
> The second result is a story from Snopes, a left-leaning "fact checker," which purports to "debunk" the Biden gaffe.

Since Breitbart put out an extensive report on this phenomenon, Google appears to have adjusted their algorithm so the plagiarism sites don't appear quite so high, so often. But(!)—they appear to have found a new way to use their search engine to advance their preferred political narratives. As of February 2021, if you search "Joe Biden Touts 'Most Extensive & Inclusive Voter Fraud Organization in History of American Politics'" (a literal Breitbart.com headline), while the Breitbart article with that exact headline is the fourth result, the top result is a Reuters fact-check titled "Fact check: Clip of Biden taken out of context to portray him as plotting a voter fraud scheme." (Here's Biden's exact quote: "We have put together, I think, the most extensive and inclusive voter fraud organization in the history of American politics." At Breitbart News, we described the Biden remark as a "slip of the tongue," not as some actual admission of massive fraud. We were having fun with the story, unlike the joyless fact-checkers at Reuters.)

As of early 2021, if you copy and paste the entire lede sentence of

Olsen's article into a Google search bar, the front page of your results won't include the Breitbart story. However, a website called NaturalNews.com, which plagiarizes the Breitbart article without our permission, shows up toward the top of the list.

Suppressing Breitbart harms the national discourse; I believe that the electorate is more poorly informed as a result of Google's decision when it comes to their search algorithm. But it also slows the growth of the conservative news business by unfairly depriving us of traffic and buzz.

The Masters of the Universe view this as a positive, no doubt.

The question becomes, if Breitbart is oppressed, arguably the biggest conservative new media platform, then how are voters who get their news online going to get their information? Evidently, they get it from CNN, the *New York Times*, Vox.com, et cetera. No "philanthropist" can cut a check big enough to benefit Democrat causes and candidates that can compete with Google et al. if they choose to pick winners and losers. Once Google (apparently) began to institutionalize political bias in their search results, it was the game changer the flailing establishment media needed.

Facebook actually beat Google to the punch in terms of suppressing Breitbart. After a 2017 study by Yochai Benkler, a professor at Harvard Law School, showed that Breitbart dominated the right-wing media sphere in the 2016 election, we saw our reach begin to diminish. The study was widely discussed in 2017. And it probably was the reason why in January 2018, again seemingly overnight, Breitbart's Facebook traffic fell. (Facebook consistently denies suppressing conservative voices.)

As of election day 2016, Breitbart was competing with CNN and the *New York Times*, *Washington Post*, and *Huffington Post* for most influential news outlets on the world's largest social media platform. No one else was close. We were going toe-to-toe with the biggest corporate media giants in the country, and arguably winning. In early 2018, we fell from the top ten publishers on Facebook to outside of the top twenty. At the same time, CNN's engagement surged about 30 percent.[50]

And we're supposed to believe all of this was a coincidence?

Democrats were no doubt thrilled, and Republicans were unable to do anything to stop Big Tech. This hurt Breitbart, but it was also a dry run for what they would do before Trump ran for reelection.

In October 2020, when bombshell information about Hunter Biden was reported by the *New York Post* and others, the censorship machine was immediately spun up. Silicon Valley was ready.

The Masters of the Universe had been waiting for this moment for four years.

Game On

On October 14, 2020, the *New York Post* reported Hunter Biden introduced a top official from the corrupt Ukrainian energy company Burisma to then–Vice President Joe Biden.[51] Vadym Pozharskyi, a purportedly high-ranking adviser to the board of Burisma, thanked Hunter profusely in an April 17, 2015, email and asked for "advice on how you could use your influence" to help the company. Hunter Biden had been on the board of Burisma since April 2014 and was paid a reported $83,000 a month to hold that position.[52] He joined the company around the time his father, then the U.S. vice president, visited Kiev to show support for the government.[53] The emails (evidence of the meeting) were found on a laptop that apparently belonged to Hunter Biden; the laptop had been allegedly dropped off at a Delaware computer repair shop in 2019 and had never been retrieved. The store owner, according to the *Post*, made a copy of the material on the laptop and then turned it over to the FBI.[54]

This meeting was a direct contradiction of Joe Biden's claims that he had never discussed Hunter's business endeavors with him.

Part of the reason this story was such a bombshell is that the Biden family was involved in all sorts of seemingly dirty deals throughout Joe's time in public office. While Joe himself managed to remain fairly clean, at least in the public's eye, several others in the Biden clan appeared to make a robust amount of cash on the family name.

Let me introduce you to the Biden Five, a term coined by Breitbart senior contributor and the author of the book *Profiles in Corruption: Abuse of Power by America's Progressive Elite*, Peter Schweizer:

Frank Biden, Joe's youngest brother:

- His businesses received millions in taxpayer-funded loans, including for companies that operate overseas.[55]

• His renewable energy companies based in Costa Rica and Jamaica got taxpayer-backed loans, even though he had no background in renewable energy.[56]

• One of his businesses also got sweetheart multimillion-dollar grants to construct charter schools.[57]

Valerie Biden, Joe's sister:

• Valerie's business bagged millions running Joe's political campaigns, which typically did not have credible challengers.[58]

• She got these gigs despite not having any other significant accomplishments as a political consultant; Schweizer referred to this as legal graft.[59]

Ashley Biden, Joe's daughter:

• StartUp Health, a company cofounded by Ashley's husband Howard Krein, scored Obama administration support after a White House meeting. He had no business plan or website, but got an Oval Office sit-down anyway.[60]

• While he was vice president, Biden made a surprise appearance at their annual conference, according to the source.[61]

• Krein advised the Biden campaign on coronavirus.[62]

James Biden, Joe's other brother:

• James's firm landed $1.5 billion in government contracts to build homes in Iraq, though he had no background in construction or international development.[63]

• It was reported just after the 2020 election that James Biden is under federal investigation for his role in a bankrupt health-care firm.[64]

And last but not least, Hunter Biden, Joe's son:

• Hunter launched a multibillion-dollar investment fund with backing from a state-run Chinese bank ten days after flying with then–Vice President Joe on Air Force Two to China in 2013.[65]

• Hunter received a million-dollars-per-year deal with a corrupt Ukrainian energy company even though he had no background in energy.[66]

• Hunter reportedly flew to capital city Astana to explore a business deal with Kazakhstani oligarchs (Breitbart reported on a photo of Joe, Hunter, and one of the oligarchs posing together in D.C. restaurant Café Milano).[67]

• Devon Archer, Hunter's business partner, was convicted for his role in defrauding the Oglala Sioux Indian tribe, which is the poorest tribe in the country.[68]

• Hunter received $3.5 million as part of a deal with Russian oligarch Yelena Baturina; she is connected to organized crime.[69]

None of these people had much expertise, if any, and they all made lots of money nonetheless. Though seemingly improper, all of this appears to be legal.

This is the pattern with the Biden family, and regular consumers of conservative news were aware of this.

But those weren't the type of people who needed to be persuaded by the information Schweizer unearthed in 2018 or the *New York Post* in 2020. The *Post*'s story was particularly important because it not only revealed alleged Biden family corruption and a media cover-up, it exposed Joe as a stone-cold liar.

And the Biden campaign wasn't even denying the story![70]

In fact, similar stories about Hunter Biden and Burisma had been reported in establishment outlets like the *New York Times* going back half a decade.[71]

The Masters of the Universe censorship machine clearly knew this, but they would not tolerate a Trump victory.

"Blip." "Hiccup."

So they kicked their censorship machine into overdrive.

It was "game on."

Facebook suppressed the story, "reducing its distribution" while its super-neutral third-party fact-checkers vetted it.[72] This is incredibly dishonest and devious. This shut down all of the story's momentum on the platform.

Twitter followed suit by blocking the story with an even more ridiculous explanation, stating that suppressing it was "in line with our Hacked Materials Policy."[73] There was no evidence the emails had been hacked. Allegedly, the information was retrieved from the laptop after it was left at a Delaware repair shop.

(John Paul Mac Isaac, the computer technician whom Hunter Biden hired to repair his laptop, claims that Twitter destroyed his business by portraying him as a hacker.[74] He maintains he obtained the information about the Bidens legally through his business's abandoned property policy. He is suing Twitter for $500 million in punitive damages.)[75]

The nation's fourth-largest newspaper remained locked out of Twitter for two weeks leading into the presidential election, despite the fact that the report did not appear to be obtained through hacking, nor was its accuracy substantively challenged.[76]

Millions upon millions of voters were prevented from seeing this accurate story likely because it just so happened to make the Bidens look really, really bad.

The day after news of the Burisma meeting broke, October 15, the *New York Post* broke another bombshell: the contents of more emails from the trove purportedly found on Hunter Biden's laptop that were arguably even juicier.[77] These emails seemed to show that Hunter had a provisional equity agreement for an endeavor with the now-defunct Shanghai-based conglomerate CEFC China Energy Company, where the "big guy" would get a 10 percent stake. One of the emails released by the *Post* contains the following text:

At the moment there is a provisional agreement that the equity will be distributed as follows:

20 H

20 RW

20 JG

20 TB

10 Jim

10 held by H for the big guy?

We don't know if "H" stands for Hunter. Nor do we know that "Jim" refers to Jim Biden, Joe's brother (more on him shortly). "TB" might be Tony Bobulinski, who was copied on the email. Bobulinski was a former Biden ally who turned on him, ultimately feeding a trove of documents to Senate investigators.[78] We also don't know that the numbers refer to percentages of equity (though the six lines in the email add up exactly to 100). And we don't know who the "big guy" is or if he was ultimately cut in.

But we do know what it looks like.

Anyone with two brain cells to rub together knows exactly what it looks like: corruption extended to the highest echelons of the American government.

Twitter memory-holed the report detailing Hunter's dealing with the Chinese energy company.[79] Sohrab Ahmari, the *Post*'s editor, tweeted, "Twitter is censoring us—again. This is what I—an editor at America's oldest continuously published newspaper, founded by Alexander Hamilton—get when I try to post our follow-up story on Hunter's financial shenanigans with the Chinese regime." Ahmari included a screenshot of a notification that "[y]our tweet couldn't be sent because this link has been identified by Twitter or our partners as being potentially harmful."

The news media played their part in the censorship campaign as well. James O'Keefe's Project Veritas released audio of a CNN conference call where network president Jeff Zucker spiked the *New York Post*'s story personally, saying it would be going down "the Breitbart, New York Post, Fox News rabbit hole of Hunter Biden." Others on the call are heard agreeing with their puppet master boss.[80] CNN's general counsel David Vigilante is heard saying that "we should be awfully careful" with the story.[81] CNN political director David Chalian agreed that the story shouldn't be touched, stating that that "Senate Committees looked at and found nothing wrong in Joe Biden's interaction with Ukrainians." (This is a distortion. A Senate report released in September 2020 stated that "Hunter Biden, his family, and [business partner Devon] Archer received millions of dollars from foreign nationals with questionable backgrounds." This includes Ukraine. The report found that Hunter "made millions of dollars" from his association with Burisma "while Joe Biden was vice president and the public face of the Obama administration's Ukraine policy.")[82]

With only weeks left until the election, the media merely had to run out the clock and make sure the story didn't become fully engrained in our cultural consciousness. In order to do that, they would need more than just the "he was hacked" lie. So, they dusted off a trusty device: blame the Russians.

Yes, the Democrat Media Complex attempted to portray actual evidence of possible actual corruption uncovered by a legitimate newspaper about the soon-to-be-president as Russian interference. According to the *Hill*, fifty deep state intelligence officials warned that the *Post*'s bombshells could be Russian disinfo.[83] The establishment press took the narrative and ran with it.[84] NBC News, the *Washington Post,* the *Washington Post* again, *Politico,* the *New York Times*, MSNBC, PBS, NPR, CBS News, CNN, *Rolling Stone*, Business Insider, *Newsweek, USA Today, Mother Jones,* Vox, and more all indulged the Democrat disinformation campaign in order to protect the Bidens and the tech elite.

Politico ran the headline "Hunter Biden story is Russian disinfo, dozens of former intel officials say."[85] The headline is wildly misleading. Here is the lede sentence of the story: "More than 50 former senior intelligence officials have signed on to a letter outlining their belief that the recent disclosure of emails allegedly belonging to Joe Biden's son 'has all the classic earmarks of a Russian information operation.'" "Has all the classic earmarks of a Russian information operation" is not proof that it's actually Russian disinformation.

The *Atlantic*'s David Frum tweeted, "The people on far right and far left who publicized the obviously bogus @nypost story were not dupes. They were accomplices. The story could not have been more obviously fake if it had been wearing dollar-store spectacles and attached plastic mustache."[86]

Wikipedia labeled the story "debunked" and a "conspiracy theory" after initially censoring it.[87] They even added the story to an article on "Russian interference in the 2020 United States elections," even though this itself was a baseless hoax.

After the election, Joe Biden mocked Fox News's Peter Doocy for asking if it was all Russian disinfo, stating categorically that it was: "Yes, yes, yes. God love you, man. You're a one horse pony," Biden said, apparently inventing a new equine species.[88]

All of these "hot takes" were fake news (a "hot take" is a quickly informed commentary tailored more toward generating attention than accuracy). It was another hoax to benefit the Left.

As it turns out, Hunter Biden had already been under investigation since 2018 for exactly this type of corruption, including tax evasion.[89] The Justice Department had been looking at Hunter for, among other things, his shady Chinese business dealings.[90] For one, he had apparently received a 2.8-carat diamond from the aforementioned CEFC company's founder, and it is unknown if he paid taxes on it.[91] News of the investigations came out—you guessed it—just after the election. "I learned yesterday for the first time that the U.S. Attorney's Office in Delaware advised my legal counsel, also yesterday, that they are investigating my tax affairs," Hunter said on December 9, 2020. Attorney General William Barr had instructed the Department of Justice not to disclose any info to that effect so as to not interfere with the election. NBC reported on December 11, 2020, that Hunter had allegedly failed to disclose $400,000 of income from Burisma from 2014.[92]

If only Barr had leaked three simple words: "Not. Russian. Disinformation." Perhaps Trump would have won.

None of this should have surprised anyone because these scandals are consistent with prior reporting on flagged transactions involving Hunter Biden and foreign oligarchs, as confirmed by years of suspicious activity reports (SARs) filed by banks. The Senate Finance Committee report on Burisma from September 2020 exposed transactions involving Hunter and a Russian oligarch with mafia ties, Elena Baturina.[93] Later reporting revealed that Syrian businessman Hares Youssef invested millions in another one of Hunter's firms.[94] Hunter himself admitted to the *New Yorker* that he received a "large diamond" from Chinese energy tycoon Ye Jianming back in 2019.[95]

Maybe Ye is simply a generous guy who didn't want anything in return.

Court documents from 2018 showed hundreds of thousands of dollars flowing to Hunter from Burisma through a pass-through LLC.

And Chinese corporate records show that Hunter had been a board member of Chinese investment firm Bohai Harvest RST since its founding in 2013. Hunter's attorney, George Mesires, has tried to downplay Hunter's financial stake in Bohai Harvest RST. In a statement posted on Medium, Mesires says Hunter paid $420,000 for his 10 percent stake—in a company with $2 billion in assets under management.[96] According to Steve Kaplan, a University of Chicago financial expert cited by FactCheck.org: "It is difficult to imagine, if not incomprehensible, that a 10% stake in those economics is worth only $420K." [97]

And it's equally hard to imagine that the potential value of this stake would diminish under a Biden administration.

According to Hunter's Secret Service travel records, which were obtained by Judicial Watch, he took 411 trips across 29 countries between 2009 and the middle of 2014.[98] That includes twenty-three flights into or out of Joint Base Andrews—home to Air Force One and Air Force Two. Did any of the journalists who sought to suppress the Hunter Biden story as Russian disinformation investigate exactly where Hunter was going on these trips and with whom?

It didn't matter to the people who had an election to win and a public to misinform.

Hunter said he never spoke to his father about business. But he revealed to the *New Yorker* that he introduced his father to his Chinese business partners during an official visit in December 2013.[99]

So Joe was lying.

Were there any other meetings between Hunter and a foreign oligarch that he discussed with Joe? Or are we simply to believe that Joe Biden had never, ever spoken to his globetrotting son about his international businesses? Aside from that one time . . .

Consistently the American public has been told that Hunter Biden was pure as the driven snow. Joe Biden called his son "the smartest guy I know." Dr. Jill (Ed.D.) and Joe both expressed confidence that Hunter had done nothing wrong.[100] And, of course, Joe said he thought it was all Russian disinformation.

None of this was fact-checked. None of this was framed as lies.

It was the factual story that was censored across the same Big Tech platforms that had been cracking down on conservatives for years.

Game Over?

So, the question is: Did it work? Did the suppression of the Hunter Biden story by the establishment media and the tech oligarchs swing the election?

According to data compiled by the conservative Media Research

Center, absolutely. The MRC surveyed 1,750 Biden voters in Arizona, Georgia, Michigan, North Carolina, Nevada, Pennsylvania, and Wisconsin, which were reported in a Newsbusters.org article titled "SPECIAL REPORT: The Stealing of the Presidency, 2020," which revealed startling data. Some key findings: [101]

- 35.4 percent of Biden voters were unaware of credible allegations that Joe Biden had sexually assaulted Tara Reade when she was on his Senate staff. (Joe Biden has denied Reade's allegations, which are unproven.)
  - 8.9 percent of those surveyed told the MRC they would have changed their vote if they had been aware of it

- 45.1 percent of Biden voters were unaware of financial scandals involving Joe and Hunter.
  - 9.4 percent of those surveyed told the MRC they would have changed their vote if they had been aware of it.

- 25.3 percent of Biden voters said they didn't know that Gov-Track had found that Kamala Harris had the most left-wing record in the Senate.
  - 4.1 percent of those surveyed told the MRC they would have changed their vote if they had been aware of it.

Other data also found broad ignorance of Trump's political victories, specifically rapid economic growth, booming jobs numbers, advances toward Middle East peace, energy independence, and progress made toward a coronavirus vaccine. In conclusion, the MRC found that 82 percent of Biden voters were unaware of at least one of the three aforementioned anti-Biden narratives or at least one of five pro-Trump narratives. This all appears to have cost Trump votes.

In total, the MRC survey showed that a whopping 17 percent of Biden voters would have switched their votes had they known about all eight items mentioned.

A Rasmussen Reports poll released shortly after the election revealed that most voters—including around a third of Democrats(!)—believed the media hid the Hunter Biden stories. [102]

If these numbers are even close to accurate, this could have easily swung the election for Biden.

This is your election right here.

This is why Facebook and Google turned down Breitbart's reach.

This is why the Masters of the Universe blocked the Hunter Biden bombshells.

This may well be why Joe Biden is president.

The establishment media and Big Tech oligarchs took control of the 2020 presidential election, and they did it legally and often in plain sight.

(Furthermore, with a diminished social media reach, each opportunity Trump had to make his own case to the public gained significance. Thus, the cancellation of the second presidential debate, ostensibly due to Donald Trump's coronavirus diagnosis, was devastating to his reelection chances.[103] This meant that there was no foreign policy–centric debate in the entire general election cycle. This was disastrous fortune for Trump, who was largely responsible for the demise of the ISIS "caliphate" and the death of their "caliph," Abu Bakr al-Baghdadi, among other highlights mentioned throughout this book.[104] The world was relatively peaceful during the Trump era, and America entered no new wars during that time. He lost out on his best chance to flaunt this record on the debate stage.)

Zuckerberg's Mailboxes

Though it is apparent to me that the suppression of conservative-friendly stories and the elevation of hoax narratives that benefit Joe Biden were enough to swing the election on its own, the Masters of the Universe and the establishment media knew better than to count their chickens before they hatched. After all, they weren't going to be blindsided this time around. They had to take other precautions.

Twitter altered their "retweet" functionality to slow the proliferation of viral stories.[105] They justified this as a means to stop disinformation online, but observers speculated this was an inelegant fail-safe that can be used in an emergency to diminish the reach of say, a story like the *New York Post*'s Hunter Biden bombshells.[106] Twitter reversed the policy shortly after the election.

Google continued to censor Breitbart articles on Joe Biden.[107] Networks continued to claim that legitimate scandals around Hunter Biden's corruption were "unfounded and baseless."[108] Joe Biden refused to take questions on the swirling controversies, and most of the media seemed to be perfectly fine with that.[109]

Mark Zuckerberg made sure that he was able to restore his credibility with the world elite by doing his part to make sure Biden won. (Facebook had laughably been portrayed as a "right-wing echo chamber" in outlets like the *Washington Post,* despite evidence to the contrary.)[110]

Though there was no indication that voting in person was particularly dangerous relative to other "essential" activities in the COVID-19 era, the Democratic Party used the pandemic as an opportunity to institutionalize mail-in voting.[111]Though most any eligible voter can vote by mail, the more often people vote by mail, the better Democrats perform in elections.

This is reminiscent of MTV's "Rock the Vote," which rose in popularity throughout the 1990s. Though a superficially nonpartisan campaign, it was designed to appeal to young people who vote overwhelmingly Democrat. It was all a ruse.

Zuckerberg pumped in hundreds of millions of dollars to pay for "safe" election administration. Local elections offices were able to apply for money from the Center for Tech and Civic Life, funded by a $350 million donation from Zuckerberg and his wife, Priscilla Chan.[112]

Sounds noble. But upon scrutiny, the funds were a de facto get-out-the-vote (GOTV) effort for Democrats. (Nothing Zuckerberg did was illegal, as far as I can tell.)

The centerpiece of the effort was COVID-safe "drop boxes." These were bins that look like aluminum public trash cans, strewn randomly throughout the country, largely unprotected and unguarded. These made it easier for people to "safely" turn in their mail-in ballots. Critics of the plan like Newt Gingrich have said that a high number of these drop boxes were placed in precincts that favor Democrats, particularly ones that were likely to be close races.

Newt was correct to raise the red flag. After all, the far-left Southern Poverty Law Center funded dozens of these drop boxes in Democrat areas themselves.[113] This is as sure a sign as any that drop boxes were installed specifically to help the Democrats.

Phill Kline, the director of the Amistad Project of the conservative Thomas More Society, broke it down as follows:[114]

Zuckerberg paid for the election judges; he purchased the drop boxes—contrary to state law; he ordered the consolidation of the counting facilities; Zuckerberg paid the local officials who boarded up the windows to the counting room; Zuckerberg money purchased the machines, Dominion and otherwise; and Zuckerberg money was contributed to secretaries of state, like Michigan's Jocelyn Benson, who has fought transparency in this election.

Perhaps Zuckerberg came up with an (ostensibly nonpartisan) way to squeeze out a few extra crucial votes for the pro–Big Tech Democrats.

Maybe he'll have finally redeemed himself for not stopping the Right from succeeding on his platform.

Tech Titans Triumph

I believe the Masters of the Universe were the single biggest deciding factor in the 2020 election. From the combination of President Trump and the Republicans' failing to curtail their monopolistic powers, the constant manipulation of their platforms to benefit Joe Biden, and Mark Zuckerberg's mystery cheat-by-mail boxes, I think I have a made a strong case.

Joe Biden certainly is behaving as though he might agree. Big Tech's loyalty is being rewarded with important jobs in the administration (and look for Biden admin alumni to find cushy gigs in Silicon Valley when they exit, too).

Jeff Zients, a former Facebook board member, is Biden's COVID czar. Erskine Bowles, a former Facebook board member, advised the transition. Jessica Hertz, formerly a government affairs executive at Facebook, served as the Biden transition team's general counsel.[115]

Amazon, Google, and Microsoft were also quickly placed in the Big Tech/Big Government revolving door.[116] During the transition, for example, Amazon hired Jeff Ricchetti, brother of White House counselor Steve Ricchetti, to lobby for them.[117]

Silicon Valley (and the rest of corporate America) stroked huge checks for Biden's inauguration.[118]

After Biden's election win, the convergence of the national security establishment and the Masters of the Universe began to reveal itself. Secretary of State Antony Blinken and Director of National Intelligence Avril Haines both worked for the consulting firm WestExec, which Blinken cofounded with Michèle Flournoy, a former undersecretary of defense under President Obama.[119] Google hired WestExec to help them land valuable Department of Defense contracts. WestExec also had a partnership with Jigsaw, Google's in-house think tank, according to the Intercept.[120] In addition, Blinken disclosed that he worked for Microsoft and Facebook.

From a Reuters report from December 2020: "Google's former Chief Executive Eric Schmidt, a billionaire who is a Silicon Valley titan, has been making personnel recommendations for appointments to the Department of Defense—as the company tries to pursue military contracts and defense work, according to three sources."[121] When Biden was sworn in, Schmidt was appointed to lead a government panel on artificial intelligence. I made contact with Schmidt's team in an effort to confirm the Reuters report; they declined to comment.[122]

Despite the fact that Joe Biden was inaugurated with elevated unemployment rates (January 2021 data showed jobs actually declining!), a partially shuttered economy, and a seemingly worsening pandemic, Biden announced that he would introduce an immigration bill immediately.[123] (Breitbart calculated between the cancellation of the Keystone XL pipeline, Trump's border wall, and other initiatives that create jobs, Biden killed about 70,000 jobs on his first day in office.)[124] Access to cheaper labor via lax immigration rules has always been the top priority for the Masters of the Universe, especially Mark Zuckerberg, who founded the pro-amnesty group FWD.us.

Looks like Joe Biden knows where his bread is buttered.

The Purge

The last act of the Trump presidency was like the last scene of *The Godfather*. Or the first scene of *The Children of the Corn*, depending on your preference. Once the narrative was set that Donald Trump was encouraging a coup, the Masters of the Universe struck Trump World and they struck them hard.

Trump was banned or restricted by Facebook, Snapchat, Instagram, Shopify, Reddit, YouTube, TikTok, Pinterest, Google, and even his beloved and powerful Twitter page.[125]

Donald Trump banned from Twitter, for life.

Regardless of your political viewpoint, it is quite frightening to see corporate America attempt to cancel the president of the United States, regardless of who it is.

Still, the Masters of the Universe always had the knives out for Trump and finally they thought they were morally justified in sending him to the gulag.

Many Trump supporters were also caught in the crossfire, particularly those seen as supporting the challenges to the Electoral College vote.

This is particularly ironic since several Democrat congresspeople went out of their way to avoid calling Donald Trump "President." Representative Hakeem Jeffries (D-NY) called him "the Grand Wizard of 1600 Pennsylvania Avenue," implying tens of millions of his fellow Americans actually voted for a Ku Klux Klansman.[126] (Many of them twice.) "Squad" member Ayanna Pressley doesn't refer to him as "President," either; she says he is merely the man "occupying the Oval Office." [127] So brave! So clever!

Facebook removed all "Stop the Steal" content.[128] "Stop the Steal" was the rallying cry for those who believed Joe Biden was not legitimately elected. "Stop the Steal" leaders Sidney Powell and General Michael Flynn were also blacklisted.

This is particularly outrageous because the last time Big Tech did a blanket content ban like this, it was of the accurate Hunter Biden scoops from the *New York Post*.

Arguably more alarming, though, was a quick and ruthless Twitter purge of countless thousands of pro-Trump accounts.[129] This appeared to be a mass blacklisting of otherwise platform-less citizens. Top Republicans saw their followings diminish rapidly. Mike Pompeo observed that follower counts for Democrats like Joe Biden, Kamala Harris, Nancy Pelosi, and Chuck Schumer soared during this time, while Republicans Tom Cotton and Kevin McCarthy saw theirs fall through the floor.[130] I personally detest Twitter and rarely tweet, but it was nonetheless shocking when I lost 25 percent of my followers in a matter of a couple of days without any explanation.

The blacklisting was met with near-universal praise from the liberal side of the aisle. Hollywood rejoiced.[131] Joe Manchin (D-WV), seen as perhaps the most moderate Democrat in the Senate, thanked Twitter for canceling the president.[132]

The social media start-up Parler, which had become a safe space for conservative social media users, was targeted with the heat of a thousand suns over calls for violence that appeared on the platform. (Twitter, at the time, still allowed accounts openly supportive of Antifa to organize on their platform.)[133] Google blacklisted Parler from the Play store.[134] Apple blacklisted it from the App store.[135] And in a blow that took Parler offline entirely, Amazon, which rarely delves into the political hysterias of the day, booted Parler from its web hosting servers.[136]

All at once, Silicon Valley had decided to destroy MAGA, or at least try to. And it was all done in concert.

Despite that fact, a few on the left like journalist Glenn Greenwald and even German chancellor Angela Merkel warned that this crackdown on free speech might not be such a great idea.[137] Mexican president Andres Manuel Lopez Obrador blasted Twitter.[138] Still, the blacklisting fervor only got more intense.

The establishment media got in on the censorship action as well. An ABC political editor called for a "cleansing" of Trump's movement.[139] The *Washington Post* called for the media to shun Republicans who deny Biden's legitimacy.[140] Simon & Schuster canceled Josh Hawley's forthcoming book on Big Tech (Hawley was seen as the face of Senate Republican objectors to the Electoral College vote).[141]

CNN shamelessly began a campaign to get cable providers to drop Fox News, typically the highest-rated network on all of cable and CNN's direct competition.[142]

The canceling wasn't merely limited to media entities, either. Payment processor Stripe shut down service to the Trump campaign.[143] Several major businesses, including Citigroup, Marriott, and Blue Cross Blue Shield, said they would stop donating to political causes.[144]

Calls flooded in to break up the Masters of the Universe—all from conservatives who were headed out of power after years of doing nothing to stop their rise. Many of them even enabled it.

So, in a way, Joe Biden did have his "unity," at least on the social web. Most everyone of prominence who remained "platformed" supported the new woke McCarthyism, or at least were going to keep quiet about it until the heat died down. Political opponents were no longer to be debated, or even tolerated. They were to be forced into submission.

The Big Tech oligarchs and their allies in the corporate media paid no mind to the fact that much of the country was appalled by what they were doing and still supported President Trump. The Rasmussen presidential tracking poll for January 11, 2021, showed Trump's approval at 48 percent, right around where it had been most of his administration.[145]

They weren't convincing many of his voters. But that was never their intent. Our weaponized news media and social media giants have wanted to crush Trump, his movement, and American individuals who dare not conform to their vision of the world.

CHAPTER 11

A TIME TO HEAL

On November 23, 2020, *Time* magazine published a "commemorative" cover image of Joe Biden and Kamala Harris holding hands with the quote "A TIME TO HEAL" in bold letters at the top of the image. The quote echoed the key line in remarks made by Joe Biden the previous night in a victory speech, one of several victory speeches he gave in the chaotic time just after the 2020 presidential election.

No civically engaged person in the country believed it was truly a "time to heal." *Time*—and Biden—were setting a narrative.

Trump is the divider, not us!

The irony of the Democrats insisting that all of us accept the results of the 2020 election before they fully accepted the results of the 2016 election is not lost on me.

There were still legal challenges that had yet to be decided, states hadn't certified their tallies, and the majority of Republicans said they doubted the election results, according to multiple surveys.[1] An NPR poll said only a quarter of Republicans said they trust the results.[2]

What's more, there were still two crucial Senate races yet to be decided in the state of Georgia. Two runoffs in the Peach State were sure to come down to razor-thin margins. Control of the Senate majority hung in the balance. While Georgia is typically a red state, it was also ground zero for Democrat activist Stacey Abrams's vote-by-mail operation. Abrams rose to prominence after losing the 2018 Georgia governorship to Brian Kemp. Abrams spent two years calling Georgia's election system fraudulent.

She never conceded.

From an interview with NPR:

You see, I'm supposed to say nice things and accept my fate. They will complain that I should not use this moment to recap what was done wrong or to demand a remedy. And I will not concede because the erosion of our democracy is not right.

Trump lost Georgia by around 12,000 votes.[3] Abrams lost by around 55,000 votes.[4]

But now we're expected to blindly trust the result, no questions asked. In fact, if you did question the results, you might get called a "traitor to democracy."

Even before the Capitol riot of January 6, 2021, words like "sedition" and "treason" swirled around Trump for casting doubt on the election, whether or not our election had integrity. By contrast, since Stacey Abrams brought our democracy to the brink of ruin by not conceding the 2018 Georgia governor race, she has published two nonfiction books, is set to release a novel, and was the subject of a fawning Amazon documentary. She's also treated with kid gloves on national media appearances.

But now is the time for unity?

No, now is the time for wild double standards. Now is the time to cancel MAGA and elevate woke activists.

Calls for unity are almost always phony. I've never met a single person who called for unity who didn't have conditions. Actually, only one condition: you agree with the person calling for unity 100 percent of the time. So long as you accept exactly the values of the person calling for unity and healing, then we can have unity and healing. And who decided unity was the ultimate goal anyway?[5] Arguably, more progress is made when we have civil disagreement.

Americans were treated to months of insistence that the election was most certainly 100 percent legitimate from the crowd that referred to themselves as the Resistance and portrayed half of their countrymen as racists and Russian stooges for the entire previous administration.

Rachel Maddow said that Putin "hacked" the 2016 election.[6] Harvard's Belfer Center wrote after the 2016 election, "emerging evidence suggests

Russia has been using cyberattacks to attempt to influence this year's election."[7] In May 2019, Pew blogged that Special Counsel Robert Mueller's findings raised hacking fears, citing technologist Maurice Turner, who claimed "interference operations targeting the 2020 presidential election already have begun."[8]

But in 2020, Trump voters weren't even allowed to wait until all the votes had been counted before we were told to accept the election results and unify with those who had been trying to nullify our vote for four years.

The establishment press also, apparently, forgot that they had insisted that there can be actual voter fraud. If the election had gone the other way, I think they would have sung a different tune.

In fact, I know it.

The *New York Times* reported in July 2019 that Russia targeted voting machines.[9] An April 2020 *Wall Street Journal* headline read, "Why a Data-Security Expert Fears U.S. Voting Will Be Hacked."[10] In June 2019, *Politico* voiced concern that that a Florida election software vendor alerted FBI about a potential hacking attempt in 2016.[11] And here's a headline from the *New York Times*, September 2020: "Ransomware Attacks Take On New Urgency Ahead of Vote."[12]

So, what is it? Are elections hackable or not? It would be good to know soon so we can get back to our quest for unity.

In August 2020, Hillary Clinton advised Joe Biden not to concede the election "under any circumstances" because Republicans are going to try to "mess up absentee balloting." "I do believe he will win," the failed former presidential candidate said, "if we don't give an inch, and if we are as focused and relentless as the other side is."[13]

If Trump had said such things as Hillary did (and he has), then he would be called a threat to democracy (and he has been). Harvard social scientist Ryan Enos was quoted November 12 in the *New York Times* as saying that Trump's refusal to concede is "one of the gravest threats to democracy."[14] Biden, always the unifier and always the healer, said it was "an embarrassment" that Trump hadn't conceded by November 11.[15]

It's almost as if the Democrats are trying to have it both ways.

In fact, Hillary wasn't entirely incorrect in her assessment about mail-in ballots.[16] NBC would later report that U.S. Postal Service delays could disenfranchise thousands of legitimate ballots. However, analysts concluded there were not enough of these ballots to call into question the overall result of the election or even a single 2020 battleground state.

Not only are breaches possible, they actually happen. Our voting systems are vulnerable. In 2017, hackers at a cybersecurity conference breached dozens of voting machines within just a few minutes.[17] Florida governor Ron DeSantis said that in 2016 "two Florida counties experienced intrusion into the supervisor of election networks"; the intrusion came from Russian hackers, but thankfully there wasn't manipulation, he said.[18]

In 2019, comedian and far-left pundit John Oliver devoted an entire episode of his HBO show to concerns about electronic voting machines. The episode included examples of results getting switched by the machine.

In February 2020, the Associated Press ran a report titled "Reliability of pricey new voting machines questioned."[19] The report broke down concerns about several voting systems, specifically highlighting Dominion Voting Systems, which was the subject of intense controversy after the 2020 election. A stunning passage:

> Some of the most popular ballot-marking machines, made by industry leaders Election Systems & Software and Dominion Voting Systems, register votes in bar codes that the human eye cannot decipher. That's a problem, researchers say: Voters could end up with printouts that accurately spell out the names of the candidates they picked, but, because of a hack, the bar codes do not reflect those choices. Because the bar codes are what's tabulated, voters would never know that their ballots benefited another candidate.
>
> Even on machines that do not use bar codes, voters may not notice if a hack or programming error mangled their choices. A University of Michigan study determined that only 7 percent of participants in a mock election notified poll workers when the names on their printed receipts did not match the candidates they voted for.[20]

ES&S rejects those scenarios. Spokesman Katina Granger said the company's ballot-marking machines' accuracy and security "have been proven through thousands of hours of testing and tens of thousands of successful elections." Dominion declined to comment for this story.

On November 7, 2016, famed *New York Times* columnist Paul Krugman, the genius economist who once declared the "Internet's impact on the economy" would be "no greater than the fax machine's," penned a piece with the title "How to Rig an Election."[21] Krugman uses the phrase "the election was rigged" six times in the column.

So maybe, just maybe, it's okay to talk about integrity.

January 6

All of these possibilities for manipulation created a haze for many Trump voters. After hearing for years that the Bad Orange Man was LITERALLY HITLER! A menace to the world! It stood to reason that the Left might be willing to cheat to make sure he lost.

That's how much they hate Trump.

Reuters/Ipsos published a poll on November 18 that had data in it that broadly summed up the mood of the moment:

- 68 percent of Republicans said they were concerned that the election was "rigged"[22]

- Even 16 percent of Democrats and 33 percent of independents thought it was "rigged"

- 52 percent of Republicans said that Trump "rightfully won"; only 29 percent of Republicans said that Biden had "rightfully won"

- 73 percent of respondents agreed that Biden won the election; just 5 percent thought Trump had won

So, by mid-November, it appears as though a slight majority of Republicans thought Trump had *rightfully* won, only a small minority thought Trump actually won. The poll is unclear on the distinction, but I take it to mean that the vast majority of GOP voters accepted that Joe Biden would get sworn in on January 20, 2021, but they also believed Trump would have won if the election had met the highest standards for integrity.

That was me: I assumed Biden would become president as scheduled, but also thought Trump got "cheated," so to speak, in a multitude of different ways, and I managed Breitbart's newsroom accordingly. We reported on most of the various lawsuits and theories, but we never gave our audience the impression that the election results were likely to get overturned.

Some on the right were prepared to throw in the towel, concede the race, and move on with their lives. Other prominent pro-Trump figures seemed to lose their minds altogether, taking dark and conspiratorial turns, suggesting violence against other conservatives and making wild accusations that people who disagreed with them are secret pedophiles. These same people suggested withholding votes from Republicans in Georgia, effectually gifting the Senate to the Democrats.

Q: Why would you vote in a broken electoral system?

A: To stop the Democrats and the Left, genius!

But many people found themselves somewhere in between, looking for ways to voice their objection to our increasingly unfree and unfair elections without necessarily delaying the inevitable.

More than one hundred House members and several senators, most notably Senators Josh Hawley (R-MO) and Ted Cruz (R-TX), said that they would raise objections during the electoral vote certification over voter integrity issues.[23] Hawley was keen to point out that Democrats had raised objections to recent elections where Republicans had won, so it wasn't entirely unprecedented.[24] Hawley noted Big Tech's interference as well as the numerous allegations of voter fraud that had been documented throughout right-wing media in the weeks following the election.[25]

Cruz took a slightly more cautious tone, stating, "I am not arguing for setting aside the results of this election." He continued that he hopes for "a conclusive determination whether and to what extent this election complied with the constitution and with federal law." He also stated that he was confident the country will have a "peaceful and orderly transition of power."[26]

Many on the left still treated this effort as undermining our democracy, standing athwart a peaceful transition of power, and even encouraging a coup.

A more charitable view of what the senators were trying to accomplish was a dramatic but symbolic gesture to represent their frustrated constituents, who felt like they had been swindled. And why wouldn't they be allowed to object, considering all that the Democrats had done to delegitimize the

2016 election? Additionally, the 2000 election narrowly won by George W. Bush over Al Gore has been consistently called "illegitimate" or "rigged" by media and Democrats. (I have always thought the "Re-defeat Bush" bumper stickers that were prominent in my Los Angeles neighborhood during the 2004 race between Bush and John Kerry were pretty genius.)

On December 20, Trump tweeted, "Statistically impossible to have lost the 2020 Election. Big protest in DC on January 6th. Be there, will be wild!"[27]

At the rally on the sixth President Trump delivered a speech in which he said, "After this, we are going to walk down, and I will be there with you, we are going to walk down, anyone you want, but I think right here, we're going to walk down to the Capitol and we're going to cheer on our brave senators and congressmen and women."[28] He did not walk with the protesters.

He continued: "We're probably not going to be cheering so much for some of them, because you'll never take back our country with weakness. You have to show strength, you have to be strong."

He then implored Congress to "confront this egregious assault on our democracy."

But most important, he said, "I know that everyone here will soon be marching over to the Capitol building to peacefully and patriotically make your voices heard."

"Peacefully."

Trump "knows" that they will march "peacefully."

Taken literally, this was Trump being Trump: not giving an inch, toying with the Democrats and the establishment, passing the buck to anyone else. Quite standard, really.

But January 6 is a solemn date on America's calendar. And some of the president's supporters had become more conspiratorial, even unruly, and some of them were heading toward the Capitol at that moment. Though it's clear (to me) that Trump did not incite violence, I don't have the foggiest idea exactly what he hoped to accomplish with the speech. It remains a mystery. This gave the media room to interpret. And when you give the media room to interpret Donald Trump, their conclusions will always be drawn in bad faith.

They quickly settled on the narrative that Trump was organizing a coup or even a civil war.[29]

The supporters did march (walk) to the Capitol and many forced their way inside (it appears others were let in). Many wore silly costumes and took silly photos; the ultimate MAGA Instagram moment. Many were disrespectful of the Capitol building and those who hold office there. One man took over Speaker Pelosi's office, wrote notes, and snapped photos. I "put my feet up on her desk and scratched my balls," the man said.[30]

A man in a Viking horn hat, clad in fur pelts and with American flag face paint, scored the biggest social media reaction, particularly after getting snapped on the dais in the Senate chamber.[31]

It was more frightening than it sounds, though. At one point Vice President Pence was rushed out of the Senate chamber while protesters stormed in.[32] Official proceedings were shut down.

Trump sent out a tweet that afternoon urging protesters to be peaceful: "Please support our Capitol Police and Law Enforcement. They are truly on the side of our Country. Stay peaceful!"[33] But he didn't yet call on them to go home.

Some outright rioting occurred, as some people brought in weapons, pipes, and pepper spray. There were around 120 arrests.[34] Five people died during the melee, including Capitol Police officer Brian Sicknick.[35] Protester Ashli Babbitt was shot dead by Capitol Police. Three others died of medical emergencies related to the day's events.

The scene was clearly the worst moment for MAGA in its history and President Trump's darkest hour.

Trump was quickly impeached for a second time for supposedly inciting the mob.

Yet the media did what they always do: exaggerate what happened. They suggested Trump hadn't been merely irresponsible, reckless, or even a little crazed; he had actively inspired an insurrection to overthrow the government (that he still controlled).

CNN's Brian Stelter said we were "minutes away from a possible massacre."[36] MSNBC's Joe Scarborough said that "we can draw the analogies" between the riot and the rise of Hitler's Nazis.[37] Alexandria Ocasio-Cortez told ABC's George Stephanopoulos, "We came close to half of the House nearly dying," then implied Trump "ordered an attack on the United States Congress"; Stephanopoulos did not push back on this.[38]

Media reports initially claimed that Sicknick had been murdered with a fire extinguisher. "He Dreamed of Being a Police Officer, Then Was Killed by a Pro-Trump Mob," read the headline in the *New York Times* on January 8.[39] "MAGA Mob Kills Capitol Police Officer Brian Sicknick, a [sic] Iraq War Veteran Defending Congress From Trump Rioters," was another headline at the *Daily Beast* and reprinted by Yahoo News.[40]

However, a CNN report from February 2, 2021, noted, "According to one law enforcement official, medical examiners did not find signs that the officer sustained any blunt force trauma, so investigators believe that early reports that he was fatally struck by a fire extinguisher are not true."[41] This bombshell information was buried deep within the article.

(Recall the media rules: "Within a given article, information that rebuts a preferred narrative or confirms an undesirable narrative is to appear deep in the article, or not at all.")

We caught the buried lede at Breitbart, but the *New York Times* didn't correct their story right away.[42] During the interim, the MURDERED BY MAGA narrative played on a loop throughout the Senate impeachment trial to determine if former president Trump was responsible for the unrest. The media rarely if ever mentioned that all five people who died during the melee were apparently Trump supporters, including Sicknick.[43] The public arguments portion of the Senate trial lasted from February 9 until Trump was acquitted on February 13. The *New York Times* finally corrected their story in the February 12 paper, when the acquittal was no longer in doubt.[44]

Back to Normal

The only surprise in this series of events, from my perspective, is the fact that Trump supporters were actually violent, which is quite rare. It did not surprise me, however, that the media seemed to have no collective memory of all the left-wing violence that had occurred all year. (Recall the aforementioned study that showed that hundreds of Black Lives Matter protests turned violent in the summer of 2020.)[45]

The memory of the widespread Black Lives Matter rampages that were encouraged by our establishment press was still fresh on the minds of Trump backers, even those like myself who disavow and condemn the Capitol violence on January 6. Our broken media spent the better part of a year extolling protests and excusing violence, looting, fires, and deaths as the language of the unheard, only to feign terror when the other side used similar tactics.

This is not mere "bias."

This is weaponized fake news.

No, Joe Biden and the Democrat Media Complex never actually wanted unity or truth or healing. They didn't want law and order or an end to violence. They wanted to punish the Bad Orange Man and his supporters.

They wanted power for power's sake.

They started flexing that power the moment they got it. After being warned about Trump's fascism and alleged dictatorial tendencies for years, America watched Joe Biden sign fifty-nine executive orders in his first month,[46] including thirty in the first three days. (By way of comparison, every president since Carter averaged less than that *per year*.) Biden rejoined the Paris Climate accords, revoked several of Donald Trump's immigration guidelines, including the policy that asylum seekers must remain in Mexico until their court hearing, and killed the Keystone XL pipeline.[47] He enacted a moratorium on oil and gas leasing on federal lands like the Arctic National Wildlife Refuge, promoted more reregulation, and expanded rights for transgendered people who want to compete in women's sports.[48] He even killed a program Trump created that carved out federal funds for apprenticeship programs; an odd move in a jobs crisis.[49]

So much for "Sleepy Joe."

The establishment media, of course, loved every minute of it.

Washington Post reporter Matt Viser waxed poetic on Twitter talking about Biden and his deceased son Beau, who had passed away of brain cancer: "Joe and Beau used to watch an eagle soar by the dock. Now, when Biden steps to a lectern, he will be greeted by a presidential seal. It features as its most prominent symbol a bald eagle, a reminder both of what he has accomplished and what he has lost."[50] Countless stories were written about the Biden family dogs, especially Major, a German shepherd who was adopted from a rescue shelter.[51] (Major Biden was temporarily sent back to Delaware in March of 2021 after having bitten someone at the White House.) Less than a month into Biden's presidency, while the coronavirus still raged and unemployment stood at an extremely elevated level, *Newsweek* put out the headline "Joe Biden, Playing as Luigi, Wins in Mario Kart Race Against Granddaughter at Camp David."[52]

The Biden administration continued Trump's tradition of being openly hostile to the media.

Fox News reporter Peter Doocy asked Biden what was discussed on a phone call with Vladimir Putin, to which Biden replied, "You. He sends his best," then walked away from the gaggling media. The implication of Biden's rib is that the Russian president and Fox News are allies.

White House deputy press secretary T. J. Ducklo resigned within weeks of the inauguration after verbally abusing a reporter. Ducklo threatened to "destroy" *Politico*'s Tera Palmeri, who was working on a story about his relationship with then-Axios reporter Alexi McCammond.[53] According to his LinkedIn, Ducklo was a corporate media veteran, having worked for NBC, Viacom, and Bloomberg, among others.[54]

Vogue editor-in-chief Anna Wintour had refused to put real-life model and First Lady Melania Trump on the cover because of political reasons. "You have to stand up for what you believe in and you have to take a point of view," Wintour said. The nation's foremost fashion magazine wasted no time giving that honor to the first female vice president; Kamala Harris got the cover of the January 2021 issue. Only, it backfired on both of them. Breitbart News "Fashion Notes" columnist John Binder described the cover:[55]

> For the magazine's print edition, Harris stands in a casual position, hands clasped, atop a pink taffeta curtain in front of a sage jacquard backdrop as a vague color reference to Alpha Kappa Alpha, her sorority. The image, shot by 26-year-old Tyler Mitchell, appears like a test shot with Harris awkwardly smiling as if she is unsure how this all works.
>
> Worse is Harris's wardrobe. Harris wears a black jacket by Donald Deal, a pair of generic brand skinny jeans, and Converse's Chuck Taylor All-Star sneakers. You are reading that correctly—sneakers on the cover of Vogue. It was not that long ago, 1988, that Vogue Editor in Chief Anna Wintour put jeans on the cover, a gasp at the time.
>
> [. . .]
>
> That is lovely for a photo on the fireplace mantel but this is high fashion.

That's a brutal take, but the Harris camp seemed to agree. They reportedly ripped *Vogue* for the cover, as did countless social media users.[56] *Vogue* buckled to the pressure and released a new cover.

The Democrat Media Complex publicly brainstormed about how the Biden administration could expand their censorship capabilities. The *New York Times* hyped the idea of a "reality czar" to tackle "disinformation" and "extremism": "Joan Donovan, the research director of Harvard University's Shorenstein Center on Media, Politics and Public Policy, suggested that the Biden administration could set up a 'truth commission,' similar to the 9/11 Commission, to investigate the planning and execution of the Capitol siege on Jan. 6," wrote columnist Kevin Roose.[57]

MSNBC's Chuck Todd was inspired by the idea. He raised the issue with his *Meet the Press* panel: "But I noticed the *New York Times* today called for something—they didn't call it this, but it almost felt like a truth and reconciliation commission. Is that something that our current politics could allow to happen?" Left-wing PBS reporter Yamiche Alcindor was pessimistic about the idea because "it's very hard to have a truth and reconciliation commission when Americans can't agree on the truth." I concur.[58]

Thirty-two-year-old freshman congresswoman Sara Jacobs (D-CA) suggested a "truth commission" specifically to examine America's past.[59] Think the revisionist history of the 1619 Project, but applied to all elements of U.S. history. She discussed the idea with CNN's Brian Stelter on the show *Reliable Sources*. "We haven't really done the reckoning with the racial injustice and white supremacy of our past that we need to do," she said, explaining the necessity for the truth commission. "Do you think the House and Senate leadership have the stomach for that?" Stelter asked. "I think so," Jacobs said.

Perhaps the quickest way to achieve unity is by banishing any dissent from the media-approved consensus.

CONCLUSION

American media is broken. It was broken by Andrew Breitbart, who inspired a generation of conservatives to fight the culture war with their keyboards and smartphone cameras, starting with systematically discrediting and rejecting the establishment press. My colleagues at Breitbart News as well as many powerful voices in conservative talk radio, cable news, and publishing continue Andrew's work, providing the information and analysis the powers-that-be don't want you to read or hear. Millions upon millions of citizens have enlisted in this fight on social media as well.

The media was broken by Donald Trump, who triggered the members of the elite American press so effortlessly and so thoroughly that they now lack any claim to objectivity. More Americans than ever now know that the media isn't simply putting their "spin" on the news; they are a weapon used by the globalist left to destroy political enemies. We can thank Trump for that.

The media was also broken by the international conglomerates that own and run most of the news business. They have pushed enterprising, freethinking, entertaining journalists off their platforms in order to protect their corporate interests and avoid the wrath of woke activists.

And finally, the media broke itself by refusing to respect their audiences. In the Trump era and beyond, the media has become angrier, more hysterical, more prone to crying wolf, and more dishonest than was previously imaginable. Instead of trying to convince their audiences to embrace their left-leaning worldview, they now use coercion and intimidation, sometimes even blacklisting, to force people to agree. Conform and obey or we will come after you. That is their mantra. This is horrifying, but it's also a sign of weakness. And they know many Americans are on to them.

Yet the conservative movement has made some significant errors during this time as well. Still, with a lot of discipline and a little time, we can make progress toward fixing these problems. First, President Trump continued to feed the media beast by giving interviews and exclusive content to establishment outlets. In order to defeat the corporate media, conservatives must interact with them only when it is strategically advantageous to do so. Key players in Trump's administration believed that gaining acceptance from brand-name journalists and outlets was of utmost importance. They were wrong—and they were never going to be accepted anyway. Recall the coronavirus task force press briefings that were almost exclusively limited to reporters from national establishment outlets; local and new media journalists were rarely included, and non-journalists (like doctors, for example) were never among those who got to ask questions about the deadly virus. Handing over the coronavirus narrative to a group of elite Washington journalists was nothing short of disastrous for Trump's reelection prospects. He also did little to bolster alternative online outlets or the vast array of conservative talk radio shows and podcasts. The next Republican standard-bearer needs to empower independent and conservative media like no one before.

The establishment media is weakened, but they are not going away. They may be disgraced, partisan, and have a failing business model, but they will get bailed out by the powerful corporate structures that back them. And these corporations are only getting bigger and stronger.

Also, as mentioned previously in this book, Trump ultimately chose not to crack down on the Masters of the Universe. The former POTUS often talked tough about Big Tech, which likely kept them somewhat in check, but ultimately, he was reluctant to curtail them in a meaningful way. I have come to the conclusion that he was willing to indulge their attacks on his own voters because those companies were driving stock markets to record highs and he didn't want to interfere. In the meantime, the Masters of the Universe were censoring stories that would benefit him and were gearing up to purge thousands (millions?) of his followers from their platforms. When conservatives take power next, their top priority should be restraining Big Tech, holding them accountable for their anti-conservative bias, favoritism toward major corporations, and monopolistic tendencies. It is not enough to have hearings that generate great sound bites but usually no progress. Every available avenue to weaken these monopolies and oligopolies should be considered. No conservative should ever accept another penny from a major Silicon Valley corporation. If they do, they should be challenged in primary races.

I opened this book discussing Mario Savio's "Bodies upon the Gears" speech. Breitbart is clearly "upon the gears," but that is only thanks to our millions of readers who empower us with their clicks, views, and shares. Now is not the time to be passive. The time to be silent is over. The globalist left is on the march. It's time to speak out for your values and your country. For us civilians, we cannot count on Republicans to efficiently and effectively roll back Big Tech's dominance. We must build our own platforms as alternatives. This task sounds impossible, and maybe it is, but we must try. The Left is awash in funding for new ideas and initiatives; this incentivizes bright people to join their cause. The Right must think similarly. And they must invest similarly.

The refrain that we must build our own should not exclusively be applied to the high-tech sector. Americans who are skeptical of the new era of hypercorporate conformity should be doing all they can to support each other with our dollars whenever we can. Buy American. Advertise on programs or platforms that share your values. Be fearless and bold about this. A 2020 survey found that "83% of Millennials find it important for the companies they buy from to align with their values."[1] There is no turning back from this reality, at least not in the short term. People are voting with their dollars; let's give them some more options. The woke-ification of corporate America provides incalculable opportunity for innovative citizens. There are billions of dollars to be made by entrepreneurs who are willing to boldly and bravely oppose the cancel culture. (And if this book inspires you to start or expand your business, I'm willing to serve on your corporate board for a nominal fee.)

The Biden years will be a challenge for conservatives. While the tight nature of the House of Representatives and the Senate mean we are not powerless, there aren't many political victories on a national level to be had. That said, Americans tend to overemphasize national politics and undervalue state and local civic engagement. Volunteer in your area. Become a precinct captain. Run for school board. Or city council. Or district attorney. Get elected to your homeowner's association! Just get involved! You never know where it might lead. You might find that you are capable of true leadership.

There are obvious steps you can take for increased personal happiness during this moment of disunity. I recommend having a big family and enjoying them as much as you can; this includes pets, but kids are better. Move to a place where you have physical (and mental) space and can commune with nature. Spend time deepening your relationship with God and contemplate America's founding documents. Buy guns (and learn to use them safely). Spend less time on social media and more time reading; books if you can, articles if you must. Exercise. Listen to music, the older the better. Despite the politics of our celebrity class, the tools of narrative are usually conservative (how many great movies have government bureaucrats or woke cancel mobs as their protagonists?), so there are plenty of films and television shows that are both diverting and enriching (though most of them weren't made recently).

Use humor and persuasion to bring people to your side, not anger or violence.

If you can move to a red or purple state, go there. But no matter where you are, vote.

And get ten thousand of your friends and family members to get their news and information from alternative sources like Breitbart News.

We can no longer hide from the Left. Time is of the essence. Though censorship mania has overwhelmed America in recent years, Breitbart has been taking these slings and arrows for a decade. One thing I can tell you from my career in independent media is that the Left cannot be appeased. They do not want compromise. They do not want to educate or reform. They want to absorb or destroy. Become one of them or they will come for you. It's only a matter of time.

America has entered a dark moment where dialogue with certain people who hold certain viewpoints is verboten. This is a dangerous trend and one that must be resisted intensely. All of the people won't agree on all of the things all of the time. So, what happens when we can't discuss and debate and argue? What happens when certain opinions are no longer allowed in the battlefield of ideas? What is the alternative to dialogue? My fear is that it's much worse than anyone wants to imagine.

That's why it's time to stand up and be heard.

It's time to put our bodies upon the gears.

ACKNOWLEDGMENTS

Breaking the News would not have been possible if not for a few people, the first of whom is Andrew Breitbart. Andrew is a towering figure, and yet he is still underrated as a cultural visionary and media pioneer. If he had not trusted me to help him on his epic but all too brief journey, I wouldn't be on mine.

Wynn and Robert Marlow gave me life, but they also gave me my values. Remarkably, we've had the opportunity to fight for them together at Breitbart News for years. My sister Molly is also one of my secret weapons.

My friend Mark Levin has said that writing a book is a family effort; having now completed my first, I can say this is undoubtedly the case. As much as anyone, I wrote this book for my wife, Mrs. Dr. Marlow, and my boys, Master Marlow and Master Marlow Jr., but they are also the ones who had to sacrifice for me to make sure it came to fruition. They are my purpose, my inspiration, and my constant source of fun. My home life would have fallen apart during this process if not for the support of Lauren Wilson and Francesco Federico. Love to you both!

My editor, Natasha Simons, saw my vision for this book, then made it much, much stronger. Her knowledge, toughness, and savvy were essential.

My agents, Tom Flannery and David Vigliano, are true pros. They got this project started and were a source of calm throughout.

I was incredibly fortunate to have the versatile and steely Jacob McLeod at my right hand as my head of research. He knew just when to follow his news nose and when to take my lead. He deserves tremendous credit.

Larry Solov, CEO of Breitbart News, gives me the honor every day of being editor-in-chief of Breitbart.com, one of the most important websites in the history of news. He also gave me the time to complete the goal of writing a book, and even gave me terrific ideas along the way. His faith in me has opened countless doors in my life.

Sometimes your heroes are also your friends. For me that is especially true of Peter Schweizer. Not only is Peter the best in the world at what he does (update: we do), he is an incredibly generous person with his time and insights.

Breitbart News is a pirate ship, but it's also a family. My colleagues are among the toughest, smartest, and most entertaining people who ever fought the culture war. Everyone there deserves acknowledgment, but I want to give special thanks to Jon David Kahn, Ezra Dulis, Elizabeth Moore, my real-life godfather John Nolte, Joel Pollak, and Matt Boyle.

Thank you to my "Breitbart News Daily" team at SiriusXM: Liz Aiello, Greg Ebben, Paul DeMilio, and Greg Sahakian.

And most important, thanks to all of you who read *Breaking the News*. Books, talk shows, and websites do not truly exist if there isn't an audience to consume, discuss, critique, and share the content. Power to the people!

NOTES

Preface

1 Jared Piazza and Neil McLatchie, "Cannibalism Is Common in the Animal Kingdom—Here's Why for Humans It's the Ultimate Taboo," *Newsweek*, August 20, 2019, https://www.newsweek.com/cannibalism-animal-kingdom -ultimate-taboo-humans-1455287.

2 Joel B. Pollak, "CNN Analyst Accuses Black SiriusXM Host David Webb of 'White Privilege,'" Breitbart, January 15, 2019, https://www.breitbart.com /the-media/2019/01/15/cnn-analyst-accuses-sirius-xm-host-david-webb-of -white-privilege-then-learns-hes-black/.

3 John Nolte, "CNN's Jake Tapper Under Fire for 'Homophobic' Roger Stone Remark," Breitbart, January 28, 2019, https://www.breitbart.com/the-media/2019 /01/28/nolte-cnns-jake-tapper-under-fire-for-homophobic-roger-stone-remark/.

4 Jon Levine, "CNN Analyst David Gergen Calls Roger Stone a "Dandy" Who May Be 'Subject to Rape' in Prison," *The Wrap*, February 20, 2019, https:// www.thewrap.com/cnn-analyst-david-gergen-calls-roger-stone-a-dandy -who-may-be-subject-to-rape-in-prison-video/.

5 "CNN's Jake Tapper Dedicates Segment to Trump's Penis," YouTube video, posted by "Politics Updates Today," September 19, 2018, https://www.youtube .com/watch?v=OKKyKuaCJW4.

Chapter 1: The Rise of Breitbart and the Fake News Hall of Shame

1 Jack Montgomery, "Nigel Farage: 'Brexit Would not Have Happened Without Breitbart,'" Breitbart, December 20, 2018, https://www.breitbart.com/europe /2018/12/20/nigel-farage-brexit-would-not-have-happened-without-breitbart/.

2 David Horowitz, "Bill Kristol: Republican Spoiler, Renegade Jew," Breitbart, May 15, 2016, https://www.breitbart.com/politics/2016/05/15/bill-kristol -republican-spoiler-renegade-jew/.

3 Wil S. Hylton, "Down the Breitbart Hole," *New York Times*, August 16, 2017,

https://www.nytimes.com/2017/08/16/magazine/breitbart-alt-right-steve
-bannon.html.

4 Sarah Rumph, "Breitbart Texas' Cartel Chronicles; Effort Begins to Help Citizen Journalists in Mexico," Breitbart, February 15, 2015, https://www.breit
bart.com/border/2015/02/15/breitbart-texas-announces-cartel-chronicles
-effort-begins-to-help-citizen-journalists-in-mexico/.

5 Sarah Posner, "How Donald Trump's New Campaign Chief Created an Online Haven for White Nationalists," Mother Jones, August 22, 2016, https://www
.motherjones.com/politics/2016/08/stephen-bannon-donald-trump-alt-right
-breitbart-news/.

6 Allum Bokhari and Milo Yiannopoulos, "An Establishment Conservative's Guide to the Alt-Right," Breitbart, March 29, 2016, https://www.breitbart.com
/tech/2016/03/29/an-establishment-conservatives-guide-to-the-alt-right/.

7 "Jealousy List 2016," Bloomberg, accessed February 8, 2021, https://www
.bloomberg.com/features/2016-jealousy-list/.

8 Joel B. Pollak, "The Vetting—Exclusive—Obama's Literary Agent in 1991 Booklet: 'Born in Kenya and Raised in Indonesia and Hawaii,'" Breitbart, May 17, 2012, https://www.breitbart.com/politics/2012/05/17/the-vetting
-barack-obama-literary-agent-1991-born-in-kenya-raised-indonesia-hawaii/.

9 Benjy Sarlin, "Analysis: Breitbart's Steve Bannon Leads the 'Alt Right' to the White House," NBC News, November 13, 2016, https://www.nbcnews.com
/politics/white-house/analysis-breitbart-s-steve-bannon-leads-alt-right
-white-house-n683316; Kim LaCapria, "Is Comet Ping Pong Pizzeria Home to a Child Abuse Ring Led by Hillary Clinton?" Snopes, November 21, 2016, https://www.snopes.com/fact-check/pizzagate-conspiracy/; Joshua Gillin, "How Pizzagate Went from Fake News to a Real Problem for a D.C. Business," PolitiFact, December 5, 2016, https://www.politifact.com/article/2016/dec/05
/how-pizzagate-went-fake-news-real-problem-dc-busin/.

10 "Trump's Comments on White Supremacists, 'Alt-Left' in Charlottesville," Politico, August 15, 2017, https://www.politico.com/story/2017/08/15/full
-text-trump-comments-white-supremacists-alt-left-transcript-241662.

11 Dan Merica, "Trump Says Both Sides to Blame Amid Charlottesville Backlash," CNN Politics, August 16, 2017, https://www.cnn.com/2017/08/15/politics
/trump-charlottesville-delay/index.html; Joel B. Pollak, "CNN's Jake Tapper Admits: Trump Did Not Call Neo-Nazis 'Very Fine People' in Charlottesville," Breitbart, April 27, 2019, https://www.breitbart.com/the-media/2019/04/27
/cnn-jake-tapper-admits-trump-did-not-call-neo-nazis-very-fine-people-in
-charlottesville/.

12 Jill Tucker, "Washington and Lincoln Are Out. S.F. School Board Tosses 44 School Names in Controversial Move," San Francisco Chronicle, January 27, 2021, https://www.sfchronicle.com/education/article/Washington-and-Lin
coln-are-out-S-F-school-board-15900963.php?utm_source=newsletter&utm
_medium=email&utm_content=headlines&utm_campaign=sfc_morningfix
&sid=5d54065e91d15c7b08162233.

13 Ken Klukowski, "Brett Kavanaugh Confirmed, Possibly Most Conservative Supreme Court Since 1934," Breitbart, October 6, 2018, https://www.breitbart .com/politics/2018/10/06/kavanaugh-confirmed-possibly-most-conservative -supreme-court-since-1934/.

14 Ken Klukowski, "Democrat Meltdown on Kavanaugh: 'Complicit in Evil,' 'Path to Tyranny,'" Breitbart, July 31, 2018, https://www.breitbart.com/poli tics/2018/07/31/democrat-meltdown-on-kavanaugh-complicit-in-evil-path -to-tyranny/; Ken Klukowski, "Democrats' Demand for 1 Million Documents on Kavanaugh Is Obstruction," Breitbart, July 20, 2018, https://www.breit bart.com/politics/2018/07/20/democrat-demand-documents-kavanaugh -obstruction/.

15 Ryan Grim, "Dianne Feinstein Withholding Brett Kavanaugh Document from Fellow Judiciary Committee Democrats," Intercept, September 12, 2018, https://theintercept.com/2018/09/12/brett-kavanaugh-confirmation-dianne -feinstein/; Alanna Durkin Richer, "When Was the Party? Kavanaugh's 1982 Summer Comes into Focus," Associated Press, September 27, 2018, https:// apnews.com/article/e8d6ebed487649f3a8ea174ec4610472.

16 Emma Brown, "California Professor, Writer of Confidential Brett Kavanaugh Letter, Speaks Out About Her Allegation of Sexual Assault," Washington Post, September 16, 2018, https://www.washingtonpost.com/investigations/cali fornia-professor-writer-of-confidential-brett-kavanaugh-letter-speaks-out -about-her-allegation-of-sexual-assault/2018/09/16/46982194-b846-11e8 -94eb-3bd52dfe917b_story.html; Eli Watkins, "Timeline: How the Kava-naugh Accusations Have Unfolded," CNN Politics, September 17, 2018, https:// www.cnn.com/2018/09/17/politics/kavanaugh-ford-timeline; Kristina Peter-son, Natalie Andrews, and Rebecca Ballhaus, "Kavanaugh Confirmation Vote Is Delayed for FBI Investigation," Wall Street Journal, September 28, 2018, https://www.wsj.com/articles/senate-judiciary-committee-prepares-to-vote -on-kavanaugh-this-morning-1538134779.

17 Ken Dilanian, Brandy Zadrozny, and Ben Popken, "Accuser's Schoolmate Says She Recalls Hearing of Alleged Kavanaugh Incident," NBC News, September 19, 2018, https://www.nbcnews.com/politics/supreme-court/accuser-s-school mate-says-she-recalls-hearing-alleged-kavanaugh-incident-n911111.

18 Ronan Farrow and Jane Mayer, "Senate Democrats Investigate a New Allega-tion of Sexual Misconduct, from Brett Kavanaugh's College Years," New Yorker, September 23, 2018, https://www.newyorker.com/news/news-desk/senate -democrats-investigate-a-new-allegation-of-sexual-misconduct-from-the -supreme-court-nominee-brett-kavanaughs-college-years-deborah-ramirez.

19 Joel B. Pollak, "NYT: New Brett Kavanaugh Accuser Claims 'Friends Pushed His Penis into the Hand of a Female Student,'" Breitbart, September 15, 2019, https://www.breitbart.com/politics/2019/09/15/nyt-new-brett-kavanaugh -accuser-claims-friends-pushed-his-penis-into-the-hand-of-a-female-stu dent/.

20 Indelible in the Hippocampus: Writings from the MeToo Movement, Shelly

Oria, ed. (San Francisco: McSweeny's, 2019), Amazon.com, accessed February 8, 2021, https://www.amazon.com/Indelible-Hippocampus-Writings-Too-Movement/dp/1944211713.

21 Sarah Fitzpatrick, Rich Schapiro, and Adiel Kaplan, "Kavanaugh Accuser Julie Swetnick Alleges He 'Spiked' Punch at Parties So Intoxicated Women Could be Raped," NBC News, September 26, 2018, https://www.nbcnews.com/politics/supreme-court/woman-alleges-kavanaugh-spiked-punch-parties-so-intoxicated-girls-could-n912491.

22 Ian Schwartz, "Swetnick: I Cannot Specifically Say That Kavanaugh Was One of the Ones Who Assaulted Me," RealClearPolitics, October 1, 2018, https://www.realclearpolitics.com/video/2018/10/01/swetnick_i_cannot_specifically_say_that_kavanaugh_was_one_of_the_ones_who_assaulted_me.html.

23 Senator Hatch Office, "A Utah man named Dennis Ketterer reached out to the Hatch office this week with information about accuser Julie Swetnick, and her allegations against Judge Kavanaugh," Twitter, October 2, 2018, https://twitter.com/senorrinhatch/status/1047225465881202689?ref_src=twsrc%5Etfw%7Ctwcamp%5Etweetembed%7Ctwterm%5E104722546588120 2689%7Ctwgr%5E%7Ctwcon%5Es1_&ref_url=https%3A%2F%2Fwww.breit bart.com%2Fpolitics%2F2018%2F10%2F03%2Fformer-dem-candidat.

24 Klukowski, "Brett Kavanaugh Confirmed, Possibly Most Conservative Supreme Court Since 1934."

25 Jerome Hudson, "'Clinton Cash,' Breitbart News, and the Narratives That Led to the Clinton Foundation's Demise," Breitbart, January 18, 2017, https://www.breitbart.com/politics/2017/01/18/clinton-cash-breitbart-news-and-the-narratives-that-led-to-the-clinton-foundations-demise/.

26 Ibid.

27 "Princeton University: Russia's Use and Stockpiles of Highly Enriched Uranium Pose Significant Nuclear Risks," Phys.org, September 13, 2017, https://phys.org/news/2017-09-russia-stockpiles-highly-enriched-uranium.html.

28 Jo Becker and Mike McIntire, "Cash Flowed to Clinton Foundation Amid Russian Uranium Deal," New York Times, April 23, 2015, https://www.nytimes.com/2015/04/24/us/cash-flowed-to-clinton-foundation-as-russians-pressed-for-control-of-uranium-company.html?_r=0; Todd Gitlin, "Op-ed: Peter Schweizer and the Gaming of the Times," Columbia Journalism Review, October 30, 2019, https://www.cjr.org/opinion/schweizer-times-biden-opinion.php.

29 Malia Zimmerman, "Hillary Clinton Sided with Russia on Sanctions as Bill Made $500G on Moscow Speech," Fox News, last updated September 27, 2017, https://www.foxnews.com/politics/hillary-clinton-sided-with-russia-on-sanctions-as-bill-made-500g-on-moscow-speech.

30 Dustin Volz, "Trump Signs into Law U.S. Government Ban on Kaspersky Lab Software," Reuters, December 12, 2017, https://www.reuters.com/article/us-usa-cyber-kaspersky/trump-signs-into-law-u-s-government-ban-on-kaspersky-lab-software-idUSKBN1E62V4?il=0.

31 "Dow Jones Industrial Average," CNBC, accessed February 8, 2021, https://www.cnbc.com/quotes/.DJI.

32 Evan Bush, Christine Clarridge, Dominic Gates, and Hal Bernton, "Russians Turned Away at Seattle Consulate After Trump Administration Announces Closure," *Seattle Times*, last updated March 28, 2018, https://www.seattle times.com/seattle-news/russians-turned-away-at-seattle-consulate-after -trump-administration-announces-closure/.

33 Gregory Hellman, "Trump Approves New Russia Sanctions for Violating Cold War Arms Pact," *Politico*, December 8, 2017, https://www.politico.com/story /2017/12/08/trump-russia-sanctions-cold-war-arms-pact-215837.

34 Josh Rogin, "Opinion: Trump Administration Approves Lethal Arms Sales to Ukraine," *Washington Post*, December 20, 2017, https://www.washington post.com/news/josh-rogin/wp/2017/12/20/trump-administration-approves -lethal-arms-sales-to-ukraine/.

35 Chris Strohm and Jennifer Jacobs, "Trump Decided Russia Indictments Should Come Pre-Summit, Sources Say," Bloomberg, July 17, 2018, https://www.bloomberg.com/news/articles/2018-07-17/trump-said-to-decide-russia -indictments-should-come-pre-summit.

36 Chris Cillizza and Brenna Williams, "15 Times Donald Trump Praised Authoritarian Rulers," CNN Politics, last updated July 2, 2019, https://www .cnn.com/2019/07/02/politics/donald-trump-dictators-kim-jong-un-vladi mir-putin/index.html.

37 Ted Johnson, "Facebook Sold Political Ads to Russian Sources During 2016 Election," *Variety*, September 6, 2017, https://variety.com/2017/politics /news/facebook-trump-russia-political-ads-1202549414/; Raphael Satter, Jeff Donn, and Chad Day, "Inside Story: How Russians Hacked the Democrats' Emails," Associated Press, November 4, 2017, https://apnews.com/article/hill ary-clinton-phishing-moscow-russia-only-on-ap-dea73efc01594839957c3c9 a6c962b8a.

38 Joshua Caplan and Ezra Dulis, "Called Shot: Watch Breitbart's Alex Marlow Predict the Russia Hoax Outcome in June 2017," Breitbart, March 26, 2019, https://www.breitbart.com/the-media/2019/03/26/called-shot-watch-breit barts-alex-marlow-predict-the-russia-hoax-outcome-in-june-2017/.

39 Neal Rothschild, "The Social-Media Spread of Trump/Mueller," Axios, March 25, 2019, https://www.axios.com/robert-mueller-donald-trump-social -media-reach-0586790d-711f-42fe-b3e1-21acc54cdfa6.html.

40 Franklin Foer, "Was a Trump Server Communicating with Russia?" *Slate*, October 31, 2016, http://www.slate.com/articles/news_and_politics/cover _story/2016/10/was_a_server_registered_to_the_trump_organization_com municating_with_russia.html#return.

41 Hillary Clinton (@HillaryClinton), "Computer scientists have apparently uncovered a covert server . . . ," Twitter, October 31, 2016, 5:36 p.m., https://twitter.com/HillaryClinton/status/793250312119263233.

42 Philip Bump, "One of the Busiest Websites in the U.S. in 2016 Regularly Linked to Russian Propaganda," *Washington Post*, November 10, 2017, https://www.washingtonpost.com/news/politics/wp/2017/11/10/one-of-the-busiest-websites-in-the-u-s-in-2016-regularly-linked-to-russia-propaganda/.

43 Andrew Beaujon, "Washington Post Appends Editor's Note to Russian Propaganda Story," *Washingtonian*, December 7, 2016, https://www.washingtonian.com/2016/12/07/washington-post-appends-editors-note-russian-propaganda-story/.

44 Juliet Eilperin and Adam Entous, "Russian Operation Hacked a Vermont Utility, Showing Risk to U.S. Electrical Grid Security, Officials Say," *Washington Post*, December 31, 2016, https://www.washingtonpost.com/world/national-security/russian-hackers-penetrated-us-electricity-grid-through-a-utility-in-vermont/2016/12/30/8fc90cc4-ceec-11e6-b8a2-8c2a61b0436f_story.html.

45 Glenn Greenwald, "Beyond BuzzFeed: The 10 Worst, Most Embarrassing U.S. Media Failures on the Trump-Russia Story," *Intercept*, January 20, 2019, https://theintercept.com/2019/01/20/beyond-buzzfeed-the-10-worst-most-embarrassing-u-s-media-failures-on-the-trumprussia-story/.

46 Matthew Boyle, "Very Fake News: CNN Pushes Refurbished Russia Conspiracy, Inaccurately Claims Investment Fund Under Investigation," Breitbart, June 23, 2017, https://www.breitbart.com/politics/2017/06/23/very-fake-news-cnn-pushes-refurbished-russia-conspiracy-inaccurately-claims-investment-fund-under-investigation/.

47 Eliza Collins, "Yes, 17 Intelligence Agencies Really Did Say Russia Was Behind Hacking," *USA Today*, last updated December 16, 2016, https://www.usatoday.com/story/news/politics/onpolitics/2016/10/21/17-intelligence-agencies-russia-behind-hacking/92514592/; Nina Agrawal, "There's More than the CIA and FBI: The 17 Agencies That Make Up the U.S. Intelligence Community," *Los Angeles Times*, January 17, 2017, https://www.latimes.com/nation/la-na-17-intelligence-agencies-20170112-story.html; Tim Hains, "Clapper Confirms: '17 Intelligence Agencies' Russia Story Was False," RealClearPolitics, July 6, 2017, https://www.realclearpolitics.com/video/2017/07/06/clapper_confirms_17_intelligence_agencies_russia_story_was_false.html.

48 Ian Hanchett, "Report: Flynn Ready to Testify Against Trump, Testify Trump 'Ordered Him' to Contact Russians," Breitbart, December 1, 2017, https://www.breitbart.com/clips/2017/12/01/report-flynn-ready-to-testify-against-trump-testify-trump-ordered-him-to-contact-russians/.

49 Joshua Caplan, "Brian Ross Resigns from ABC News After False Report on Mike Flynn," Breitbart, July 2, 2018, https://www.breitbart.com/the-media/2018/07/02/brian-ross-resign-abc-news-mike-flynn/.

50 John Carney, "Huckabee Sanders Vindicated: Bloomberg and WSJ Walk Back Deutsche Bank Subpoena Story," Breitbart, December 6, 2017, https://www.breitbart.com/politics/2017/12/06/huckabee-sanders-vindicated-bloomberg-and-wsj-walk-back-deutsche-bank-subpoena-story/.

51 Jenny Strasburg, "Mueller Subpoenas Deutsche Bank Records Related to

Trump," *Wall Street Journal*, December 6, 2017, https://www.wsj.com/articles /trumps-deutsche-bank-records-subpoenaed-by-mueller-1512480154.

52 Adam Shaw, "CNN Issues Correction over Trump Wikileaks Email Story," Breitbart, December 8, 2017, https://www.breitbart.com/the-media/2017/12 /08/cnn-issues-correction-over-trump-wikileaks-email-story/.

53 Rosalind S. Helderman and Tom Hamburger, "Email Pointed Trump Campaign to Wikileaks Documents That Were Already Public," *Washington Post*, December 8, 2017, https://www.washingtonpost.com/politics/email -offering-trump-campaign-wikileaks-documents-referred-to-information -already-public/2017/12/08/61dc2356-dc37-11e7-a841-2066faf731ef_story .html?utm_term=.cb8edb7de666.

54 Manu Raju and Jeremy Herb, "Email Pointed Trump Campaign to WikiLeaks Documents," CNN Politics, December 8, 2017, https://www.cnn.com/2017 /12/08/politics/email-effort-give-trump-campaign-wikileaks-documents /index.html; Matthew Boyle, "Three Employees Resign from CNN amid Very Fake News Scandal," Breitbart, June 26, 2017, https://www.breitbart.com/the -media/2017/06/26/three-employees-resign-from-cnn-amid-very-fake-news -scandal/.

55 Kristina Wong, "Deep State: Feds Wiretapped President Trump Personal Lawyer Michael Cohen," Breitbart, May 3, 2018, https://www.breitbart.com /politics/2018/05/03/deep-state-feds-wiretapped-president-trump-personal -lawyer-michael-cohen/.

56 Luke Harding and Dan Collyns, "Manafort Held Secret Talks with Assange in Ecuadorian Embassy, Sources Say," *Guardian*, November 27, 2018, https:// www.theguardian.com/us-news/2018/nov/27/manafort-held-secret-talks -with-assange-in-ecuadorian-embassy.

57 Esther Addley, "The Seven-Year Itch: Assange's Awkward Stay in the Embassy," *Guardian*, April 11, 2019, https://www.theguardian.com/media/2019/apr/11 /how-ecuador-lost-patience-with-houseguest-julian-assange.

58 Peter Stone and Greg Gordon, "Cell Signal Puts Cohen Outside Prague Around Time of Purported Russian Meeting," McClatchy DC, last updated April 18, 2019, https://www.mcclatchydc.com/news/investigations/article219016820.html.

59 John Nolte, "Top 51 Fake News 'Bombshells' the Media Spread About Russiagate," Breitbart, April 22, 2019, https://www.breitbart.com/the-media/2019 /04/22/top-51-fake-news-bombshells-media-spread-russiagate/.

60 Sharon LaFraniere, Kenneth P. Vogel, and Maggie Haberman, "Manafort Accused of Sharing Trump Polling Data with Russian Associate," *New York Times*, January 8, 2019, https://www.nytimes.com/2019/01/08/us/politics /manafort-trump-campaign-data-kilimnik.html.

61 Joshua Caplan, "Mueller: BuzzFeed Report Claiming Trump Directed Michael Cohen Testimony 'Not Accurate,'" Breitbart, January 18, 2019, https://www .breitbart.com/politics/2019/01/18/mueller-disputes-buzzfeed-news-report -claiming-trump-directed-michael-cohen-testimony/.

62 Aaron Klein, "Hillary's Law Firm That Paid for Dossier Also Recruited

Crowdstrike to Probe DNC Hack," Breitbart, May 12, 2020, https://www.breit
bart.com/politics/2020/05/12/hillarys-law-firm-that-paid-for-dossier-also
-recruited-crowdstrike-to-probe-dnc-hack/.

63 "The Cast of the Trump-Russia Collusion Hoax," Capital Research Center,
August 6, 2020, https://capitalresearch.org/article/the-cast-of-the-trump-rus
sia-collusion-hoax/.

64 "Staffs of The New York Times and The Washington Post," Pulitzer Prizes,
accessed February 8, 2021, https://www.pulitzer.org/winners/staffs-new-york
-times-and-washington-post.

65 Justin Caruso, "Flashback: 50 Hollywood Stars Who Accused Trump of Treason, Collusion with Russia," Breitbart, March 25, 2019, https://www.breitbart
.com/entertainment/2019/03/25/flashback-50-hollywood-stars-who-accused
-trump-of-treason-collusion-with-russia/.

66 Colin Madine, "The Media Is Ignoring the 500-Pound Surveillance Elephant
in the Room," Breitbart, April 3, 2017, https://www.breitbart.com/politics
/2017/04/03/media-ignoring-500-pound-surveillance-elephant-room/.

67 Joshua Green, "No One Cares About Russia in the World Breitbart Made,"
New York Times, July 15, 2017, https://www.nytimes.com/2017/07/15/opinion
/sunday/no-one-cares-about-russia-in-the-world-breitbart-made.html.

68 Mollie Hemingway (@MZHemingway), "Shorter NYT: Please don't sue us,"
Twitter, January 20, 2019, 6:53 p.m., https://twitter.com/MZHemingway/sta
tus/1087181286559698944/photo/1.

69 SE Cupp Unfiltered (@UnfilteredSE), "Teens in MAGA gear mock a Native
American Vietnam vet. . . ." Twitter, January 19, 2019, 4:57 p.m., https://twit
ter.com/UnfilteredSE/status/1086789656207810561.

70 Representative Deb Haaland (@RepDebHaaland), "This Veteran put his life
on the line for our country . . . ," Twitter, January 19, 2019, 8:31 a.m., https://
twitter.com/RepDebHaaland/status/1086662398071566337.

71 Maggie Haberman (@maggieNYT), "There are dozens of students laughing
and egging on the behavior . . . ," January 19, 2019, 4:08 p.m., https://twitter
.com/maggienyt/status/1086777325356752897?lang=en.

72 Chris Evans (@ChrisEvans), "This is appalling. This is ignorance. The gall. The
disrespect. It's shameful . . . ," Twitter, January 19, 2019, 2:51 p.m., https://twit
ter.com/ChrisEvans/status/1086758159891320832.

73 ROSIE (@Rosie), "horrible smug asswipe," Twitter, January 19, 2019, 1:52 p.m.,
https://twitter.com/Rosie/status/1086743221802336258.

74 "Ed Asner's Message to the 9/11 Truth Movement," YouTube video,
posted by "911REICHSTAG," March 6, 2007, https://www.youtube.com
/watch?v=8dVNDQWhtMc; Ed Asner (@theOnlyEdAsner), "This is a disgrace
. This is not America," Twitter, January 19, 2019, 11:01 a.m., https://twitter.com
/TheOnlyEdAsner/status/1086700192827551745.

75 Valerie Richardson, "Ex-CNN Host 'Likely' to Be Sued over Now-Deleted
'Punchable Face' Tweet: Sandmann Attorney," Washington Times, January 13,

2020, https://www.washingtontimes.com/news/2020/jan/13/reza-aslan-likely
-be-sued-over-now-deleted-punchab/.

76   Ruth Graham, "The MAGA Teenager Who Harassed a Native American Veteran Is Still Unnamed, but We've Seen His Face Before," *Slate,* January 19, 2019,
https://slate.com/news-and-politics/2019/01/maga-teenager-native-american
-veteran-harassment-smile.html.

77   Matt Wolking (@MattWolking), "Just @CNN employee @Bakari_Sellers fantasizing about punching a 15-year-old in the face," Twitter, January 21, 2019,
4:32 a.m., https://twitter.com/MattWolking/status/1087327139937030144.

78   Tim Robbins (@TimRobbins1), "Who are these good Christians? What
school is teaching them to hate with such contempt and ignorance? . . ."
Twitter, January 19, 2019, 7:09 a.m., https://twitter.com/timrobbins1/status
/1086641857189289985?lang=en.

79   Jeffrey Wright (@jfreewright), "Since they're in DC, they should take the
phucking red hats . . . ," Twitter, January 19, 2019, 3:36 p.m., https://twitter
.com/jfreewright/status/1086769367788982272.

80   Francesca Paris, "Video of Kentucky Students Mocking Native American
Man Draws Outcry," NPR, January 20, 2019, https://www.npr.org/2019/01
/20/686988268/video-of-kentucky-students-mocking-native-american-man
-draws-outcry.

81   Daniel Nussbaum, "Kathy Griffin Beheads Donald Trump in Bloody Shock
Photo," Breitbart, May 30, 2017, https://www.breitbart.com/entertainment
/2017/05/30/kathy-griffin-beheads-donald-trump-shock-bloody-photo/;
Kathy Griffin (@kathygriffin), "Names please. And stories from people who
can identify them and vouch for their identity. Thank you," Twitter, January 20,
2019, https://twitter.com/kathygriffin/status/1086932616392011776?s=20.

82   Ben Kesslen, "Gay Valedictorian Banned from Speaking at Covington
Graduation 'Not Surprised' by D.C. Controversy," NBC News, January 22,
2019, https://www.nbcnews.com/feature/nbc-out/gay-valedictorian-banned
-speaking-covington-graduation-not-surprised-d-c-n961446.

83   "SEE IT: Covington Catholic High Students in Blackface at Past Basketball
Game," *New York Daily News,* January 21, 2019, https://www.nydailynews
.com/news/national/ny-sports-covington-nathan-phillips-nick-sandmann
-20190121-story.html; Jennifer Smith, "PICTURED: Kentucky Students from
the Same Catholic High School As the Teens Who Taunted a Native American Man Were Allowed to Don BLACKFACE at Their Sports Events—and
Openly Goaded African American Players," *Daily Mail,* January 21, 2019,
https://www.dailymail.co.uk/news/article-6616793/Kentucky-Catholic-high
-school-Lincoln-Memorial-clash-allowed-blackface-pep-rallies.html; Joel B.
Pollak, "Covington Catholic High School Alumni Push Back Against Media's
New 'Blackface' Claim," Breitbart, January 22, 2019, https://www.breitbart
.com/politics/2019/01/22/alunmni-covington-catholic-high-school-push
-back-against-medias-new-blackface-claim/; Martin Gould, "EXCLUSIVE: 'It

Was Not About Race.' Black Basketball Player Who Was Jeered by Covington Catholic Students Painted in Blackface Depicted in Shocking Photo Believes They Were Just 'Spirited' Fans Supporting Their Team," *Daily Mail*, January 24, 2019, https://www.dailymail.co.uk/news/article-6625071/Black-basketball -player-jeered-Covington-fans-blackface-says-wasnt-race.html.

84 Max Londberg, "'Blatant Racism': Ky. High School Apologizes Following Backlash After Video Shows Students Surrounding Indigenous Marchers," *Cincinnati Enquirer*, January 19, 2019, https://www.cincinnati.com/story /news/nation/2019/01/19/kentucky-diocese-incident-indigenous-peoples -march-covington-catholic-high-school/2624503002/.

85 Michelle Boorstein, "'Opposed to the Dignity of the Human Person': Kentucky Catholic Diocese Condemns Teens Who Taunted Vet at March for Life," *Washington Post*, January 20, 2019, https://www.washingtonpost.com/reli gion/2019/01/20/opposed-dignity-human-person-kentucky-catholic-diocese -condemns-teens-who-taunted-vet-march-life/.

86 Cleve R. Wootson, Jr., Antonio Olivo, and Joe Heim, "'It Was Getting Ugly': Native American Drummer Speaks on His Encounter with MAGA-Hat -Wearing Teens," *Washington Post*, January 22, 2019, https://www.washing tonpost.com/nation/2019/01/20/it-was-getting-ugly-native-american-drum mer-speaks-maga-hat-wearing-teens-who-surrounded-him/.

87 Hugh Hewitt (@hughhewitt), "Agree but it would be useful to train every high schooler in Proverbs 15:1 . . . ," Twitter, January 20, 2019, 9:35 a.m., https:// twitter.com/hughhewitt/status/1087040902231552001; Proverbs 15:1, https:// www.kingjamesbibleonline.org/Proverbs-15-1/.

88 Joel B. Pollak, "Critics Push Back Against Media Reports Covington Catholic High School Students Racist Toward Native American Drummer," Breitbart, January 20, 2019, https://www.breitbart.com/the-media/2019/01/20 /critics-covington-maga-critics-push-back-against-portrayal-of-catholic -high-school-as-racist-to-native-american/.

89 Nicholas Frankovich, "The Covington Students Might as Well Have Just Spit on the Cross," *National Review* (archive), January 20, 2019, https://archive.is /tlwIV#selection-897.1-904.0.

90 Kristina Wong, "Report: Native American Nathan Phillips Has Criminal Background," Breitbart, January 24, 2019, https://www.breitbart.com/politics /2019/01/24/report-native-american-nathan-phillips-criminal-background/; Alana Goodman, "Native American Activist Nathan Phillips Has Violent Criminal Record and Escaped from Jail as Teenager," *Washington Examiner*, January 23, 2019, https://www.washingtonexaminer.com/politics/native -american-activist-nathan-phillips-has-violent-criminal-record-and-escaped -from-jail-as-teenager.

91 Joshua Caplan, "Washington Post Correction: Nathan Phillips 'Was Never Deployed to Vietnam,'" Breitbart, January 22, 2019, https://www.breitbart .com/the-media/2019/01/22/washington-post-correction-nathan-phillips -was-never-deployed-to-vietnam/.

92 Phil Kerpen (@kerpen), "Don Shipley got the DD-214 . . . ," Twitter, January 22, 2019, 5:15 p.m., https://twitter.com/kerpen/status/1087881473225572352 /photo/4.

93 Dan Lamothe, "Nathan Phillips, Man at Center of Standoff with Coving-ton Teens, Misrepresented His Military History," *Washington Post*, Janu-ary 24, 2019, https://www.washingtonpost.com/national-security/2019/01/23 /nathan-phillips-man-standoff-with-covington-teens-faces-scrutiny-his-mil itary-past/.

94 Phil Kerpen (@kerpen), "Nathan Phillips, October 29, 2018 . . . ," Twitter, January 24, 2019, 7:51 p.m., https://twitter.com/kerpen/status/10886455192 18536448.

95 Gerald D. Jaynes, *Encyclopaedia Britannica*, s.v. "Black Hebrew Israelites," accessed February 9, 2021, https://www.britannica.com/topic/Black-Hebrew -Israelites.

96 "Racist Black Hebrew Israelites Becoming More Militant," Southern Poverty Law Center, August 29, 2008, https://www.splcenter.org/fighting-hate/intelli gence-report/2008/racist-black-hebrew-israelites-becoming-more-militant.

97 John Eligon, "Hebrew Israelites See Divine Intervention in Lincoln Memorial Confrontation," *New York Times*, January 23, 2019, https://www.nytimes.com /2019/01/23/us/black-hebrew-israelites-covington-catholic.html.

98 Michelle Mark, "Here's What to Know About the Black Hebrew Israelites, the Group of Protesters That Has Shot to the Center of the Covington Catho-lic Controversy," Insider, January 24, 2019, https://www.insider.com/black -hebrew-israelites-covington-students-hate-group-2019-1.

99 "Nick Sandmann: The Truth in 15 Minutes," YouTube video, posted by "Lin-wood Pc," February 1, 2019, https://www.youtube.com/watch?v=lSkpPaiUF8s &feature=emb_logo.

100 Pam Key, "Behar: Covington Students Attacked Because 'We're Desperate to Get Trump Out of Office,'" Breitbart, January 22, 2019, https://www.breit bart.com/clips/2019/01/22/behar-covington-students-attacked-because-were -desperate-to-get-trump-out-of-office/.

101 Joshua Caplan, "CNN Settles Lawsuit with Covington Catholic Student Nick Sandmann," Breitbart, January 7, 2020, https://www.breitbart.com/the-media /2020/01/07/cnn-settles-lawsuit-with-covington-catholic-student-nick-sand mann/.

102 Kristina Wong, "Covington Teen Nicholas Sandmann Settles $250M Defama-tion Lawsuit with the Washington Post on 18th Birthday," Breitbart, July 24, 2020, https://www.breitbart.com/politics/2020/07/24/covington-teen-sand mann-settles-lawsuit-washington-post/.

103 Ibid.

104 "Hate Crimes," FBI.gov, accessed February 9, 2021, https://www.fbi.gov/inves tigate/civil-rights/hate-crimes.

105 Aemer Madhani, "Jussie Smollett Purposely Misled Police by Saying Assail-ants Were White, Lawsuit Alleges," *USA Today*, last updated April 17, 2019,

https://www.usatoday.com/story/news/nation/2019/04/11/jussie-smollett
-lawsuit-actor-falsely-described-attackers-white/3442179002/.

106 Mathew Silver, "Jussie Smollett Details Assault, Says Attackers Yelled 'This Is MAGA Country,'" *Vulture*, February 14, 2019, https://www.vulture.com/2019 /02/jussie-smollet-attack-good-morning-america-interview-video.html.

107 Kamala Harris (@KamalaHarris), "@JussieSmollett is one of the kindest, most gentle human beings I know . . . ," Twitter, January 29, 2019, 1:30 p.m., https:// twitter.com/kamalaharris/status/1090361495119187969?lang=en.

108 Avery Anapol, "Kamala Harris: Violent Attack on 'Empire' Star Is 'Attempted Modern Day Lynching,'" *Hill*, January 29, 2019, https://thehill.com/homenews /senate/427538-kamala-harris-violent-attack-on-empire-star-is-attempted -modern-day-lynching.

109 Joel B. Pollak, "NAACP Blames President Donald Trump for Alleged Racist, Homophobic Attack on Actor Jussie Smollett," Breitbart, January 29, 2019, https://www.breitbart.com/politics/2019/01/29/naacp-blames-president -donald-trump-for-alleged-racist-homophobic-attack-on-actor-jussie-smollett/.

110 Pam Key, "Maxine Waters Blames Trump for Smollett Incident—'He's Dog Whistling Every Day,'" Breitbart, February 1, 2019, https://www.breitbart.com /clips/2019/02/01/maxine-waters-blames-trump-for-smollett-incident-hes -dog-whistling-every-day/.

111 Joe Biden (@JoeBiden), "What happened today to @JussieSmollett must never be tolerated in this country . . . ," Twitter, January 29, 2019, 5:31 p.m., https:// twitter.com/joebiden/status/1090422326783606784?lang=en.

112 Erin Jenson, "'Red Table Talk': Don Lemon Tells Jada Pinkett Smith He Texts Jussie Smollett Daily," *USA Today*, February 11, 2019, https://www.usato day.com/story/life/tv/2019/02/11/red-table-don-lemon-jussie-smollett-jada -pinkett-smith/2837561002/.

113 Yamiche Alcindor (@Yamiche), "Hoping for a full recovery for @JussieSmollett, who TMZ is reporting was brutally attacked . . . ," Twitter, January 29, 2019, 8:41 a.m., https://twitter.com/yamiche/status/1090288879482085377?lang=en.

114 Jamil Smith (@JamilSmith), "Thankfully, @JussieSmollett is reportedly in good condition . . . ," Twitter, January 29, 2019, 10:12 a.m., https://twitter.com /JamilSmith/status/1090311656830160901.

115 Ben Kew, "Ellen Page Blames Pence, Trump for 'Hate' That Led to Smollett Attack: 'This Needs to F*cking Stop,'" Breitbart, February 1, 2019, https:// www.breitbart.com/entertainment/2019/02/01/ellen-page-blames-pence -trump-for-hate-that-led-to-smollett-attack-this-needs-to-fcking-stop/; Cher (@cher), "Jussie Smollett, 'Empire' Actor, Reportedly Attacked in Possible Hate Crime . . . ," Twitter, January 29, 2019, 8:13 p.m., https://twitter.com/cher/sta tus/1090463098224500736?lang=en; Katy Perry (@katyperry), "Standing with and sending love to @JussieSmollett today . . . ," Twitter, January 29, 2019, 11:55 a.m., https://twitter.com/katyperry/status/1090337590958448641; O M (@oliviamunn), "Jussie Smollett was violently attacked by two white men who poured bleach on him . . . ," Twitter, January 29, 2019, 12:15 p.m., https://twit

ter.com/oliviamunn/status/1090342691030806528; Justin Caruso, "15 Celebrities Who Blamed Trump, Deplorables for Hoax Attack on Jussie Smollett," *Breitbart*, February 17, 2019, https://www.breitbart.com/entertainment/2019 /02/17/15-celebrities-who-blamed-trump-deplorables-for-hoax-attack-on -jussie-smollett/.

116 Rob Elgas (@RobElgasABC7), "As Chicago police expand their search for the men who allegedly attacked Jussie Smollett . . . ," Twitter, January 30, 2019, 10:13 a.m., https://twitter.com/robelgasabc7/status/1090674476486979584.

117 Rosemary Sobol and Tracy Swartz, "Week Before Reported Attack, Jussie Smollett Got Threatening Letter with 'MAGA' Written for Return Address," *Chicago Tribune*, February 4, 2019, https://www.chicagotribune.com/news /breaking/ct-met-jussie-smollett-alleged-attack-20190204-story.html.

118 "Jussie Smollett Tells ABC News' Robin Roberts He's 'Pissed Off' After Vicious Attack," *Good Morning America*, February 13, 2019, https://www.goodmorni ngamerica.com/culture/video/jussie-smollett-speaks-robin-roberts-abc -news-exclusive-61052883.

119 Charlie De Mar (@CharlieDeMar), "BREAKING: Police raided the home of two persons of interest in Jussie Smollett case last night . . . ," Twitter, February 14, 2019, 2:57 p.m., https://twitter.com/CharlieDeMar/status/1096181650 390765570.

120 Joshua Caplan, "Report: 'Empire' Extras Detained for Alleged Staged Attack on Jussie Smollett to Be Charged," *Breitbart*, February 15, 2019, https://www .breitbart.com/entertainment/2019/02/15/report-empire-extras-detained-for -alleged-staged-attack-on-jussie-smollett-to-be-charged/.

121 Tracy Swartz, Jeremy Gorner, and Annie Sweeney, "Chicago Police Investigating Whether 'Empire' Actor Jussie Smollett Paid Brothers to Stage Attack," *Chicago Tribune*, February 17, 2019, https://www.chicagotribune.com/news /local/breaking/ct-met-jussie-smollett-police-question-20190216-story.html.

122 Lucas Nolan, "Instagram Deletes Donald Trump Jr. Post About Jussie Smollett, Claims 'Error,'" *Breitbart*, February 18, 2019, https://www.breitbart.com/tech /2019/02/18/instagram-deletes-donald-trump-jr-post-about-jussie-smollett -claims-error/.

123 Dominic Patten, "Fox Backs Jussie Smollett Anew as "Consummate Professional" While Police Attack Probe Continues & Lawyers Talk," *Deadline*, February 20, 2019, https://deadline.com/2019/02/jussie-smollett-fox-backs -empire-star-chicago-investigation-1202560587/.

124 Cynthia Littleton, "Chicago Police: Jussie Smollett Staged Attack Because He Was 'Dissatisfied with His Salary,'" *Variety*, February 21, 2019, https:// variety.com/2019/tv/news/chicago-police-jussie-smollett-salary-dissatis fied-1203144826.

125 Megan Crepeau, "Jussie Smollett Indicted on 16 Counts over Allegedly Phony Claims of Racist, Homophobic Attack," *Chicago Tribune*, March 9, 2019, https://www.chicagotribune.com/news/breaking/ct-met-jussie-smollett -indicted-20190308-story.html.

126 "Jussie Smollett Update: Charges Against 'Empire' Actor Dropped; 'Not an Exoneration,' Prosecutor Says," ABC 7 Chicago, March 26, 2019, https://abc7 chicago.com/charges-against-jussie-smollett-dropped/5218125/.

127 Justin Caruso, "CNN's Brian Stelter on Jussie Smollett: 'We May Never Know What Really Happened,'" Breitbart, March 26, 2019, https://www.breitbart .com/the-media/2019/03/26/cnns-brian-stelter-on-jussie-smollett-we-may -never-really-know-what-happened/.

128 Joe Otterson, "Jussie Smollett Will Not Return to 'Empire,' Lee Daniels Says," *Variety*, June 4, 2019, https://variety.com/2019/tv/news/jussie-smollett -empire-season-6-1203232805/.

129 "Jussie Smollett Pleads Not Guilty to New Charges," NBC 5 Chicago, February 24, 2020, https://www.nbcchicago.com/news/local/jussie-smollett-to-appear -in-court-in-chicago-for-arraignment-on-new-charges/2224644/.

130 John Nolte, "A History of the Woke Taliban's 'Noose' Hoaxes," Breitbart, June 24, 2020, https://www.breitbart.com/politics/2020/06/24/nolte-a-history -of-the-woke-talibans-noose-hoaxes/.

131 Richie Duchon, " 'Nooses' Found Hanging on University of Delaware Campus Were Lanterns," NBC News, September 22, 2015, https://www.nbcnews.com /news/us-news/nooses-found-hanging-tree-university-delaware-campus -n432041.

132 Tom Ciccotta, "Depaul Students Traumatized by Pro-Trump Message, Rope Found After Milo Visit," Breitbart, June 1, 2016, https://www.breitbart.com /social-justice/2016/06/01/depaul-students-traumatized-by-pro-trump-mes sage-rope-found-after-milo-visit/.

133 Tom Ciccotta, "University of Maryland Police Investigate Discarded Plastic Wrap as a 'Hate-Bias' Incident," Breitbart, June 28, 2017, https://www.breit bart.com/tech/2017/06/28/university-of-maryland-police-investigate-dis carded-plastic-wrap-as-a-hate-bias-incident/.

134 Christina Sturdivant, "Police Say Reported Noose in Ivy City Was Rope Used for Moving Equipment," *DCist*, August 9, 2017, https://dcist.com/story/17/08 /09/reported-ivy-city-noose/.

135 " 'Nooses' in Oakland Park Were Exercise Aids, Man Says," Associated Press, June 18, 2020, https://www.usnews.com/news/politics/articles/2020-06-18 /nooses-in-oakland-park-were-exercise-aids-man-says.

136 Joel B. Pollak, "Oakland Investigates Exercise Ropes in Trees as 'Hate Crime'; 'Intentions Do Not Matter,'" Breitbart, June 19, 2020, https://www.breitbart .com/politics/2020/06/19/oakland-investigates-exercise-ropes-in-trees-as -hate-crime-intentions-do-not-matter/.

137 Jeff Poor, "Nascar: Noose Found in Black Driver Bubba Wallace's Garage Still at Talladega," Breitbart, June 21, 2020, https://www.breitbart.com/sports/2020 /06/21/nascar-noose-found-in-black-driver-bubba-wallaces-garage-stall-at -talladega/.

138 Juliet Macur, "Bubba Wallace Thankful for Flag Ban, but NASCAR's Fans Might Not Be," *New York Times*, June 13, 2020, https://www.nytimes.com

/2020/06/13/sports/bubba-wallace-nascar-confederate-flag.html; Tadd Hais-lop, "Bubba Wallace's Black Lives Matter Car: Why He Changed No. 43 Paint Scheme for the Martinsville Race," *Sporting News,* June 10, 2020, https://www .sportingnews.com/us/nascar/news/bubba-wallaces-black-lives-matter-car -paint-scheme-martinsville/kwriho0g7ov516p1oo4g4alyq; "Bubba Wallace Wants Confederate Flags Removed from NASCAR Tracks," ESPN, June 9, 2020, https://www.espn.com/racing/nascar/story/_/id/29287025/bubba-wal lace-wants-confederate-flags-removed-nascar-tracks.

139 Dylan Gwinn, "'No Hate Crime': FBI Determines 'Noose' in Bubba Wallace's Garage to Be a Rope Handle," Breitbart, June 23, 2020, https://www.breit bart.com/sports/2020/06/23/no-hate-crime-fbi-determines-noose-in-bubba -wallaces-garage-to-be-a-rope-handle/.

140 John Nolte, "Bubba Wallace Continues to Insist 'It's a Noose!'" Breitbart, June 24, 2020, https://www.breitbart.com/politics/2020/06/24/nolte-bubba -wallace-continues-to-insist-its-a-noose/.

141 Milo, "There Have Been over 100 Hate Crime Hoaxes in the Past Decade," Breitbart, May 2, 2016, https://www.breitbart.com/social-justice/2016/05/02 /hate-crime-hoaxes-growing-epidemic/.

142 Jennifer Kabbany, "Here Are 50 Campus Hate Crime Hoaxes Since 2012," RealClearEducation, February 20, 2019, https://www.realcleareducation.com /2019/02/20/here_are_50_campus_hate-crime_hoaxes_since_2012_46850 .html.

143 Darren Samuelsohn, "Could Trump Be Impeached Shortly After He Takes Office?" *Politico,* April 17, 2016, https://www.politico.com/magazine/story /2016/04/donald-trump-2016-impeachment-213817.

144 Matea Gold, "The Campaign to Impeach President Trump Has Begun," *Wash-ington Post,* January 20, 2017, https://www.washingtonpost.com/news/post -politics/wp/2017/01/20/the-campaign-to-impeach-president-trump-has -begun/.

145 J. Edward Moreno, "U.S. Rep. Al Green Tried for Two Years to Impeach Donald Trump. Is That Hurting Democrats Now?" *Texas Tribune,* December 10, 2019, https://www.texastribune.org/2019/12/10/al-green-pushed-impeachment -years-ago-hurting-democrats-now/.

146 Haris Alic, "Hunter Biden Admits Father's Position Helped Secure $83K Per Month Burisma Role: 'It's a Swamp in Many Ways,'" Breitbart, October 15, 2019, https://www.breitbart.com/politics/2019/10/15/hunter-biden-admits -fathers-position-helped-secure-83k-per-month-burisma-role-its-a-swamp -in-many-ways/.

147 Robert Kraychik, "'The Biden Five': The Definitive Breakdown of One of America's Most Corrupt Families," Breitbart, October 28, 2020, https://www .breitbart.com/clips/2020/10/28/the-biden-five-the-definitive-breakdown-of -one-of-americas-most-corrupt-families/.

148 Tim Hains, "FLASHBACK, 2018: Joe Biden Brags at CFR Meeting About Withholding Aid to Ukraine to Force Firing of Prosecutor," RealClearPoli-

tics, September 27, 2019, https://www.realclearpolitics.com/video/2019/09/27/flashback_2018_joe_biden_brags_at_cfr_meeting_about_withholding_aid_to_ukraine_to_force_firing_of_prosecutor.html.

149 Melanie Arter, "Trump to Ukraine: 'There's a Lot of Talk About Biden's Son, That Biden Stopped the Prosecution,'" Media Research Center, September 25, 2019, https://www.cnsnews.com/news/article/melanie-arter/trump-ukraine-theres-lot-talk-about-bidens-son-biden-stopped-prosecution.

150 Olivia Rubin, "White House Official Ordered Aid to Ukraine Be Withheld 91 Minutes After Trump Call with Ukraine President, Documents Show," ABC News, December 22, 2019, https://abcnews.go.com/Politics/trump-admin-forced-turn-ukraine-aid-documents/story?id=67869710.

151 "Whistleblower Filed Complaint Despite Only Hearing About Trump-Zelensky Call Secondhand. Their Account of It Is Completely Accurate," Week, September 26, 2019, https://theweek.com/speedreads/867931/whistleblower-filed-complaint-despite-only-hearing-about-trumpzelensky-call-secondhand-account-completely-accurate.

152 Kristina Wong, "RealClear Investigations Suggests 'Whistleblower' Likely 33-Year-Old CIA Analyst Eric Ciaramella," Breitbart, October 30, 2019, https://www.breitbart.com/politics/2019/10/30/realclear-investigations-suggests-whistleblower-likely-33-year-old-cia-analyst-eric-ciaramella/.

153 Joel B. Pollak, "Fox News: IG Found 'Whistleblower' Had 'Political Bias' in Favor of Trump 2020 Rival," Breitbart, September 24, 2019, https://www.breitbart.com/politics/2019/09/24/fox-news-ig-found-whistleblower-had-political-bias-in-favor-of-trump-2020-rival/.

154 Zachary B. Wolf and Curt Merrill, "The Whistleblower Complaint, Annotated," CNN, September 26, 2019, https://www.cnn.com/interactive/2019/09/politics/whistleblower-complaint-annotated/.

155 Sean Davis, "Intel Community Secretly Gutted Requirement of First-Hand Whistleblower Knowledge," Federalist, September 27, 2019, https://thefederalist.com/2019/09/27/intel-community-secretly-gutted-requirement-of-first-hand-whistleblower-knowledge/.

156 ForAmerica (@ForAmerica), "Ladies and gentlemen, JIM. JORDAN. GAME. OVER . . . ," Twitter, November 13, 2019, 10:42 a.m., https://twitter.com/ForAmerica/status/1194686899744575488.

157 Joshua Caplan, "Volodomyr Zelensky: I Never Talked to Trump About 'Position of a Quid Pro Quo,'" Breitbart, December 2, 2019, https://www.breitbart.com/politics/2019/12/02/volodomyr-zelensky-i-never-talked-to-trump-about-position-of-a-quid-pro-quo/.

158 "The Real Bombshell: 'I Want Nothing. I Want Nothing. I Want No Quid Pro Quo,'" Rush Limbaugh Show, November 20, 2019, https://www.rushlimbaugh.com/daily/2019/11/20/the-real-bombshell-i-want-nothing-from-ukraine-no-quid-pro-quo/.

159 Edwin Mora, "Media, Dems Moving Away from July 25 Call: Quid Pro Quo

'Evolved over Time,' " Breitbart, October 28, 2019, https://www.breitbart.com /politics/2019/10/28/media-dems-moving-away-from-july-25-call-quid-pro -quo-evolved-over-time/.

160 John Nolte, "No Legitimate Media Would Accept Adam Schiff's Impeachment Lies and Secrecy," Breitbart, October 8, 2019, https://www.breitbart.com /politics/2019/10/08/nolte-no-legitimate-media-would-accept-adam-schiffs -impeachment-lies-and-secrecy/.

161 Kristina Wong, "Adam Schiff Performs Fake Conversation Between Trump and Ukraine President," Breitbart, September 26, 2019, https://www.breitbart .com/politics/2019/09/26/adam-schiff-performs-fake-conversation-between -trump-and-ukraine-president/.

162 Joel B. Pollak, "Adam Schiff Tries to Make Impeachment About 'Russia Collusion' Hoax," Breitbart, January 22, 2020, https://www.breitbart.com/politics /2020/01/22/adam-schiff-tries-to-make-impeachment-about-russia-collu sion-hoax/.

163 Hannah Bleau, "Fake News: CNN Analyst Makes Up Conversation Between Republican Senators on Impeachment," Breitbart, January 22, 2020, https:// www.breitbart.com/politics/2020/01/22/cnn-analyst-makes-up-conversation -between-republican-senators/.

164 John Nolte, "Embattled CNN Fails to Attract One Million Viewers During Impeachment Month," Breitbart, November 27, 2019, https://www.breitbart .com/the-media/2019/11/27/nolte-embattled-cnn-fails-to-attract-one-mil lion-viewers-during-impeachment-month/.

165 Joel B. Pollack, "For Mainstream Media, Everything About Impeaching Trump Has Been 'Historic,' " Breitbart, December 18, 2019, https://www.breit bart.com/the-media/2019/12/18/for-mainstream-media-everything-about -impeaching-trump-has-been-historic/.

166 Ibid.; Susan B. Glasser, "The Trumperdammerung Is a Fitting End to 2020," New Yorker, December 29, 2020, https://www.newyorker.com/news/letter -from-trumps-washington/the-trumperdammerung-is-a-fitting-end-to -2020; Dave Barry, "Dave Barry's Year in Review 2020," Washington Post Magazine, December 27, 2020, https://www.washingtonpost.com/magazine/2020 /12/27/dave-barrys-year-review-2020/?arc404=true.

167 "Read the Articles of Impeachment Against President Trump," New York Times, last updated December 13, 2019, https://www.nytimes.com/interactive /2019/12/10/us/politics/articles-impeachment-document-pdf.html.

168 Ralph Ketcham, "James Madison: The Unimperial President," Virginia Quarterly Review, Winter 1978, https://www.vqronline.org/essay/james-madison -unimperial-president; Nat Hentoff, "James Madison Warned of Abuse of Power," Arizona Daily Sun, January 28, 2006, https://azdailysun.com/james -madison-warned-of-abuse-of-power/article_bfde8694-63cf-5e22-a6a5 -b253e79fbf4a.html.

169 Charlie Spiering, "Trump Campaign Manager Rips Washington Post Report-

ers Celebrating 'Merry Impeachmas,'" Breitbart, December 18, 2019, https://www.breitbart.com/the-media/2019/12/18/trump-campaign-manager-rips-washington-post-reporters-celebrating-merry-impeachmas/.

170 John Nolte, "Washpost's Rachael Bade Says Her 'Merry Impeachmas' Celebration Wasn't What Everyone Knows It Was," Breitbart, December 19, 2019, https://www.breitbart.com/the-media/2019/12/19/nolte-washposts-rachael-bade-says-her-merry-impeachmas-celebration-wasnt-what-everyone-knows-it-was/.

171 John Nolte, "ABC News Forced to Correct 'Bombshell' About Trump's Ukraine Call," Breitbart, September 26, 2019, https://www.breitbart.com/the-media/2019/09/26/nolte-abc-news-forced-to-correct-bombshell-about-trumps-ukraine-call/.

172 Patrick Reevell and Lucien Bruggeman, "Ukrainians Understood Biden Probe Was Condition for Trump-Zelenskiy Talks, Says Former Ukrainian Adviser," ABC News, September 25, 2019, https://abcnews.go.com/Politics/ukrainians-understood-biden-probe-condition-trump-zelenskiy-phone/story?id=65863043.

173 Mike Brest, "Jake Tapper Accuses Jim Jordan of Spreading 'Wild Allegations' Against Hunter Biden," Washington Examiner, September 29, 2019, https://www.washingtonexaminer.com/news/jake-tapper-accuses-jim-jordan-of-spreading-wild-allegations-against-hunter-biden.

174 John Solomon, "These Once-Secret Memos Cast Doubt on Joe Biden's Ukraine Story," Hill, September 26, 2019, https://thehill.com/opinion/campaign/463307-solomon-these-once-secret-memos-cast-doubt-on-joe-bidens-ukraine-story.

175 Paul Callan, "How a Trump Impeachment Could Lead to a Pelosi Presidency," CNN, October 31, 2019, https://edition.cnn.com/2019/10/30/opinions/25th-amendment-impeachment-opinion-callan/index.html.

176 Pam Key, "FNC's Wallace: There Is 'Meat on the Bones' of Trump Impeachment Inquiry," Breitbart, September 24, 2019, https://www.breitbart.com/clips/2019/09/24/fncs-wallace-there-is-meat-on-the-bones-of-trump-impeachment-inquiry/.

177 Allum Bokhari, "YouTube 'Error' Takes Breitbart Impeachment Stream Offline," Breitbart, January 23, 2020, https://www.breitbart.com/politics/2020/01/23/youtube-error-takes-breitbart-impeachment-stream-offline/.

178 Allum Bokhari, "Google Censors the Congressional Record," Breitbart, February 4, 2020, https://www.breitbart.com/tech/2020/02/04/google-censors-the-congressional-record/.

179 Allum Bokhari, "Facebook Blacklists Conservative News Organizations with 3.4 Million Followers," Breitbart, November 13, 2019, https://www.breitbart.com/tech/2019/11/13/facebook-blacklists-conservative-news-organization-with-3-4-million-followers/.

180 Joel B. Pollak, "Nancy Pelosi Uses More than a Dozen Commemorative Pens to Sign 'Sad' Articles of Impeachment," Breitbart, January 15, 2020, https://

www.breitbart.com/politics/2020/01/15/nancy-pelosi-uses-more-than-a-dozen-commemorative-pens-to-sign-sad-articles-of-impeachment/.

181 James Risen, "Joe Biden, His Son and the Case Against a Ukrainian Oligarch," *New York Times*, December 8, 2015, https://www.nytimes.com/2015/12/09/world/europe/corruption-ukraine-joe-biden-son-hunter-biden-ties.html; "Joe Biden Lectures Ukraine," *New York Times*, December 11, 2015, https://www.nytimes.com/2015/12/12/opinion/joe-biden-lectures-ukraine.html; Helene Cooper, "Biden's Son 'Embarrassed' over Navy Ouster," *New York Times*, October 16, 2014, https://www.nytimes.com/2014/10/17/us/bidens-son-embarrassed-over-navy-ouster.html; Adam Taylor, "Hunter Biden's New Job at a Ukrainian Gas Company Is a Problem for U.S. Soft Power," *Washington Post*, May 14, 2014, https://www.washingtonpost.com/news/worldviews/wp/2014/05/14/hunter-bidens-new-job-at-a-ukrainian-gas-company-is-a-problem-for-u-s-soft-power/; Katie Zezima and Missy Ryan, "Biden's Son Discharged from Navy After Positive Cocaine Test," *Washington Post*, October 16, 2014, https://www.washingtonpost.com/news/post-politics/wp/2014/10/16/report-bidens-son-discharged-from-navy-after-positive-cocaine-test/.

182 James Risen, "I Wrote About the Bidens and Ukraine Years Ago. Then the Right-Wing Spin Machine Turned the Story Upside Down," *Intercept*, September 25, 2019, https://theintercept.com/2019/09/25/i-wrote-about-the-bidens-and-ukraine-years-ago-then-the-right-wing-spin-machine-turned-the-story-upside-down/.

183 Adam Entous, "Will Hunter Biden Jeopardize His Father's Campaign?" *New Yorker*, July 1, 2019, https://www.newyorker.com/magazine/2019/07/08/will-hunter-biden-jeopardize-his-fathers-campaign.

184 Andrew Duehren and Dustin Volz, "Hunter Biden's Ukraine Work Raised Concerns with Obama Officials, GOP-Led Probe Confirms," *Wall Street Journal*, last updated September 23, 2020, https://www.wsj.com/articles/republican-probe-finds-hunter-bidens-ukraine-work-raised-concerns-with-obama-officials-11600859178.

185 John Hudson, Rachael Bade, and Matt Viser, "Diplomat Tells Investigators He Raised Alarms in 2015 About Hunter Biden's Ukraine Work but Was Rebuffed," *Washington Post*, October 18, 2019, https://www.washingtonpost.com/politics/diplomat-tells-investigators-he-raised-alarms-in-2015-about-hunter-bidens-ukraine-work-but-was-rebuffed/2019/10/18/81e35be9-4f5a-4048-8520-0baabb18ab63_story.html.

186 Dan Mangan, "'You're a Damn Liar, Man!' – Joe Biden Blasts Iowa Voter, Calls Him 'Fat' After Man Repeats Ukraine Smear," CNBC, December 5, 2019, https://www.cnbc.com/2019/12/05/biden-calls-iowa-voter-damn-liar-and-fat-after-ukraine-accusation.html.

187 Sarah Chayes, "Hunter Biden's Perfectly Legal, Socially Acceptable Corruption," *Atlantic*, September 27, 2019, https://www.theatlantic.com/ideas/archive/2019/09/hunter-bidens-legal-socially-acceptable-corruption/598804/.

188 Joel B. Pollack, "Democrats Pushed Impeachment While Coronavirus Spread," Breitbart, March 13, 2020, https://www.breitbart.com/politics/2020/03/13 /pollak-democrats-pushed-impeachment-while-coronavirus-spread/.

189 Joel B. Pollak, "Democrats Fail to Mention Impeachment During Convention," Breitbart, August 23, 2020, https://www.breitbart.com/2020-election /2020/08/23/democrats-fail-to-mention-impeachment-during-convention/.

190 Joe Garofoli, "Remember Trump's Impeachment? Democrats Aren't Going There at Convention," *San Francisco Chronicle*, August 18, 2020, https://www .sfchronicle.com/politics/article/Remember-Trump-s-impeachment-Demo crats-15490886.php.

Chapter 2: Meet the Press

1 "Jennifer Brown, Jacob Tapper," *New York Times*, September 3, 2006, https:// www.nytimes.com/2006/09/03/fashion/weddings/03brown.html.

2 John Nolte, "CNN's Jim Sciutto Busted for Two Fake News Scoops in One Week," Breitbart, August 24, 2018, https://www.breitbart.com/politics/2018/08 /24/nolte-cnns-jim-sciutto-busted-for-two-fake-news-scoops-in-one-week/.

3 Hannah Bleau, "The Year of Fredo: Chris Cuomo's 7 Embarrassing 2019 Moments," Breitbart, December 30, 2019, https://www.breitbart.com/poli tics/2019/12/30/the-year-of-fredo-chris-cuomos-7-embarrassing-2019 -moments/.

4 Michael M. Grynbaum, "CNN Moves Chris Cuomo to Prime Time," *New York Times*, March 14, 2018, https://www.nytimes.com/2018/03/14/business /media/chris-cuomo-cnn.html?mtrref=undefined.

5 John Nolte, "CNN's Chris Cuomo Defends Left-Wing Terrorist Group Antifa as 'Good Cause,'" Breitbart, on Internet Archive, April 30, 2019, https://www .breitbart.com/the-media/2019/04/30/nolte-cnns-chris-cuomo-defends-left -wing-terrorist-group-antifa-as-good-cause/ (the screenshot of the site was captured on February 5, 2021); Christopher C. Cuomo (@ChrisCuomo), "Let's not forget," Twitter, August 16, 2017, 6:59 a.m., https://twitter.com /ChrisCuomo/status/897820041273626626.

6 John Nolte, "Watch CNN's Chris Cuomo Encourage More Riots in Democrat -Run Cities," Breitbart, June 3, 2020, https://www.breitbart.com/the-media /2020/06/03/nolte-watch-cnns-chris-cuomo-encourage-more-riots-in-dem ocrat-run-cities/.

7 John Nolte, "CNN Stages Chris Cuomo's Phony Exit from Basement Quaran-tine," Breitbart, April 21, 2020, https://www.breitbart.com/the-media/2020/04 /21/nolte-cnn-stages-chris-cuomos-phony-exit-from-basement-quarantine/.

8 Jeff Poor, "Watch: FNC's Carlson Exposes CNN's Cuomo Hypocrisy on Masks," Breitbart, October 22, 2020, https://www.breitbart.com/clips/2020/10 /22/watch-fncs-carlson-exposes-cnns-cuomo-hypocrisy-on-masks/.

9 Beth DeFalco, "CNN President Jeff Zucker's Teenage Son Resigns from Cushy Consulting Gig as 'Millennial Adviser' at Cory Booker Start-up Waywire—

Twitter Critics Blast Hire as 'Gross Nepotism Alert,'" *New York Post*, August 8, 2013, https://nypost.com/2013/08/08/cnn-president-jeff-zuckers-teenage-son-resigns-from-cushy-consulting-gig-as-millennial-adviser-at-cory-booker-start-up-waywire-twitter-critics-blast-hire-as-gross-nepotism-alert/.

10 "Drake Makes Huge Fee for Party Appearance," *Elle*, May 9, 2011, https://www.ellecanada.com/culture/music/drake-makes-huge-fee-for-party-appearance#:~:text=Drake%20made%20%24250%2C000%20for%20one,to%20appear%20from%20Kanye%20West.&text=Drake%20made%20%24250%2C000%20performing%20at,Kanye%20West's%20%241%20millio.

11 "Virginia Moseley," CNN, profile, accessed February 11, 2021, https://www.cnn.com/profiles/virginia-moseley-profile.

12 "Volunteer Fundraisers," Biden Harris, accessed February 11, 2021, https://joebiden.com/asmfr200830jkl/; "Members of the Biden Institute Policy Advisory Board," Biden School of Public Policy and Administration, accessed February 11, 2021, https://www.bidenschool.udel.edu/bideninstitute/Documents/Biden%20Institute%20Policy%20Advisory%20Board.pdf.

13 "WikiLeaks Emails Show Clinton Camp Tipped Off on CNN Poll—and Even More Moderator Questions," Fox News, November 8, 2016, https://www.foxnews.com/politics/wikileaks-emails-show-clinton-camp-tipped-off-on-cnn-poll-and-even-more-moderator-questions.

14 Emma Powys Maurice, "Joe Biden Names Karine Jean-Pierre, a Proud Black Lesbian Immigrant, As Deputy White House Press Secretary," Yahoo News, November 30, 2020, https://uk.news.yahoo.com/joe-biden-names-karine-jean-111519643.html.

15 Brian Flood, "Critics Call Out Revolving Door of Ex-Pundits Jumping from Liberal Networks to Biden Administration," Fox News, November 23, 2020, https://www.foxnews.com/media/biden-administration-pundits-liberal-news-organizations.

16 Ted Johnson, "Obama's 'Bundlers,'" *Variety*, November 13, 2007, https://variety.com/2007/biz/opinion/obamas-bundlers-44679/.

17 Alex Weprin, "Hollywood Heavyweights Among Biden Campaign Bundlers," *Hollywood Reporter*, November 1, 2020, https://www.hollywoodreporter.com/news/hollywood-heavyweights-among-biden-campaign-bundlers.

18 Adam Kredo, "U.S. Ambassador, Obama Holdover, Signals Disdain for Representing Trump," *Washington Free Beacon*, May 15, 2017, https://freebeacon.com/national-security/u-s-ambassador-obama-holdover-signals-disdain-representing-trump/; Johnson, "Obama's 'Bundlers.'"

19 "Who We Are," Maverick Strategies and Mail, on Internet Archive, accessed February 11, 2021, http://web.archive.org/web/20100722040443/http://www.maverickstrat.com/index.php?option=com_content&task=blogsection&id=1&Itemid=6 (the screenshot of the site was captured July 22, 2010).

20 Opensecrets.org, "Vendor/Recipient: Maverick Strategies & Mail," 2020, accessed February 11, 2021, https://www.opensecrets.org/campaign-expenditures/vendor?year=2016&vendor=Maverick%20Strategies%20%26%20Mail.

21 Ian Mohr, "Debate Moderator Chuck Todd Was Amy Klobuchar's Landlord in Arlington," *Page Six*, February 20, 2020, https://pagesix.com/2020/02/20 /debate-moderator-chuck-todd-was-amy-klobuchars-landlord-in-arlington/.

22 Dylan Byers, "BuzzFeed News Editor Ben Smith to Join New York Times as Media Columnist," NBC News, January 28, 2020, https://www.nbcnews.com /news/all/buzzfeed-editor-ben-smith-join-new-york-times-media-columnist -n1124796.

23 Ben Smith, "Is Ronan Farrow Too Good to Be True?" *New York Times*, May 17, 2020, https://www.nytimes.com/2020/05/17/business/media/ronan-farrow.html.

24 Brian Flood, "NBC Raises Eyebrows over $400 Million Relationship with BuzzFeed," Fox News, January 22, 2019, https://www.foxnews.com/entertain ment/nbc-raises-eyebrows-over-400-million-relationship-with-buzzfeed.

25 Joel B. Pollak, "The Stunning Synergy of the Atlantic's Anonymous Attack on Trump," Breitbart, September 4, 2020, https://www.breitbart.com/poli tics/2020/09/04/pollak-the-stunning-synergy-of-the-atlantics-anonymous -attack-on-president-donald-trump/.

26 UPI, "U.S. Economy Adds 1.4 Million Jobs in August; Unemployment at 8.4%," Breitbart, September 4, 2020, https://www.breitbart.com/news/u-s -economy-adds-1-4-million-jobs-in-august-unemployment-at-8-4/.

27 Jennifer Epstein (@jeneps), "The Biden Campaign is holding a press call this morning . . . ," Twitter, September 4, 2020, 5:30 a.m., https://twitter.com/jen eps/status/1301860171262689280.

28 Haris Alic, " 'Deplorable': Joe Biden Chides Trump over 'The Atlantic' Story," Breitbart, September 4, 2020, https://www.breitbart.com/2020-election/2020 /09/04/deplorable-joe-biden-chides-trump-atlantic-story/.

29 Peter Alexander (@PeterAlexander), "NEW: "When my son volunteered and joined the United States military . . . ," Twitter, September 4, 2020, https:// twitter.com/PeterAlexander/status/1301928728679784448?ref_src=twsrc% 5Etfw%7Ctwcamp%5Etweetembed%7Ctwterm%5E1301928728679784448 %7Ctwgr%5E%7Ctwcon%5Es1_&ref_url=https%3A%2F%2Fwww.breitbart .com%2Fclips%2F2020%2F09%2F04%2Fnbcs-peter-alexander-.

30 Joseph Wulfsohn, "Reporters Blasted for 'Shamefully Embarrassing' Softball Questions at Rare Biden Press Conference," Fox News, September 4, 2020, https:// www.foxnews.com/media/biden-press-conference-shamefully-embarrass ing-questions-reporters; Robert Kraychik, "NBC's Peter Alexander Asks Trump to 'Apologize' to Veterans for Atlantic Story; Whether True or Not, It 'Reso- nates,' " Breitbart, September 4, 2020, https://www.breitbart.com/clips/2020/09 /04/nbcs-peter-alexander-asks-trump-apologize-veterans-atlantic-story -whether-true-not-resonates/

31 Jeremy Barr, "Jennifer Griffin Defended by Fox News Colleagues After Trump Twitter Attack over Her Confirmation of Atlantic Reporting," *Seattle Times*, September 5, 2020, https://www.seattletimes.com/nation-world/jennifer-grif fin-defended-by-fox-news-colleagues-after-trump-twitter-attack-over-her -confirmation-of-atlantic-reporting/.

32 Techno Fog (@Techno_Fog), "On that Atlantic Story . . .," Twitter, September 3, 2020, 9:37 p.m., https://twitter.com/Techno_Fog/status/1301741080577 298437.

33 Matthew Boyle, "Exclusive—U.S. Ambassador to France Denies the Atlantic Story: 'Potus Has Never Denigrated Any Member of U.S. Military,'" Breitbart, September 7, 2020, https://www.breitbart.com/politics/2020/09/07/u -s-ambassador-france-denies-atlantic-story-potus-never-denigrated-any -member-us-military/.

34 Charlie Spiering, "On the Record: Sources Traveling with Donald Trump Deny 'The Atlantic' Story," Breitbart, September 4, 2020, https://www.breit bart.com/politics/2020/09/04/on-record-sources-traveling-donald-trump -deny-atlantic-story/.

35 Jeff Poor, "Bolton: The Atlantic Report Claiming Trump Disparaged Military 'Simply False,'" Breitbart, September 8, 2020, https://www.breitbart.com/clips /2020/09/08/bolton-the-atlantic-report-claiming-trump-disparaged-military -simply-false/.

36 Jake Tapper, "Former White House Chief of Staff Tells Friends That Trump 'Is the Most Flawed Person' He's Ever Met," CNN Politics, October 16, 2020, https://www.cnn.com/2020/10/16/politics/donald-trump-criticism-from -former-administration-officials/index.html; John Parkinson, "Former Trump Chief of Staff John Kelly to Voters: 'Look Harder' at Who You Elect," ABC News, June 5, 2020, https://abcnews.go.com/Politics/trump-chief-staff-john -kelly—harder-elect/story?id=71093630; Jake Tapper, "John Kelly Blasts Trump for Not Helping with the Transition: 'The Downside to Not Doing So Could Be Catastrophic,'" CNN Politics, November 14, 2020, https://www.cnn .com/2020/11/13/politics/john-kelly-transition/index.html.

37 "Robert Michael Kelly," Arlington National Cemetery website, November 10, 2010, http://www.arlingtoncemetery.net/rmkelly.htm.

38 Mimi Montgomery, "The Atlantic Has Added 300,000 New Subscriptions in the Last Year," Washingtonian, September 10, 2020, https://www.washingto nian.com/2020/09/10/the-atlantic-has-added-300000-new-subscriptions-in -the-last-year/; Kathryn Lundstrom, "The Atlantic's Jeffrey Goldberg on Subscription Strategy, Editorial Values and Interviewing Obama," Adweek, December 9, 2020, https://www.adweek.com/media/the-atlantics-jeffrey-goldberg -on-subscription-strategy-editorial-values-and-interviewing-obama/.

39 Kerry Flynn, "The Atlantic Gained 20,000 Subscribers After Trump Dismissed It as a 'Dying' Magazine," CNN Business, September 9, 2020, https://www.cnn .com/2020/09/09/media/the-atlantic-subscriptions/index.html.

40 Joel B. Pollak, "Fact Check: Obama Repeats Debunked Atlantic 'Suckers' Story," Breitbart, October 21, 2020, https://www.breitbart.com/2020-election /2020/10/21/fact-check-obama-repeats-debunked-atlantic-suckers-story/.

41 Thomas D. Williams, Ph.D., "Atlantic Fake News: Fetal Heartbeats Are 'Imaginary,'" Breitbart, January 25, 2017, https://www.breitbart.com/politics/2017 /01/25/atlantic-fake-news-fetal-heartbeats-imaginary/.

42 Kyle Morris, "25 Times 'The Atlantic' Used Single Anonymous Sources to Smear Trump Family," Breitbart, September 10, 2019, https://www.breitbart .com/politics/2019/09/10/25-times-the-atlantic-used-single-anonymous -sources-to-smear-trump-family/.

43 John Nolte, "Atlantic Mag Hopes Coronavirus Leads America to China-Style Speech Censorship," Breitbart, April 27, 2020, https://www.breitbart.com/the -media/2020/04/27/nolte-atlantic-mag-hopes-coronavirus-leads-america-to -china-style-speech-censorship/.

44 "Freedom on the Net 2020," Freedom House, accessed February 11, 2021, https://freedomhouse.org/country/china/freedom-net/2020.

45 Paige Leskin, "These Are the 11 Richest Women in Tech," Business Insider, February 5, 2019, https://www.businessinsider.com/richest-women-in-tech -according-to-forbes-list-2019-1#1-laurene-powell-jobs-185-billion-11.

46 Aaron Klein, "Green New Deal, Healthcare for Illegals: Soros-Funded Groups Push Dems to Use Virus to Achieve Progressive Wish List," Breitbart, May 5, 2020, https://www.breitbart.com/politics/2020/05/05/green-new-deal -healthcare-for-illegals-soros-funded-groups-push-dems-to-use-virus-to -achieve-progressive-wish-list/; Aaron Klein, "George Soros Groups Pushing Democrat Scheme for Mail-in Voting," Breitbart, April 3, 2020, https://www .breitbart.com/politics/2020/04/03/george-soros-groups-pushing-democrat -scheme-mail-voting/.

47 "Our Team," Emerson Collective, accessed February 11, 2021, https://www .emersoncollective.com/our-team/.

48 Gillian B. White, "Emerson Collective Acquires Majority Stake in The Atlantic," Atlantic, July 28, 2017, https://www.theatlantic.com/business/ar chive/2017/07/emerson-collective-atlantic-coalition/535215/.

49 "Our Team," Emerson Collective, accessed March 11, 2021, https://www .emersoncollective.com/our-team/.

50 OpenSecrets.org, "Emerson Collective: Contributions," accessed March 11, 2021, https://www.opensecrets.org/orgs/emerson-collective/totals?id=D000068512.

51 Kristin Stoller, "The Top 10 Richest Women in the World," Forbes, accessed February 11, 2021, https://www.forbes.com/sites/kristinstoller/2020/04/07/the-top -10-richest-women-in-the-world-2020/?sh=710b4eb34776.

52 Kara Swisher, "Laurene Powell Jobs's Emerson Collective Bought Pop-Up Magazine Productions," Vox, November 27, 2018, https://www.vox.com/2018 /11/27/18114661/laurene-powell-jobs-emerson-collective-pop-up-maga zine-productions.

53 Kara Swisher, "Can Laurene Powell Jobs Save Storytelling?" New York Times, November 27, 2018, https://www.nytimes.com/2018/11/27/opinion/laurene -powell-jobs-emerson-pop-up.html.

54 Sara Fischer, "Scoop: Emerson Collective Initial Launch Partner for New NowThis Division," Axios, January 7, 2020, https://www.axios.com/emer son-collective-nowthis-non-profits-media-9bef74ac-925c-4dcf-a588 -269f2c98fe82.html.

55 "Stacey Abrams Fights for a Fair Count in the 2020 Census," Emerson Collective, accessed February 11, 2021, https://www.emersoncollective.com/now this-stacey-abrams-fights-for-a-fair-count-in-the-2020-census/.

56 Eric Newcomer, "Tech Execs Rally Behind Harris as Known Quantity for VP Pick," Bloomberg, August 19, 2020, https://www.bloomberg.com/news/arti cles/2020-08-19/tech-execs-rally-behind-harris-as-known-quantity-for-vp -pick.

57 Elizabeth Weil, "Kamala Harris Takes Her Shot," *Atlantic*, May 2019, https:// www.theatlantic.com/magazine/archive/2019/05/kamala-harris-2020-cam paign/586033/.

58 Emily Jane Fox, "Exclusive: Jim Vandehei and Mike Allen Bring on Washington Insiders to Help Run Axios," *Vanity Fair*, January 3, 2017, https://www .vanityfair.com/news/2017/01/jim-vandehei-and-mike-allen-hire-washing ton-insiders-to-run-axios; "Evan Ryan," Axios, accessed February 11, 2021, https://schedule.sxsw.com/2018/speakers/1937671.

59 Fox, "Exclusive: Jim Vandehei and Mike Allen Bring on Washington Insiders to Help Run Axios."

60 U.S. Office of Government Ethics, Public Financial Disclosure Report for Antony Blinken, accessed February 11, 2021, https://extapps2.oge.gov/201 /Presideñ.nsf/PAS+Index/DB768AE135A5BA8C8525864F008104D6/$FILE /Blinken,%20Antony%20%20final%20278.pdf.

61 Theodore Schleifer, "Tech Billionaires Are Plotting Sweeping, Secret Plans to Boost Joe Biden," *Vox*, May 27, 2020, https://www.vox.com/recode/2020 /5/27/21271157/tech-billionaires-joe-biden-reid-hoffman-laurene-powell -jobs-dustin-moskovitz-eric-schmidt; Jim Rutenberg and Matthew Rosenberg, "Trump Won the Internet. Democrats Are Scrambling to Take It Back," *New York Times*, March 30, 2020, https://www.nytimes.com/2020/03/30/us /politics/democrats-digital-strategy.html; Gabby Deutch, "Opinion: A Website Wanted to Restore Trust in the Media. It's Actually a Political Operation," *Washington Post*, February 6, 2020, https://www.washingtonpost.com/opin ions/2020/02/06/is-it-local-journalism-or-just-local-propaganda/.

62 Joshua Green, "The Left's Plan to Slip Vote-Swaying News into Facebook Feeds," *Bloomberg Businessweek*, November 25, 2019, https://www.bloomberg .com/news/features/2019-11-25/acronym-s-newsrooms-are-a-liberal-digital -spin-on-local-news.

63 Charles Fain Lehman, "Why Is Laurene Powell Jobs Funding Fake News?" *Washington Free Beacon*, June 11, 2020, https://freebeacon.com/media/why-is -laurene-powell-jobs-funding-fake-news/.

64 Michelle Ye Hee Lee, "Network of News Sites Must Register as a Political Committee Due to Democratic Links, Complaint Alleges," *Washington Post*, September 3, 2020, https://www.washingtonpost.com/politics/courier-newsroom -complaint-fec/2020/09/02/afa2305c-ed2e-11ea-ab4e-581edb849379_story .html.

65 Soo Rin Kim, "What to Know About Shadow Inc., the Vendor Behind Iowa

Democrats' Caucus App," ABC News, February 4, 2020, https://abcnews.go.com
/Politics/shadow-vendor-iowa-dems-reporting-app/story?id=68754002.

66 Brianne Pfannenstiel, "Audit Finds National Democratic Party Slowed, Complicated Iowa's Caucus Efforts," *Des Moines Register*, last updated December 14, 2020, https://www.desmoinesregister.com/story/news/politics/2020
/12/12/national-democratic-party-complicated-iowas-caucus-efforts
-dnc/6509514002/.

67 Kristina Wong, "#Mayorcheat Trends After Buttigieg Campaign Is Tied to
Company Behind Iowa Caucus App Failure," Breitbart, February 4, 2020,
https://www.breitbart.com/politics/2020/02/04/mayorcheat-trends-after-but
tigieg-campaign-is-tied-to-company-behind-iowa-caucus-app-failure/.

68 Maggie Astor, "D.N.C. Leader Now Calls for 'Surgical' Recanvass in Iowa," *New
York Times*, February 7, 2020, https://www.nytimes.com/live/2020/iowa-cau
cus-nh-primary-02-06#ap-unable-to-declare-a-winner; Wong, "#Mayorcheat
Trends After Buttigieg Campaign Is Tied to Company Behind Iowa Caucus App
Failure."

Chapter 3: Mob Rule Media: *The New York Times* in the Age of Woke

1 Sydney Ember, "A.G. Sulzberger, 37, to Take Over as New York Times Publisher," *New York Times*, December 14, 2017, https://www.nytimes.com/2017
/12/14/business/media/a-g-sulzberger-new-york-times-publisher.html;
Ian Mason, "5th Generation of Sulzberger Family to Take the Reins at the
New York Times," Breitbart, December 15, 2017, https://www.breitbart.com
/politics/2017/12/15/5th-generation-of-sulzberger-family-to-take-the-reins
-at-the-new-york-times/.

2 Marc Tracy, "Arthur Sulzberger Jr. to Retire as New York Times Company
Chairman," *New York Times*, September 23, 2020, https://www.nytimes.com
/2020/09/23/business/media/arthur-sulzberger-retirement.html.

3 "Board of Directors," *New York Times*, accessed February 11, 2021, https://
www.nytco.com/board-of-directors/.

4 "John Rogers Has Deep Ties to Obama Administration," *Pensions & Investments*, April 15, 2013, https://www.pionline.com/article/20130415/PRINT
/304159974/john-rogers-has-deep-ties-to-obama-administration.

5 Ibid.

6 David Gelles, "Melody Hobson of Ariel Investments: 'Capitalism Needs to
Work for Everyone,'" *New York Times*, July 18, 2019, https://www.nytimes
.com/2019/07/18/business/mellody-hobson-ariel-investments-corner-office
.html?searchResultPosition=5.

7 Azam Ahmed, "Harbinger's Falcone Sells Down Stake in Times Co.," *New
York Times*, November 24, 2010, https://dealbook.nytimes.com/2010/11/24
/harbingers-falcone-sells-down-times-co-stake/.

8 "Philip Falcone and Harbinger Capital Agree to Settlement," U.S. Securities

and Exchange Commission, press release, August 19, 2013, https://www.sec.gov/news/press-release/2013-159.

9 Maureen Farrell, "SEC Bans Phil Falcone from Trading for 5 Years," CNN Business, August 19, 2013, https://money.cnn.com/2013/08/19/investing/phil-falcone-sec/index.html.

10 "Carlos Slim Becomes Top New York Times Shareholder," Reuters, January 14, 2015, https://www.reuters.com/article/us-new-york-times-warrants-carlos-slim/carlos-slim-becomes-top-new-york-times-shareholder-idUSK BN0KN2M820150114.

11 Tae Kim, "Mexican Billionaire Carlos Slim Reportedly Will Cut His Stake in New York Times Nearly in Half," CNBC, December 19, 2017, https://www.cnbc.com/2017/12/19/billionaire-carlos-slim-reportedly-cutting-his-stake-in-new-york-times-roughly-in-half.html.

12 "New York Times Net Worth 2006–2020," Macrotrends, accessed February 11, 2021, https://www.macrotrends.net/stocks/charts/NYT/new-york-times/net-worth.

13 Tony Lee, "Mexican Billionaire, NYT Minority Owner Launches Campaign to Bring Dreamers into US Workforce," Breitbart, August 14, 2014, https://www.breitbart.com/politics/2014/08/14/Mexican-Billionaire-NYT-Minority-Owner-Launching-Campaign-to-Bring-DREAMers-into-US-Workforce/.

14 "America's Test at the Border," New York Times, July 20, 2014, https://www.nytimes.com/2014/07/21/opinion/Americas-Test-Children-at-the-Border.html; John Binder, "NYT: Amnesty Is the 'Only Long-Term Solution,'" Breitbart, March 21, 2017, https://www.breitbart.com/border/2017/03/21/nyt-amnesty-long-term-solution/.

15 Patricia Laya, "Mexico's Richest Man Urges Young U.S. Immigrants into Workforce," Bloomberg, August 13, 2014, https://www.bloomberg.com/news/articles/2014-08-13/mexico-s-richest-man-urges-young-u-s-immigrants-into-workforce.

16 Dolia Estevez, "Is Mexican Billionaire Carlos Slim the New Role Model for Facebook's Mark Zuckerberg?" Forbes, September 8, 2014, https://www.forbes.com/sites/doliaestevez/2014/09/08/is-mexican-billionaire-carlos-slim-the-new-role-model-for-facebooks-mark-zuckerberg/?sh=43a946614b4c.

17 Lucas Matney, "Former Facebook Brand Marketing Head Is New Oculus CMO," TechCrunch, August 31, 2017, https://techcrunch.com/2017/08/31/former-facebook-brand-marketing-head-to-become-new-cmo-at-oculus/.

18 Michael Patrick Leahy, "New York Times Admits It Lied About Crowd Size at Nashville Trump Rally, Corrects After President Calls Them Out," Breitbart, May 30, 2018, https://www.breitbart.com/politics/2018/05/30/new-york-times-admits-it-lied-about-crowd-size-at-nashville-trump-rally-corrects-after-president-calls/.

19 Joel B. Pollak, "Very Fake News: New York Times Revives 'Blood Libel' Against Sarah Palin," Breitbart, June 14, 2017, https://www.breitbart.com

/the-media/2017/06/14/very-very-fake-news-new-york-times-revives-blood
-libel-against-sarah-palin/.

20 Ibid.

21 Joel B. Pollak, "Judge Allows Sarah Palin's Defamation Lawsuit Against New
York Times to Proceed," Breitbart, August 28, 2020, https://www.breitbart
.com/the-media/2020/08/28/judge-allows-sarah-palins-defamation-lawsuit
-against-new-york-times-to-proceed/.

22 Joseph Goldstein, "Alt-Right Gathering Exults in Trump Election with Nazi
-Era Salute," New York Times, November 20, 2016, https://www.nytimes.com
/2016/11/21/us/alt-right-salutes-donald-trump.html?_r=1.

23 Joel B. Pollak, "Fake News: New York Times Falsely Claims Breitbart 'Birther'
Site," Breitbart, November 21, 2016, https://www.breitbart.com/the-media
/2016/11/21/fake-news-new-york-times-joseph-goldstein-falsely-claims
-breitbart-birther/.

24 John Nolte, "Bombshell: 'Washington Post' Confirms Hillary Clinton Started
the Birther Movement," Breitbart, September 26, 2015, https://www.breitbart
.com/politics/2015/09/26/washington-post-confirms-hillary-clinton-started
-the-birther-movement/.

25 Peter Baker, Katie Rogers, David Enrich, and Maggie Haberman, "Trump's
Aggressive Advocacy of Malaria Drug for Treating Coronavirus Divides Medical Community," New York Times, April 6, 2020, https://www.nytimes.com
/2020/04/06/us/politics/coronavirus-trump-malaria-drug.html.

26 Julia Carrie Wong, "Hydroxychloroquine: How an Unproven Drug Became
Trump's Coronavirus 'Miracle Cure,'" Guardian, April 7, 2020, https://www
.theguardian.com/world/2020/apr/06/hydroxychloroquine-trump-corona
virus-drug.

27 Alex Kasprak, "Does Trump Benefit Financially by Promoting Hydroxychloroquine as COVID-19 Treatment?" Snopes, April 7, 2020, https://www
.snopes.com/fact-check/trump-profit-hydroxychloroquine/.

28 Steve Goldstein, "Trump's Personal Stake in the Malaria-Drug Maker Sanofi
Could Be as Small as $99," MarketWatch, April 7, 2020, https://www.market
watch.com/story/trumps-personal-stake-in-the-malaria-drug-maker-sanofi
-could-be-as-small-as-99-2020-04-07.

29 Joseph Wulfsohn, "Reporters Blasted for 'Shamefully Embarrassing' Softball
Questions at Rare Biden Press Conference," Fox News, September 4, 2020,
https://www.foxnews.com/media/biden-press-conference-shamefully-em
barrassing-questions-reporters.

30 https://www.breitbart.com/clips/2020/09/04/nbcs-peter-alexander-asks
-trump-apologize-veterans-atlantic-story-whether-true-not-resonates/.

31 Joe Pompeo, "Is Trump-Whisperer Maggie Haberman Changing the New York
Times?" Vanity Fair, October 5, 2017, https://www.vanityfair.com/news/2017
/10/is-trump-whisperer-maggie-haberman-changing-the-new-york-times.

32 Glenn Greenwald and Lee Fang, "Exclusive: New Email Leak Reveals Clinton Campaign's Cozy Press Relationship," Intercept, October 9, 2016, https://

theintercept.com/2016/10/09/exclusive-new-email-leak-reveals-clinton-cam paigns-cozy-press-relationship/.

33 John Nolte, "5 Reasons Our Lapdog Media Agreed to Hillary's Leash," Breit-bart, July 6, 2015, https://www.breitbart.com/the-media/2015/07/06/5-rea sons-our-lapdog-media-agreed-to-hillarys-leash/.

34 John Nolte, "New York Times' Maggie Haberman Blames Trump for Media's 'Animal' Fake News," Breitbart, May 19, 2018, https://www.breitbart.com/the -media/2018/05/19/nyts-haberman-blames-trump-medias-animal-fake-news/.

35 Maggie Haberman (@maggieNYT), "This is the same thing Trump has done since fall 2015 . . . ," Twitter, May 18, 2018, 6:13 a.m., https://twitter.com/mag gieNYT/status/997465119989878784.

36 Jamie DeRosa (@JamieDeRosa), "The FBI just thwarted a plot by Trump . . . ," Twitter, October 8, 2020, https://twitter.com/realDonaldTrump/status/1314 252606110412806.

37 Joy Pullmann, "With Baseless Claim of 'Digital Backdrop' for Trump, NYT Enters Then Scrubs Bizarre Conspiracy," Federalist, October 9, 2020, https:// thefederalist.com/2020/10/09/with-baseless-claim-of-digital-backdrop-for -trump-nyt-enters-then-scrubs-bizarre-conspiracy/.

38 Trent Baker, "NYT's Haberman: Mattis Resignation an 'Astonishing Rebuke of Trumpism,'" Breitbart, December 21, 2018, https://www.breitbart.com/clips /2018/12/21/nyts-haberman-mattis-resignation-an-astonishing-rebuke-of -trumpism/.

39 Joel B. Pollack, "James Mattis: Joe Biden Must Eliminate 'America First' from U.S. Foreign Policy," Breitbart, November 23, 2020, https://www.breitbart .com/national-security/2020/11/23/james-mattis-joe-biden-must-eliminate -america-first-from-u-s-foreign-policy/.

40 Trent Baker, "NYT's Haberman: 'This Is Certainly the Worst Week' of Trump's Presidency," Breitbart, July 20, 2018, https://www.breitbart.com/clips/2018/07 /20/nyts-haberman-this-is-certainly-worst-week-trumps-presidency/.

41 Mary Margaret Olohan, "Maggie Haberman Floats Baseless Theory About Trump Getting Advance on Job Numbers," Daily Caller, September 5, 2019, https://dailycaller.com/2019/09/05/haberman-trump-jobs/.

42 John Nolte, "NYT's Maggie Haberman Suggests White House Played Pro -Nazi Anthem 'Edelweiss,'" Breitbart, April 19, 2019, https://www.breitbart .com/the-media/2019/04/19/nolte-nyts-maggie-haberman-suggests-white -house-played-pro-nazi-anthem-edelweiss/.

43 Ibid.

44 Hannah Bleau, "Covington Catholic Students Take Legal Action Against Eliz-abeth Warren, Kathy Griffin, and Others," Breitbart, August 3, 2019, https:// www.breitbart.com/politics/2019/08/03/covington-catholic-students-take -legal-action-against-elizabeth-warren-kathy-griffin-and-others/.

45 Zach Haberman's Twitter page, Twitter, accessed February 11, 2021, https:// twitter.com/ZHaberman?ref_src=twsrc%5Egoogle%7Ctwcamp%5Eserp%7C twgr%5Eauthor.

46 "WEDDINGS/CELEBRATIONS; Maggie Haberman, Dareh Gregorian," *New York Times*, November 9, 2003, https://www.nytimes.com/2003/11/09/style/weddings-celebrations-maggie-haberman-dareh-gregorian.html; Dareh Gregorian's Twitter page, Twitter, accessed February 11, 2021, https://twitter.com/darehgregorian.

47 "WEDDINGS/CELEBRATIONS; Maggie Haberman, Dareh Gregorian."

48 "Founders," Aurora Humanitarian Initiative, accessed February 11, 2021, https://auroraprize.com/en/prize/detail/founders.

49 Peter Schweizer, "Uncovering the Russia Ties of Hillary's Campaign Chief," *New York Post*, July 5, 2017, https://nypost.com/2017/07/05/uncovering-the-russia-ties-of-hillarys-campaign-chief/; Jerome Hudson, "Putin-Funded Company John Podesta Received 75,000 Shares from Has Collapsed," Breitbart, July 19, 2017, https://www.breitbart.com/politics/2017/07/19/putin-funded-company-john-podesta-received-75000-shares-collapsed/; Michael Patrick Leahy, "Collusion? Russians Gave $35 Million to Company with John Podesta on Board," Breitbart, April 3, 2019, https://www.breitbart.com/politics/2019/04/03/collusion-russians-gave-35-million-to-company-with-john-podesta-on-board/.

50 "Re: Follow-up Media Call," WikiLeaks, January 14, 2015, https://wikileaks.org/podesta-emails/emailid/7524.

51 "Who We Are," Rubenstein, accessed February 11, 2021, https://rubenstein.com/who-we-are/nancy-haberman-2/; Ken Auletta, "The Fixer," *New Yorker*, February 5, 2007, https://www.newyorker.com/magazine/2007/02/12/the-fixer.

52 Rachael Combe, "Wanna Know What Donald Trump Is Really Thinking? Read Maggie Haberman," *Elle*, May 24, 2017, https://www.elle.com/culture/career-politics/a45485/maggie-haberman-new-york-times-trump-profile/.

53 "Hult Global Case Challenge: Solutions to the Water Crisis," *Business Wire*, April 20, 2011, https://www.businesswire.com/news/home/20110420006349/en/Hult-Global-Case-Challenge-Solutions-to-the-Water-Crisis.

54 Ashley Feinberg, "The New York Times Unites vs. Twitter," *Slate*, August 15, 2019, https://slate.com/news-and-politics/2019/08/new-york-times-meeting-transcript.html.

55 Zach Goldberg, "How the Media Led the Great Racial Awakening," *Tablet Mag*, August 4, 2020, https://www.tabletmag.com/sections/news/articles/media-great-racial-awakening.

56 "Americans' View of Black-White Race Relations Hits a 20-Year Low," *Economist*, September 8, 2020, https://www.economist.com/graphic-detail/2020/09/08/americans-view-of-black-white-race-relations-hits-a-20-year-low.

57 Ibid.

58 Goldberg, "How the Media Led the Great Racial Awakening."

59 Haris Alic, "Exclusive—Another New York Times Editor Made Racist, Anti-Semitic Comments," Breitbart, September 22, 2019, https://www.breitbart.com/the-media/2019/09/22/another-new-york-times-editor-made-racist-anti-semitic-comments/.

60 Matthew Boyle, "'Douche Zest': New York Times Politics Editor Describes What His Newspaper Publishes," Breitbart, August 23, 2019, https://www.breit bart.com/the-media/2019/08/23/douche-zest-new-york-times-politics-editor -describes-what-newspaper-publishes/.

61 Joshua Caplan, "NYT: New Hire Sarah Jeong 'Regrets' Professing Hate for 'Dumbass F*cking White People,'" Breitbart, August 2, 2018, https://www .breitbart.com/the-media/2018/08/02/sarah-jeong-new-york-times-dumb-ss -f-ing-white-people/.

62 Sarah Jeong (@sarahjeong), "Hi all, I have a statement about the tweets that have been going around . . . ," Twitter, August 2, 2018, https://twitter.com /sarahjeong/status/1025050118989332480/.

63 Joe Concha, "Sarah Jeong out at New York Times Editorial Board," Hill, Sep- tember 28, 2019, https://thehill.com/homenews/media/463503-sarah-jeong -out-at-new-york-times-editorial-board.

64 John Cardillo (@johncardillo), "THREAD: WHOA, @nytimes fact checker @jeanuh_ has a nearly decade long history . . . ," Twitter, September 17, 2019, https://twitter.com/johncardillo/status/1174104343752126466.

65 Kyle Morris, "New York Times Publishes Antisemitic, 'Offensive' Cartoon, Fails to Apologize," Breitbart, April 27, 2019, https://www.breitbart.com /politics/2019/04/27/new-york-times-publishes-antisemitic-offensive-car toon-forced-to-apologize/.

66 Matthew Boyle, "Under Fire, New York Times Finally Apologizes for Anti- semitic Cartoon After Days of Failing to Do So," Breitbart, April 28, 2019, https://www.breitbart.com/the-media/2019/04/28/under-fire-new-york -times-finally-apologizes-antisemitic-cartoon-after-days-refusing-do-so/.

67 "Our International Edition Will Stop Publishing Syndicated Cartoons," New York Times, April 29, 2019, https://www.nytimes.com/2019/04/29/reader-cen ter/anti-semitic-cartoon-apology.html.

68 Matthew Boyle, "New York Times Ducks Transparency, Accountability for Antisemitic Cartoon," Breitbart, April 27, 2019, https://www.breitbart.com /the-media/2019/04/27/new-york-times-ducks-transparency-accountability -for-antisemitic-cartoon/.

69 Charles M. Blow, "Exit Polls Point to the Power of White Patriarchy," New York Times, November 4, 2020, https://www.nytimes.com/2020/11/04/opin ion/election-2020-exit-polls.html.

70 Penny Starr, "New York Times: Lawns Are Symbols of Racism and Bad for Global Warming," Breitbart, August 13, 2019, https://www.breitbart.com/the -media/2019/08/13/new-york-times-lawns-are-symbols-of-racism-and-bad-for -global-warming/; Penelope Green, "Do Americans Need Air-Conditioning?" New York Times, July 3, 2019, https://www.nytimes.com/2019/07/03/style/air -conditioning-obsession.html.

71 Michael Goodwin, "The Family That Owns the New York Times Were Slave- holders," New York Post, July 18, 2020, https://nypost.com/2020/07/18/the -family-that-owns-the-new-york-times-were-slaveholders-goodwin/.

72 Nikole Hannah-Jones, "Our Democracy's Founding Ideals Were False When They Were Written. Black Americans Have Fought to Make Them True," *New York Times*, August 14, 2019, https://www.nytimes.com/interactive/2019/08/14/magazine/black-history-american-democracy.html.

73 "The 1619 Project Curriculum," Pulitzer Center, accessed February 12, 2021, https://pulitzercenter.org/lesson-plan-grouping/1619-project-curriculum.

74 "We Respond to the Historians Who Critiqued the 1619 Project," *New York Times*, last updated January 19, 2021, https://www.nytimes.com/2019/12/20/magazine/we-respond-to-the-historians-who-critiqued-the-1619-project.html.

75 Ida Bae Wells (@nhannahjones), "It's a rhetorical question, a bit of a troll of old, white male historians . . . ," Twitter, on Internet Archive, November 25, 2019, https://web.archive.org/web/20191126011251if_/https:/twitter.com/nhannahjones/status/1199130592299962368.

76 Nikole Hannah-Jones, "Our Democracy's Founding Ideals Were False When They Were Written. Black Americans Have Fought to Make Them True," *New York Times*, on Internet Archive, August 14, 2019, https://web.archive.org/web/20190814050033/https:/www.nytimes.com/interactive/2019/08/14/magazine/black-history-american-democracy.html (the screenshot of the site was captured on August 14, 2019).

77 Jeff Barrus, "Nikole Hannah-Jones Wins Pulitzer Prize for 1619 Project," Pulitzer Center, May 4, 2020, https://pulitzercenter.org/blog/nikole-hannah-jones-wins-pulitzer-prize-1619-project.

78 Joel B. Pollak, "Pulitzer Prize to New York Times Essay Falsely Claiming American Revolution Was Fought to Preserve Slavery," Breitbart, May 4, 2020, https://www.breitbart.com/the-media/2020/05/04/pulitzer-prize-to-new-york-times-essay-falsely-claiming-american-revolution-was-fought-to-preserve-slavery/; Joel B. Pollak, "New York Times' '1619 Project' Named to 'Top Ten Works of Journalism of the Decade,' " Breitbart, October 14, 2020, https://www.breitbart.com/the-media/2020/10/14/new-york-times-1619-project-named-to-top-ten-works-of-journalism-of-the-decade/.

79 Leslie M. Harris, "I Helped Fact-Check the 1619 Project. The Times Ignored Me," *Politico*, March 6, 2020, https://www.politico.com/news/magazine/2020/03/06/1619-project-new-york-times-mistake-122248.

80 Noam Blum (@neontaster), "Just letting her talk does way more heavy lifting . . . ," Twitter, July 27, 2020, 7:42 a.m., https://twitter.com/neontaster/status/1287760191514202113.

81 "We Respond to the Historians Who Critiqued the 1619 Project."

82 Cliff Levy (@cliffordlevy), "A note to the NYT newsroom about the 1619 Project . . . ," Twitter, October 13, 2020, 7:07 a.m., https://twitter.com/cliffordlevy/status/1316017794664652800.

83 "Flight from the Cities," Breitbart, accessed February 11, 2021, https://www.breitbart.com/tag/flight-from-the-cities/.

84 Joe Gabriel Simonson (@SaysSimonson), "Remember she's going to be in pub-

lic school textbooks," Twitter, June 20, 2020, 8:13 a.m., https://mobile.twitter
.com/SaysSimonson/status/1274359677493575680.

85 Gabriella Lewis, "Hannah-Jones Implores Nuanced View of MLK," *Emory
    Wheel*, January 22, 2020, https://emorywheel.com/hannah-jones-implores
    -nuanced-view-of-mlk/.

86 Joshua Caplan, "NYT's Nikole Hannah-Jones: Looting from Big-Name Stores
    Is 'Symbolic' for Black Americans," Breitbart, June 2, 2020, https://www.breit
    bart.com/the-media/2020/06/02/nyts-nikole-hannah-jones-looting-symbolic
    -black-americans/.

87 CBS News (@CBSNews), "Violence is when an agent of the state kneels on
    a man's neck . . . ," Twitter, June 2, 2020, 10:55 a.m., https://twitter.com
    /CBSNews/status/1267877443911778306.

88 Jordan Davidson, "In Racist Screed, NYT's 1619 Project Founder calls 'White
    Race' 'Barbaric Devils,' 'Bloodsuckers,' Columbus 'No Different Than Hit-
    ler,'" *Federalist*, June 25, 2020, https://thefederalist.com/2020/06/25/in-racist
    -screed-nyts-1619-project-founder-calls-white-race-barbaric-devils-blood
    suckers-no-different-than-hitler/#.XvT-UWykKKs.twitter.

89 Kyle Morris, "NYT's Nikole Hannah-Jones Confirms She Called Europeans
    'Barbaric Devils,' Linked Africa to Aztec Temples," Breitbart, July 15, 2020,
    https://www.breitbart.com/politics/2020/07/15/nyts-nikole-hannah-jones
    -confirms-she-called-europeans-barbaric-devils-linked-africa-to-aztec-tem
    ples/.

90 Jake Silverstein, "On Recent Criticism of the 1619 Project," *New York Times*,
    October 16, 2020, https://www.nytimes.com/2020/10/16/magazine/criticism
    -1619-project.html.

91 Conor Friedersdorf (@conor64), "How do you call other people liars . . . ,"
    Twitter, September 18, 2020, 1:37 p.m., https://twitter.com/conor64/status
    /1307056277848297473.

92 Rod Dreher, "Not So Fast, Nikole Hannah-Jones," *American Conserva-
    tive*, September 18, 2020, https://www.theamericanconservative.com/dreher
    /nikole-hannah-jones-1619-project-history-trump-live-not-by-lies/; CNN
    (@CNN), "The 1619 Project 'does not argue that 1776 was not the founding
    of the country . . . , '" Twitter, September 18, 2020, 11:52 a.m., https://twitter
    .com/CNN/status/1307029623943831552.

93 CNN (@CNN), "The 1619 Project 'does not argue that 1776 was not the
    founding of the country . . . '"

94 Twitter, photograph, accessed February 12, 2021, https://twitter.com/nhanna
    hjones/header_photo.

95 Nikole Hannah-Jones, "What Is Owed," *New York Times*, June 30, 2020,
    https://www.nytimes.com/interactive/2020/06/24/magazine/reparations
    -slavery.html.

96 Ashley Feinberg, "The New York Times Unites vs. Twitter," *Slate,* August 15,
    2019, https://slate.com/news-and-politics/2019/08/new-york-times-meeting
    -transcript.html.

97　Nancy Coleman, "Why We're Capitalizing Black," *New York Times*, July 5, 2020, https://www.nytimes.com/2020/07/05/insider/capitalized-black.html.

98　"About Tom," Tom Cotton's Senator page, accessed March 11, 2021, https://www.cotton.senate.gov/about; Molly Ball, "The Making of a Conservative Superstar," *Atlantic*, September 17, 2014, https://www.theatlantic.com/politics/archive/2014/09/the-making-of-a-conservative-superstar/380307/.

99　Tom Cotton, "Send in the Troops," *New York Times*, June 3, 2020, https://www.nytimes.com/2020/06/03/opinion/tom-cotton-protests-military.html.

100　Zack Beauchamp, "The New York Times Staff Revolt over Tom Cotton's Op-ed, Explained," *Vox*, June 7, 2020, https://www.vox.com/2020/6/5/21280425/new-york-times-tom-cotton-send-troops-staff-revolt.

101　Charlie Spiering, "Donald Trump Honors Former Police Captain David Dorn—Shot, Killed by Rioters," Breitbart, June 2, 2020, https://www.breitbart.com/politics/2020/06/02/donald-trump-honors-former-police-captain-david-dorn-shot-killed-by-rioters/; Joel B. Pollak, "Minneapolis: Minority-Owned Businesses Destroyed by Rioters," Breitbart, June 2, 2020, https://www.breitbart.com/politics/2020/06/02/minneapolis-minority-owned-businesses-destroyed-by-rioters/.

102　Joel B. Pollak, "New York Times, Journalists Freak Out over Tom Cotton Op-ed Calling for Military to Restore Order," Breitbart, June 4, 2020, https://www.breitbart.com/the-media/2020/06/04/new-york-times-journalists-freak-out-over-tom-cotton-op-ed-calling-for-military-to-restore-order/.

103　James Bennet (@JBennet), "I want to explain why we published the piece today by Senator Tom Cotton," Twitter, June 3, 2020, 4:46 p.m., https://twitter.com/JBennet/status/1268328278730866689.

104　Jerry Dunleavy (@JerryDunleavy), "An op-ed from a U.S. senator did not meet the editorial standards of the @NYTimes . . . ," Twitter, June 4, 2020, 3:34 p.m., https://twitter.com/JerryDunleavy/status/1268672423617900544.

105　Marc Tracy, Rachel Abrams, and Edmund Lee, "New York Times Says Senator's Op-Ed Did Not Meet Standards," *New York Times*, June 4, 2020, https://www.nytimes.com/2020/06/04/business/new-york-times-op-ed-cotton.html.

106　Ibid.

107　"The New York Times Announces First Narrative Nonfiction Podcast, 'Caliphate' with Rukmini Callimachi," *New York Times* (Investors), March 10, 2018, https://investors.nytco.com/news-and-events/press-releases/news-details/2018/THE-NEW-YORK-TIMES-ANNOUNCES-FIRST-NARRATIVE-NONFICTION-PODCAST-CALIPHATE-WITH-RUKMINI-CALLIMACHI/default.aspx.

108　Leyland Cecco, "Did the 'Caliphate Executioner' Lie About His Past as an Isis Killer?" *Guardian*, October 2, 2020, https://www.theguardian.com/world/2020/oct/02/canada-isis-killer-story-police-hoax.

109　"Finalist: Rescinded," Pulitzer Prizes, accessed February 12, 2021, https://www.pulitzer.org/finalists/rukmini-callimachi-new-york-times; "The New York Times' Rukmini Callimachi to Receive the ICFJ Integrity in Journalism

Award in Partnership with the Aurora Prize," International Center for Journalists, April 23, 2016, https://www.icfj.org/news/new-york-times-rukmini -callimachi-receive-icfj-integrity-journalism-award-partnership-aurora.

110 "Caliphate (The New York Times)," Peabody, accessed February 12, 2021, http://www.peabodyawards.com/award-profile/caliphate.

111 House of Commons Debates, Canada, 42nd Parliament, 1st Session, May 11, 2018, https://www.ourcommons.ca/DocumentViewer/en/42-1/house/sitting -297/hansard.

112 "Canadian Police Arrest Shehroze Chaudhry from Caliphate Podcast for Alleged Islamic State Terrorism Hoax," ABC News, September 26, 2020, https://www.abc.net.au/news/2020-09-27/canada-police-arrest-man-for -hoax-terrorism-isis/12707648.

113 Ibid.

114 Rukmini Callimachi (@rcallimachi), "1. Big news out of Canada: Abu Huzayfah has been arrested . . . ," Twitter, September 25, 2020, 3:27 p.m., https:// twitter.com/rcallimachi/status/1309620500176556032.

115 "BenSmithing," Urban Dictionary, accessed February 12, 2021, https://www .urbandictionary.com/define.php?term=BenSmithing; John Nolte, "Ben Smith's BuzzFeed Politics Loves Seamus, Ignore Obama Eating Dog," Breitbart, April 18, 2012, https://www.breitbart.com/the-media/2012/04/18/ben -smith-ignores-obama-eats-dog-story/; John Nolte, "'New York Times' Writes of Ben Smith and Bensmithing," Breitbart, February 16, 2013, https:// www.breitbart.com/the-media/2013/02/16/the-new-york-times-writes-of -ben-smith-and-bensmithing/.

116 Ben Smith, "An Arrest in Canada Casts a Shadow on a New York Times Star, and The Times," New York Times, last update December 18, 2020, https://www .nytimes.com/2020/10/11/business/media/new-york-times-rukmini-callima chi-caliphate.html.

117 Erik Wemple, "Opinion: Rukmini Callimachi's Reporting Troubles," Washington Post, September 30, 2020, https://www.washingtonpost.com/opinions /2020/09/30/rukmini-callimachis-reporting-troubles/.

118 Ivan Nechepurenko and Rukmini Callimachi, "Website with Qaeda Ties Publishes Claim on St. Petersburg Bombing," New York Times, April 25, 2017, https://www.nytimes.com/2017/04/25/world/europe/st-petersburg-metro-al -qaeda.html.

119 Erik Wemple, "Opinion: The Strange Story Behind the Departure of the New York Times's Baghdad Bureau Chief," Washington Post, October 13, 2018, https://www.washingtonpost.com/blogs/erik-wemple/wp/2018/10/13 /the-strange-story-behind-the-departure-of-the-new-york-timess-baghdad -bureau-chief/.

120 Associated Press, "New York Times: 'Caliphate' Podcast Didn't Meet Standards," Breitbart, December 21, 2020, https://www.breitbart.com/news/new -york-times-caliphate-podcast-didnt-meet-standards/.

121 David Folkenflik, "2 Prominent 'New York Times' Journalists Depart over

Past Behavior," NPR, February 6, 2021, https://www.npr.org/2021/02/06
/964618301/two-prominent-new-york-times-journalists-depart-over-past
-behavior.

122   Tamar Lapin, "New York Times Reporter Donald McNeil Jr. Accused of Making Racist Comments," *New York Post*, January 28, 2021, https://nypost.com
/2021/01/28/new-york-times-reporter-donald-mcneil-jr-accused-of-racist
-comments/.

123   Marc Tracy, "Two Journalists Exit New York Times After Criticism of Past
Behavior," *New York Times*, February 5, 2021, https://www.nytimes.com/2021
/02/05/business/media/donald-mcneil-andy-mills-leave-nyt.html.

124   Bret Stephens, "Read the Column the New York Times Didn't Want You to
See," *New York Post*, February 11, 2021, https://nypost.com/2021/02/11/read
-the-column-the-new-york-times-didnt-want-you-read/.

125   Scott Alexander, "NYT Is Threatening My Safety by Revealing My Real Name,
So I Am Deleting the Blog," *Slate Star Codex*, June 22, 2020, https://slate
starcodex.com/2020/06/22/nyt-is-threatening-my-safety-by-revealing-my
-real-name-so-i-am-deleting-the-blog/.

126   Jeff Poor, "Tucker Carlson: NY Times Threatening to Reveal Where I Live—
'To Hurt Us, to Injure My Wife and Kids,'" Breitbart, July 20, 2020, https://
www.breitbart.com/clips/2020/07/20/tucker-carlson-ny-times-threatening-to
-reveal-where-i-live-to-hurt-us-to-injure-my-wife-and-kids/.

127   Ibid.; Kyle Morris, "Watch: 'Knock Knock Tucker': Leftists Protest Tucker
Carlson at His Home," Breitbart, November 8, 2018, https://www.breitbart
.com/politics/2018/11/08/watch-knock-knock-tucker-leftists-protest-tucker
-carlson-at-his-home/.

128   Allyson Chiu, "'They Were Threatening Me and My Family': Tucker Carlson's
Home Targeted by Protesters," *Washington Post*, November 8, 2018, https://
www.washingtonpost.com/nation/2018/11/08/they-were-threatening-me
-my-family-tucker-carlsons-home-targeted-by-protesters/.

129   Ibid.

130   "Bret Stephens Joins NYT Opinion," *New York Times*, April 12, 2017, https://
www.nytco.com/press/bret-stephens-joins-nyt-opinion/.

131   Bret Stephens, "Climate of Complete Certainty," *New York Times*, April 28,
2017, https://www.nytimes.com/2017/04/28/opinion/climate-of-complete
-certainty.html.

132   Benjamin Mullin, "New York Times Journalists Immediately Begin Subtweet-
ing Bret Stephens' Defense of Climate Change Skepticism," Poynter, April 28,
2017, https://www.poynter.org/reporting-editing/2017/new-york-times-jour
nalists-immediately-begin-subtweeting-bret-stephens-defense-of-climate
-skepticism/.

133   Michael Calderone (@mlcalderone), "NYT opinion has hired another from
the WSJ . . . ," Twitter, April 14, 2017, 11:21 a.m., https://twitter.com/mlcal
derone/status/852949886794379264.

134   Glenn Greenwald, "The NY Times's Newest Op-Ed Hire, Bari Weiss, Embodies

Its Worst Failings—and Its Lack of Viewpoint Diversity," *Intercept*, August 31, 2017, https://theintercept.com/2017/08/31/nyts-newest-op-ed-hire-bari-weiss -embodies-its-worst-failings-and-its-lack-of-viewpoint-diversity/.

135 Joel B. Pollak, "Bari Weiss Hurts Fight Against Antisemitism with Anti-Trump Smears," Breitbart, September 15, 2019, https://www.breitbart.com/the-media /2019/09/15/pollak-bari-weiss-hurts-fight-against-antisemitism-with-anti -trump-smears/.

136 Bari Weiss, "When Progressives Embrace Hate," *New York Times*, August 1, 2017, https://www.nytimes.com/2017/08/01/opinion/womens-march-pro gressives-hate.html.

137 Bari Weiss, "Aziz Anzari Is Guilty. Of Not Being a Mind Reader," *New York Times*, January 15, 2018, https://www.nytimes.com/2018/01/15/opinion/aziz -ansari-babe-sexual-harassment.html.

138 Bari Weiss, "Meet the Renegades of the Intellectual Dark Web," *New York Times*, May 8, 2018, https://www.nytimes.com/2018/05/08/opinion/intellec tual-dark-web.html.

139 Weiss, "When Progressives Embrace Hate"; Weiss, "Aziz Anzari Is Guilty. Of Not Being a Mind Reader"; "A Sexual Encounter, and a Dispute," *New York Times*, January 19, 2018, https://www.nytimes.com/2018/01/19/opinion/me too-ansari-harassment.html.

140 Bari Weiss Resignation Letter, Bari Weiss's website, accessed February 12, 2021, https://www.bariweiss.com/resignation-letter.

141 Regina Ip, "Hong Kong Is China, Like It or Not," *New York Times*, October 1, 2020, https://www.nytimes.com/2020/10/01/opinion/hong-kong-china-secu rity-law.html.

142 Helen Gao, "How Did Women Fare in China's Communist Revolution?" *New York Times*, September 25, 2017, https://www.nytimes.com/2017/09/25/opin ion/women-china-communist-revolution.html.

143 New York Times Opinion (@nytopinion), "For all its flaws, the Communist revolution taught Chinese women to dream big," Twitter, September 25, 2017, 5:11 p.m., https://twitter.com/nytopinion/status/912469539283177472.

144 John Hayward, "New York Times Columnist Parrots North Korean Propa ganda from Pyongyang," Breitbart, October 3, 2017, https://www.breitbart .com/national-security/2017/10/03/new-york-times-columnist-parrots -north-korean-propaganda-pyongyang/.

145 Yuichiro Kakutani, "NYT Quietly Scrubs Chinese Propaganda," *Washing ton Free Beacon*, August 4, 2020, https://freebeacon.com/media/nyt-quietly -scrubs-chinese-propaganda/.

146 Ibid.

147 Jim Waterson and Dean Sterling Jones, "Daily Telegraph Stops Publishing Sec tion Paid for by China," *Guardian*, April 14, 2020, https://www.theguardian .com/media/2020/apr/14/daily-telegraph-stops-publishing-section-paid-for -by-china.

148 Max Fisher, "What Happens When You Fight a 'Deep State' That Doesn't

Exist," *New York Times*, March 10, 2017, https://www.nytimes3xbfgragh.onion /2017/03/10/world/americas/what-happens-when-you-fight-a-deep-state -that-doesnt-exist.html.

149 Michelle Cottle, "They Are Not the Resistance. They Are Not a Cabal. They Are Public Servants," *New York Times*, October 20, 2019, https://www.nytimes .com/2019/10/20/opinion/trump-impeachment-testimony.html?smid=tw -nytopinion&smtyp=cur.

150 "I Am Part of the Resistance Inside the Trump Administration," *New York Times*, September 5, 2018, https://www.nytimes.com/2018/09/05/opinion /trump-white-house-anonymous-resistance.html.

151 Anthony Zurcher, "The Whodunnit Editorial Puzzling Washington," BBC News, September 6, 2018, https://www.bbc.com/news/world-us-canada-454 36245.

152 Allum Bokhari, "'Anonymous' Never Trumper Miles Taylor Now Works for Google," Breitbart, October 29, 2020, https://www.breitbart.com/tech/2020 /10/29/anonymous-never-trumper-miles-taylor-now-works-for-google/.

Chapter 4: NBC "News" and the Corporatization of Mass Media

1 Ben Kew, "Couple Ejected from Sixers Game for Shouting 'Free Hong Kong,'" Breitbart, October 9, 2019, https://www.breitbart.com/sports/2019/10/09 /couple-ejected-from-sixers-game-for-shouting-free-hong-kong/.

2 Manish Singh, "Chinese Firms Tencent, Vivo and CCTV Suspend Ties with the NBA over Hong Kong Tweet," *TechCrunch*, October 8, 2019, https://tech crunch.com/2019/10/08/chinese-firms-tencent-vivo-and-cctv-suspend-ties -with-the-nba-over-hong-kong-tweet/.

3 Patrick Brzeski, "NBA's Apology to China Draws Outrage Across Political Spectrum," *Hollywood Reporter*, October 6, 2019, https://www.hollywoodreporter .com/news/nbas-apology-china-draws-outrage-political-spectrum-1245772.

4 Andy Lack, "Journalism Is Under Attack from Coronavirus and the White House. But We're Winning," NBC News, April 27, 2020, https://www.nbc news.com/think/opinion/journalism-under-attack-coronavirus-white-house -we-re-winning-ncna1192306.

5 Kurt Bardella, "Trump's Delusional Assault on the Press Should Get Him Banned from the White House Correspondents' Dinner," NBC News, April 4, 2018, https://www.nbcnews.com/think/opinion/trump-s-delusional-assault -press-should-get-him-banned-white-ncna862721.

6 Kristina Wong, "White House Suspends Jim Acosta's Press Pass After Combative Briefing," Breitbart, November 7, 2018, https://www.breitbart.com/politics /2018/11/07/white-house-suspends-jim-acostas-press-pass-after-combative -briefing/; Joshua Caplan, "White House Reinstates Jim Acosta's Press Pass, CNN Dropping Lawsuit," Breitbart, November 19, 2018, https://www.breit bart.com/the-media/2018/11/19/jim-acosta-white-house-press-pass-cnn -dropping-lawsuit/.

7 "Murdered Mexican Journalists," Breitbart, accessed February 12, 2021, https://www.breitbart.com/tag/murdered-mexican-journalists/; Carrie Kahn, "12 Journalists Have Been Killed in Mexico This Year, the World's Highest Toll," NPR, September 12, 2019, https://www.npr.org/2019/09/12/759882660/12 -journalists-have-been-killed-in-mexico-this-year-the-worlds-highest-toll.

8 Ildefonso Ortiz and Brandon Darby, "Free Press Group Documents 249 Aggressions Against Mexican Media in 2019," Breitbart, September 7, 2019, https://www.breitbart.com/border/2019/09/07/press-freedom-org-docu ments-249-aggressions-against-mexican-media-in-2019/.

9 "China, Turkey, Saudi Arabia, Egypt Are World's Worst Jailers of Journalists," Committee to Protect Journalists, December 11, 2019, https://cpj.org/reports /2019/12/journalists-jailed-china-turkey-saudi-arabia-egypt/.

10 John Hayward, "China Leads the World in Jailing Journalists for Second Year Running," Breitbart, December 15, 2020, https://www.breitbart.com/asia /2020/12/15/china-leads-world-jailing-journalists-second-year-running/.

11 John Hayward, "China Dethrones Turkey as World's Worst Jailer of Jour-nalists," Breitbart, December 11, 2019, https://www.breitbart.com/national -security/2019/12/11/china-dethrones-turkey-as-worlds-worst-jailer-of -journalists/.

12 Mathew Ingram, "White House Revokes Press Passes for Dozens of Journal-ists," Columbia Journalism Review, May 9, 2019, https://www.cjr.org/the_media _today/white-house-press-passes.php; Josh Gerstein, "Court Grapples with White House's Right to Suspend Press Passes," Politico, March 23, 2020, https:// www.politico.com/news/2020/03/23/court-white-house-press-passes-144848.

13 Michelle Castillo, "Trump's 'Fake News' Fight Has Helped Media Ratings and Readership," CNBC, last updated April 27, 2018, https://www.cnbc.com/2018/04 /23/trumps-fake-news-fight-has-helped-media-ratings-and-readership.html.

14 Benjamin Mullin and Joe Flint, "2020 Is Proving How Much MSNBC's Rat-ings Hinge on Politics," Wall Street Journal, October 1, 2020, https://www.wsj .com/articles/2020-is-proving-how-much-msnbcs-ratings-hinge-on-politics -11601580214.

15 Sara Fischer, "Trump bump: NYT and WaPo digital subscriptions tripled since 2016," Axios, November 24, 2020, https://www.axios.com/washington-post -new-york-times-subscriptions-8e888fd7-5484-44c7-ad43-39564e06c84f.html.

16 Marc Tracy, "The New York Times Tops 6 Million Subscribers as Ad Rev-enue Plummetes," New York Times, May 6, 2020, https://www.nytimes.com /2020/05/06/business/media/new-york-times-earnings-subscriptions-coro navirus.html.

17 Joshua Benton, "The Wall Street Journal Joins the New York Times in the 2 Million Digital Subscriber Club," NiemanLab, February 10, 2020, https:// www.niemanlab.org/2020/02/the-wall-street-journal-joins-the-new-york -times-in-the-2-million-digital-subscriber-club/.

18 "Apple Podcasts—United States of America—All Podcasts," Chartable, accessed February 12, 2021, https://chartable.com/charts/itunes/us-all-podcasts-podcasts.

19 Benedict Nicholson, "These Were the Top Publishers on Facebook in August 2020," Newswhip, September 17, 2020, https://www.newswhip.com/2020/09 /top-publishers-facebook-august-2020/.

20 Michael Barthel and Galen Stocking, "Key Facts About Digital-Native News Outlets amid Staff Cuts, Revenue Losses," Pew Research Center, July 14, 2020, https://www.pewresearch.org/fact-tank/2020/07/14/key-facts-about-digital -native-news-outlets-amid-staff-cuts-revenue-losses/.

21 John Nolte, "NBC Shock: Brian Williams Forced to Recant Iraq War Lie Repeated for 12 Years," Breitbart, February 4, 2015, https://www.breitbart.com /the-media/2015/02/04/nbc-shock-brian-williams-forced-to-recant-iraq-war -lie-repeated-for-12-years/.

22 Travis J. Tritten, "NBC's Brian Williams Recants Iraq Story After Soldiers Protest," *Stars and Stripes,* February 4, 2015, https://www.stripes.com/news/us /nbc-s-brian-williams-recants-iraq-story-after-soldiers-protest-1.327792.

23 Jordan Chariton, "Inside MSNBC's Impending Shakeup: Cancellations, Reboots and Chief Phil Griffin," *The Wrap,* last updated November 25, 2015, https://www.thewrap.com/inside-msnbcs-impending-shakeup-cancellations -reboots-and-chief-phil-griffin/.

24 John Nolte, "NBC News's Homophobe: 11 Times Joy Reid Bashed Gays," Breitbart, December 7, 2017, https://www.breitbart.com/the-media/2017/12 /07/sam-seder-fired-joy-reid-not-fired-yep-nbc-news-hates-gays/.

25 Brooke Sopelsa, "MSNBC's Joy Reid Apologizes for 'Insensitive' LGBT Blog Posts," NBC News, December 3, 2017, https://www.nbcnews.com/feature /nbc-out/msnbc-s-joy-reid-apologizes-insensitive-lgbt-blog-posts-n826091; Caleb Ecarma, "EXCLUSIVE: Joy Reid Claims Newly Discovered Homopho-bic Posts from Her Blog Were 'Fabricated,'" *Mediaite,* April 23, 2018, https:// www.mediaite.com/online/exclusive-joy-reid-claims-newly-discovered -homophobic-posts-from-her-blog-were-fabricated/.

26 Josh Meyer, "Flashback: September 30, 2001," *Reid Report* (blog), on Internet Archive, March 4, 2006, http://web.archive.org/web/20130121062440/http:/ blog.reidreport.com/2006/03/flashback-september-30-2001.html (the screen-shot of the site was captured on January 21, 2013).

27 "The Official Story," *Reid Report* (blog), on Internet Archive, March 22, 2006, http://web.archive.org/web/20130121064446/http:/blog.reidreport.com/2006 /03/official-story.html (the screenshot of the site was captured on January 21, 2013).

28 Tom Kludt, "MSNBC Host Joy Reid Apologizes for Incendiary Old Blog Posts," CNN Business, June 1, 2018, https://money.cnn.com/2018/06/01/media/joy -reid-blog-msnbc/index.html.

29 Alexis C. Madrigal, "The Evidence Is Not with Joy Reid," *Atlantic,* April 25, 2018, https://www.theatlantic.com/technology/archive/2018/04/the-evidence -is-not-with-joy-reid/558935/; Amy B. Wang, "Joy Reid Apologizes for Anti-LGBT Posts, Says She Can't Prove Her Blog Was Hacked," *Washington Post,* April 28, 2018, https://www.washingtonpost.com/news/arts-and-entertain

ment/wp/2018/04/28/joy-reid-apologizes-for-anti-lgbt-posts-says-she-cant-prove-her-blog-was-hacked/.

30 Tom Kludt, "Joy Reid's Attorney Says FBI Has Opened Investigation into Hacking Claim," CNN Business, April 26, 2018, https://money.cnn.com/2018/04/26/media/joy-reid-hacking-fbi-investigation/index.html?iid=EL.

31 Hayley Miller, "Daily Beast Suspends Joy Reid Column amid Scrutiny over Her Hacking Claims," *Huffington Post*, April 26, 2018, https://www.huffpost.com/entry/joy-reid-cancels-event_n_5ae1d916e4b055fd7fc90c67; Kludt, "Joy Reid's Attorney Says FBI Has Opened Investigation into Hacking Claim"; Joshua Caplan, "MSNBC Absolves Joy Reid of 'Hateful' Writings," Breitbart, June 1, 2018, https://www.breitbart.com/the-media/2018/06/01/msnbc-refuses-to-punish-joy-reid-after-new-controversial-blog-posts-surface/.

32 Joy-Ann Pro-Democracy & Masks Reid (@JoyAnnReid) "Violence and mayhem, perpetrated by people who support HIM, unleashed at night and let's just be clear . . . ," Twitter, August 30, 2020, 9:54 a.m., https://twitter.com/joyannreid/status/1300114583764570112?lang=en.

33 Rebecca Morrin, "USA TODAY/Ipsos Poll: A Majority of Americans Say Cities Under Siege by Protesters," *USA Today*, September 22, 2020, https://www.usatoday.com/story/news/politics/2020/09/22/usa-today-ipsos-poll-majority-americans-say-cities-under-siege/3483172001/.

34 John Nolte, "Poll Shows Majority Turn Against Rioters, Media," Breitbart, September 23, 2020, https://www.breitbart.com/law-and-order/2020/09/23/nolte-poll-shows-majority-turn-against-rioters-media/.

35 John Koblin, "How Did NBC Miss Out on a Harvey Weinstein Exposé?" *New York Times*, October 11, 2017, https://www.nytimes.com/2017/10/11/business/media/nbc-news-harvey-weinstein.html.

36 John Koblin, "Ronan Farrow's Ex-Producer Says NBC Impeded Weinstein Reporting," *New York Times*, August 30, 2018, https://www.nytimes.com/2018/08/30/business/media/ronan-farrow-weinstein-producer.html.

37 "The New York Times, for Reporting Led by Jodi Kantor and Megan Twohey, and The New Yorker, for Reporting by Ronan Farrow," Pulitzer Prizes, accessed February 14, 2021, https://www.pulitzer.org/winners/new-york-times-reporting-led-jodi-kantor-and-megan-twohey-and-new-yorker-reporting-ronan.

38 Erik Ortiz and Corky Siemaszko, "NBC News Fires Matt Lauer After Sexual Misconduct Review," NBC News, November 29, 2017, https://www.nbcnews.com/storyline/sexual-misconduct/nbc-news-fires-today-anchor-matt-lauer-after-sexual-misconduct-n824831.

39 Sarah Ellison, "'Everybody Knew': Inside the Fall of *Today*'s Matt Lauer," *Vanity Fair*, November 30, 2017, https://www.vanityfair.com/news/2017/11/inside-the-fall-of-todays-matt-lauer; Hunter Harris, "NBC Investigation Says Management Didn't Know About Matt Lauer Accusations," *Vulture*, May 9, 2018, https://www.vulture.com/2018/05/nbc-says-management-didnt-know-about-matt-lauer-accusations.html.

40 Ramin Setoodeh and Elizabeth Wagmeister, "Matt Lauer Accused of Sexual

Harassment by Multiple Women (EXCLUSIVE)," *Variety*, November 29, 2017, https://variety.com/2017/biz/news/matt-lauer-accused-sexual-harassment-multiple-women-1202625959/.

41 Kaitlin Menza, "Matt Lauer Wasn't the Only One with a Button Under His Desk at NBC," *Architectural Digest*, December 1, 2017, https://www.architecturaldigest.com/story/matt-lauer-wasnt-the-only-one-with-a-button-under-his-desk-at-nbc.

42 Ramin Setodoeh and Elizabeth Wagmeister, "Matt Lauer Accused of Sexual Harassment by Multiple Women (EXCLUSIVE)," *Variety*, November 29, 2017, https://variety.com/2017/biz/news/matt-lauer-accused-sexual-harassment-multiple-women-1202625959/.

43 Tony Ortega, "Matt Lauer's Roast: Tom Cruise, Katie Couric, and 3 Hours of Dick Jokes," *Village Voice*, October 24, 2008, https://www.villagevoice.com/2008/10/24/matt-lauers-roast-tom-cruise-katie-couric-and-3-hours-of-dick-jokes/.

44 Madeleine Aggeler, "In 2008, Matt Lauer Joked That He Had Slept with Both Katie Couric and Ann Curry," *Cut*, November 29, 2017, https://www.thecut.com/2017/11/matt-lauer-once-joked-about-sleeping-with-his-colleagues.html.

45 "Matt Lauer Once Boasted of Sleeping with Katie Couric and Ann Curry at His 2008 Roast in New York City," *Daily Mail*, November 29, 2017, https://www.dailymail.co.uk/news/article-5130885/Matt-Lauer-boasted-sleeping-Katie-Couric.html.

46 Setoodeh and Wagmeister, "Matt Lauer Accused of Sexual Harassment by Multiple Women (EXCLUSIVE)."

47 Ej Dickson, "Matt Lauer Accused of Rape According to New Ronan Farrow Book," *Rolling Stone*, October 9, 2019, https://www.rollingstone.com/culture/culture-news/matt-lauer-ronan-farrow-book-rape-allegation-sochi-brooke-nevils-896853/.

48 Marisa Guthrie, "Ronan Farrow Strikes Again: A New Book Targets NBC News and How Harvey Weinstein May Have Leveraged Matt Lauer," *Hollywood Reporter*, October 9, 2019, https://www.hollywoodreporter.com/features/ronan-farrow-book-how-harvey-weinstein-may-have-leveraged-matt-lauer-1246149.

49 Cynthia Littleton, "Andy Lack: Ronan Farrow's 'Catch and Kill' Paints 'Fundamentally Untrue' Picture of NBC News," *Variety*, October 9, 2019, https://variety.com/2019/biz/news/andy-lack-ronan-farrow-nbc-harvey-weinstein-1203365158/.

50 Gerry Smith, "NBC Pushes Back Against Ronan Farrow Book's Claims on Matt Lauer Handling," Yahoo Finance, October 14, 2019, https://finance.yahoo.com/news/nbc-pushes-back-against-ronan-150019827.html.

51 Smith, "Is Ronan Farrow Too Good to Be True?"

52 Jaclyn Peiser, "BuzzFeed's First Round of Layoffs Puts an End to Its National News Desk," *New York Times*, January 25, 2019, https://www.nytimes.com/2019/01/25/business/media/buzzfeed-layoffs.html.

53 Smith, "Is Ronan Farrow Too Good to Be True?"

54 Ben Smith, "We Worked Together on the Internet. Last Week, He Stormed the Capitol," *New York Times*, last updated January 12, 2021, https://www.nytimes.com/2021/01/10/business/media/capitol-anthime-gionet-buzzfeed-vine.html.

55 Laura Bradley, "Tom Brokaw Accused of Sexual Harassment by Two Former NBC Colleagues," *Vanity Fair*, April 27, 2018, https://www.vanityfair.com/hollywood/2018/04/tom-brokaw-sexual-harassment-allegations-linda-vester.

56 Emily Smith, "NBC Staffers Felt Pressured to Sign Letter Defending Brokaw," *Page Six*, April 30, 2018, https://pagesix.com/2018/04/30/nbc-staffers-felt-pressured-to-sign-letter-defending-brokaw/.

57 Associated Press, "Fox News Anchor Ed Henry Fired After Sexual-Misconduct Investigation," MarketWatch, July 1, 2020, https://www.marketwatch.com/story/fox-news-ed-henry-fired-after-sexual-misconduct-investigation-2020-07-01; Alex Weprin and Hadas Gold, "It's Official: Roger Ailes to Step Down at Fox News," *Politico*, July 21, 2016, https://www.politico.com/blogs/on-media/2016/07/draft-its-official-roger-ailes-to-step-down-at-fox-news-225886; Victor Garcia, "Megyn Kelly Calls on NBC News to Have 'Outside Investigator' Look into Shocking Allegations at Network," Fox News, October 16, 2019, https://www.foxnews.com/media/nbc-allegations-outside-investigator-megyn-kelly; Justin Baragona, "Megyn Kelly Calls for 'Outside Investigation' of NBC in Return to Fox News Airwaves," *Daily Beast,* October 16, 2019, https://www.thedailybeast.com/megyn-kelly-calls-for-outside-investigation-of-nbc-in-return-to-fox-news-airwaves.

58 Christina Zhao, "Megyn Kelly Slams NBC, Calls for Outside Investigation into Network During Tucker Carlson Appearance," *Newsweek*, October 16, 2019, https://www.newsweek.com/megyn-kelly-slams-nbc-calls-outside-investigation-network-during-tucker-carlson-appearance-1465837.

59 Kenzie Bryant, "NBC Chairman Andrew Lack Accused of Mishandling Sexual Harassment as Sony Music C.E.O.," *Vanity Fair*, September 22, 2018, https://www.vanityfair.com/news/2018/09/nbc-chairman-andrew-lack-accused-of-mishandling-sexual-harassment-claims-as-sony-music-ceo.

60 Jason Newman, "Charlie Walk: Top Music Executive Accused of Sexual Misconduct over Decades," *Rolling Stone*, February 22, 2018, https://www.rollingstone.com/culture/culture-features/charlie-walk-top-music-executive-accused-of-sexual-misconduct-over-decades-202979/.

61 Sarah Ellison and Elahe Izadi, "Andy Lack, Longtime NBC News and MSNBC Executive, Steps Down from Chairmanship After Internal, External Criticism," *Washington Post*, May 4, 2020, https://www.washingtonpost.com/lifestyle/media/andy-lack-longtime-nbc-news-and-msnbc-executive-steps-down-from-chairmanship/2020/05/04/b30e5b9e-8e3d-11ea-a0bc-4e9ad4866d21_story.html.

62 David Folkenflik, "NBC News Chief Andrew Lack Out After Tenure Marked by Scandal," NPR, May 4, 2020, https://www.npr.org/2020/05/04/850292571/nbc-news-chief-andrew-lack-out-after-tenure-marked-by-scandal.

63 Kat Stoeffel, "The Age of the MSNBC Mom," *New York Times*, June 8, 2018, https://www.nytimes.com/2018/06/08/opinion/sunday/msnbc-cable-news -viewers-moms.html.

64 John Nolte, "Rachel Maddow's 17 Most Audacious and Paranoid Russia Hoax Lies," Breitbart, May 2, 2019, https://www.breitbart.com/the-media/2019/05/02 /nolte-rachel-maddows-17-most-audacious-and-paranoid-russia-hoax-lies/.

65 "Will 'Kompromat' Make It into the Dictionary?" Merriam-Webster, accessed February 14, 2021, https://www.merriam-webster.com/words-at-play/what -does-kompromat-mean.

66 Aaron Maté (@aaronjmate), "20/ Speaking of installing Tillerson, remember when you also speculated . . . ," Twitter, April 28, 2019, 6:51 p.m., https://twit ter.com/aaronjmate/status/1122679649035747328.

67 Aaron Maté, "MSNBC's Rachel Maddow Sees a 'Russia Connection' Lurk-ing Around Every Corner," *Intercept*, April 12, 2017, https://theintercept .com/2017/04/12/msnbcs-rachel-maddow-sees-a-russia-connection-lurking -around-every-corner/.

68 Avi Selk, "MSNBC Host's Conspiracy Theory: What If Putin Planned the Syrian Chemical Attack to Help Trump?" *Washington Post*, April 8, 2017, https://www .washingtonpost.com/news/the-fix/wp/2017/04/08/msnbc-hosts-conspiracy -theory-what-if-putin-planned-the-syrian-chemical-attack-to-help-trump/.

69 John Nolte, "Russia Hoax Queen Rachel Maddow's Ratings Crash to Trump -Era Low," Breitbart, June 4, 2019, https://www.breitbart.com/the-media/2019 /06/04/nolte-russia-hoax-queen-rachel-maddows-ratings-crash-to-trump -era-low/; "Ratings," TVNewser, accessed February 15, 2021, https://www .adweek.com/tvnewser/category/ratings/.

70 Will Thorne, "TV Ratings: Rachel Maddow Interview with Mary Trump Breaks Viewership Record," *Variety*, July 17, 2020, https://variety.com/2020 /tv/news/rachel-maddow-mary-trump-interview-breaks-viewership-record -1234709901/.

71 John Nolte, "MSNBC's Chris Hayes Spreads Conspiracy Theory to Explain Trump's Booming Economy," Breitbart, May 4, 2019, https://www.breitbart .com/the-media/2019/05/04/msnbcs-chris-hayes-spreads-conspiracy-theory -explain-trumps-booming-economy/.

72 Joel B. Pollak, "MSNBC Chyron: 'Trump-Inspired Terrorism,'" Breitbart, August 6, 2019, https://www.breitbart.com/the-media/2019/08/06/msnbc -chyron-trump-inspired-terrorism/.

73 David Schanzer, "We Must Call the El Paso Shooting What It Is: Trump-Inspired Terrorism," *Guardian,* August 5, 2019, https://www.theguardian.com /commentisfree/2019/aug/05/trump-inspired-terrorism-el-paso.

74 Joel B. Pollak, "Report: El Paso Shooter Claimed to Be Radicalized Before Trump," Breitbart, August 4, 2019, https://www.breitbart.com/crime/2019/08 /04/report-el-paso-shooter-claimed-to-be-radicalized-before-trump/.

75 John Nolte, "Nolte: MSNBC's Lawrence O'Donnell Lets Conspiracy Spread Online After TV Retraction," Breitbart, August 29, 2019, https://www.breit

bart.com/the-media/2019/08/29/nolte-msnbcs-lawrence-odonnell-lets-con
spiracy-spread-online-after-tv-retraction/.

76 Matthew Boyle, "President Trump Demands Retraction from MSNBC for
O'Donnell's Deutsche Bank Claims," Breitbart, August 28, 2019, https://www
.breitbart.com/the-media/2019/08/28/president-trump-demands-retraction
-from-msnbc-for-odonnells-deutsche-bank-claims/.

77 Warner Todd Huston, "Rob Reiner Demands Trump Indictment over Bogus
MSNBC Russia Story," Breitbart, August 28, 2019, https://www.breitbart.com
/entertainment/2019/08/28/rob-reiner-demands-trump-indictment-over
-bogus-msnbc-russia-story/.

78 Hannah Bleau, "Trump Breaks MSNBC: Lawrence O'Donnell Apologizes for
Deutsche Bank Claims," Breitbart, August 28, 2019, https://www.breitbart
.com/the-media/2019/08/28/trump-breaks-msnbc-lawrence-odonnell-apol
ogizes-for-deutsche-bank-claims/.

79 Nolte, "Nolte: MSNBC's Lawrence O'Donnell Lets Conspiracy Spread Online
After TV Retraction."

80 Jeff Poor, "MSNBC's Velshi as Minneapolis Burns Behind Him: 'This Is Mostly
a Protest—It Is Not Generally Speaking Unruly,'" Breitbart, May 28, 2020,
https://www.breitbart.com/clips/2020/05/28/msnbcs-velshi-as-minneapolis
-burns-behind-him-this-is-mostly-a-protest-it-is-not-generally-speaking
-unruly/.

81 Craig Melvin, "This will guide our reporting in MN . . . ," Twitter, May 28,
2020, 8:37 a.m., https://twitter.com/craigmelvin/status/1266030830473940993
?lang=en.

82 Pam Key, "MSNBC's Figliuzzi: 'Notion' Antifa Is Some Kind of 'Organized
Group Is Laughable,'" Breitbart, September 30, 2020, https://www.breitbart
.com/clips/2020/09/30/msnbcs-figliuzzi-notion-antifa-is-some-kind-of-orga
nized-group-is-laughable/.

83 Hannah Bleau, "AG Barr: Antifa Violence Is Domestic Terrorism and Will
Be 'Treated Accordingly,'" Breitbart, May 31, 2020, https://www.breitbart.com
/politics/2020/05/31/ag-barr-antifa-violence-is-domestic-terrorism-and-will
-be-treat-accordingly/.

84 Kristina Wong, "DHS Official Called Portland Violence 'Organized' in Leaked
Email," Breitbart, September 15, 2020, https://www.breitbart.com/politics
/2020/09/15/former-dhs-official-portland-violence-organized/.

85 Lucas Nolan, "Facebook Removes Antifa and Qanon Groups," Breitbart,
August 20, 2020, https://www.breitbart.com/tech/2020/08/20/facebook-re
moves-antifa-and-qanon-groups/.

86 Penny Starr, "CNN's Don Lemon Defends Violent Antifa: 'No Organization Is
Perfect,'" Breitbart, August 29, 2018, https://www.breitbart.com/politics/2018
/08/29/cnns-don-lemon-defends-violent-antifa-no-organization-is-perfect/.

87 Joy-Ann Pro-Democracy & Masks Reid (@JoyAnnReid), "And they would
happily trade a million more . . . ," Twitter, October 13, 2020, 8:52 a.m., https://
twitter.com/JoyAnnReid/status/1316044121291845633?.

88 Adele-Momoko Fraser, "Google Bans Two Websites from Its Ad Platform over Protest Articles," NBC News, on Internet Archive, June 16, 2020, https://web .archive.org/web/20200616191520/https:/www.nbcnews.com/tech/tech-news /google-bans-two-websites-its-ad-platform-over-protest-articles-n1231176 (the screenshot of the site was captured on June 16, 2020).

89 Eric Rosenberg, "How Google Makes Money," Investopedia, June 23, 2020, https://www.investopedia.com/articles/investing/020515/business-google .asp.

90 NBC News VC (@NBC_VC), "Two far-right sites, ZeroHedge and The Federalist, will no longer be able . . . ," Twitter, June 16, 2020, 11:42 a.m., https:// twitter.com/NBC_VC/status/1272962743436374016.

91 Joel B. Pollak, "NBC News Reporter Thanks Foreign Groups for 'Collaboration' in Pushing Google to 'Defund' the Federalist," Breitbart, June 16, 2020, https://www.breitbart.com/the-media/2020/06/16/nbc-news-reporter-thanks -foreign-groups-for-collaboration-in-pushing-google-to-defund-the-federal ist-twitter/.

92 Megan Graham, "Google Says Zero Hedge Can Run Google Ads Again After Removing 'Derogatory' Comments," CNBC, July 14, 2020, https://www.cnbc .com/2020/07/14/google-reinstates-zero-hedge-ad-monetization.html.

93 Brian Fung (@b_fung), "NBC seems to have updated its story on Google . . . ," Twitter, June 16, 2020, 1:32 p.m., https://twitter.com/b_fung/status/1272990 537440772099.

94 Stop Funding Fake News (@SFFakeNews), "THREAD: These brands all support #BlackLivesMatter . . . ," Twitter, June 16, 2020, 1:24 a.m., https://twitter .com/SFFakeNews/status/1272807322876882944.

95 "Defund Racism: Black Lives Matter," Stop Funding Fake News, accessed March 11, 2021, https://www.stopfundingfakenews.com/defund-racism.

96 Joshua Caplan, "NBC News' Adele-Momoko Fraser Walks Back Touted 'Collaboration' with Activist Group on Google Story," Breitbart, June 17, 2020, https://www.breitbart.com/tech/2020/06/17/nbc-news-adele-momoko-fraser -walks-back-touted-collaboration-with-activist-group-on-google-story/.

97 NBC News VC's Twitter page, accessed February 15, 2021, https://twitter.com /NBC_VC.

98 Andy Eckardt, "Breitbart Blacklisted by Germany's BMW and Deutsche Telekom," NBC News, December 8, 2016, https://www.nbcnews.com/news/world /breitbart-blacklisted-germany-s-bmw-deutsche-telekom-n693531; Dennis Romero, "Los Angeles Police Recruitment Ad on Breitbart Prompts Inquiry," NBC News, September 28, 2019, https://www.nbcnews.com/news/us-news /los-angeles-police-recruitment-ad-breitbart-prompts-inquiry-n1060026.

99 Claire Atkinson, "Advertisers Between Rock and Hard Place over 'Hannity' Sponsorship," NBC News, November 12, 2017, https://www.nbcnews.com /news/us-news/advertisers-between-rock-hard-place-over-hannity-sponsor ship-n820126; Ben Popken, "Advertisers Flee Fox's Bill O'Reilly Show amid Sexual Harassment Lawsuits," NBC News, April 4, 2017, https://www.nbc

news.com/business/business-news/advertisers-start-flee-bill-o-reilly-s-show
-after-more-n742461; Tim Stelloh, "Advertisers Bail on Fox News' Tucker
Carlson over Immigration Comments," NBC News, December 17, 2018,
https://www.nbcnews.com/news/all/advertisers-bail-fox-news-tucker-carl
son-over-immigration-comments-n949171; Ali Velshi, "Advertisers Boycott
Laura Ingraham Show After Taunts to Parkland Teen," NBC News, video,
March 29, 2018, https://www.nbcnews.com/flashback/video/advertisers-boy
cott-laura-ingraham-show-after-taunts-to-parkland-teen-1198067267911.

100 Kaelin Tully, "27 Cats Who Are a Better Human than You," BuzzFeed, April 2,
2015, https://www.buzzfeed.com/kaelintully/these-cats-are-almost-as-good
-as-freddie-mercury; Kirby Beaton, "Will Smith Just Listed the 'Fresh Prince'
Mansion on Airbnb and My Quarantine Just Got Turned Upside Down,"
BuzzFeed, September 14, 2020, https://www.buzzfeed.com/kirbybeaton/fresh
-prince-mansion-airbnb; Chris Spags, "BuzzFeed Had People Drink Their
Own Piss for One of Those In-Studio Viral Videos," Barstool Sports, January 6, 2016, https://www.barstoolsports.com/blog/449426/buzzfeed-had-peo
ple-drink-their-own-piss-for-one-of-those-in-studio-viral-videos.

101 Kayleigh Barber, "BuzzFeed Wants to Become an Authority of Sexual Well-
ness for Millennials with a New Branded Sex Toy," Digiday, November 11,
2020, https://digiday.com/media/buzzfeed-wants-to-become-an-authority-of
-sexual-wellness-for-millennials-with-a-new-branded-sex-toy/.

102 "BuzzFeed + NBCUniversal," NBCUniversal, accessed February 15, 2021,
https://together.nbcuni.com/capabilities/buzzfeed-nbcu/.

103 LollapaRooza, "24 Bizarre Pogs That Will Leave You Scratching Your Head,"
BuzzFeed, January 20, 2013, https://www.buzzfeed.com/lollaparooza/24
-bizarre-pogs-that-will-leave-you-scratching-you-8s5g; Austin Gebbia, "Can
We Guess What Your Pubes Look Like Based on Some of Your Lifestyle
Choices?" BuzzFeed, June 19, 2017, https://www.buzzfeed.com/austingebbia1
/take-this-quiz-and-well-tell-you-what-your-pube-style.

104 Joshua Caplan, "BuzzFeed Staff Eviscerate CEO Jonah Peretti over Handling
of Mass Layoffs," Breitbart, January 25, 2019, https://www.breitbart.com/the
-media/2019/01/25/buzzfeed-staff-eviscerate-ceo-jonah-peretti-over-han
dling-of-mass-layoffs/; Janko Roettgers, "BuzzFeed Layoffs Gut National
News Desk, National Security Team," Variety, January 25, 2019, https://variety
.com/2019/digital/news/buzzfeed-layoffs-national-news-desk-1203118080/.

105 "Top Digital Publishers Join Concert to Create the Largest Premium Advertising Marketplace Online," Vox Media, May 31, 2018, https://www.voxme
dia.com/about-vox-media/2018/5/31/17413008/top-digital-publishers-join
-concert-to-create-largest-premium-advertising-marketplace-online.

106 John McCarthy, "Sleeping Giants on Breitbart and Brand Safety: 'It's Not Our
Job to Police Your Ads,'" Drum, September 4, 2019, https://www.thedrum
.com/news/2019/09/04/sleeping-giants-breitbart-and-brand-safety-its-not
-our-job-police-your-ads.

107 John Nolte, "Jon Meacham Loses MSNBC Contributor Gig for Failure to Dis-

close Biden Work," Breitbart, November 10, 2020, https://www.breitbart.com /the-media/2020/11/10/nolte-jon-meacham-loses-msnbc-contributor-gig -for-failure-to-disclose-biden-work/.

108 Patrick Gavin, "Jon Meacham's 'Week from Hell,'" *Politico*, May 15, 2010, https://www.politico.com/story/2010/05/jon-meachams-week-from-hell -037292; Mike Allen and Keach Hagey, "Sidney Harman Buys Newsweek," *Politico*, last updated April 30, 2012, https://www.politico.com/story/2010/08 /sidney-harman-buys-newsweek-040552.

109 Jonathan Easley, "MSNBC Cuts Ties with Three Contributors Joining Team Biden," *Hill*, November 11, 2020, https://thehill.com/homenews/campaign /525462-msnbc-cuts-ties-with-three-contributors-joining-team-biden.

110 Erik Wemple, "Opinion: MSNBC's John Meacham Problem," *Washington Post*, November 11, 2020, https://www.washingtonpost.com/opinions/2020 /11/11/msnbcs-jon-meacham-problem/.

111 Annie Karni and John Koblin, "The Historian John Meacham, Who Wrote 'The Soul of America,' Has Been Working on Biden's Speeches," *New York Times*, November 9, 2020, https://www.nytimes.com/2020/11/09/us/politics /the-historian-jon-meacham-who-wrote-of-the-soul-of-america-has-been -working-on-bidens-speeches.html.

112 Malcolm Nance (@MalcolmNance), "READ: Glen Greenwald shows his true colors . . . ," Twitter, July 7, 2018, 7:27 a.m., https://twitter.com/MalcolmNance /status/1015603194557153280.

113 Glenn Greenwald, "MSNBC Does Not Merely Permit Fabrications Against Democratic Party Critics. It Encourages and Rewards Them," *Intercept*, July 8, 2018, https://theintercept.com/2018/07/08/msnbc-does-not-merely-permit -fabrications-against-democratic-party-critics-it-encourages-and-rewards -them/.

Chapter 5: Beijing Bloomberg

1 "Sen. Kamala Harris Announces 2020 Presidential Candidacy," NPR, January 21, 2019, https://www.npr.org/2019/01/21/677834764/sen-kamala-harris -announces-2020-presidential-candidacy.

2 Joshua Caplan, "Bloomberg Campaign Manager: Trump Is on a 'Path to Victory' Right Now," Breitbart, November 25, 2019, https://www.breitbart.com /politics/2019/11/25/bloomberg-campaign-manager-trump-is-on-a-path-to -victory-right-now/.

3 Awr Hawkins, "Michael Bloomberg's Top 10 Gun Controls," Breitbart, November 9, 2019, https://www.breitbart.com/politics/2019/11/09/michael -bloomberg-gun-control/.

4 Awr Hawkins, "Bloomberg Enjoys Armed Guards While Fighting to Disarm Americans," Breitbart, February 3, 2020, https://www.breitbart.com/politics /2020/02/03/bloomberg-enjoys-armed-guards-while-fighting-disarm-ameri cans/.

5   "Mr. Bloomberg's Third Term," *New York Times*, December 31, 2009, https:// www.nytimes.com/2010/01/01/opinion/01fri1.html.

6   Javier C. Hernández, "Once Again, City Voters Approve Term Limits," *New York Times*, November 3, 2010, https://www.nytimes.com/2010/11/03/ny region/03limits.html.

7   "Bloomberg," *Forbes*, accessed February 15, 2021, https://www.forbes.com /companies/bloomberg/#aa5fd4174a13.

8   Emily Peck, "Billionaire Media Moguls Shouldn't Run for President," *Huffington Post*, November 26, 2019, https://www.huffpost.com/entry/billionaire -media-moguls-shouldnt-run-for-president_n_5ddd49e2e4b0913e6f7486ef.

9   Charlie Spiering, "CNN Poll: Michael Bloomberg Enters Presidential Race with Three Percent," Breitbart, November 27, 2019, https://www.breitbart.com /politics/2019/11/27/cnn-poll-michael-bloomberg-enters-presidential-race -with-three-percent/.

10 Scott Shackford, "Bloomberg's Awful Old Quotes Defending Unconstitutional Stop-and-Frisk Are Coming Back to Haunt Him," *Reason*, February 11, 2020, https://reason.com/2020/02/11/bloombergs-awful-old-quotes-defending -unconstitutional-stop-and-frisk-are-coming-back-to-haunt-him/.

11 Ann Coulter, "Stop Apologizing for Saving Black Lives," Breitbart, February 12, 2020, https://www.breitbart.com/politics/2020/02/12/ann-coulter -stop-apologizing-for-saving-black-lives/.

12 Alex Pareene, "Michael Bloomberg's Polite Authoritarianism," *Soapbox*, February 13, 2020, https://newrepublic.com/article/156560/michael-bloombergs -polite-authoritarianism.

13 John Nolte, "No One Has to Lie to Prove Michael Bloomberg's a Racist," Breitbart, February 13, 2020, https://www.breitbart.com/politics/2020/02/13/nolte -no-one-has-to-lie-to-prove-michael-bloombergs-a-racist/.

14 UPI, "Bloomberg Apologizes for Stop-and-Frisk Policy," Breitbart, November 17, 2019, https://www.breitbart.com/news/bloomberg-apologizes-for -stop-and-frisk-policy/.

15 "China's Xi Allowed to Remain 'President for Life' as Term Limits Removed," BBC News, March 11, 2018, https://www.bbc.com/news/world-asia-china -43361276.

16 Eric Levitz, "In Appeal to Hard Left, Bloomberg Praises Chinese Communism," *New York*, December 2, 2019, https://nymag.com/intelligencer/2019/12 /michael-bloomberg-china-pbs-climate-xi-dictator.html.

17 "A Global Town Hall," Bloomberg, accessed February 15, 2021, https://www .neweconomyforum.com/.

18 Sarah Zheng, "Why Chinese Vice-President Wang Qishan Can't Take Praise— Even from Michael Bloomberg," *South China Morning Post*, November 6, 2018, https://www.scmp.com/news/china/diplomacy/article/2171922/chinese-vice -president-unmoved-bloombergs-sweet-talk-singapore.

19 John Hayward, "Billionaire Guo Wengui Asks U.S. for Asylum After Accusing Top Chinese Officials of Corruption," Breitbart, September 7, 2017, https://

www.breitbart.com/national-security/2017/09/07/billionaire-guo-wengui
-asks-u-s-asylum-accusing-top-chinese-officials-corruption/; Frances Martel,
"China's Anti-Corruption Chief Out of Powerful Communist Politburo After
Corruption Accusations," Breitbart, October 24, 2017, https://www.breitbart
.com/national-security/2017/10/24/chinas-anti-corruption-chief-power
ful-communist-politburo-corruption-accusations/.

20　Jun Mai and Wendy Wu, "Is 'Firefighter' Wang Qishan Working Behind the
Scenes on Trade Talks?" *South China Morning Post*, July 2, 2019, https://
www.scmp.com/news/china/politics/article/3017001/firefighter-wang-qishan
-working-behind-scenes-trade-talks; Katsuji Nakazawa, "Xi Brings in 'Firefighter' Wang Qishan in Bid to Calm Hong Kong," Nikkei Asia, September 6, 2019, https://asia.nikkei.com/Spotlight/Hong-Kong-protests/Xi-brings
-in-firefighter-Wang-Qishan-in-bid-to-calm-Hong-Kong.

21　"Provisions on Administration of Provision of Financial Information Services in China by Foreign Institutions," Chinalawinfo, accessed February 15,
2021, http://www.lawinfochina.com/display.aspx?lib=law&id=9559&CGid
=#menu3http://www.gov.cn/flfg/2009-04/30/content_1300556.htmhttps://
translate.google.com/translate?sl=auto&tl=en&u=http%3A%2F%2Fwww.gov
.cn%2Fflfg%2F2009-04%2F30%2Fcontent_1300556.htm.

22　"List of permits for foreign (overseas) to provide financial information services in China: Bloomberg Limited Partnership," National Cyberspace
Administration of China, May 24, 2014, http://www.cac.gov.cn/2014-05/23/c
_133355715.htm.

23　"Jiang Jianguo Met with the Founder of Bloomberg L.P.," State Council Information Office of the People's Republic of China, August 20, 2015, http://www
.scio.gov.cn/32618/Document/1445192/1445192.htm.

24　"Jiang Jianguo Meets with Bloomberg Vice President," State Council Information Office of the People's Republic of China, December 21, 2015, http://www
.scio.gov.cn/32618/Document/1459587/1459587.htm.

25　http://www.gov.cn/xinwen/2016-07/14/content_5091218.htm.

26　Edwin Mora, "Expert: China Using Belt and Road to Build 'Imperialism 3.0,'"
Breitbart, May 10, 2019, https://www.breitbart.com/national-security/2019
/05/10/expert-china-using-belt-road-build-imperialism-3-0/.

27　Edwin Mora, "Uganda Trying to Attract Chinese Tourists to Make Up for
Money Lost on Belt and Road," Breitbart, May 8, 2019, https://www.breitbart
.com/national-security/2019/05/08/uganda-trying-to-attract-chinese-tourists
-to-make-up-for-money-lost-on-belt-and-road/.

28　Andrew Chatzky and James McBride, "China's Massive Belt and Road Initiative," Council on Foreign Relations, last updated January 28, 2020, https://
www.cfr.org/backgrounder/chinas-massive-belt-and-road-initiative.

29　Gabrielle Reyes, "Chinese State Media: China Must Prepare for War," Breitbart, September 11, 2020, https://www.breitbart.com/asia/2020/09/11/chi
nese-state-media-china-must-prepare-war/.

30　AFP, "US Brands Beijing's South China Sea Claims Illegal," Breitbart, July 13,

2020, https://www.breitbart.com/news/raising-stakes-us-brands-china-claims -in-south-china-sea-illegal/.

31 Frances Martel, "Indians, Vietnamese, Tibetans Rally in D.C. Against Chinese Aggression," Breitbart, August 10, 2020, https://www.breitbart.com/asia/2020 /08/10/indians-vietnamese-tibetans-rally-d-c-against-chinese-aggression/.

32 "Jiang Jianguo Meets Senior Executive of Bloomberg L.P.," State Council Information Office, People's Republic of China, last updated June 8, 2017, http:// english.scio.gov.cn/aboutscio/2017-06/08/content_40988903.htm.

33 "Guo Weimin Meets Bloomberg Delegation," State Council Information Office of the People's Republic of China, July 11, 2017, http://www.scio.gov.cn /32618/Document/1558080/1558080.htm.

34 "Guo Weimin Meets Editor-in-Chief of Bloomberg News," State Council Information Office of the People's Republic of China, last updated April 13, 2018, http://english.scio.gov.cn/m/aboutscio/2018-04/13/content_50876003 .htm.

35 "Jiang Jianguo Meets with Bloomberg Delegation," State Council Information Office of the People's Republic of China, last updated May 9, 2018, http://english.scio.gov.cn/aboutscio/2018-05/09/content_51190876_0.htm.

36 http://www.scio.gov.cn/jrxx/xkmd/Document/517300/517300.htm.

37 Steve Stecklow, "SPECIAL REPORT—Refinitiv created filter to block Reuters amid Hong Kong protests," Reuters, December 12, 2019, https://www.reuters .com/article/hongkong-protests-media/special-report-refinitiv-created-filter -to-block-reuters-stories-amid-hong-kong-protests-idUSL1N28M1EZ.

38 http://english.scio.gov.cn/aboutscio/2019-12/06/content_75484685.htm.

39 Tony Owusu, "Dow Jones CEO William Lewis to Leave Company After Contract Isn't Renewed," Street, April 8, 2020, https://www.thestreet.com/investing /dow-jones-ceo-to-leave-company.

40 Marc Tracy and Edmund Lee, "Dow Jones Chief, William Lewis, to Step Down," New York Times, April 8, 2020, https://www.nytimes.com/2020/04/08/busi ness/media/dow-jones-wall-street-journal-william-lewis.html.

41 Edward Wong, "Bloomberg News Is Said to Curb Articles That Might Anger China," New York Times, November 8, 2013, https://www.nytimes.com/2013 /11/09/world/asia/bloomberg-news-is-said-to-curb-articles-that-might -anger-china.html.

42 "Xi Jinping Millionaire Relations Reveal Fortunes of Elite," Bloomberg, June 29, 2012, https://www.bloomberg.com/news/articles/2012-06-29/xi-jin ping-millionaire-relations-reveal-fortunes-of-elite.

43 David Folkenflik, "Bloomberg News Killed Investigation, Fired Reporter, Then Sought to Silence His Wife," NPR, April 14, 2020, https://www.npr.org /2020/04/14/828565428/bloomberg-news-killed-investigation-fired-reporter -then-sought-to-silence-his-wi.

44 Tania Branigan, "China Blocks Bloomberg for Exposing Financial Affairs of Xi Jinping's Family," Guardian, June 29, 2012, https://www.theguardian.com /world/2012/jun/29/china-bloomberg-xi-jinping.

45 Howard W. French, "Bloomberg's Folly," *Columbia Journalism Review* (archive), May/June 2014, https://archives.cjr.org/feature/bloombergs_folly.php.

46 Folkenflik, "Bloomberg News Killed Investigation, Fired Reporter, Then Sought to Silence His Wife."

47 John Nolte, "Bloomberg News Caught on Tape Telling Reporters to Preserve Access to China's 'Nazis,'" Breitbart, April 15, 2020, https://www.breitbart .com/the-media/2020/04/15/nolte-bloomberg-news-caught-on-tape-telling -reporters-to-preserve-access-to-chinas-nazis/.

48 Eli Lake, "Trump's New Slogan Has Old Baggage from Nazi Era," Bloomberg Opinion, April 27, 2016, https://www.bloomberg.com/opinion/articles/2016 -04-27/trump-s-america-first-slogan-has-nazi-era-baggage; Billy House, Margaret Talev, and Jennifer Epstein, "Stung by Criticism, White House Says Trump Abhors Neo-Nazis," Bloomberg, August 13, 2017, https://www.bloom berg.com/news/articles/2017-08-13/trump-criticized-for-not-denouncing -white-nationalists-at-rally; Timothy L. O'Brien, "Trump's Racism Infests the Republican Party," Bloomberg, July 29, 2019, https://www.bloomberg.com /opinion/articles/2019-07-29/trump-s-baltimore-elijah-cummings-racism-is -fine-with-republicans.

49 Joshua Caplan, "Left-Wing Media Admit Bloomberg's Benjamin Penn Falsely Smeared a Trump Official," Breitbart, September 4, 2019, https://www.breit bart.com/the-media/2019/09/04/left-wing-media-admit-bloombergs-benja min-penn-falsely-smeared-a-trump-official/; "Trump Labor Aide Quits After Facebook Posts Surface (Retracted)," Bloomberg Law, last updated October 4, 2019, https://news.bloomberglaw.com/daily-labor-report/trump-labor-aide -quits-after-facebook-posts-surface.

50 Robert Kraychik, "Bloomberg Compares America to Nazi Germany on Holo-caust Remembrance Day Address," Breitbart, January 27, 2020, https://www .breitbart.com/2020-election/2020/01/27/bloomberg-compares-america-to -nazi-germany-on-holocaust-remembrance-day-address/.

51 Wong, "Bloomberg News Is Said to Curb Articles That Might Anger China."

52 Leta Hong Fincher, "When Bloomberg News's Reporting on China Was Chal-lenged, Bloomberg Tried to Ruin Me for Speaking Out," *Intercept*, February 18, 2020, https://theintercept.com/2020/02/18/mike-bloomberg-lp-nda-china/.

53 Wong, "Bloomberg News Is Said to Curb Articles That Might Anger China."

54 Marc Tracy, Edward Wong, and Lara Jakes, "China Announces That It Will Expel American Journalists," *New York Times*, March 17, 2020, https://www.nytimes .com/2020/03/17/business/media/china-expels-american-journalists.html.

55 Lauren Hirsch and Brian Schwartz, "Bloomberg News Will Not Investigate Mike Bloomberg or His Democratic Rivals During Primary," CNBC, Novem-ber 24, 2019, https://www.cnbc.com/2019/11/24/bloomberg-news-will-not -investigate-mike-bloomberg-or-his-democratic-rivals-during-primary.html.

56 Ibid.

57 Andrew Beaujon, "Which Bloomberg News Staffers Have Started Working for Mike Bloomberg's Campaign?" *Washingtonian*, February 28, 2020, https://

www.washingtonian.com/2020/02/28/which-bloomberg-news-staffers-have
-started-working-for-mike-bloombergs-campaign/; Maxwell Tani, "Bloomberg Continues to Poach His Newsroom to Staff Up 2020 Campaign," *Daily
Beast,* last updated January 13, 2020, https://www.thedailybeast.com/bloom
berg-continues-to-poach-his-newsroom-to-staff-up-2020-campaign.

58 Lauren Hirsch, "Trump Campaign Revokes Credentials for Bloomberg News
Reporters over Decision Not to Investigate 2020 Dems," CNBC, December 2,
2019, https://www.cnbc.com/2019/12/02/trump-campaign-revokes-creden
tials-for-bloomberg-news-reporters.html.

59 Tal Axelrod, "Trump Campaign Removes Bloomberg News Reporter from Iowa
Event," *Hill,* February 3, 2020, https://thehill.com/homenews/campaign/481285
-trump-campaign-removes-bloomberg-news-reporter-from-iowa-event.

60 jimrutenberg (@jimrutenberg), "Bloomberg News exits political investigation
biz for primaries at least . . . ," Twitter, November 24, 2019, 12:46 p.m., https://
twitter.com/jimrutenberg/status/1198704496681062401.

61 Jerome Hudson, "Bill Maher: Bloomberg's Soda Ban 'Makes Liberals Look
Bad,'" Breitbart, March 17, 2013, https://www.breitbart.com/blog/2013/03/17
/bill-maher-bloomberg-s-soda-ban-makes-liberals-look-bad/.

62 John Washington, "Mike Bloomberg Exploited Prison Labor to Make 2020
Presidential Campaign Phone Calls," The Intercept, December 24, 2019,
https://theintercept.com/2019/12/24/mike-bloomberg-2020-prison-labor/.

63 Ibid.

64 Taylor Lorenz, "Michael Bloomberg's Campaign Suddenly Drops Memes
Everywhere," *New York Times,* February 13, 2020, https://www.nytimes.com
/2020/02/13/style/michael-bloomberg-memes-jerry-media.html?auth=login
-email&login=email.

65 Jeff Horwitz and Georgia Wells, "Bloomberg Bankrolls a Social-Media Army
to Push Message," *Wall Street Journal,* last updated February 19, 2020, https://
www.wsj.com/articles/bloomberg-bankrolls-a-social-media-army-to-push
-message-11582127768.

66 Suhauna Hussain and Jeff Bercovici, "Twitter Is Suspending 70 Pro-Bloomberg
Accounts, Citing 'Platform Manipulation,'" *Los Angeles Times,* February 21,
2020, https://www.latimes.com/business/technology/story/2020-02-21/twitter
-suspends-bloomberg-accounts.

67 Jim VandeHei, Alexi McCammond, and Alayna Treene, "Bloomberg's Historic Bust," Axios, March 4, 2020, https://www.axios.com/mike-bloomberg
-super-tuesday-bust-16a35376-95f7-425e-a5c1-bc78249c6553.html; "Who's
Winning the 2020 Presidential Delegate Count?" Bloomberg, last updated
August 14, 2020, https://www.bloomberg.com/graphics/2020-presidential
-delegates-tracker/.

68 Chelsea Stahl, "Meet the Press Blog: Latest News, Analysis and Data Driving
the Political Discussion," NBC News, last updated February 15, 2021, https://
www.nbcnews.com/politics/meet-the-press/blog/meet-press-blog-latest
-news-analysis-data-driving-political-discussion-n988541/ncrd1164846.

69 Michael Scherer, "Mike Bloomberg to Spend at Least $100 Million in Florida to Benefit Joe Biden," *Washington Post*, September 13, 2020, https://www.washingtonpost.com/politics/bloomberg-money-florida-biden/2020/09/12/af51bb50-f511-11ea-bc45-e5d48ab44b9f_story.html.

70 Ina Cordle, "Making Hay in Washington," *Real Deal*, June 17, 2019, https://therealdeal.com/miami/issues_articles/making-hay-in-wellington/.

71 Rashaan Ayesh, "Bloomberg Pledges $60 Million in Bid to Help Democrats Retain House," Axios, August 18, 2020, https://www.axios.com/bloomberg-pledge-house-democrats-36ae09a3-edb5-467a-a082-aef826513189.html.

72 Joshua Klein, "Michael Bloomberg Funding Helps Florida Felons Vote Due to Groundwork by George Soros," Breitbart, September 29, 2020, https://www.breitbart.com/politics/2020/09/29/bloomberg-funds-help-florida-felons-vote-due-soros-groundwork/.

73 Joel B. Pollak, "Mike Bloomberg Raises $16 Million to Pay Fines of Black, Hispanic Felons to Vote in Florida," Breitbart, September 22, 2020, https://www.breitbart.com/politics/2020/09/22/mike-bloomberg-raises-16-million-to-pay-fines-of-black-hispanic-felons-to-vote-in-florida/.

74 John Binder, "Florida to Investigate Mike Bloomberg's Donations to Black, Hispanic Felons So They Can Vote," Breitbart, September 23, 2020, https://www.breitbart.com/politics/2020/09/23/florida-to-investigate-mike-bloombergs-donations-to-black-hispanic-felons-so-they-can-vote/.

75 David Wainer, "Michael Bloomberg Re-Appointed as United Nations Climate Envoy," Bloomberg, February 5, 2021, https://www.bloomberg.com/news/articles/2021-02-05/michael-bloomberg-re-appointed-as-united-nations-climate-envoy.

76 Morgan Phillips, "Michael Bloomberg, UN Climate Envoy, Shuns Commercial Travel for Private Jets," Fox News, February 5, 2021, https://www.foxnews.com/politics/michael-bloomberg-un-climate-envoy-private-jets.

Chapter 6: Sleeping Giants and the Cancellation of MAGA

1 Natalle Jackson, "HuffPost Forecasts Hillary Clinton Will Win with 323 Electoral Votes," *HuffPost*, November 7, 2016, https://www.huffpost.com/entry/polls-hillary-clinton-win_n_5821074ce4b0e80b02cc2a94; Josh Katz, "Who Will Be President?" *New York Times*, November 8, 2016, https://www.nytimes.com/interactive/2016/upshot/presidential-polls-forecast.html; "Betting sites see record wagering on US presidential election," CNBC, November 7, 2016, https://www.cnbc.com/2016/11/07/betting-sites-see-record-wagering-on-us-presidential-election.html.

2 Nate Silver, "Why FiveThirtyEight Gave Trump a Better Chance than Almost Anyone Else," FiveThirtyEight, November 11, 2016, https://fivethirtyeight.com/features/why-fivethirtyeight-gave-trump-a-better-chance-than-almost-anyone-else/.

3 Jen Doll, "Is protesting the new brunch?" *Week*, February 23, 2017, https://

theweek.com/articles/678868/protesting-new-brunch; John Favreau (@jonfavs), "'Protest is the new brunch' is up! Joined by @SabrinaSiddiqui and @realdgray to talk #MuslimBan and SCOTUS . . . ," Twitter, January 30, 2017, 3:51 p.m., https://twitter.com/jonfavs/status/826171089310998528?lang=en.

4 Ian Mason, "Hillary Spokesman: Clinton Campaign Didn't Appreciate 'Profound' Impact of the 'Breitbart Effect,'" Breitbart, March 29, 2017, https://www.breitbart.com/politics/2017/03/29/hillary-spokesman-clinton-campaign-didnt-appreciate-profound-impact-of-the-breitbart-effect/.

5 Charlie Spiering, "Barack Obama: Breitbart News Shifted Entire Media Narrative During 2016 Election," Breitbart, November 2, 2017, https://www.breitbart.com/politics/2017/11/02/barack-obama-breitbart-news-shifted-entire-media-narrative-during-2016-election/.

6 David Weigel, "Democratic donors plot the future—out-thinking the right," Washington Post, January 21, 2017, https://www.washingtonpost.com/politics/democratic-donors-plot-the-future—out-thinking-the-right/2017/01/21/6d0d14ea-df5f-11e6-ad42-f3375f271c9c_story.html.

7 Nina Nguyen, "Inside the rise of the 'Breitbart of the Left,'" Vanity Fair, January 5, 2017, https://www.vanityfair.com/news/2017/01/david-brock-breitbart-interview-shareblue.

8 "Ads Shown Before YouTube ISIS Videos Catch Companies Off-Guard," NBC, March 10, 2015, https://www.nbcnews.com/storyline/isis-terror/ads-shown-isis-videos-youtube-catch-companies-guard-n320946.

9 Jack Marshall, "IAB Chief Calls On Online Ad Industry to Fight Fake News," Wall Street Journal, January 30, 2017, https://www.wsj.com/articles/iab-chief-calls-on-online-ad-industry-to-fight-fake-news-1485812139.

10 Ibid.

11 Chriss W. Street, "Facebook's Mark Zuckerberg Attacked by Left for Lacking Bias to Help Hillary Win," Breitbart, November 12, 2016, https://www.breitbart.com/local/2016/11/12/facebooks-zuckerberg-attacked-lacking-bias-hillary-clinton-win/; Sarah Perez, "Rigged," TechCrunch, November 9, 2016, https://techcrunch.com/2016/11/09/rigged/.

12 Joel B. Pollak, "It Begins: College Professor Lists Breitbart as 'Fake News' Site," Breitbart, November 15, 2016, https://www.breitbart.com/the-media/2016/11/15/fake-news-begins-college-professor-lists-breitbart/.

13 Chriss W. Street, "Google, Facebook to Defund Conservative Sites as 'Fake News,'" Breitbart, November 16, 2016, https://www.breitbart.com/local/2016/11/16/google-facebook-to-defund-conservative-sites-as-fake-news/.

14 Joel B. Pollak, "Fake News: New York Times Falsely Claims Breitbart 'Birther' Site," Breitbart, November 21, 2016, https://www.breitbart.com/the-media/2016/11/21/fake-news-new-york-times-joseph-goldstein-falsely-claims-breitbart-birther/.

15 Joel B. Pollak, "More Fake News: New York Times Calls Bannon 'White Nationalist,'" Breitbart, November 21, 2016, https://www.breitbart.com/the-media/2016/11/21/fake-news-new-york-times-calls-bannon-white-nationalist/.

16 John Hayward, "12 Fake News Stories from the Mainstream Media," Breitbart, November 22, 2016, https://www.breitbart.com/the-media/2016/11/22/12-fake -news-stories-from-the-mainstream-media/.

17 Sheila Coronel, Steve Coll, and Derek Kravitz, "Rolling Stone's Investigation: 'A Failure That Was Avoidable,'" *Columbia Journalism Review*, April 5, 2015, https://www.cjr.org/investigation/rolling_stone_investigation.php.

18 Tom Ciccotta, "Flashback: New York Times Bigot Sarah Jeong Defended UVA Rape Hoaxer," Breitbart, August 3, 2018, https://www.breitbart.com /tech/2018/08/03/flashback-new-york-times-bigot-sarah-jeong-defended -uva-rape-hoaxer/.

19 John Hayward, "Exclusive—Ann Coulter Post-Election Review: Media Bias, 'Fake News,' and Burning Down the Conservative Establishment," Breitbart, November 25, 2016, https://www.breitbart.com/radio/2016/11/25/exclu sive-ann-coulter-post-election-review-media-bias-fake-news-and-burning -down-the-conservative-establishment/.

20 Callum Borchers, "How Hillary Clinton might have inspired Trump's 'fake news' attacks," *Washington Post*, January 3, 2018, https://www.washington post.com/news/the-fix/wp/2018/01/03/how-hillary-clinton-might-have -inspired-trumps-fake-news-attacks/.

21 Ezra Dulis, "8 Times Hillary Clinton Pushed Fake News," Breitbart, December 10, 2016, https://www.breitbart.com/the-media/2016/12/10/hillary-clin ton-fake-news/.

22 Matthew Boyle, "Fake Newsman Brian Williams Slams Fake News," Breitbart, December 8, 2016, https://www.breitbart.com/politics/2016/12/08/fake -newsman-brian-williams-slams-fake-news/.

23 Joel B. Pollak, "10 Ways the CIA's 'Russian Hacking' Story Is Left-Wing 'Fake News,'" Breitbart, December 12, 2016, https://www.breitbart.com/politics /2016/12/12/cia-russian-hacking-story-sham/.

24 Borchers, "How Hillary Clinton might have inspired Trump's 'fake news' attacks."

25 John McCarthy, "Sleeping Giants on Breitbart and brand safety: 'It's not our job to police your ads,'" *The Drum*, September 4, 2019, https://www.thedrum. com/news/2019/09/04/sleeping-giants-breitbart-and-brand-safety-its-not -our-job-police-your-ads#:~:text=Watch%20Now-,Sleeping%20Giants%20 on%20Breitbart%20and%20brand%20safety%3A%20'It's%20not%20 our,job%20to%20police%20your%20ads.

26 Nandini Jammi, "I'm leaving Sleeping Giants, but not because I want to," Nandini Jammi, July 9, 2020, https://nandoodles.medium.com/im-leaving-sleep ing-giants-but-not-because-i-want-to-d9c4f488642.

27 Shareen Pathak, "In response to complaints, some brands are pulling ads placed on Breitbart," Digiday, November 22, 2016, https://digiday.com/mar keting/brands-pulling-ads-placed-breitbart/.

28 Jay Willis, "How an Activist Group Turned to the Dark Side to Hit Breitbart Where It Hurts," *GQ*, March 2, 2018, https://www.gq.com/story/sleeping -giants-breitbart-nra-interview; Wil S. Hylton, "Down the Breitbart Hole,"

New York Times, August 16, 2017, https://www.nytimes.com/2017/08/16 /magazine/breitbart-alt-right-steve-bannon.html.

29 Eric Johnson, "How a Twitter account convinced 4,000 companies to stop advertising on Breitbart," *Vox,* September 4, 2018, https://www.vox.com /2018/9/3/17813124/sleeping-giants-breitbart-advertising-matt-rivitz-kara -swisher-recode-decode-podcast.

30 McCarthy, "Sleeping Giants on Breitbart and brand safety: 'It's not our job to police your ads.'"

31 Sapna Maheshwari, "Revealed: The People Behind an Anti-Breitbart Twitter Account," *New York Times,* July 20, 2018, https://www.nytimes.com/2018/07 /20/business/media/sleeping-giants-breitbart-twitter.html.

32 "Hemingway: Sleeping Giants 'Delusional or Dishonest' to Claim 'Apolitical' Mission," Breitbart, February 22, 2019, https://www.breitbart.com/the-media /2019/02/22/hemingway-sleeping-giants-delusional-or-dishonest-to-claim -apolitical-mission/.

33 Sleeping Giants (@slpng_giants), "TIME OUT. @united, didn't you say that you would no longer fly children separated from their parents from ICE . . . ," Twitter, June 26, 2018, 12:24 a.m., https://twitter.com/slpng_giants/status /1011465290314633216?lang=en.

34 Sleeping Giants (@slpng_giants), "Here's our comment: If @nbc brass is found to have known about Lauer's actions and covered them up . . . ," Twitter, October 9, 2019, 2:59 p.m., https://twitter.com/slpng_giants/status /1182007796381839360; Mike Shields, "An activist group that holds companies involved in #metoo allegations accountable explains why it hasn't gone after CBS and Les Moonves," Business Insider, August 2, 2018, https://www .businessinsider.com/why-activist-group-sleeping-giants-hasnt-gone-after -cbs-and-les-moonves-2018-8.

35 Melody Hahm, "How a group of marketers jumpstarted a Twitter campaign against Bill O'Reilly," Yahoo Finance, April 19, 2017, https://finance.yahoo .com/news/bill-oreilly-oreilly-report-sleeping-giants-twitter-campaign -165628232.html.

36 Wieden+Kennedy's Portland office has represented SG targets:

• SG tweet attacking Coke. "You might want to check with your agency." Wieden+Kennedy's Portland office, where Britton Taylor works, lists Coca Cola as a client.

• SG also approached Nike, a W+K client.
• Turbotax.
• American Indian College Fund.
• W+K's NY office represents Fox Sports.

As well as Spotify.

37 Brian O'Kelley, "My company was one of the first to pull advertising from Breitbart—here's why," *Independent,* December 19, 2016, https://www.inde

pendent.co.uk/voices/breitbart-steve-bannon-donald-trump-hate-speech-ad
-tech-a7484766.html.

38 Russell Brandom, "AT&T restores service to Breitbart after buying out upstart
ad company," *Verge*, August 21, 2019, https://www.theverge.com/2019/8/21
/20826484/att-breitbart-service-appnexus-xandr-deplatform-hate-speech.

39 Jim Rutenberg, "News Outlets to Seek Bargaining Rights Against Google and
Facebook," *New York Times*, July 9, 2017, https://www.nytimes.com/2017/07
/09/business/media/google-facebook-news-media-alliance.html; Jim Rutenberg, "Sean Hannity, a Murder, and Why Fake News Endures," *New York
Times,* May 24, 2017, https://www.nytimes.com/2017/05/24/business/media
/seth-rich-fox-news-sean-hannity.html.

40 Glenn Fleishman, "Thousands of Advertisers Shun Breitbart, but Amazon
Remains," *Fast Company*, April 16, 2018, https://www.fastcompany.com
/40535815/thousands-of-advertisers-shun-breitbart-but-amazon-remains.

41 "About half of all digital display ad revenue goes to Facebook, Google," Pew
Research Center, July 14, 2020, https://www.pewresearch.org/ft_20-07-10
_digitalnative_feature_new/.

42 Pagan Kennedy, "How to Destroy the Business Model of Breitbart and Fake
News," *New York Times,* January 1, 2017, https://www.nytimes.com/2017/01
/07/opinion/sunday/how-to-destroy-the-business-model-of-breitbart-and
-fake-news.html.

43 Andy Eckhardt, "Breitbart Blacklisted by Germany's BMW and Deutsche
Telekom," NBC News, December 8, 2016, https://www.nbcnews.com/news
/world/breitbart-blacklisted-germany-s-bmw-deutsche-telekom-n693531.

44 Peter Hasson, "Sleeping Giants' Anonymous Founder Unmasked; Top Ad
Writer Behind Boycott Campaign Targeting Breitbart, Ingraham," *Daily Caller,*
July 16, 2018, https://dailycaller.com/2018/07/16/sleeping-giants-founder
-rivitz/; Maheshwari, "Revealed: The People Behind an Anti-Breitbart Twitter
Account."

45 Patrick Coffee, "Inside an Anonymous Marketing Group's Efforts to Take
Down Breitbart One Ad at a Time," *Ad Week,* March 26, 2017, https://www
.adweek.com/performance-marketing/inside-an-anonymous-marketing
-groups-efforts-to-take-down-breitbart-one-ad-at-a-time/.

46 Fleishman, "Thousands of Advertisers Shun Breitbart, but Amazon Remains."

47 Johnson, "How a Twitter account convinced 4,000 companies to stop advertising on Breitbart."

48 Gilad Edelman, "She Helped Wreck the News Business. Here's Her Plan to Fix
It," *Wired,* August 13, 2020, https://www.wired.com/story/she-helped-wreck
-the-news-business-heres-her-plan-to-fix-it/.

49 Suzanne Vranica, "'Shooting,' 'Bomb,' 'Trump': Advertisers Blacklist News
Stories Online," *Wall Street Journal*, August 15, 2019, https://www.wsj.com
/articles/advertisers-blacklist-hard-news-including-trump-fearing-backlash
-11565879086.

50 Jonty Bloom, "Coronavirus: How the advertising industry is changing," BBC, May 27, 2020, https://www.bbc.com/news/business-52806115.

51 Craig Silverman, "Coronavirus Ad Blocking Is Starving Some News Sites of Revenue," BuzzFeed News, March 26, 2020, https://www.buzzfeednews.com /article/craigsilverman/news-sites-need-ads-to-survive-the-coronavirus -more-than-35.

52 Ibid.

53 Jackie Wattles, "Sleeping Giants founder talks online ads in first on-camera interview," CNN, September 2, 2018, https://money.cnn.com/2018/09/02 /media/matt-rivitz-sleeping-giants-google-ads-breitbart/index.html.

54 Lucinda Southern, "Keyword Block Lists Still Cause Headaches for Publishers," Digiday, November 22, 2019, https://digiday.com/media/keyword-block -lists-still-cause-headaches-publishers/.

55 Tim Peterson, " 'Keywords are still a pretty blunt tool': Agencies work to refine brand-safety blocklists," Digiday, May 9, 2019, https://digiday.com/marketing /keywords-still-pretty-blunt-tool-agencies-work-refine-brand-safety-block lists/.

56 "Coronavirus: When using the c-word gets you blacklisted," Deutsche Welle, accessed February 21, 2020, https://www.dw.com/en/coronavirus-pandemic -blacklist-advertising-news-digital-covid-19/a-53056149.

57 George P. Slefo, "Publishers Complain About Media Buyers Blacklisting Coronavirus Content," AdAge, March 20, 2020, https://adage.com/article/media /publishers-complain-about-media-buyers-blacklisting-coronavirus-content /2245406.

58 Sheila Dang, Kate Holton, and Helen Coster, "Advertisers shun coronavirus coverage, hastening news media battle for survival," Reuters, April 9, 2020, https://www.reuters.com/article/us-health-coronavirus-media-blacklisting /advertisers-shun-coronavirus-coverage-hastening-news-media-battle-for -survival-idUSKCN21R0HC.

59 Mark Sweney, "UK publishers losing digital ad revenue due to content 'blacklists,' " Guardian, January 20, 2020, https://www.theguardian.com/media/2020 /jan/20/uk-publishers-losing-digital-ad-revenue-due-to-content-blacklists.

60 Slefo, "Publishers Complain About Media Buyers Blacklisting Coronavirus Content."

61 Megha Rajagopalan, "The Leaders of Sleeping Giants Are Splitting over a Dispute on Credit and Titles," BuzzFeed News, July 10, 2020, https://www .buzzfeednews.com/article/meghara/nandini-jammi-leaving-sleeping-giants.

62 Allum Bokhari, "Matt Rivitz of Far-left 'Sleeping Giants' Admits Discriminating Against Woman of Color," Breitbart, July 13, 2020, https://www.breit bart.com/tech/2020/07/13/matt-rivitz-of-far-left-sleeping-giants-admits-dis criminating-against-woman-of-color/.

63 Sleeping Giants (@slpng_giants), "A letter of apology," Twitter, July 10, 2020, 11:35 a.m., https://twitter.com/slpng_giants/status/1281613023770284035.

64 Patrick Kulp, "Sleeping Giants Co-Founder Sees Natural Language AI as Next Step in War on Disinformation," *Ad Week,* June 12, 2020, https://www.adweek .com/programmatic/sleeping-giants-founder-sees-natural-language-ai-as -next-step-in-war-on-disinformation/.

65 "Largest Funders of Poynter," Poynter, accessed February 22, 2021, https:// www.poynter.org/major-funders/; Jerome Hudson, "Facebook Fact-Checker PolitiFact Funded by Clinton Foundation Donor," Breitbart, December 16, 2016, https://www.breitbart.com/the-media/2016/12/16/facebook-fact -checker-politifact-funded-by-clinton-foundation-donor/; "Facebook's Third -Party Fact-Checking Program," Facebook, accessed February 22, 2021, https://www.facebook.com/journalismproject/programs/third-party-fact -checking.

66 Erica Anderson, "Building trust online by partnering with the International Fact Checking Network," Google, October 26, 2017, https://blog.google/out reach-initiatives/google-news-initiative/building-trust-online-partnering -international-fact-checking-network/.

67 Mathew Ingram, "NewsGuard wants to rank the news based on credibility," *Columbia Journalism Review,* March 4, 2018, https://www.cjr.org/the_new _gatekeepers/newsguard-news-ranking-credibility.php.

68 Allum Bokhari, "Microsoft Teams with Establishment 'NewsGuard' to Create News Blacklist," Breitbart, January 23, 2019, https://www.breitbart.com/tech /2019/01/23/microsoft-teams-with-establishment-newsguard-to-create-news -blacklist/.

69 Sean Moran, "Five News Publications Deemed 'Trustworthy' by NewsGuard That Posted Fake News," Breitbart, January 24, 2020, https://www.breitbart .com/tech/2019/01/24/five-news-publications-deemed-trustworthy-by -newsguard-that-posted-fake-news/; Allum Bokhari, "NewsGuard Defends New York Times Stealth Edit of Blackface Story: 'Not All Changes Necessar- ily Corrections,'" Breitbart, February 7, 2019, https://www.breitbart.com/tech /2019/02/07/newsguard-defends-new-york-times-stealth-edit-of-blackface -story-not-all-changes-necessarily-corrections/; John Nolte, "Nolte: Black- listers at Microsoft's NewsGuard Label Proven Hoaxes 'Credible,'" Breitbart, January 28, 2019, https://www.breitbart.com/the-media/2019/01/28/nolte -blacklisters-microsofts-newsguard-label-proven-hoaxes-credible/.

70 Nolte, "Nolte: Blacklisters at Microsoft's NewsGuard Label Proven Hoaxes 'Credible.'"

71 Lucas Nolan, "Microsoft Blacklist: NewsGuard Warns Breitbart Is 'Fake News' 29 Times on Single Google Page," Breitbart, February 1, 2019, https://www .breitbart.com/tech/2019/02/01/microsoft-blacklist-newsguard-warns-breit bart-is-fake-news-29-times-on-single-google-page/.

72 "France Relaxes Its Ban on Trucks Entering from Britain," *U.S. News & World Report,* December 22, 2020, https://www.usnews.com/news/world/articles /2020-12-22/still-stuck-1-500-france-bound-trucks-stranded-in-england; "France relaxes its ban on trucks entering from Britain," Breitbart, Decem-

ber 22, 2020, https://www.breitbart.com/news/still-stuck-1500-france-bound
-trucks-stranded-in-england/.

73 Allum Bokhari, "NewsGuard Labels Bogus BuzzFeed Moscow Tower Story
'Trustworthy,' Breitbart Fact Check 'Untrustworthy,'" Breitbart, January 29,
2019, https://www.breitbart.com/tech/2019/01/29/newsguard-labels-bogus
-buzzfeed-moscow-tower-story-trustworthy-breitbart-fact-check-untrust
worthy/.

74 Allum Bokhari, "NewsGuard Packs Board with Neo Conservatives, D.C.
Power Players," Breitbart, January 24, 2019, https://www.breitbart.com/tech
/2019/01/24/newsguard-packs-board-with-neo-conservatives-d-c-power
-players/.

75 Charlie Nash, "NewsGuard's Advisory Board Has History of Fake News,
Unethical Journalism," Breitbart, January 25, 2019, https://www.breitbart.com
/tech/2019/01/25/newsguards-advisory-board-has-history-of-fake-news
-unethical-journalism/.

76 "Fourteen Clear Factual Errors in Richard Stengel's Essay on the Constitution
(And I Am Looking for Your Help)," Breitbart, June 29, 2011, https://www
.breitbart.com/the-media/2011/06/29/fourteen-clear-factual-errors-in-rich
ard-stengel-s-essay-on-the-constitution-and-i-am-looking-for-your-help/.

77 Nash, "NewsGuard's Advisory Board Has History of Fake News, Unethical
Journalism."

78 "Brand Safety," NewsGuard, accessed February 22, 2021, https://www.news
guardtech.com/.

Chapter 7: Mostly Peaceful Riots: The Story of Black Lives Matter

1 Jeff Poor, "MSNBC's Velshi as Minneapolis Burns Behind Him: 'This Is Mostly
a Protest—It Is Not Generally Speaking Unruly,'" Breitbart, May 28, 2020,
https://www.breitbart.com/clips/2020/05/28/msnbcs-velshi-as-minneapolis
-burns-behind-him-this-is-mostly-a-protest-it-is-not-generally-speaking
-unruly/.

2 Jeff Poor, "MSNBC's Haake Near White House as St. John's Church Burns:
'This Is Still Peaceful Protesters,'" Breitbart, May 31, 2020, https://www.breit
bart.com/clips/2020/05/31/msnbcs-haake-near-white-house-as-st-johns
-church-burns-this-is-still-peaceful-protesters/.

3 Steve Guest (@steveguest), "While protesters in St. Paul, Minnesota held a
moment of silence, CNN goes there live for an interview only to get shouted
down for ruining the silence . . . ," Twitter, June 2, 2020, 4:54 p.m., https://twit
ter.com/SteveGuest/status/1267922509845934081.

4 Peter Wade, "Obama Rails Against Government Attacks on Protesters and
Voter Suppression During John Lewis Eulogy," Rolling Stone, July 30, 2020,
https://www.rollingstone.com/politics/politics-news/obama-government
-attacks-protesters-voter-suppression-john-lewis-eulogy-1036913/.

5 Neal Augenstein (@AugensteinWTOP), "First on WTOP: U.S. Park Police is

expanding its decision-making . . . ," Twitter, June 2, 2020, 5:13 a.m., https://twitter.com/AugensteinWTOP/status/1267791336146636800.

6 Philip Melanchthon Wegmann (@philipWegmann), "Protesters were warned 3 times over loud speaker by park service . . . ," Twitter, June 1, 2020, 4:53 p.m., https://twitter.com/PhilipWegmann/status/1267605295863300096; Neal Augenstein (@AugensteinWTOP), "First on WTOP: U.S. Park Police is expanding its decision-making . . ."

7 Penny Starr, "US Park Police Corrects Record: Tear Gas Not Used in Lafayette Park," Breitbart, June 2, 2020, https://www.breitbart.com/politics/2020/06/02/us-park-police-corrects-record-tear-gas-not-used-in-lafayette-park/.

8 Joel B. Pollak, "Nancy Pelosi Admits to MSNBC: 'Maybe They Didn't Have Tear Gas,'" Breitbart, June 3, 2020, https://www.breitbart.com/politics/2020/06/03/nancy-pelosi-admits-to-msnbc-maybe-they-didnt-have-tear-gas/.

9 Alana Mastrangelo, "Mia Farrow: If Trump Were a 'Real Leader,' He Would Listen to 'Peaceful Protesters' Outside White House," Breitbart, June 1, 2020, https://www.breitbart.com/entertainment/2020/06/01/mia-farrow-if-trump-were-a-real-leader-he-would-listen-to-peaceful-protesters-outside-white-house/.

10 Charlie Spiering, "Violent Protesters Fail to Tear Down White House Barriers," Breitbart, June 3, 2020, https://www.breitbart.com/politics/2020/06/03/violent-protesters-fail-to-tear-down-white-house-barriers/.

11 Jaclyn Cosgrove, "A Peaceful Protest, Then Looting, on Van Nuys Boulevard," Los Angeles Times, June 1, 2020, https://www.latimes.com/california/story/2020-06-01/peaceful-protest-then-looting-on-van-nuys-boulevard.

12 Chris Rickert, "Third night of looting follows third night of mostly peaceful protest," Wisconsin State Journal, June 2, 2020, https://madison.com/wsj/news/local/crime-and-courts/third-night-of-looting-follows-third-night-of-mostly-peaceful-protest/article_c19bcd26-f454-58dd-abf8-40eeef596f3c.html.

13 "Peaceful Protesters Defy Curfews as Violence Ebbs," New York Times, June 2, 2020, https://www.nytimes.com/2020/06/02/us/george-floyd-video-autopsy-protests.html.

14 "Peaceful Protests of George Floyd's Death Take Place Across the World | TODAY," YouTube video, posted by Today, June 2, 2020, https://www.youtube.com/watch?v=jOfymJ1X6Io.

15 "Peaceful protests seen across Los Angeles, OC, over George Floyd's death | ABC7," YouTube video, posted by "ABC7," June 1, 2020, https://www.youtube.com/watch?v=MGwQZfrdl8Y.

16 "Peaceful protests in L.A. County overshadowed by violence," YouTube video, posted by "KTLA 5," May 31, 2020, https://www.youtube.com/watch?v=alEYSlvYD70.

17 "Peaceful Protests Turn Violent in Fairfax District | NBCLA," YouTube video, posted by "NBCLA," May 31, 2020, https://www.youtube.com/watch?v=IfQZ7q87GEs.

18 "Peaceful California protests overshadowed by violence and looting," CBS News, June 1, 2020, https://www.cbsnews.com/video/peaceful-california-pro tests-overshadowed-by-violence-and-looting/.

19 "Police use tear gas, push back peaceful protesters for Trump church visit | ABC News," YouTube video, posted by "ABC News," June 2, 2020, https:// www.youtube.com/watch?v=hblX9QwPDaw.

20 "NYPD Commissioner Says Bricks 'Are Being Placed and Then Transported to Peaceful Protests,' Councilman Then Calls Them 'Construction Debris,'" CBS News, June 3, 2020, https://newyork.cbslocal.com/2020/06/03/nypd -shea-bricks-strategically-placed-at-protests/.

21 John Nolte, "Nolte: Watch CNN's Chris Cuomo Encourage More Riots in Democrat-Run Cities," Breitbart, June 3, 2020, https://www.breitbart.com/the -media/2020/06/03/nolte-watch-cnns-chris-cuomo-encourage-more-riots-in -democrat-run-cities/.

22 Tom Ciccotta, "Poll: 58% of Young, College-Educated Americans Say Riots Are Justified," Breitbart, June 3, 2020, https://www.breitbart.com/tech/2020 /06/03/poll-58-of-young-college-educated-americans-say-riots-are-justified/.

23 Ibid.

24 Robert Kraychik, "AOC Shares 'Protesting Safely' Guidelines, Warns of 'White Supremacist' Infiltration," Breitbart, May 30, 2020, https://www.breitbart.com /politics/2020/05/30/aoc-shares-protesting-safely-guidelines-warns-white -supremacist-infiltration/.

25 Joy-Ann Pro-Democracy and Masks Area (@JoyAnnReid), "So now, the attorney general, Bill Barr, is attempting to pin the anarchy and infiltration . . . ," Twitter, May 30, 2020, https://twitter.com/JoyAnnReid/sta tus/1266794420457873408?ref_src=twsrc%5Etfw.

26 Edwin Mora, "Minnesota Democrats: 'White Supremacists' Instigating Race Riots over Black Man's Death," Breitbart, May 30, 2020, https://www .breitbart.com/politics/2020/05/30/minnesota-democrats-white-suprema cists-instigating-race-riots-over-black-mans-death/; Keynode's TechTalk (@_techtalkng), "RT QuickTake Asked whether there were white suprema- cists causing destruction in the Minneapolis protests Minnesota Gov. Tim Walz said he suspected so, but couldn't confirm . . . ," Twitter, May 30, 2020, 4:57 a.m., https://twitter.com/_techtalkng/status/1266654878035841026.

27 Edwin Mora, "Even Far-Left Southern Poverty Law Center Says No Evidence White Supremacists Sparking Riots," Breitbart, June 2, 2020, https://www .breitbart.com/politics/2020/06/02/even-far-left-southern-poverty-law-cen ter-says-no-evidence-white-supremacists-sparking-riots/.

28 Gabe Gutierrez, David K. Li, and Dennis Romero, "Minneapolis police pre- cinct burns as George Floyd protests rage; CNN crew arrested," NBC, May 28, 2020, https://www.nbcnews.com/news/us-news/protests-looting-erupt-again -minneapolis-area-following-death-george-floyd-n1216881.

29 Terry Flores, "Damage due to rioting, unrest in Kenosha tops $50 million; 200 Guard assisted here," Kenosha News, September 9, 2020, https://www

.kenoshanews.com/news/local/damage-due-to-rioting-unrest-in-kenosha
-tops-50-million-2-000-guard-assisted-here/article_26473ec9-c08a-5490
-9d09-cc2b840b65f1.html.

30 Noah Manskar, "450 NYC businesses damaged during George Floyd protests,"
New York Post, June 12, 2020, https://nypost.com/2020/06/12/450-nyc-busi
nesses-damaged-during-george-floyd-protests/.

31 Zack Budryk, "Over 90 Percent of Protests This Summer Were Peaceful,
Report Shows," *Hill,* September 3, 2020, https://thehill.com/homenews/state
-watch/515082-over-90-percent-of-protests-this-summer-were-peaceful
-report-shows.

32 Joseph Wulfsohn, "CNN Panned for On-Air Graphic Reading 'Fiery But
Mostly Peaceful Protest' in Front of Kenosha Fire," Fox News, August 27, 2020,
https://www.foxnews.com/media/cnn-panned-for-on-air-graphic-reading
-fiery-but-mostly-peaceful-protest-in-front-of-kenosha-fire.

33 Megan Garber, "Don't Fall for the 'Chaos' Theory of the Protests," *Atlantic,*
June 2, 2020, https://www.theatlantic.com/culture/archive/2020/06/george
-floyd-protests-are-not-chaos-trump-new-york-times/612544/.

34 "Ferguson Effect," Wikipedia, accessed February 24, 2021, https://en.wikipedia
.org/wiki/Ferguson_effect#:~:text=The%20Ferguson%20effect%20refers%20
to,distrust%20and%20hostility%20towards%20police.

35 Ali Watkins, "N.Y.P.D. Disbands Plainclothes Units Involved in Many Shootings," *New York Times,* June 15, 2020, https://www.nytimes.com/2020/06
/15/nyregion/nypd-plainclothes-cops.html.

36 Frank Main and Fran Spielman, "Chicago Cops Are Retiring at 'Unheard
of' Twice the Usual Rate," *Chicago Sun-Times,* August 17, 2020, https://chi
cago.suntimes.com/politics/2020/8/17/21372795/chicago-police-department
-retirements-policemens-annuity-benefit-fund-michael-lappe; Anthony M.
DeStefano, "NYPD Officers Retiring in Large Numbers, Officials Say," *News-
day,* last updated September 15, 2020, https://www.newsday.com/news/new
-york/nypd-retirements-shea-1.49362848.

37 Dara Lind, "The 'Ferguson Effect,' a Theory That's Warping the American
Crime Debate, Explained," *Vox,* May 18, 2016, https://www.vox.com/2016/5
/18/11683594/ferguson-effect-crime-police.

38 Shaila Dewan, "Deconstructing the 'Ferguson Effect,'" *New York Times,*
March 29, 2017, https://www.nytimes.com/interactive/2017/us/politics/fer
guson-effect.html.

39 Ibid.; Mihir Zaveri, "A Violent August in N.Y.C.: Shootings Double, and Murder Is Up by 50%," *New York Times,* September 2, 2020, https://www.nytimes
.com/2020/09/02/nyregion/nyc-shootings-murders.html.

40 Holly Bailey, "Minneapolis Violence Surges as Police Officers Leave Department in Droves," *Washington Post,* November 12, 2020, https://www.washing
tonpost.com/national/minneapolis-police-shortage-violence-floyd/2020/11
/12/642f741a-1a1d-11eb-befb-8864259bd2d8_story.html.

41 Lia Eustachewich, "Seattle Sees 525 Percent Spike in Crime Thanks to CHOP:

Mayor Durkan," *New York Post*, July 2, 2020, https://nypost.com/2020/07/02/seattle-sees-525-percent-spike-in-crime-thanks-to-chop-mayor-durkan/.

42 ABC News (@ABC), "Protesters in California set fire to a courthouse, damaged a police station and assaulted officers after a peaceful demonstration intensified," Twitter, July 26, 2020, 10:36 a.m., https://twitter.com/ABC/status/1287396378407243777/.

43 Bob Price, "Antifa Attacks Democrat HQ in Portland—Wants Revenge, Not Biden," Breitbart, January 20, 2021, https://www.breitbart.com/law-and-order/2021/01/20/antifa-attacks-democrat-hq-in-portland-wants-revenge-not-biden/; Andy Ngo (@MrAndyNgo), "Small random selection of those arrested in Portland . . . ," Twitter, January 9, 2021, 5:42 a.m., https://twitter.com/MrAndyNgo/status/1347901451188776962.

44 Rabbi Aryeh Spero, "Rabbi Spero: Leaders Are Silent on Antisemitism, Violence of Black Lives Matter Protests," Breitbart, June 6, 2020, https://www.breitbart.com/politics/2020/06/06/rabbi-spero-leaders-are-silent-on-anti semitism-violence-of-black-lives-matter-protests/; Tom Tugend, "LA Jews Reeling After Local Institutions Looted and Burned in Floyd Protests," *Times of Israel*, June 3, 2020, https://www.timesofisrael.com/la-jews-take-stock-after-george-floyd-protests-batter-local-institutions/.

45 Tugend, "LA Jews Reeling After Local Institutions Looted and Burned in Floyd Protests."

46 Joel B. Pollak, "Kenosha Rioters Vandalize Synagogue ('Free Palestine'), Church ('BLM')," Breitbart, August 27, 2020, https://www.breitbart.com/crime/2020/08/27/kenosha-rioters-vandalize-synagogue-free-palestine-church-blm/.

47 Joel B. Pollak, "WATCH: BLM Protesters Target Jews in Philadelphia While Yelling 'Synagogue of Satan,'" Breitbart, October 28, 2020, https://www.breitbart.com/law-and-order/2020/10/28/watch-blm-protesters-target-jews-in-philadelphia-while-yelling-synagogue-of-satan/.

48 Hollie McKay, "Behind Susan Rosenberg and the Roots of Left-wing Domestic Extremism," Fox News, November 17, 2020, https://www.foxnews.com/us/susan-rosenberg-left-wing-domestic-extremism-roots.

49 Lila Thulin, "In the 1980s, a Far-Left, Female-Led Domestic Terrorism Group Bombed the U.S. Capitol," *Smithsonian Magazine*, January 6, 2020, https://www.smithsonianmag.com/history/1980s-far-left-female-led-domestic-terrorism-group-bombed-us-capitol-180973904/; "How the All-Female Terror Group M19 Formed and Operated in the US in the '70s and '80s," *Inside Edition*, July 4, 2020, https://www.insideedition.com/how-the-all-female-terror-group-m19-formed-and-operated-in-the-us-in-the-70s-and-80s-60519.

50 "Amazon Donates $10 Million to Organizations Supporting Justice and Equity," Amazon, June 3, 2020, https://www.aboutamazon.com/news/policy-news-views/amazon-donates-10-million-to-organizations-supporting-justice-and-equity; John Carney, "$1.175 Billion: Corporate America Floods Social Justice Causes with Cash amid Floyd Protests," Breitbart, June 11, 2020,

https://www.breitbart.com/economy/2020/06/11/corporate-donations-to-social-justice/.

51 Kate Cox, "Amazon Cuts Off Parler's Web Hosting Following Apple, Google Bans," Ars Technica, January 9, 2021, https://arstechnica.com/tech-policy/2021/01/amazon-cuts-off-parlers-web-hosting-following-apple-google-bans/.

52 Jonah Gottschalk, "Democrats Block Resolution Condemning Mob Violence," Federalist, July 2, 2020, https://thefederalist.com/2020/07/02/democrats-block-resolution-condemning-mob-violence/#.X_ZsyWk6V8I.twitter.

53 Haris Alic, "Harris Urged Supporters to Donate to Group Pushing Defunding Police," Breitbart, August 11, 2020, https://www.breitbart.com/2020-election/2020/08/11/harris-urged-supporters-to-donate-to-group-pushing-defunding-police/.

54 Anthony Adragna and Zack Colman, "Ocasio-Cortez, Youth Protesters Storm Pelosi Office to Push for Climate Plan," Politico, November 13, 2018, https://www.politico.com/story/2018/11/13/ocasio-cortez-climate-protestors-push-pelosi-962915.

55 Robert Gearty, "Anti-Kavanaugh Protesters Accosting Senators Have Ties to Soros," Fox News, October 2, 2018, https://www.foxnews.com/politics/anti-kavanaugh-protesters-accosting-senators-have-ties-to-soros.

56 Tal Axelrod, "Pelosi Says Dems 'Have to Be Ready to Throw a Punch—for the Children' in 2020," Hill, August 23, 2019, https://thehill.com/homenews/house/458594-pelosi-says-dems-have-to-be-ready-to-throw-a-punch-for-the-children-in-2020.

57 Dan Merica, "Eric Holder on Republicans: 'When they go low, we kick them,'" CNN, October 10, 2018, https://www.cnn.com/2018/10/10/politics/eric-holder-republicans-when-they-go-low/index.html.

58 Rachel Ventresca, "Clinton: 'You Cannot Be Civil with a Political Party That Wants to Destroy What You Stand for,'" CNN, October 9, 2018, https://www.cnn.com/2018/10/09/politics/hillary-clinton-civility-congress-cnntv/index.html.

59 Pam Key, "Maxine Waters: People Are 'Going to Harass' Trump Administration Officials at Restaurants, Stores, and Gas Stations," Breitbart, June 24, 2018, https://www.breitbart.com/clips/2018/06/24/maxine-waters-people-are-going-to-harass-trump-administration-officials-at-restaurants-stores-and-gas-stations/.

60 CBS News (@CBSNews), "Violence is when an agent of the state kneels on a man's neck until all of the life is leached out of his body. Destroying property . . . ," Twitter, June 2, 2020, 1:55 p.m., https://twitter.com/CBSNews/status/1267877443911778306.

61 Brent Baker (@BrentHBaker), "Our country was started because, the Boston tea party. Rioting. So do not get it twisted and think this is something that has never happened before and this is so terrible and these savages and all of that. This is how this country was started"—@DonLemon on @CNN . . . ," Twitter, May 31, 2020, 11:53 p.m., https://twitter.com/BrentHBaker/status/1266945397609635840?ref_src=twsrc%5Etfw%7Ctwcamp%5Etweetem

bed%7Ctwterm%5E1266945397609635840%7Ctwgr%5E%7Ctwcon%5Es1
_&ref_url=https%3A%2F%2Fthefederalist.com%2F2021%2F01%2F07%2F28
-times-media-and-democrats-exc.

62 Laura Basset, "Why Violent Protests Work," *GQ*, June 2, 2020, https://www.gq
.com/story/why-violent-protests-work.

63 Cam Edwards (@CamEdwards), "You can't govern a nation with two
sets of rules," Twitter, January 7, https://twitter.com/CamEdwards/status
/1347056977097199618?ref_src=twsrc%5Etfw%7Ctwcamp%5Etweetem
bed%7Ctwterm%5E1347056977097199618%7Ctwgr%5E%7Ctwcon%5Es1
_&ref_url=https%3A%2F%2Fthefederalist.com%2F2021%2F01%2F07%2F28
-times-media-and-democrats-excu.

Chapter 8: Cheat by Mail and the True Story of the 2020 Election

1 Molly Ball, "The Secret History of the Shadow Campaign That Saved the 2020
Election," *Time*, February 4, 2021, https://time.com/5936036/secret-2020
-election-campaign/.

2 Jeffery Martin, "Trump Lashes Out at Bookies for Predicting 97% Chance He'd
Win Election," *Newsweek*, December 9, 2020, https://www.newsweek.com
/trump-lashes-out-bookies-predicting-97-chance-hed-win-election-1553663.

3 Dante Chinni, "Poll: Half of voters have already decided against Trump in
2020," NBC News, November 3, 2019, https://www.nbcnews.com/politics
/meet-the-press/poll-half-voters-have-already-decided-against-trump-2020
-n1075746.

4 Catherine Thorbecke, "Unemployment rate falls to its lowest level in 50 years,"
ABC News, October 4, 2019, https://abcnews.go.com/Business/unemploy
ment-rate-falls-lowest-level-50-years/story?id=66058946.

5 Jeanna Smialek and Ben Casselman, "Black Workers' Wages Are Finally Rising," *New York Times*, February 7, 2020, https://www.nytimes.com/2020/02/07
/business/black-unemployment-wages.html.

6 Charlie Spiering, "Donald Trump Previews Declaration: Islamic State Is 100
Percent Defeated," Breitbart, February 6, 2019, https://www.breitbart.com
/politics/2019/02/06/donald-trump-previews-declaration-islamic-state-is
-100-percent-defeated/.

7 Joel B. Pollak, "Trump Confirms More Federal Judges in First Term than Any
President in 40 Years," Breitbart, October 20, 2020, https://www.breitbart.com
/politics/2020/10/20/trump-federal-judges/.

8 Jeffery M. Jones, "Donald Trump, Michelle Obama Most Admired in 2020,"
Gallup, December 29, 2020, https://news.gallup.com/poll/328193/donald
-trump-michelle-obama-admired-2020.aspx.

9 John Nolte, "Nolte: 7 Reasons Pollsters Deliberately Lie to Us," Breitbart,
November 6, 2020, https://www.breitbart.com/2020-election/2020/11/06/nolte
-7-reasons-pollsters-deliberately-lie-us/.

10 "Biden leads Trump by 17 points in Wisconsin in ABC News/Washington

Post poll," ABC, October 28, 2020, https://www.wbay.com/2020/10/28/biden -leads-trump-by-17-points-in-wisconsin-in-abc-newswashington-post-poll/.

11 "2020 Wisconsin President Election Results," RealClear Politics, accessed February 22, 2021, https://www.realclearpolitics.com/elections/live_results/2020 /state/wi/president/.

12 Katherine Rodriguez, "Pollster: Major Polls Are Wrong Because People Fear Being Canceled," Breitbart, November 5, 2020, https://www.breitbart.com /2020-election/2020/11/05/pollster-says-major-polls-wrong-because-people -fear-canceled/.

13 John Nolte, "Rap Sheet: **389** Media-Approved Hate Crimes Against Trump Supporters," Breitbart, February 14, 2020, https://www.breitbart.com/the-media /2020/02/14/rap-sheet-389-media-approved-hate-crimes-trump-supporters/.

14 Tracey Kornet, "Woman punches man in Broadway bar over MAGA-style birthday hat," NBC Nashville, February 11, 2020, https://www.wsmv.com /news/woman-punches-man-in-broadway-bar-over-maga-style-birthday /article_e2ac313a-4d53-11ea-84b4-0b82e9d6d71a.html.

15 Students for Trump at ASU (@sft_asu), "ASU Police told us yesterday that they need help identifying this student who threatened to 'slash Republican throats,'" Twitter, February 13, 2020, 12:31 p.m., https://twitter.com/sft_asu /status/1228008808116473856.

16 Daniel Dahm, "Man stabs, kills pro-Trump boss, drapes American flag over him, deputies say," CBS Orlando, January 21, 2020, https://www.clickorlando .com/news/local/2020/01/21/man-stabs-kills-pro-trump-boss-drapes-ameri can-flag-over-him-deputies-say/.

17 Danielle Wallace, "Florida schoolboy, 14, beaten over MAGA hat, parent claims, as shocking video goes viral," Fox News, December 14, 2019, https:// www.foxnews.com/us/florida-teen-maga-hat-bullies-bus-attack-video-ham ilton-county.

18 Joel B. Pollak, "WATCH: Black Lives Matter Protesters Surround Rand Paul for Several Minutes After RNC," Breitbart, August 27, 2020, https://www.breit bart.com/law-and-order/2020/08/27/watch-black-lives-matter-protesters -surround-rand-paul-for-several-minutes-after-rnc/.

19 Shomik Mukherjee, "GOP headquarters vandalism will cost thousands to repair, chair says," Times Standard, February 10, 2020, https://www.times -standard.com/2020/02/10/gop-headquarters-vandalism-will-cost-thou sands-to-repair-chair-says/.

20 "National General Election Polls," RealClearPolitics, accessed February 22, 2021, https://www.realclearpolitics.com/epolls/2020/president/National.html.

21 Zeke Miller and Jill Colvin, "Trump insists, falsely, that Pence can decertify results," AP News, January 5, 2021, https://apnews.com/article /election-2020-joe-biden-donald-trump-senate-elections-elections-aaa00b 96179c454426453a99ca1e2e30.

22 Joel B. Pollak, "Sidney Powell Files Lawsuits Challenging Election Results in Georgia, Michigan," Breitbart, November 26, 2020, https://www.breitbart

.com/politics/2020/11/26/sidney-powell-files-lawsuits-challenging-election -results-in-georgia-michigan/.

23 Ali Swenson and Jude Joffe-Block, "Lengthy video makes false claims about 2020 election," AP News, December 24, 2020, https://apnews.com/article/fact -checking-afs:Content:9900544617.

24 "Fact check: TV news clip does not show 'live computerized fraud' on Election Day 2020," Reuters, November 9, 2020, https://www.reuters.com/article /uk-factcheck-cnn-not-evidence-vote-fraud/fact-check-tv-news-clip-does -not-show-live-computerized-fraud-on-election-day-2020-idUSKBN27P2TI.

25 Jon Levine, "Confessions of a voter fraud: I was a master at fixing mail-in ballots," *New York Post*, August 29, 2020, https://nypost.com/2020/08/29/political -insider-explains-voter-fraud-with-mail-in-ballots/.

26 David Litt (@davidlitt), "Anyone in Georgia? Team Joe needs people to go door to door helping voters fix their mail in ballots so they count . . . ," Twitter, November 4, 2020, 5:32 p.m., https://twitter.com/davidlitt/status/132 4117440297639940.

27 Jeff Poor, "Rudy Giuliani on Break with Sidney Powell: 'We're Pursuing Two Different Theories,'" Breitbart, November 23, 2020, https://www.breitbart .com/clips/2020/11/23/rudy-giuliani-on-break-with-sidney-powell-were -pursuing-two-different-theories/.

28 Patrick Basham, "Reasons Why the 2020 Presidential Election Is Deeply Puzzling," *Spectator*, November 27, 2020, https://spectator.us/topic/reasons-why -the-2020-presidential-election-is-deeply-puzzling/.

29 Ari Berman, "Trump's Strategy for Contesting the Election: Throw Out Black People's Votes," *Mother Jones*, November 18, 2020, https://www.motherjones .com/politics/2020/11/trumps-strategy-for-contesting-the-election-throw -out-black-peoples-votes/; Juana Summers, "Trump Push to Invalidate Votes in Heavily Black Cities Alarms Civil Rights Groups," NPR, November 24, 2020, https://www.npr.org/2020/11/24/938187233/trump-push-to-invalidate -votes-in-heavily-black-cities-alarms-civil-rights-group.

30 Jeff Poor, "Local News Affiliate at AZ Event Attended by Biden, Harris: 'Technically a Big Event but Not a Lot of Fanfare'—'Can't Tell Anything Much Is Going On,'" Breitbart, October 11, 2020, https://www.breitbart.com/clips /2020/10/11/local-news-affiliate-at-az-event-attended-by-biden-harris-tech nically-a-big-event-but-not-a-lot-of-fanfare-cant-tell-anything-much-is -going-on/.

31 Camille Caldera, "Fact check: Biden won the most total votes—and the fewest total counties—of any president-elect," *USA Today*, December 9, 2020, https:// www.usatoday.com/story/news/factcheck/2020/12/09/fact-check-joe-biden -won-most-votes-ever-and-fewest-counties/3865097001/.

32 Drew Desilver, "Mail-in voting became much more common in 2020 primaries as COVID-19 spread," Pew Research Center, October 13, 2020, https:// www.pewresearch.org/fact-tank/2020/10/13/mail-in-voting-became-much -more-common-in-2020-primaries-as-covid-19-spread/.

33 Quinn Scanlan, "Here's how states have changed the rules around voting amid the coronavirus pandemic," ABC, September 22, 2020, https://abcnew s.go.com/Politics/states-changed-rules-voting-amid-coronavirus-pandemic /story?id=72309089.

34 "Changes to Election Dates, Procedures, and Administration in Response to the Coronavirus (COVID-19) Pandemic, 2020," Ballotpedia, accessed February 22, 2021, https://ballotpedia.org/Changes_to_election_dates, _procedures,_and_administration_in_response_to_the_coronavirus _(COVID-19)_pandemic,_2020.

35 Rebecca Mansour and James P. Pinkerton, "Mansour and Pinkerton: The Democrats' 7-Step Strategy to Win the Election Using Vote-by-Mail Chaos," Breitbart, September 25, 2020, https://www.breitbart.com/2020-election/2020 /09/25/mansour-and-pinkerton-the-democrats-7-step-strategy-to-win-the -election-using-vote-by-mail-chaos/.

36 Shane Devine, "Soros Aims to Transform the Justice System by Funding DA Races," Capital Research Center, December 17, 2019, https://capitalresearch .org/article/soros-aims-to-transform-the-justice-system-by-funding-da-races/.

37 "Dirty Tricks: 9 Falsehoods That Could Undermine the 2020 Election," Brennan Center for Justice, May 14, 2020, https://www.brennancenter.org/our -work/research-reports/dirty-tricks-9-falsehoods-could-undermine-2020 -election?ms=gad_election%20facts_437214061573.

38 Klein, "George Soros Groups Pushing Democrat Scheme for Mail-in Voting."

39 Gabriel Debenedetti, "Ranking the Most Influential Democratic Donors in the 2020 Race," Intelligencer, August 22, 2019, https://nymag.com/intelli gencer/2019/08/most-influential-democratic-donors-2020-elections.html.

40 Hans von Spakovsky, "Vote Harvesting: A Recipe for Intimidation, Coercion, and Election Fraud," Heritage Foundation, October 8, 2019, https://www.heri tage.org/election-integrity/report/vote-harvesting-recipe-intimidation-coer cion-and-election-fraud.

41 Simon Kent, "Democrat Primary: Arrests Made in Illegal Ballot Harvesting Scheme," Breitbart, September 25, 2020, https://www.breitbart.com/politics /2020/09/25/democrat-primary-arrests-made-in-illegal-ballot-harvesting -scheme/.

42 Willie Brown, "Why Democrats Own the GOP in Mail Voting," San Francisco Chronicle, August 2, 2020, https://www.sfchronicle.com/bayarea/williesworld /article/Willie-Brown-Why-Democrats-own-the-GOP-in-mail-15450612 .php.

43 Joel B. Pollak, "Pennsylvania Supreme Court Allows Mail-in Ballots to Be Counted After Election Day Without Evidence of Postmark," Breitbart, September 17, 2020, https://www.breitbart.com/2020-election/2020/09/17/penn sylvania-supreme-court-postmark/.

44 Ibid.

45 Kyle Olson, "Watch: Detroit Absentee Ballot Counting Chaos as Workers Block Windows, Bar Observers," Breitbart, November 4, 2020, https://www

.breitbart.com/politics/2020/11/04/watch-detroit-absentee-ballot-counting
-chaos-as-workers-block-windows-bar-observers/.

46 "Why is the Nevada vote count taking so long," *Guardian*, November 6, 2020, https://www.theguardian.com/us-news/2020/nov/06/why-is-the-nevada -vote-count-taking-so-long-us-election-2020.

47 Sam Gringlas and Bill Chappell, "When Will We Know the Winner? Time Frames for Key States," NPR, November 4, 2020, https://www.npr.org/2020 /11/04/931288362/when-will-we-know-the-winner-timeframes-for-6-key -states.

48 Bruce Golding, "Philadelphia vote count resumes after temporary stoppage as Democrats appeal ruling," *New York Post*, November 5, 2020, https://nypost .com/2020/11/05/philadelphia-vote-count-stopped-as-democrats-appeal -ruling/.

49 Pam Fessler, "A 2020 Surprise: Fewer Absentee Ballot Rejections than Expected," NPR, December 31, 2020, https://www.npr.org/2020/12/31/951 249068/a-2020-surprise-fewer-absentee-ballots-rejections-than-expected.

50 "Election Results, 2020: Analysis of Rejected Ballots," Ballotpedia, last updated February 10, 2021, https://ballotpedia.org/Election_results,_2020:_Analysis _of_rejected_ballots.

51 Elections Division web page, Georgia Secretary of State, accessed February 24, 2021, https://elections.sos.ga.gov/Elections/voterabsenteefile.do.

52 Martin, "Trump Lashes Out at Bookies for Predicting 97% Chance He'd Win Election."

53 Carter-Baker Commission Report, *Building Confidence in U.S. Elections: Report of the Commission on Federal Election Reform* (September 2005), p. 46.

54 See *Crawford v. Marion County Election Board*, 553 U.S. 181, 194 & n.10, 197 (2008) (plurality opinion); *id.* at 231, 232 (Souter, J., dissenting); *id.* at 240, 241 (Breyer, J., dissenting).

55 Complaint, *Trump v. Raffensperger*, No. 2020cv34355 (Fulton Cty. Ga. Super. Ct.), 17–29.

56 Ibid.

57 Ibid., 33–36.

58 Ibid.

59 Supreme Court of the United States, Petition for a Writ of Certiorari, *Trump v. Biden*, December 29, 2020, https://cdn.donaldjtrump.com/public-files/press _assets/trump-v-biden-petition-appendix-final.pdf.

60 *Trump v. Evers*, Case No. 2020AP1971-OA, December 3, 2020, https://www .democracydocket.com/wp-content/uploads/sites/45/2020/12/2020AP1971 -OA.pdf.

61 *Supreme Court of Wisconsin, Trump et al. v. Biden et al.*, Case No. 2020AP2038, majority opinion, December 14, 2020, https://www.wicourts.gov/sc/opinion /DisplayDocument.pdf?content=pdf&seqNo=315395.

62 Ibid., dissenting opinion.

63 Marc Levy, "Pennsylvania: Mail Ballots Can't Be Discarded over Signa-

ture," Associated Press, September 15, 2020, https://apnews.com/article /pennsylvania-election-2020-pittsburgh-elections-presidential-elections -fc464c287c18823ff57fedc13facf7e5.

64 Ibid.

65 25 P.S. § 3146.8(g)(1.1).

66 Commonwealth Court of Pennsylvania, "In Re: Canvassing Observation," Appeal of Donald J. Trump for President, Inc., No. 1094 C.D. 2020, https:// electionlawblog.org/wp-content/uploads/PA-Canvassing-20201105-appeal .pdf.

67 Supreme Court of Pennsylvania, "In Re: Canvassing Observation," Appeal of City of Philadelphia Board of Elections, No. 30 EAP 2020, submitted November 13, 2020, http://www.pacourts.us/assets/opinions/Supreme/out/J-116 -2020mo%20-%20104608159120049033.pdf?cb=1.

68 Jack Rodgers, "High Court Refuses to Limit Pennsylvania Ballot Counting," Courthouse News Service, October 28, 2020, https://www.courthousenews .com/high-court-refuses-to-limit-pennsylvania-ballot-counting/.

69 Marc E. Elias (@marceelias), "BREAKING: Trump and his allies have now lost . . . ," Twitter, January 4, 2021, 11:21 a.m., https://twitter.com/marceelias /status/1346174890068611073?lang=en.

70 Joel B. Pollak, "Democrat Lawyer Marc Elias Claims Faulty Voting Machines in New York Race," Breitbart, February 3, 2021, https://www.breitbart.com /2020-election/2021/02/03/democrat-lawyer-marc-elias-claims-faulty-voting -machines-in-new-york-race/.

71 Michael Balsamo, Mary Clare Jalonick, and Nomaan Merchant, "Chief: Police Heeded Capitol Attack Warnings but Overwhelmed," Associated Press, February 25, 2021, https://apnews.com/article/capitol-assault-hearing-intelligence -8389c3a618c655e25c1956e94c00add5.

72 Alana Mastrangelo, "Leftist Activist Among Those Arrested in Capitol Riot," Breitbart, January 15, 2021, https://www.breitbart.com/politics/2021/01/15 /leftist-activist-among-those-arrested-in-capitol-riot/.

73 "The Capitol Siege: The Arrested and Their Stories," NPR, February 24, 2021, https://www.npr.org/2021/02/09/965472049/the-capitol-siege-the-arrested -and-their-stories.

Chapter 9: The Trump Virus

1 Warner Todd Huston, "Watch: Biden Fundraiser Jane Fonda Says COVID-19 Is 'God's Gift to the Left,'" Breitbart, October 7, 2020, https://www.breitbart .com/entertainment/2020/10/07/jane-fonda-says-covid-19-is-gods-gift-to -the-left/.

2 Jeffery Martin, "More than Half of Americans Would Support National One -Month Lockdown: Poll," Newsweek, December 24, 2020, https://www.news week.com/more-half-americans-would-support-national-one-month-lock down-poll-1557262.

3   Joshua Potash (@JoshuaPotash), "Wow. In Staten Island, New York someone came to a grocery store without a mask. And other patrons drove them out," Twitter, May 25, 2020, 8:01 a.m., https://twitter.com/JoshuaPotash/status /1264889424468459520.

4   Eddie Zipperer (@EddieZipperer), "'INSTANT CLASSIC FROM @MSNBC ANCHOR: 'Are the people there just not worried about it? Are they not worried about their personal safety?'. . .'" Twitter, May 26, 2020, 4:10 p.m., https:// twitter.com/EddieZipperer/status/1265374806662397953.

5   Spencer Neale, "Man derides MSNBC reporter as maskless crew films segment criticizing people not wearing masks," *Washington Examiner*, May 26, 2020, https://www.washingtonexaminer.com/news/man-derides-msnbc-reporter -as-maskless-crew-films-segment-criticizing-people-not-wearing-masks.

6   Philip Ellis, "Tom Hanks Has a Very Simple Message for Anti-Mask Crowd: 'Don't Be a Pussy,'" *Men's Health*, July 2, 2020, https://www.menshealth.com /entertainment/a33077436/tom-hanks-face-mask-social-distancing-corona virus-pandemic/.

7   Trip Gabriel, "Trump May Have Covid, but Many of His Supporters Still Scoff at Masks," *New York Times*, October 6, 2020, https://www.nytimes.com/2020 /10/06/us/politics/trump-voters-face-masks.html.

8   Sara Pequeño, "Instagram Account Calling Out Partying UNC–Chapel Hill Students Leads to University Investigation," INDY Week, January 29, 2021, https://indyweek.com/news/orange/unc-chapel-hill-where-yall-goin-insta gram/.

9   Rebecca Mansour, "2020's Big Winners: Billionaires, Silicon Valley Tech Lords, and Communist China," Breitbart, December 31, 2020, https://www .breitbart.com/economy/2020/12/31/2020s-big-winners-billionaires-silicon -valley-tech-lords-and-communist-china/.

10 "Nielsen COVID-19 Beverage Alcohol Insights," Wine Industry Network, November 16, 2020, https://wineindustryadvisor.com/2020/11/16/nielsen -covid-beverage-alcohol-insights.

11 Jane Wells, "Legal cannabis industry sees record sales as customers facing coronavirus crisis stock up," CNBC, March 25, 2020, https://www.cnbc.com /2020/03/25/legal-cannabis-industry-sees-record-sales-in-coronavirus-crisis .html.

12 John Hayward, "Hayward: Six Ways China Profited from the Wuhan Pandemic," Breitbart, December 31, 2020, https://www.breitbart.com/national -security/2020/12/31/hayward-six-ways-china-profited-wuhan-pandemic/.

13 Keith Bradsher, "Coronavirus Battle Creates a Global 'Free-for-All' to Find Masks," *New York Times*, April 1, 2020, https://www.nytimes.com/2020/04/01 /business/coronavirus-china-masks.html.

14 Naomi Xu Elegant, "COVID-era exports are fueling China's economic recovery. What happens when the pandemic ends?" *Fortune*, December 13, 2020, https://fortune.com/2020/12/13/china-economy-growth-covid-export -demand/.

15 Rebecca Mansour, "Coronavirus Outbreak Exposes China's Monopoly on U.S. Drug, Medical Supplies," Breitbart, February 13, 2020, https://www.breitbart.com/asia/2020/02/13/coronavirus-outbreak-exposes-chinas-monopoly-on-u-s-drug-medical-supplies/.

16 Yanzhong Huang, "U.S. Dependence on Pharmaceutical Products From China," Council on Foreign Relations, August 14, 2019, https://www.cfr.org/blog/us-dependence-pharmaceutical-products-china.

17 "Rosemary Gibson: America's Dependence on China for Essential Medicines Is a Growing Safety Threat," *Greeley Tribune*, February 12, 2021, https://www.greeleytribune.com/2021/02/12/rosemary-gibson-americas-dependence-on-china-for-essential-medicines-is-a-growing-safety-threat/.

18 Keith Bradsher, "China Dominates Medical Supplies, in This Outbreak and the Next," *New York Times*, July 5, 2020, https://www.nytimes.com/2020/07/05/business/china-medical-supplies.html.

19 Edward Wong and Paul Mozur, "China's 'Donation Diplomacy' Raises Tensions with the U.S.," *New York Times*, April 14, 2020, https://www.nytimes.com/2020/04/14/us/politics/coronavirus-china-trump-donation.html.

20 Paul Wiseman, "US trade deficit up to $67.1 billion in August, 14-year high," AP News, October 6, 2020, https://apnews.com/article/donald-trump-global-trade-north-america-china-united-states-c6d5a4d935d8d3bca966d2395deee68d.

21 "Covid Winner: China Is Only Major Economy to Grow in 2020," Breitbart, January 18, 2021, https://www.breitbart.com/news/china-economy-grows-in-2020-as-rebound-from-virus-gains/.

22 Huileng Tan, "China's says its economy grew 6.1% in 2019, in line with expectations," CNBC, January 16, 2020, https://www.cnbc.com/2020/01/17/china-gdp-for-full-year-and-q4-2019.html#:~:text=China%20said%20Friday%20its%20economy,the%20National%20Bureau%20of%20Statistics.

23 Alice Han and Eyck Freymann, "Coronavirus Hasn't Killed Belt and Road," *Foreign Policy*, January 6, 2021, https://foreignpolicy.com/2021/01/06/coronavirus-hasnt-killed-belt-and-road/.

24 Jonathan Cheng, "China Finishes Off a Wild Year with More Manufacturing Growth," *Wall Street Journal*, December 30, 2020, https://www.wsj.com/articles/china-finishes-off-a-wild-year-with-more-manufacturing-growth-11609383751.

25 Rebecca Davis, "China Box Office Poised to Surpass U.S. as World's Largest Moviegoing Market Amid Pandemic," *Variety*, October 12, 2020, https://variety.com/2020/film/news/china-box-office-surpass-us-my-people-my-homeland-1234801700/.

26 Frances Martel, "Reports: Virus Death Toll in Wuhan over 10x China's Official Number," Breitbart, March 30, 2020, https://www.breitbart.com/asia/2020/03/30/reports-virus-death-toll-in-wuhan-over-10x-chinas-official-number/.

27 Kashmira Gander, "How China Beat Coronavirus Over the Last Six Months," *Newsweek*, September 19, 2020, https://www.newsweek.com/china-coronavirus-six-months-pandemic-beat-virus-1532874.

28 Stella Yifan Xie, "China Beat Back Covid-19, but It's Come at a Cost—Growing Inequality," *Wall Street Journal*, October 21, 2020, https://www.wsj.com/articles/china-beat-back-covid-19-but-its-come-at-a-costgrowing-inequality-11603281656.

29 David Crawshaw and Miriam Berger, "China beat back covid-19 in 2020. Then it really flexed its muscles at home and abroad," *Washington Post*, December 28, 2020, https://www.washingtonpost.com/world/2020/12/28/china-2020-major-stories/.

30 Steven Lee Myers, Keith Bradsher, Sui-Lee Wee, and Chris Buckley, "Power, Patriotism and 1.4 Billion People: How China Beat the Virus and Roared Back," *New York Times*, February 14, 2021, https://www.nytimes.com/2021/02/05/world/asia/china-covid-economy.html.

31 Ibid.

32 Jeff Poor, "Zakaria: China Has 'Essentially Vanquished the Virus Without a Vaccine,'" Breitbart, January 1, 2021, https://www.breitbart.com/clips/2021/01/01/zakaria-china-has-essentially-vanquished-the-virus-without-a-vaccine/.

33 Zhuang Pinghui, "Coronavirus: Beijing goes into emergency mode after five new cases recorded," *South China Morning Post*, December 27, 2020, https://www.scmp.com/news/china/politics/article/3115474/coronavirus-beijing-goes-emergency-mode-after-five-new-cases.

34 Dan Mangan, "Trump issues 'Coronavirus Guidelines' for next 15 days to slow pandemic," CNBC, March 16, 2020, https://www.cnbc.com/2020/03/16/trumps-coronavirus-guidelines-for-next-15-days-to-slow-pandemic.html.

35 Zachary Basu, "Trump announces 30-day extension of coronavirus guidelines," Axios, March 29, 2020, https://www.axios.com/trump-coronavirus-social-distancing-30-days-29cb77cd-39fb-4ae7-9ab7-eb6cdd314e80.html.

36 "March 2020: Dr. Anthony Fauci Talks with Dr. Jon LaPook About Covid-19," YouTube video, posted by "60 Minutes," March 8, 2020. https://www.youtube.com/watch?v=PRa6t_e7dgI.

37 Ibid.

38 Quint Forgey, "Fauci says he wears mask as 'symbol' of good behavior," *Politico*, May 27, 2020, https://www.politico.com/news/2020/05/27/fauci-wears-mask-as-symbol-of-good-behavior-283847.

39 Colin Dwyer and Allison Aubrey, "CDC Now Recommends Americans Consider Wearing Cloth Face Coverings in Public," NPR, April 3, 2020, https://www.npr.org/sections/coronavirus-live-updates/2020/04/03/826219824/president-trump-says-cdc-now-recommends-americans-wear-cloth-masks-in-public.

40 Edwin Mora, "CDC Journal: Cloth Masks 'May Give Users a False Sense of Protection' Against Coronavirus," Breitbart, October 28, 2020, https://www.breitbart.com/health/2020/10/28/cdc-journal-cloth-masks-may-give-users-a-false-sense-of-protection-against-coronavirus/.

41 Ed Kilgore, "Trump's 'Love It or Leave It' Jingoism Was Predictable All Along," *Intelligencer*, July 17, 2019, https://nymag.com/intelligencer/2019/07/trumps-love-it-or-leave-it-jingoism-was-predictable.html.

42 Andrew Cuomo (@NYGovCuomo), "This July 4th remember—real patriots wear masks," Twitter, July 4, 2020, 4:32 p.m., https://twitter.com/nygovcuomo /status/1279513499169947649?lang=en.

43 Gavin Newsom (@GavinNewsom), "Couldn't agree more. Be a Patriot. Wear a mask," Twitter, August 13, 2020, 4:38 p.m., https://twitter.com/gavinnewsom /status/1294010347578200064?lang=en.

44 Joe Biden (@JoeBiden), "Be a patriot. Wear a mask," Twitter, October 31, 2020, 10:18 a.m., https://twitter.com/joebiden/status/1322543347236438016 ?lang=en.

45 Hannah Bleau, "Maskless Nancy Pelosi Goes to San Francisco Hair Salon Despite Coronavirus Restrictions," Breitbart, September 1, 2020, https:// www.breitbart.com/politics/2020/09/01/maskless-nancy-pelosi-goes-to-san -francisco-hair-salon-despite-coronavirus-restrictions/; Travis Pittman, "Fauci calls criticism over photo of him with mask down 'mischievous,'" WUSA 9, July 24, 2020, https://www.wusa9.com/article/news/health/coro navirus/anthony-fauci-face-mask-down-photo-coronavirus/507-e33379cb -d79e-479b-9960-13293c96572f; Marina Villeneuve, "Cuomo defends not wearing a mask at indoor presser," AP News, October 5, 2020, https://apnews .com/article/virus-outbreak-new-york-albany-new-york-city-andrew-cuomo -d8ac03e71e65e2ba1413c8febf4abeb3.

46 John Nolte, "Nolte: CNN's Typhoid Kaitlan Collins Caught Removing Mask After White House Briefing," Breitbart, May 18, 2020, https://www.breitbart .com/the-media/2020/05/18/cnns-typhoid-kaitlan-collins-caught-removing -mask-white-house-briefing/.

47 Kate Ferguson, "MASK UP Brits could wear Covid face masks FOREVER as coronavirus will 'always be with us', warns JVT," U.S. Sun, January 13, 2021, https://www.the-sun.com/news/2133933/brits-covid-mask-jonathan-van -tam/.

48 Caitlin O'Kane, "California governor's office tells diners to wear masks 'in between bites,'" CBS News, October 6, 2020, https://www.cbsnews.com/news /gavin-newsom-california-face-mask-restaurant/.

49 Bill Melugin and Shelly Insheiwat, "FOX 11 obtains exclusive photos of Gov. Newsom at French restaurant allegedly not following COVID-19 protocols," Fox News, November 17, 2020, https://www.foxla.com/news/fox-11-obtains -exclusive-photos-of-gov-newsom-at-french-restaurant-allegedly-not-fol lowing-covid-19-protocols.

50 Lucy Nicholson, "ICUs clogged on the way in, morgues on the way out in California's COVID crisis," MSN, January 9, 2021, https://www.msn.com/en -us/news/us/icus-clogged-on-the-way-in-morgues-on-the-way-out-in-cali fornias-covid-crisis/ar-BB1cB8zM.

51 Frances Martel, "Hong Kong Expands Power to Isolate Individuals to Fight Chinese 'Mystery Pneumonia,'" Breitbart, January 7, 2020, https://www.breit bart.com/asia/2020/01/07/hong-kong-expands-power-to-isolate-individuals -to-fight-chinese-mystery-pneumonia/.

52 Matthew Boyle, "Exclusive—Tom Cotton Urges Trump Administration to Consider Banning Travel from China over Coronavirus," Breitbart, January 22, 2020, https://www.breitbart.com/politics/2020/01/22/exclusive-tom-cotton-urges-trump-administration-to-consider-banning-travel-from-china-over-coronavirus/.

53 John Binder, "Fact Check: Joe Biden Did Oppose Trump's Travel Ban on China," Breitbart, October 7, 2020, https://www.breitbart.com/politics/2020/10/07/fact-check-joe-biden-did-oppose-trumps-travel-ban-on-china/.

54 Tom Elliott, "Flashback: Joe Biden Calls Trump's China Travel Restrictions 'Hysterical Xenophobia,'" Grabie News, March 12, 2020, https://news.grabien.com/story-flashback-joe-biden-calls-trumps-china-travel-restrictions-h.

55 Emily Vaughn, "Coronavirus 101: What We Do—and Don't—Know About the Outbreak of COVID-19," NPR, January 24, 2020, https://www.npr.org/sections/goatsandsoda/2020/01/24/798661901/wuhan-coronavirus-101-what-we-do-and-dont-know-about-a-newly-identified-disease.

56 Natalie Escobar, "When Xenophobia Spreads Like a Virus," NPR, March 4, 2020, https://www.npr.org/2020/03/02/811363404/when-xenophobia-spreads-like-a-virus.

57 Robert Dingwall, "We Should Deescalate the War on the Coronavirus," Wired, January 29, 2020, https://www.wired.com/story/opinion-we-should-deescalate-the-war-on-the-coronavirus/.

58 Jessie Yeung, "As the coronavirus spreads, fear is fueling racism and xenophobia," CNN, January 31, 2020, https://www.cnn.com/2020/01/31/asia/wuhan-coronavirus-racism-fear-intl-hnk/index.html.

59 Farhad Manjoo, "Beware the Pandemic Panic," New York Times, January 29, 2020, https://www.nytimes.com/2020/01/29/opinion/coronavirus-panic.html.

60 Farhad Manjoo, "Admit It: You Don't Know What Will Happen Next," New York Times, February 26, 2020, https://www.nytimes.com/2020/02/26/opinion/coronavirus-panic.html.

61 Nylah Burton, "The coronavirus exposes the history of racism and 'cleanliness,'" Vox, February 7, 2020, https://www.vox.com/2020/2/7/21126758/coronavirus-xenophobia-racism-china-asians.

62 Barbie Latza Nadeau, "Italy Shows Just How Crazy Coronavirus Panic Can Get," Daily Beast, February 29, 2020, https://www.thedailybeast.com/italy-shows-just-how-crazy-coronavirus-panic-can-get.

63 Frances D'Emilio, "Italy surpasses UK for worst COVID-19 death toll in Europe," AP News, December 13, 2020, https://apnews.com/article/pandemics-europe-italy-coronavirus-pandemic-082c94d925eab4d791f28d2b2729b655.

64 Kyle Olson, "Donald Trump Vowed Coronavirus Action in SOTU Speech Nancy Pelosi Ripped Up," Breitbart, April 2, 2020, https://www.breitbart.com/politics/2020/04/02/donald-trump-vowed-coronavirus-action-sotu-speech-nancy-pelosi-ripped/.

65 Pam Key, "Pelosi: Trump's China Travel Ban Wasn't the 'Great Moment,'"

Breitbart, April 26, 2020, https://www.breitbart.com/clips/2020/04/26/pelosi -trumps-china-travel-ban-wasnt-the-great-moment/.

66   "Pelosi: My Chinatown Visit Didn't Downplay Coronavirus. It Helped Prevent It," YouTube video, posted by "Josh Christenson," April 19, 2020, https://www .youtube.com/watch?v=y7ID6Mu7gKs.

67   Pam Key, "Pelosi: 'Trump Virus' Is 'Rolling Like a Freight Train'—'Biggest Failure' in History," Breitbart, July 23, 2020, https://www.breitbart.com/clips /2020/07/23/pelosi-trump-virus-is-rolling-like-a-freight-train-biggest-failure -in-history/.

68   "De Blasio in February: Don't Let Coronavirus Stop You from Eating in Chinatown," Grabien, accessed February 23, 2021, https://grabien.com/story .php?id=280695.

69   John Nolte, "Nolte: 53 Times the Establishment Media Said 'Chinese' or 'Wuhan' Virus," Breitbart, March 18, 2020, https://www.breitbart.com/the -media/2020/03/18/nolte-53-times-the-establishment-media-said-chinese-or -wuhan-virus/.

70   Alex Berenson (@AlexBerenson), "3/ And how WE WERE ALL GOING TO DIE WITHOUT THEM . . . ," Twitter, August 23, 2020, 10:25 p.m., https:// twitter.com/AlexBerenson/status/1297721687803338753.

71   Joshua Caplan, "Neil Cavuto Stunned by Trump Taking Hydroxychloroquine: 'It Will Kill You,'" Breitbart, May 18, 2020, https://www.breitbart.com/the -media/2020/05/18/neil-cavuto-stunned-by-trump-taking-hydroxychloro quine-it-will-kill-you/.

72   "Trump drug hydroxychloroquine raises death risk in Covid patients, study says," BBC, May 22, 2020, https://www.bbc.com/news/world-52779309.

73   "Study on safety of malaria drugs for coronavirus retracted," Breitbart, June 4, 2020, https://www.breitbart.com/news/study-on-safety-of-malaria-drugs-for -coronavirus-retracted/.

74   Scott Neuman, "Man Dies, Woman Hospitalized After Taking Form of Chloro-quine to Prevent COVID-19," NPR, March 24, 2020, https://www.npr.org /sections/coronavirus-live-updates/2020/03/24/820512107/man-dies-woman -hospitalized-after-taking-form-of-chloroquine-to-prevent-covid-19.

75   Caplan, "Neil Cavuto Stunned by Trump Taking Hydroxychloroquine: 'It Will Kill You.'"

76   Joel B. Pollak, "Max Boot: Coronavirus Outbreak 'Wouldn't Have Happened if Hillary Clinton Had Won,'" Breitbart, March 22, 2020, https://www.breitbart .com/the-media/2020/03/22/max-boot-coronavirus-outbreak-wouldnt-have -happened-if-hillary-clinton-had-won/.

77   Kyle Olson, "Hillary Clinton: Saying 'Chinese Virus' Is 'Racist Rhetoric,'" Breitbart, March 18, 2020, https://www.breitbart.com/politics/2020/03/18 /hillary-clinton-saying-chinese-virus-is-racist-rhetoric/.

78   Hannah Bleau, "Hillary Clinton: 'I Would Have Done a Better Job' than Trump on Coronavirus," Breitbart, July 3, 2020, https://www.breitbart.com/politics/2020/07 /03/hillary-clinton-i-would-have-done-a-better-job-than-trump-on-coronavirus/.

79 David Ng, "New York Times Authors Deceptively Edit Trump's Advice to Governors on Medical Ventilators," Breitbart, March 16, 2020, https://www .breitbart.com/the-media/2020/03/16/new-york-times-authors-deceptively -edit-trumps-advice-to-governors-on-medical-ventilators/.

80 Tim Morrison, "No the White House didn't 'dissolve' its pandemic response office. I was there," *Washington Post*, March 16, 2020, www.washingtonpost .com/opinions/2020/03/16/no-white-house-didnt-dissolve-its-pandemic -response-office/.

81 Meg Kelly, "Biden ad manipulates video to slam Trump," *Washington Post*, March 13, 2020, https://www.washingtonpost.com/politics/2020/03/13/biden -ad-manipulates-video-slam-trump/.

82 Ian Hanchett, "Fauci: 'I'm Not Being Muzzled'—The U.S. Will 'See Additional Cases' of Coronavirus," Breitbart, February 28, 2020, https://www.breitbart .com/clips/2020/02/28/fauci-im-not-being-muzzled-the-u-s-will-see-addi tional-cases-of-coronavirus/; Edwin Mora, "Fact Check: Joe Biden Falsely Claims Fauci Didn't Flip-Flop on Efficacy of Masks," Breitbart, September 30, 2020, https://www.breitbart.com/politics/2020/09/30/fact-check-joe-biden -falsely-claims-fauci-didnt-flip-flop-on-efficacy-of-masks/.

83 Joseph Wulfsohn, "CBS News Admits 'Mistake' After Airing Footage of Over-crowded Italian Hospital in Report About NYC," Fox News, March 30, 2020, https://www.foxnews.com/media/cbs-news-admits-mistake-after-airing -footage-of-overcrowded-nyc-hospital-that-was-actually-in-italy.

84 John Nolte, "Nolte: CBS News Plays Italy Hospital Footage—Again—for Report on U.S. Coronavirus Response," Breitbart, April 9, 2020, https://www .breitbart.com/the-media/2020/04/09/cbs-news-caught-broadcasting-fake -hospital-footage-second-time/.

85 Joel B. Pollak, "New York Times Stealth Edits Article Blaming Sean Hannity for Man's Death from Coronavirus," Breitbart, April 19, 2020, https://www .breitbart.com/the-media/2020/04/19/new-york-times-stealth-edits-article -blaming-sean-hannity-for-mans-death-from-coronavirus/.

86 Ibid.

87 Joel B. Pollak, "New York Times Blames Evangelical Christians for Coronavi-rus," Breitbart, March 27, 2020, https://www.breitbart.com/faith/2020/03/27 /new-york-times-blames-evangelical-christians-for-coronavirus-pandemic/.

88 John Nolte, "Nolte: New York Times Demonizes the South with Misleading Coronavirus Map," Breitbart, April 3, 2020, https://www.breitbart.com/the -media/2020/04/03/nolte-new-york-times-demonizes-the-south-with-mis leading-coronavirus-map/.

89 "Hospitals and Health Systems Face Unprecedented Financial Pressures Due to COVID-19," American Hospital Association, accessed February 22, 2021, https://www.aha.org/guidesreports/2020-05-05-hospitals-and-health-sys tems-face-unprecedented-financial-pressures-due.

90 Amit Jain, Tinglong Dai, Kristin Bibee, and Christopher G. Myers, "Covid-19 Created an Elective Surgery Backlog. How Can Hospitals Get Back on Track?"

Harvard Business Review, August 10, 2020, https://hbr.org/2020/08/covid-19 -created-an-elective-surgery-backlog-how-can-hospitals-get-back-on-track.

91 Sarah Kliff, "Hospitals Knew How to Make Money. Then Coronavirus Happened," *New York Times,* May 15, 2020, https://www.nytimes.com/2020/05/15 /us/hospitals-revenue-coronavirus.html.

92 Jain, Dai, Bibee, and Myers, "Covid-19 Created an Elective Surgery Backlog. How Can Hospitals Get Back on Track?"

93 "States Limiting Elective Procedures in Hospitals, Resuming Surgery in All Settings," American Academy of Ophthalmology, July 16, 2020, https://www .aao.org/practice-management/article/states-begin-easing-elective-proce dure-restriction.

94 Jain, Dai, Bibee, and Myers, "Covid-19 Created an Elective Surgery Backlog. How Can Hospitals Get Back on Track?"

95 Martel, "Reports: Virus Death Toll in Wuhan over 10x China's Official Number"; Kurt Zindulka, "'Unreliable Data': Britain Drops China From Official Coronavirus Death Toll," Breitbart, April 27, 2020, https://www.breitbart.com /europe/2020/04/27/unreliable-data-britain-drops-china-from-official-coro navirus-death-toll/.

96 Allum Bokhari, "5 Times Facebook Didn't Fact Check Coronavirus Fake News," Breitbart, April 14, 2020, https://www.breitbart.com/tech/2020/04/14 /5-times-facebook-didnt-fact-check-coronavirus-fake-news/.

97 John Nolte, "Nolte: NBC News Uncritically Spreads Chinese Coronavirus Death Toll Figures," Breitbart, April 7, 2020, https://www.breitbart.com/the -media/2020/04/07/nolte-nbc-news-uncritically-spreads-chinese-coronavi rus-death-toll-figures/.

98 Patrick Boyle, "How Are Covid-19 Deaths Counted? It's Complicated," Association of American Medical Colleges, February 18, 2021, https://www.aamc .org/news-insights/how-are-covid-19-deaths-counted-it-s-complicated.

99 Center for Evidence-Based Medicine, home page, accessed February 24, 2021, https://www.cebm.net/.

100 "Heart Disease Facts," Centers for Disease Control and Prevention, accessed February 21, 2021, https://www.cdc.gov/heartdisease/facts.htm#: ~:text=Heart%20Disease%20in%20the%20United%20States&text=One%20 person%20dies%20every%2036,1%20in%20every%204%20deaths..

101 "Cancer Facts & Figures 2020," American Cancer Society, accessed February 21, 2021, https://www.cancer.org/research/cancer-facts-statistics/all-can cer-facts-figures/cancer-facts-figures-2020.html.

102 "For Specific Groups," Centers for Disease Control and Prevention, accessed February 21, 2021, https://www.cdc.gov/tobacco/campaign/tips /groups/index.html#:~:text=Smoking%20remains%20the%20single%20 largest,from%20exposure%20to%20secondhand%20smoke.

103 Edwin Mora, "CDC Data Shows High Virus Survival Rate: 99%-Plus for Ages 69 and Younger, 94.6% for Older," Breitbart, September 25, 2020, https://www

.breitbart.com/politics/2020/09/25/cdc-data-shows-high-virus-survival-rate
-99-plus-for-ages-69-and-younger-94-6-for-older/.

104 Dave Bondy, "CDC: 94% of Covid-19 Deaths Had Underlying Medical Conditions," Fox, August 30, 2020, https://nbc25news.com/news/local/cdc-94-of
-covid-19-deaths-had-underlying-medical-conditions.

105 Laura Giella and Graham McNally, "Fact Check: Did CNN Remove COVID
-19 Tracker After Joe Biden Took Office," *Newsweek*, January 25, 2021, https://
www.newsweek.com/fact-check-did-cnn-remove-covid-19-tracker-after-joe
-biden-took-office-1564233.

106 Kate Sheehy, "'I Hate Bullies': Bicyclist Verbally Attacked by Chris Cuomo
Fires Back," *New York Post*, April 14, 2020, https://nypost.com/2020/04/14
/long-island-bicyclist-verbally-attacked-by-chris-cuomo-fires-back/.

107 David NG, "Greta Thunberg Will Headline CNN's Town Hall 'Coronavirus:
Facts and Fears,'" Breitbart, May 13, 2020, https://www.breitbart.com/health
/2020/05/13/greta-thunberg-will-headline-cnns-town-hall-coronavirus-facts
-and-fears/.

108 John E. Hall, Jussara M. do Carmo, Alexandre A. da Silva, Zhen Wang, and
Michael E. Hall, "Obesity-Induced Hypertension," *AHA Journals*, March 13,
2015, https://www.ahajournals.org/doi/10.1161/circresaha.116.305697; Ser-
ena Gordon, "Why Does Obesity Cause Diabetes?" MedicineNet, accessed
February 24, 2021, https://www.medicinenet.com/script/main/art.asp?article
key=39840; "People with Certain Medical Conditions," CDC, accessed February 22, 2021, https://www.cdc.gov/coronavirus/2019-ncov/need-extra-pre
cautions/people-with-medical-conditions.html.

109 Alana Mastrangelo, "Cosmopolitan Cover Promotes Plus Size Women as
'Healthy,'" Breitbart, January 4, 2021, https://www.breitbart.com/entertain
ment/2021/01/04/cosmopolitan-cover-celebrates-11-plus-size-women-as
-healthy/.

110 Martha Bebinger, "Opioid Addiction Is 'A Disease Of Isolation,' So Pandemic
Puts Recovery At Risk," NPR, March 27, 2020, https://www.npr.org/sections
/health-shots/2020/03/27/820806440/opioid-addiction-is-a-disease-of-iso
lation-so-pandemic-puts-recovery-at-risk; "Missing Vaccinations During
COVID-19 Puts Our Children & Communities at Risk," Blue Cross Blue
Shield, November 18, 2020, https://www.bcbs.com/the-health-of-america
/infographics/missing-vaccinations-during-covid-19-puts-our-children-and
-communities-at-risk#:~:text=Doses%20of%20vaccine%20administered%20
in%202019%20and%202020&text=The%20same%20decrease%20was%20
seen,Ado; Abbot Koloff and Scott Fallon, "Coronavirus Canceled Her Chemotherapy. Should Cancer Patients Still Go to Appointments?" *USA Today*,
March 23, 2020, https://www.usatoday.com/story/news/health/2020/03/23
/cancer-patients-chemo-during-coronavirus-outbreak-canceled-appoint
ments/2897880001/.

111 Dr. Mary Gillis, D.Ed., "Mask Mandates May Affect a Child's Emotional, Intel-

lectual Development," Wish TV, July 23, 2020, https://www.wishtv.com/news /mask-mandates-may-affect-a-childs-emotional-intellectual-development/; Rachael Katz and Helen Shwe Hadani, "Are You Happy or Sad? How Wearing Face Masks Can Impact Children's Ability to Read Emotions," Brookings Institution, April 21, 2020, https://www.brookings.edu/blog/education-plus -development/2020/04/21/are-you-happy-or-sad-how-wearing-face-masks -can-impact-childrens-ability-to-read-emotions/.

112 Erin Einhorn, "Covid Is Having a Devastating Impact on Children—and the Vaccine Won't Fix Everything," NBC News, December 15, 2020, https://www .nbcnews.com/news/education/covid-having-devastating-impact-children -vaccine-won-t-fix-everything-n1251172.

113 Stacy Frances, "Op-ed: Uptick in Domestic Violence amid Covid-19 Isolation," CNBC, October 30, 2020, https://www.cnbc.com/2020/10/30/uptick-in -domestic-violence-amid-covid-19-isolation.html.

114 Julie Bosman, "Domestic Violence Calls Mount as Restrictions Linger: 'No One Can Leave,'" *New York Times*, May 15, 2020, https://www.nytimes.com /2020/05/15/us/domestic-violence-coronavirus.html.

115 Ritwik Ghosh, Mahua J Dubey, Subhankar Chatterjee, and Souvik Dubey, "Impact of COVID-19 on Children: Special Focus on the Psychosocial Aspect," National Library of Medicine, June 2020, https://pubmed.ncbi.nlm .nih.gov/32613821/.

116 Anya Kamenetz, "Are The Risks of Reopening Schools Exaggerated," NPR, October 21, 2020, https://www.npr.org/2020/10/21/925794511/were-the -risks-of-reopening-schools-exaggerated.

117 Pam Key, "Watch: MSNBC's Melvin Stunned Top Pediatricians Unanimously Saying They Would Send Kids Back to School," Breitbart, July 13, 2020, https:// www.breitbart.com/clips/2020/07/13/watch-msnbcs-melvin-stunned-top -pediatricians-unanimously-saying-they-would-send-kids-back-to-school/.

118 Charlie Spiering, "CDC Director Robert Redfield: Schools the 'Safest Places' for Children During Coronavirus Pandemic," Breitbart, November 19, 2020, https://www.breitbart.com/clips/2020/07/13/watch-msnbcs-melvin-stunned -top-pediatricians-unanimously-saying-they-would-send-kids-back-to-school/.

119 Noah Higgins-Dunn, "New York City Will Close Schools for In-person Learning to Curb Covid Outbreak, Mayor de Blasio Says," CNBC, November 18, 2020, https://www.cnbc.com/2020/11/18/coronavirus-new-york-city-will-close -schools-for-in-person-learning-mayor-says-.html.

120 Higgins-Dunn, "New York City Will Close Schools for In-person Learning to Curb Covid Outbreak, Mayor de Blasio Says"; Dr. Susan Berry, "Chicago Teachers Union Deletes Tweet: Reopening Schools 'Rooted in Sexism, Racism, Misogyny,'" Breitbart, December 7, 2020, https://www.breitbart .com/politics/2020/12/07/chicago-teachers-union-deletes-tweet-reopening -schools-rooted-in-sexism-racism-misogyny/.

121 Kyle Olson, "Socialist Chicago Teachers Union Leader Resists 'Unsafe' Schools Reopening—From Puerto Rico Poolside," Breitbart, January 1, 2021, https://

www.breitbart.com/politics/2021/01/01/socialist-chicago-teachers-union
-leader-resists-unsafe-schools-reopening-from-puerto-rico-poolside/.

122 Luke Money and Rong-Gong Lin II, "LA County on Verge of Becoming
COVID 19 Epicenter: 'We Are Getting Crushed,'" *Los Angeles Times*, December 18, 2020, https://www.latimes.com/california/story/2020-12-18/we-are
-getting-crushed-covid-19-is-hammering-l-a-countys-healthcare-system-as
-deaths-soar-statewide.

123 Berkeley Lovelace Jr., "CDC Director Says Schools Can Safely Reopen Without Vaccinating Teachers," CNBC, February 3, 2021, https://www.cnbc.com
/2021/02/03/cdc-director-says-schools-can-safely-reopen-without-vaccinat
ing-teachers.html.

124 Edwin Mora, "CDC: In-Person Schools May Reopen with Precautions as Data
Shows Scant Virus Spread," Breitbart, January 29, 2021, https://www.breit
bart.com/education/2021/01/29/cdc-schools-reopen-precautions-data-scant
-spread-virus/.

125 Charlie Spiering, "Jen Psaki Refuses to Say Whether Joe Biden Prioritizes
Teachers or Students for Reopening Schools," Breitbart, February 4, 2021,
https://www.breitbart.com/politics/2021/02/04/jen-psaki-refuses-say
-whether-joe-biden-prioritizes-teachers-students-reopening-schools/.

126 Dan Diamond, "Trump Officials Interfered with CDC Reports on Covid-19,"
Politico, September 11, 2020, https://www.politico.com/news/2020/09/11
/exclusive-trump-officials-interfered-with-cdc-reports-on-covid-19-412809.

127 Nick Valencia, Sara Murray, and Kristen Holmes, "CDC Was Pressured 'from
the Top Down' to Change Coronavirus Testing Guidance, Official Says," CNN,
August 27, 2020, https://www.cnn.com/2020/08/26/politics/cdc-coronavirus
-testing-guidance/index.html.

128 Mark Mazzetti, Sharon LaFraniere, and Noah Weiland, "Behind the White
House Effort to Pressure the C.D.C. on School Openings," *New York Times*,
September 28, 2020, https://www.nytimes.com/2020/09/28/us/politics/white
-house-cdc-coronavirus-schools.html.

129 Erica L. Green, "Surge of Student Suicides Pushes Las Vegas Schools to
Reopen," *New York Times*, January 24, 2021, https://www.nytimes.com/2021
/01/24/us/politics/student-suicides-nevada-coronavirus.html.

130 Isabella Kwai and Elian Peltier, "'What's the Point?' Young People's Despair
Deepens as Covid-19 Crisis Drags On," *New York Times*, February 14, 2021,
https://www.nytimes.com/2021/02/14/world/europe/youth-mental-health
-covid.html.

131 Eric Ravenscraft, "It's Not Just You: Everyone's Mental Health Is Suffering,"
Wired, January 18, 2021, wired.com/story/mental-health-coronavirus-pan
demic-tips/.

132 Sharon Epperson, "Nearly Half of U.S. Workers Suffer from Mental Health
Issues Since Covid-19 Pandemic Hit, Report Finds," CNBC, February 10,
2021, https://www.cnbc.com/2021/02/10/half-of-us-workers-suffer-mental
-health-issues-since-covid-19-hit.html.

133 Alison Abbott, "COVID's Mental-health Toll: How Scientists Are Tracking a Surge in Depression," *Nature*, February 3, 2021, https://www.nature.com/articles/d41586-021-00175-z.

134 Dr. Antonis Kousoulis, Professor Tine Van Bortel, and Professor Ann John, "Covid-19 Has Put a Major Strain on Mental Health," *Guardian*, February 11, 2021, https://www.theguardian.com/society/2021/feb/11/covid-19-has-put-a-major-strain-on-mental-health.

135 Kaia Hubbard, "Children's Hospitals Battle COVID-19 Surging Mental Health Needs," *U.S. News & World Report*, January 29, 2021, https://www.usnews.com/news/health-news/articles/2021-01-29/childrens-hospitals-battle-covid-19-surging-mental-health-needs.

136 Kate Larsen, "Pandemic-fueled Drinking Causes Wave of Alcohol-related Liver Disease and Hospitalizations, Report Says," ABC 7, February 19, 2021, https://abc7news.com/covid-19-alcohol-consumption-liver-disease-hospitalizations/10355901/.

137 Finbarr Toesland, "Covid Exacerbating LGBTQ Alcohol Abuse, Studies Find," NBC News, February 9, 2021, https://news.yahoo.com/covid-exacerbating-lgbtq-alcohol-abuse-145333661.html.

138 Nellie Andreeva, "MTV Sets Timely 'Each And Every Day' Documentary About Teen Depression & Suicide," *Deadline*, February 3, 2021, https://deadline.com/2021/02/each-and-every-day-timely-mtv-documentary-teen-depression-suicide-1234686832/.

139 Patrick Boyle, "How Are Covid-19 Deaths Counted? It's Complicated," Association of American Medical Colleges, February 18, 2021, https://www.aamc.org/news-insights/how-are-covid-19-deaths-counted-it-s-complicated.

140 Eliza Shapiro, Erica L. Green, and Juliana Kim, "Missing in School Reopening Plans: Black Families' Trust," *New York Times*, February 1, 2021, https://www.nytimes.com/2021/02/01/us/politics/school-reopening-black-families.html.

141 Rafi Kabarriti, MD; N. Patrik Brodin, PhD, Maxim I. Maron, MSc, et al., "Association of Race and Ethnicity With Comorbidities and Survival Among Patients With COVID-19 at an Urban Medical Center in New York," *JAMA*, September 25, 2020, https://jamanetwork.com/journals/jamanetworkopen/fullarticle/2770960.

142 "Risk for COVID-19 Infection, Hospitalization, and Death by Race/Ethnicity," CDC, accessed February 22, 2021, https://www.cdc.gov/coronavirus/2019-ncov/covid-data/investigations-discovery/hospitalization-death-by-race-ethnicity.html.

143 Eliza Shapiro, Erica L. Green, and Juliana Kim, "Missing in School Reopening Plans: Black Families' Trust," *New York Times*, February 1, 2021, https://www.nytimes.com/2021/02/01/us/politics/school-reopening-black-families.html.

144 Hannah Bleau, "1,000-Bed USNS Comfort Only Had 20 Patients Aboard," Breitbart, April 3, 2020, https://www.breitbart.com/politics/2020/04/03/1000-bed-usns-comfort-only-had-20-patients-aboard/.

145 Karen Dewitt, "Cuomo Receives Record High Approval Rating for Han-

dling of Covid-19," NPR, April 27, 2020, https://news.wbfo.org/post/cuomo
-receives-record-high-approval-rating-handling-covid-19.

146 Reed Abelson , "Why People Are Still Avoiding the Doctor (It's Not the Virus),"
New York Times, June 16, 2020, https://www.nytimes.com/2020/06/16/health
/coronavirus-insurance-healthcare.html.

147 J. David Goodman, "How Delays and Unheeded Warnings Hindered New
York's Virus Fight," *New York Times*, April 8, 2020, https://www.nytimes.com
/2020/04/08/nyregion/new-york-coronavirus-response-delays.html.

148 "Video, Audio, Photos & Rush Transcript: Amid Ongoing COVID-19 Pandemic, Governor Cuomo Announces New Hospital Network Central Coordi-
nating Team," New York State, March 31, 2020, https://www.governor.ny.gov
/news/video-audio-photos-rush-transcript-amid-ongoing-covid-19-pan
demic-governor-cuomo-announces-new.

149 "Unemployment Rates During the COVID-19 Pandemic: In Brief," Congressional Research Service, last updated January 12, 2021, https://fas.org
/sgp/crs/misc/R46554.pdf; Mayra Rodriguez Valladares, "New York State
Unemployment Rate Is at Highest Level Since the Great Depression," *Forbes*,
April 26, 2020, https://www.forbes.com/sites/mayrarodriguezvalladares/2020
/04/26/new-york-state-unemployment-rate-is-at-highest-level-since-the
-great-depression/?sh=268bad4676f2.

150 Anjali Sundaram, "Yelp Data Shows 60% of Business Closures Due to the
Coronavirus Pandemic Are Now Permanent," CNBC, December 11, 2020,
https://www.cnbc.com/2020/09/16/yelp-data-shows-60percent-of-business
-closures-due-to-the-coronavirus-pandemic-are-now-permanent.html;
"Reasons We've Loved New York," *Curbed*, December 7, 2020, https://www
.curbed.com/article/nyc-businesses-closed-2020-pandemic.html.

151 Bernard Condon and Jennifer Peltz, "AP: Over 9,000 Virus Patients Sent into
NY Nursing Homes," Associated Press, February 11, 2021, https://apnews.com
/article/new-york-andrew-cuomo-us-news-coronavirus-pandemic-nursing
-homes-512cae0abb55a55f375b3192f2cdd6b5.

152 Robert Kraychik, "Seema Verma: Science Is Clear, Cuomo's Nursing Home
Policy Was Wrong," Breitbart, June 24, 2020, https://www.breitbart.com/radio
/2020/06/24/seema-verma-science-clear-cuomos-nursing-home-policy-wrong/.

153 Hannah Bleau, "Watch Andrew Cuomo: 'Donald Trump Caused the Covid
Outbreak in New York,'" Breitbart, September 8, 2020, https://www.breitbart
.com/politics/2020/09/08/watch-andrew-cuomo-donald-trump-caused-the
-covid-outbreak-in-new-york/.

154 Jeff Poor, "PBS's Heffner: Trump Coronavirus Response 'Genocidal,' 'Mass
Murder,'" Breitbart, August 1, 2020, https://www.breitbart.com/clips/2020/08
/01/pbss-heffner-trump-coronavirus-response-genocidal-mass-murder/.

155 Louis Jacobson and Amy Sherman, "Ron DeSantis Stated on November 30,
2020 in a Press Conference," PolitiFact, December 2, 2020, https://www.politi
fact.com/factchecks/2020/dec/02/ron-desantis/florida-doing-better-covid-19
-locked-down-states/.

156 "New York Coronavirus Map and Case Count," *New York Times*, accessed March 11, 2021, https://www.nytimes.com/interactive/2020/us/new-york -coronavirus-cases.html?action=click&module=covid_tracking&pgtype=Int eractive&region=TableRowLink#county.

157 "Florida Coronavirus Map and Case Count," *New York Times*, accessed March 11, 2021, https://www.nytimes.com/interactive/2020/us/florida-corona virus-cases.html?action=click&module=covid_tracking&pgtype=Interactive &region=TableRowLink.

158 Jesse McKinley and Luis Ferré-Sadurní, "N.Y. Severely Undercounted Virus Deaths in Nursing Homes, Report Says," *New York Times*, January 28, 2021, https://www.nytimes.com/2021/01/28/nyregion/nursing-home-deaths -cuomo.html.

159 Bernadette Hogan, Carl Campanile, and Bruce Golding, "Cuomo Aide Melissa DeRosa Admits They Hid Nursing Home Data So Feds Wouldn't Find Out," *New York Post*, February 11, 2021, https://nypost.com/2021/02/11/cuomo -aide-admits-they-hid-nursing-home-data-from-feds/.

160 "Chris Cuomo Explains Why He Can't Cover Recent Allegations About His Brother," CNN Politics, accessed March 11, 2021, https://www.cnn.com/vid eos/politics/2021/03/02/governor-andrew-cuomo-news-cuomo-cpt-sot-vpx .cnn; Charlotte Klein, "Oh, So Now Chris Cuomo Can't Cover His Brother for CNN," *Vanity Fair*, March 2, 2021, https://www.vanityfair.com/news/2021/03 /so-now-chris-cuomo-cant-cover-brother-andrew-cuomo-for-cnn.

161 "Chris Cuomo Teases Brother Andrew with Giant Test Swab," YouTube video, posted by "CNN," May 21, 2020, https://www.youtube.com/watch?v=thv_gJ4 EpHw&list=PL6XRrncXkMaVTxK67HPBMRmJBar_wBwbx&index=417.

162 Joel B. Pollak, "Politico: Ron Desantis Was 'More Right' About Coronavirus; Victim of Media Bias," Breitbart, May 14, 2020, https://www.breitbart.com/the -media/2020/05/14/politico-ron-desantis-was-more-right-about-coronavirus -victim-of-media-bias/.

163 Lauren Theisen, "Twitter Is Furious with Florida After Beaches Reopen Despite Coronavirus," *New York Daily News*, April 19, 2020, https://www.nydailynews .com/coronavirus/ny-twitter-is-furious-with-florida-after-beaches-reopen -amid-coronavir-20200420-vbhs725xzrga5bk343uv3kckri-story.html.

164 David Meyer, "MIT Study: Subways a 'Major Disseminator' of Coronavirus in NYC," *New York Post*, April 15, 2020, https://nypost.com/2020/04/15/mit -study-subways-a-major-disseminator-of-coronavirus-in-nyc/.

165 Tamara Lush, Daniela Flamini, and Mike Schneider, "Disney Reopens Despite Worsening Virus Outbreak in Florida, Faces Backlash," NBC Miami, July 13, 2020, https://www.nbcmiami.com/news/local/disney-reopens-despite-wors ening-virus-outbreak-in-florida-faces-backlash/2261391/.

166 Carlye Wisel, "Should Disney World Even Be Open," *Vox*, July 30, 2020, https://www.vox.com/the-goods/21346476/disney-world-reopening-magic -kingdom-covid-florida.

167 Ally Mauch, "Walt Disney World Officially Reopens amid Coronavirus Con-

cerns: See Photos of Opening Day," *People*, July 11, 2020, https://people.com /travel/floridas-walt-disney-world-officially-reopens-see-the-photos/.

168 Greg Allen, "Disney World Orlando to Reopen Despite COVID-19 Surge in Florida," NPR, July 11, 2020, https://www.npr.org/2020/07/10/889653184/dis ney-world-orlando-to-reopen-despite-covid-19-surge-in-florida.

169 Jennifer Hassen, "Disney World Set to Reopen Despite Severe Outbreak Unfolding in Florida," *Washington Post*, July 10, 2020, https://www.washing tonpost.com/travel/2020/07/10/disney-world-set-reopen-despite-severe-out break-unfolding-florida/.

170 Nicole Acevedo, "Disney World Reopens Even as Coronavirus Cases Soar in Florida and Across U.S.," NBC, July 11, 2020, https://www.nbcnews.com/news /us-news/disney-world-reopens-even-coronavirus-cases-rise-florida-across -u-n1233579.

171 Richard Luscombe, "Disney World Set to Reopen at Weekend Despite Corona- virus Surge in Florida," *Guardian,* July 10, 2020, https://www.theguardian.com /us-news/2020/jul/10/disney-world-reopen-weekend-despite-coronavirus -surge-florida.

172 Frank Pallotta, " 'It's the Heart of the Brand': Disney World Reopens as Corona- virus Cases Spike in Florida," CNN, July 9, 2020, https://www.cnn.com/2020 /07/09/media/disney-world-reopening/index.html.

173 Brooks Barnes, "Disney World Opens Its Gates, with Virus Numbers Rising," *New York Times*, July 11, 2020, https://www.nytimes.com/2020/07/11/busi ness/florida-coronavirus-disney-world-reopening.html.

174 Anne Rimoin, "At Disney World, 'Worst Fears' About Virus Have Not Come True," *New York Times*, October 9, 2020, https://www.nytimes.com/2020/10 /09/business/disney-world-coronavirus.html.

175 Brady MacDonald, "Disneyland to Remain Closed More Than a Year, Disney Official Says," *East Bay Times*, February 12, 2021, https://www.eastbaytimes .com/2021/02/12/disneyland-to-remain-closed-more-than-a-year-disney -official-says/.

176 Sarah Whitten, "Disney Said Covid-related Costs Shaved $2.6 Billion from Parks' Operating Income in Latest Quarter," CNBC, February 11, 2021, https://www.cnbc.com/2021/02/11/coronavirus-hurt-theme-parks-costing -disney-2point6-billion.html.

177 Hannah Bleau, "Gov. Ron DeSantis Lifts Key Coronavirus Restrictions Across Florida," Breitbart, September 25, 2020, https://www.breitbart.com /politics/2020/09/25/gov-ron-desantis-lifts-key-coronavirus-restrictions -florida/.

178 Hannah Bleau, "No Spike in Florida Coronavirus Cases Despite Lack of Enforceable Mask Mandate," Breitbart, October 9, 2020, https://www.breit bart.com/politics/2020/10/09/no-spike-in-florida-coronavirus-cases-despite -lack-of-enforceable-mask-mandate/.

179 Beth Landman, "New Yorkers Are Fleeing to Palm Beach—and NYC Busi- nesses Are Following," *New York Post*, February 13, 2021, https://nypost.com

/2021/02/13/new-yorkers-are-fleeing-to-palm-beachand-businesses-are
-too/.

180 "Disney May Relocate Some Operations from California to Florida," Fox 35,
February 12, 2021, https://www.fox35orlando.com/news/disney-may-relocate
-some-operations-from-california-to-florida.

181 "New York Governor Andrew M. Cuomo to Receive International EMMY®
Founders Award," Emmys, November 20, 2020, https://www.iemmys.tv/new
-york-governor-andrew-m-cuomo-to-receive-2020-international-emmy
-founders-award/.

182 Kevin Rector, "LAPD Coronavirus Cases Spike, Adding to Debate over Role of
Protests in Spread," *Los Angeles Times*, June 23, 2020, https://www.latimes.com
/california/story/2020-06-23/lapd-coronavirus-cases-spike-adding-to-debate
-over-role-of-protests-in-spread.

183 Tom Lyden, "Minnesota Nonprofit with $35M Bails Out Those Accused of
Violent Crimes," Fox 9, August 9, 2020, https://www.fox9.com/news/minne
sota-nonprofit-with-35m-bails-out-those-accused-of-violent-crimes.

Chapter 10: The Masters of the Universe

1 Jeff Sessions, "Don't Give the Masters of the Universe Their Amnesty," *National
Review*, September 11, 2014, https://www.nationalreview.com/2014/09/dont
-give-masters-universe-their-amnesty-jeff-sessions/.

2 Olivia Solon, "As Peter Thiel ditches Silicon Valley for LA, locals tout 'conservative renaissance,'" *Guardian,* February 16, 2018, https://www.theguardian
.com/technology/2018/feb/16/peter-thiel-silicon-valley-move-la-conserva
tives-welcome.

3 Patti Domm, "Trump Heaps Praise on Trillion Dollar Tech Club—Calling
Four Big Companies MAGA," CNBC, February 11, 2020, https://www.cnbc
.com/2020/02/11/trump-heaps-praise-on-trillion-dollar-tech-club-calling
-four-big-companies-maga.html.

4 Allum Bokhari, "Sundar Pichai Confirms Google Gave Money to National
Review Institute," Breitbart, February 18, 2019, https://www.breitbart.com
/tech/2019/02/18/sundar-pichai-confirms-google-gave-money-to-national
-review-institute/.

5 Rich Lowry, "Don't Break Up Big Tech," *Politico*, March 13, 2019, https://www
.politico.com/magazine/story/2019/03/13/dont-break-up-big-tech-225808/.

6 Ibid.; Allum Bokhari, "Don't Regulate Google, Says Google-Funded National
Review Editor," Breitbart, March 16, 2019, https://www.breitbart.com/tech
/2019/03/16/bokhari-dont-regulate-google-says-google-funded-national
-review-editor/.

7 Milo, "EXCLUSIVE: Twitter Shadowbanning 'Real and Happening Every
Day' Says Inside Source," Breitbart, February 16, 2016, https://www.breitbart
.com/tech/2016/02/16/exclusive-twitter-shadowbanning-is-real-say-inside
-sources/.

8 Alex Thompson, "Twitter Appears to Have Fixed 'Shadow ban' of Prominent Republicans Like the RNC Chair and Trump Jr's Spokesman," Vice, July 25, 2018, https://www.vice.com/en/article/43paqq/twitter-is-shadow-banning-prominent-republicans-like-the-rnc-chair-and-trump-jrs-spokesman.

9 Avie Schneider, "Twitter Bans Alex Jones and InfoWars; Cites Abusive Behavior," NPR, September 6, 2018, https://www.npr.org/2018/09/06/645352618/twitter-bans-alex-jones-and-infowars-cites-abusive-behavior; Yoree Koh, "Twitter Permanently Bans Blogger Milo Yiannopoulos on Abusive-Content Grounds," Wall Street Journal, July 20, 2016, https://www.wsj.com/articles/twitter-permanently-bans-controversial-blogger-milo-yiannopoulos-1469025620.

10 Georgia Wells, "Writer Sues Twitter Over Ban for Criticizing Transgender People," Wall Street Journal, February 11, 2019, https://www.wsj.com/articles/writer-sues-twitter-over-ban-for-mocking-transgender-people-11549946725.

11 Allum Bokhari, "Twitter Suspends Washington Examiner Contributor for Tweeting 'Learn to Code,'" Breitbart, March 10, 2019, https://www.breitbart.com/tech/2019/03/10/twitter-suspends-washington-examiner-contributor-for-tweeting-learn-to-code/.

12 Allum Bokhari, "Bokhari: By Suppressing Medical Debate, It Is Twitter That Endangers Americans," Breitbart, August 1, 2020, https://www.breitbart.com/tech/2020/08/01/bokhari-twitter-censor-medical-debate-hydroxychloroquine/.

13 "Twitter Under Fire for Flagging Trump Posts but Not Iran Ayatollah Demanding Israel's Genocide," Breitbart, July 30, 2020, https://www.breitbart.com/middle-east/2020/07/30/twitter-under-fire-for-flagging-trump-posts-but-not-iran-ayatollah-calling-for-genocide-of-israel/.

14 Lucas Nolan, "Midterm Meddling: Facebook Blacklists 800+ Grassroots Accounts and Pages to Fight 'Fake News,'" Breitbart, October 12, 2018, https://www.breitbart.com/tech/2018/10/12/midterm-meddling-facebook-blacklists-800-accounts-and-pages-to-fight-fake-news/.

15 Allum Bokhari, "EXCLUSIVE: More Names on FACEBOOK 'Hate Agents' List Revealed, Including Brigitte Gabriel," Breitbart, May 20, 2019, https://www.breitbart.com/tech/2019/05/20/exclusive-more-names-on-facebook-hate-agents-list-revealed-including-brigitte-gabriel/.

16 Lucas Nolan, "Facebook Whistleblower: Staff 'Deboost' Unwanted Content–and I Saw Same Code Used on Conservatives," Breitbart, February 27, 2019, https://www.breitbart.com/tech/2019/02/27/facebook-whistleblower-staff-deboost-unwanted-content-and-i-saw-same-code-used-on-conservatives/.

17 Ibid.

18 Sarah Perez, "Facebook News Launches to All in US with Addition of Local News and Video," Tech Crunch, June 9, 2020, https://techcrunch.com/2020/06/09/facebook-news-launches-to-all-in-u-s-with-addition-of-local-news-and-video/.

19 Benjamin Mullin and Sahil Patel, "Facebook Offers News Outlets Millions of

Dollars a Year to License Content," *Wall Street Journal,* August 8, 2019, https://www.wsj.com/articles/facebook-offers-news-outlets-millions-of-dollars-a-year-to-license-content-11565294575.

20 Allum Bokhari, "Facebook 'Supreme Court' Packed with Anti-Trump, Progressive Figures," Breitbart, May 6, 2020, https://www.breitbart.com/tech/2020/05/06/facebook-supreme-court-packed-with-anti-trump-progressive-figures/.

21 Lucas Nolan, "Facebook Bans 'Dangerous' Conservative Figures but Continues to Allow Leftist Calls for Violence," Breitbart, May 3, 2019, https://www.breitbart.com/tech/2019/05/03/facebook-bans-dangerous-conservative-figures-but-continues-to-allow-leftist-calls-for-violence/.

22 Peter Hasson, "EXCLUSIVE: Google Employees Debated Burying Conservative Media in Search," *Daily Caller,* November 29, 2018, https://dailycaller.com/2018/11/29/google-censorship-conservative-media/.

23 Allum Bokhari, "LEAKED AUDIO: Google Discusses 'Steering' the Conservative Movement," Breitbart, March 7, 2019, https://www.breitbart.com/tech/2019/03/07/leaked-audio-google-discusses-steering-the-conservative-movement/.

24 Allum Bokhari, "'THE GOOD CENSOR': Leaked Google Briefing Admits Abandonment of Free Speech for 'Safety and Civility,'" Breitbart, October 9, 2018, https://www.breitbart.com/tech/2018/10/09/the-good-censor-leaked-google-briefing-admits-abandonment-of-free-speech-for-safety-and-civility/.

25 Allum Bokhari, "'THE SMOKING GUN': Google Manipulated YouTube Search Results for Abortion, Maxine Waters, David Hogg," Breitbart, January 16, 2019, https://www.breitbart.com/tech/2019/01/16/google-youtube-search-blacklist-smoking-gun/.

26 Allum Bokhari, "Google Insider to Project Veritas: YouTube Deliberately Suppresses PragerU, Dave Rubin, Tim Pool," Breitbart, June 24, 2019, https://www.breitbart.com/tech/2019/06/24/google-insider-to-project-veritas-youtube-deliberately-suppresses-prageru-dave-rubin-tim-pool/.

27 Alana Matstrangelo, "Project Veritas: 1,000 Google Employees Signed Internal Anti-Breitbart Petition," Breitbart, July 10, 2019, https://www.breitbart.com/tech/2019/07/10/poject-veritas-1000-google-employees-signed-internal-anti-breitbart-petition/.

28 Allum Bokhari, "STUDY: The CNN Search Engine—Google Search Results Overwhelmingly Favor Mainstream Media," Breitbart, May 12, 2019, https://www.breitbart.com/tech/2019/05/12/study-the-cnn-search-engine-google-search-results-overwhelmingly-favor-mainstream-media/.

29 T. D Adler, "Analysis: Wikipedia Articles on American Politicians Mostly Cite Leftist Media," Breitbart, August 17, 2020, https://www.breitbart.com/tech/2020/08/17/analysis-wikipedia-articles-on-american-politicians-mostly-cite-leftist-media/.

30 Matt Southern, "Facebook Search Results Now Include Wikipedia Knowledge

Panels," *Search Engine Journal*, June 11, 2020, https://www.searchenginejour nal.com/facebook-search-results-now-include-wikipedia-knowledge-panels /371898/#close.

31 Salvador Rodriguez, "Rejected Again by Apple, Gab Says It's a Victim of Anti -Trump Bias," *Inc.*, accessed February 22, 2021, https://www.inc.com/salvador -rodriguez/gab-apple-inauguration.html.

32 Frances Martel, "Study: Nike, Apple, BMW Among 83 Brands Using Chinese Muslim Slave Labor," Breitbart, March 2, 2020, https://www.breitbart.com /asia/2020/03/02/study-nike-apple-bmw-among-83-brands-using-chinese -muslim-slave-labor/.

33 Lucas Molan, "Apple Under Fire for Sending User Data to Chinese Company," Breitbart, October 14, 2019, https://www.breitbart.com/tech/2019/10 /14/apple-under-fire-for-sending-user-data-to-chinese-company/.

34 Allum Bokhari, "Amazon Removes Mike Cernovich's Documentary 'Hoaxed' from Prime Video," Breitbart, April 9, 2020, https://www.breitbart.com/tech /2020/04/09/amazon-removes-mike-cernovichs-documentary-hoaxed-from -prime-video/.

35 Alana Mastrangelo, "Amazon Boots Parler Off Web Hosting Service," Breitbart, January 9, 2021, https://www.breitbart.com/tech/2021/01/09/amazon -boots-parler-off-web-hosting-service/.

36 Allum Bokhari, "Mainstream Media Meltdown: Journos Freak Out over Breitbart's Inclusion in Facebook News Tab," Breitbart, October 27, 2019, https:// www.breitbart.com/tech/2019/10/27/mainstream-media-meltdown-journos -freak-out-over-breitbarts-inclusion-in-facebook-news-tab/.

37 Allum Bokhari, "THE GOOGLE TAPE: Google Global Affairs VP Kent Walker—'History Is on Our Side,'" Breitbart, September 12, 2018, https:// www.breitbart.com/tech/2018/09/12/the-google-tape-google-global-affairs -vp-kent-walker-history-is-on-our-side/.

38 Lucas Nolan, "Dr. Robert Epstein Tells Tucker Carlson: Big Tech Could 'Shift 15 Million Votes' in 2020 Election," Breitbart, October 31, 2020, https://www .breitbart.com/tech/2020/10/31/dr-robert-epstein-tells-tucker-carlson-big -tech-could-shift-15-million-votes-in-2020-election/.

39 John Hayward, "Dr. Robert Epstein: 'The More Google Knows About You, the Easier It Is for Them to Manipulate You,'" Breitbart, April 6, 2018, https:// www.breitbart.com/tech/2018/04/06/dr-robert-epstein-the-more-google -knows-about-you-the-easier-it-is-for-them-to-manipulate-you/.

40 Jack Hadfield, "Report: Google Search Bias Protecting Hillary Clinton Confirmed in Experiment," Breitbart, September 13, 2016, https://www.breitbart .com/tech/2016/09/13/hillary-google-bias-confirmed-experiment/.

41 Allum Bokhari, "Robert Epstein: Google Shifted a 'Minimum' of 6 Million Votes in 2020," Breitbart, November 24, 2020, https://www.breitbart.com/tech /2020/11/24/robert-epstein-google-shifted-a-minimum-of-6-million-votes -in-2020/.

42 Allum Bokhari, "Election Interference: Google Purges Breitbart from Search

Results," Breitbart, July 28, 2020, https://www.breitbart.com/tech/2020/07/28/election-interference-google-purges-breitbart-from-search-results/.

43 Ibid.

44 Ibid.

45 UPI, "Justice Dept. Sues Google over 'Monopoly' on U.S. Web Search Market," Breitbart, October 20, 2020, https://www.breitbart.com/news/justice-dept-sues-google-over-monopoly-on-u-s-web-search-market/.

46 Allum Bokhari, "Google Displays Plagiarized Versions of Breitbart Articles Ahead of Original Stories," Breitbart, November 2, 2020, https://www.breitbart.com/tech/2020/11/02/google-displays-plagiarized-versions-of-breitbart-articles-ahead-of-original-stories/.

47 Allum Bokhari, "Election Interference: Google Suppresses Breitbart News in Search–Even with Exact Headline," Breitbart, October 27, 2020, https://www.breitbart.com/tech/2020/10/27/election-interference-google-suppresses-breitbart-news-in-search-even-with-exact-headline/.

48 Kyle Olson, "Joe Biden Touts 'Most Extensive & Inclusive Voter Fraud Organization in History of American Politics,'" Breitbart, October 24, 2020, https://www.breitbart.com/politics/2020/10/24/joe-biden-touts-most-extensive-inclusive-voter-fraud-organization-in-history-of-american-politics/.

49 "Joe Biden Touts 'Most Extensive & Inclusive Voter Fraud Organization in History of American Politics,'" Geopolitics News, October 25, 2020, https://archive.is/Ssd3h.

50 Allum Bokhari, "Report: Establishment Media Soaring on Facebook, Conservative Media in Decline Following Algorithm Change," Breitbart, April 9, 2018, https://www.breitbart.com/tech/2018/04/09/report-establishment-media-soaring-on-facebook-conservative-media-in-decline-following-algorithm-change/.

51 Emma-Jo Morris and Gabrielle Fonrouge, "Smoking-gun Email Reveals How Hunter Biden Introduced Ukrainian Businessman to VP Dad," *New York Post,* October 14, 2020, https://nypost.com/2020/10/14/email-reveals-how-hunter-biden-introduced-ukrainian-biz-man-to-dad/.

52 Haris Alic, "Hunter Biden's $83K per Month Burisma Salary Raises Questions About Role," Breitbart, September 25, 2019, https://www.breitbart.com/politics/2019/09/25/hunter-bidens-83k-per-month-burisma-salary-raises-questions-about-role/.

53 Stephan Braun, "Ukrainian Energy Firm Hires Biden Son as Lawyer," Associated Press, June 8, 2014, https://apnews.com/article/c49555d51eb243e09a42f7577fc5937f.

54 Emma-Jo Morris and Gabrielle Fonrouge, "Emails Reveal How Hunter Biden Tried to Cash in Big on Behalf of Family with Chinese Firm," *New York Post,* October 15, 2020, https://nypost.com/2020/10/15/emails-reveal-how-hunter-biden-tried-to-cash-in-big-with-chinese-firm/.

55 Peter Schweizer, "How Five Members of Joe Biden's Family Got Rich Through His Connections," *New York Post,* January 18, 2020, https://nypost.com/2020

/01/18/how-five-members-of-joe-bidens-family-got-rich-through-his-con
nections/; James Freeman, "'Fact-Checking' Biden Family Business," *Wall
Street Journal*, February 11, 2021, https://www.wsj.com/articles/fact-checking
-biden-family-business-11613082711.

56 Schweizer, "How Five Members of Joe Biden's Family Got Rich Through His
Connections"; Freeman, "'Fact-Checking' Biden Family Business."

57 Valerie Strauss, "Brother of VP Biden Promotes Charters, Invoking Family Name," *Washington Post*, December 11, 2011, https://www.washington
post.com/blogs/answer-sheet/post/brother-of-vp-biden-promotes-charters
-invoking-family-name/2011/11/22/gIQAnhLFfO_blog.html.

58 Schweizer, "How Five Members of Joe Biden's Family Got Rich Through His
Connections."

59 Robert Kraychik, "'The Biden Five': The Definitive Breakdown of One of
America's Most Corrupt Families," Breitbart, October 28, 2020, https://www
.breitbart.com/clips/2020/10/28/the-biden-five-the-definitive-breakdown-of
-one-of-americas-most-corrupt-families/.

60 Schweizer, "How Five Members of Joe Biden's Family Got Rich Through His
Connections."

61 Ibid.

62 Ben Schreckinger, "Biden's Son-in-law Advises Campaign on Pandemic While
Investing in Covid-19 Startups," *Politico*, October 13, 2020, https://www.polit
ico.com/news/2020/10/13/howard-krein-covid-startups-biden-429123.

63 Schweizer, "How Five Members of Joe Biden's Family Got Rich Through His
Connections"; Ben Schreckinger, "Biden Inc.," *Politico*, August 2, 2019, https://
www.politico.com/magazine/story/2019/08/02/joe-biden-investigation
-hunter-brother-hedge-fund-money-2020-campaign-227407.

64 Ben Schreckinger, "Justice Department's Interest in Hunter Biden Covered
More Than Taxes," *Politico*, December 9, 2020, https://www.politico.com
/news/2020/12/09/justice-department-interest-hunter-biden-taxes-444139.

65 James T. Areddy, "What We Know About Hunter Biden's Dealings in China,"
Wall Street Journal, October 4, 2019, https://www.wsj.com/articles/what-we
-know-about-hunter-bidens-dealings-in-china-11570181403.

66 Schweizer, "How Five Members of Joe Biden's Family Got Rich Through His
Connections."

67 Guy Adams, "Prince Andrew, the Oligarchs and a New Bombshell for Joe
Biden: America's Convulsed over Pictures of the Former Vice President's
Son. But as GUY ADAMS Uncovers His Links to a Suspect Regime (and the
Duke of York) Just How Much Damage Can He Cause?" *Daily Mail* (UK),
October 16, 2020, https://www.dailymail.co.uk/news/article-8849097/As
-GUY-ADAMS-uncovers-links-suspect-regime-just-damage-Hunter-Biden
-cause.html; Joel B. Pollak, "PHOTO: Joe Biden Meets Hunter Biden's Busi-
ness Associate from Kazakhstan," Breitbart, October 20, 2020, https://www
.breitbart.com/politics/2020/10/20/photo-joe-biden-meets-hunter-bidens
-business-associate-from-kazakhstan/; Jon Levine, "Hunter Biden Also Had

Business Dealings in Kazakhstan: Report," *New York Post*, October 17, 2020, https://nypost.com/2020/10/17/hunter-biden-reportedly-also-had-business -ties-in-kazakhstan/.

68 Ben Schreckinger, "Court Reinstates Fraud Conviction for Hunter Biden Business Partner," *Politico*, October 8, 2020, https://www.politico.com/news/2020 /10/08/hunter-biden-business-partner-fraud-428154.

69 Emily Jacobs, "Hunter Biden Received $3.5M Wire Transfer from Russian Billionaire: Senate Report," *New York Post*, September 23, 2020, https:// nypost.com/2020/09/23/hunter-biden-received-3-5m-from-russian-billion aire-report/; Schweizer, "How Five Members of Joe Biden's Family Got Rich Through His Connections."

70 "Notice Biden Campaign Not Denying Post's Scoop Facts on Hunter Biden's Sleaze," *New York Post*, October 14, 2020, https://nypost.com/2020/10/14 /notice-biden-campaign-not-denying-posts-scoop-facts-on-hunter-bidens -sleaze/.

71 James Risen, "Joe Biden, His Son and the Case Against a Ukrainian Oligarch," *New York Times*, December 8, 2015, https://www.nytimes.com/2015/12/09 /world/europe/corruption-ukraine-joe-biden-son-hunter-biden-ties.html.

72 Allum Bokhari, "Election Interference? Facebook and Twitter Suppressing New York Post Bombshell Story of Damaging Hunter Biden Emails," Breitbart, October 14, 2020, https://www.breitbart.com/tech/2020/10/14/elec tion-interference-facebook-suppressing-new-york-post-bombshell-story-of -damaging-hunter-biden-emails/.

73 Tom Ciccotta, "Twitter Cities 'Hacked Info' Policy to Defend Censorship of New York Post Biden Bombshell," Breitbart, October 15, 2020, https://www .breitbart.com/tech/2020/10/15/twitter-cites-hacked-info-policy-to-defend -censorship-of-new-york-post-biden-bombshell/.

74 Robert Kraychik, "Computer Repairman with Hunter Biden's Laptop: Twitter Smearing Me as 'Hacker' Destroyed My Business," Breitbart, January 5, 2021, https://www.breitbart.com/radio/2021/01/05/computer-repairman-hunter -biden-laptop-twitter-smearing-me-as-hacker-destroyed-my-business/.

75 Kate Cox, "Computer Repairman Suing Twitter for Defamation, Seeks $500 Million," *Ars Technica*, December 29, 2020, https://arstechnica.com/tech-pol icy/2020/12/source-in-controversial-ny-post-laptop-story-sues-twitter-for -defamation/.

76 "Leading Daily Newspapers in the United States in September 2017 and January 2019, by Circulation," *Statista*, accessed February 22, 2021, https://www .statista.com/statistics/184682/us-daily-newspapers-by-circulation/; Robert McMillan, "Twitter Unlocks New York Post Account After Two-Week Stand-off," *Wall Street Journal*, October 30, 2020, https://www.wsj.com/articles/twit ter-reinstates-new-york-post-account-11604096659.

77 Emma-Jo Morris and Gabrielle Fonrouge, "Emails Reveal How Hunter Biden Tried to Cash in Big on Behalf of Family with Chinese Firm," *New York Post*,

October 15, 2020, https://nypost.com/2020/10/15/emails-reveal-how-hunter
-biden-tried-to-cash-in-big-with-chinese-firm/.

78 Matthew Boyle, "Biden Insider Tony Bobulinski Provides Trove of Documents
to Senate Investigators," Breitbart, October 22, 2020, https://www.breitbart
.com/politics/2020/10/22/biden-insider-tony-bobulinski-provides-trove-doc
uments-senate-investigators/.

79 Alana Mastrangelo, "Twitter Censors Second New York Post Bombshell Story
About Hunter Biden," Breitbart, October 15, 2020, https://www.breitbart.com
/tech/2020/10/15/twitter-censors-second-new-york-post-bombshell-story
-about-hunter-biden/.

80 Joel B. Pollak, "Listen: CNN Execs Spike 'Breitbart, New York Post, Fox News'
Hunter Biden Laptop Story," Breitbart, December 2, 2020, https://www.breit
bart.com/the-media/2020/12/02/listen-cnn-execs-spike-breitbart-new-york
-post-hunter-biden-laptop-story-emails/.

81 Joseph A. Wulfsohn, "CNN Boss, Political Director Spiked Hunter Biden
Controversy, Audiotapes Reveal: 'We're Not Going with' Story," Fox News,
December 3, 2020, https://www.foxnews.com/media/cnn-jeff-zucker-david
-chalian-hunter-biden-project-veritas.

82 Joel B. Pollak, "Senate Report Says Joe Biden Allowed Family to Enrich Themselves Abroad While He Was VP," Breitbart, September 23, 2020, https://www
.breitbart.com/politics/2020/09/23/senate-report-says-joe-biden-allowed
-family-to-enrich-themselves-abroad-while-he-was-vp/.

83 Zack Budryk, "50 Former Intelligence Officials Warn NY Post Story Sounds
Like Russian Disinformation," Hill, October 20, 2020, https://thehill.com
/homenews/campaign/521823-50-former-intelligence-officials-warn-ny-post
-story-sounds-like-russian.

84 John Nolte, "14 Media Outlets That Lied About Hunter Biden's Laptop Scandal
Being Russian Disinformation," Breitbart, December 10, 2020, https://www
.breitbart.com/the-media/2020/12/10/14-media-outlets-lied-hunter-bidens
-laptop-being-russian-disinformation/.

85 Natasha Bertrand, "Hunter Biden Story Is Russian Disinfo, Dozens of Former
Intel Officials Say," Politico, October 19, 2020, https://www.politico.com/news
/2020/10/19/hunter-biden-story-russian-disinfo-430276.

86 David Frum (@davidfrum), "The people on far right and far left who publicized the obviously bogus @nypost story were not dupes . . . ," Twitter,
October 18, 2020, 4:39 p.m., https://twitter.com/davidfrum/status/13179
73670019670016?lang=en.

87 T. D. Adler, "Wikipedia Editors Call NY Post's Biden Bombshells 'Russian Interference,'" Breitbart, November 2, 2020, https://www.breitbart.com
/tech/2020/11/02/wikipedia-editors-call-ny-posts-biden-bombshells-russian
-interference/.

88 Edwin Mora, "Joe Biden: Some Claims About Hunter's Dealings 'Russian Disinformation,' No Discussion of Son in Search for AG," Breitbart, December 22,

2020, https://www.breitbart.com/politics/2020/12/22/joe-biden-some-claims
-about-hunters-dealings-russian-disinformation-no-discussion-of-son-in
-search-for-ag/.

89 Sadie Gurman and Aruna Viswanatha, "Barr Kept Hunter Biden Probes from
    Public to Avoid Election Politics," *Wall Street Journal*, December 14, 2020,
    https://www.wsj.com/articles/barr-kept-biden-probes-from-public-to-avoid
    -election-politics-11607951984.

90 Eric Tucker, Michael Balsamo, and Jonathan Lemire, "Hunter Biden Tax
    Probe Examining Chinese Business Dealings," Associated Press, Decem-
    ber 9, 2020, https://apnews.com/article/hunter-biden-federal-tax-investiga
    tion-87c200c919aa61396b5d43077bc5b0ff.

91 Evan Perez and Pamela Brown, "Federal Criminal Investigation into Hunter
    Biden Focuses on His Business Dealings in China," CNN Politics, last updated
    December 10, 2020, https://www.cnn.com/2020/12/09/politics/hunter-biden
    -tax-investigtation/index.html.

92 Tom Winter, "Email to Hunter Biden Raises Fresh Questions About His Tax
    Dealings," NBC News, December 11, 2020, https://www.nbcnews.com/poli
    tics/politics-news/email-hunter-biden-raises-fresh-questions-about-his-tax
    -dealings-n1250973.

93 U.S. Senate Committee on Homeland Security and Governmental Affairs and
    U.S. Senate Committee on Finance, "Hunter Biden, Burisma, and Corruption:
    The Impact on U.S. Government Policy and Related Concerns," Majority Staff
    Report, accessed February 22, 2021, https://www.hsgac.senate.gov/imo/media
    /doc/HSGAC_Finance_Report_FINAL.pdf.

94 Graham Stack, "Hunter Biden Partner Secured Millions for Fund from Busi-
    nessman with Reputed Organized Crime Ties," OCCRP, November 1, 2020,
    https://www.occrp.org/en/the-fincen-files/hunter-biden-partner-secured
    -millions-for-fund-from-businessman-with-reputed-organized-crime-ties.

95 Adam Entous, "Will Hunter Biden Jeopardize His Father's Campaign?" *New
    Yorker*, July 1, 2019, https://www.newyorker.com/magazine/2019/07/08/will
    -hunter-biden-jeopardize-his-fathers-campaign.

96 George Mesires, "A Statement on Behalf of Hunter Biden, Dated Octo-
    ber 13, 2019," Medium, October 13, 2019, https://medium.com/@george
    .mesires/a-statement-on-behalf-of-hunter-biden-dated-october-13-2019
    -d80bc11087ab.

97 Robert Farley, "Trump's Claim About Hunter Biden in China," FactCheck.org,
    October 10, 2019, https://www.factcheck.org/2019/10/trumps-claims-about
    -hunter-biden-in-china/.

98 Peter Schweizer and Jacob McLeod, "New Evidence Makes Hunter Biden's
    'Business' Deals Reek Worse Than Ever," *New York Post*, September 14, 2020,
    https://nypost.com/2020/09/14/new-evidence-makes-hunter-bidens-busi
    ness-deals-reek-worse-than-ever/.

99 Entous, "Will Hunter Biden Jeopardize His Father's Campaign?"

100 Ian Hanchett, "Jill Biden: 'Hunter Did Nothing Wrong,'" Breitbart, Decem-

ber 14, 2019, https://www.breitbart.com/clips/2019/12/14/jill-biden-hunter-did-nothing-wrong/; Charlie Spiering, "Joe Biden 'Confident' That Son Hunter Biden Did Nothing Wrong," Breitbart, December 16, 2020, https://www.breitbart.com/politics/2020/12/16/joe-biden-confident-son-hunter-biden-did-nothing-wrong/.

101 "Special Report: The Stealing of the Presidency, 2020," Media Research Center, November 24, 2020, https://www.newsbusters.org/blogs/nb/rich-noyes/2020/11/24/special-report-stealing-presidency-2020.

102 "Most Think Media Hid Hunter Biden Story Before Election Day," Rasmussen Reports, December 15, 2020, https://www.rasmussenreports.com/public_content/politics/elections/election_2020/most_think_media_hid_hunter_biden_story_before_election_day.

103 Michael C. Bender and Joshua Jamerson, "Trump Plans In-Person White House Event, Rally in Florida," *Wall Street Journal*, last updated October 9, 2020, https://www.wsj.com/articles/trump-plans-in-person-white-house-event-for-saturday-11602275494?mod=hp_lead_pos1.

104 Frances Martel and Edwin Mora, "The Collapse of ISIS: Terrorist Group Sees 60% Drop in Casualties, over 70% Drop in Beheadings in Trump Era," Breitbart, October 28, 2020, https://www.breitbart.com/national-security/2020/10/28/the-collapse-of-isis-terrorist-group-sees-60-drop-in-casualties-over-70-drop-in-beheadings-in-trump-era/.

105 Jay Peters, "How to Retweet Using Twitter's New Temporary Format," *Verge*, last updated October 21, 2020, https://www.theverge.com/21524092/twitter-temporarily-changing-retweet-quote-tweet-election.

106 Lucas Nolan, "Twitter Changes Retweet Functionality to Add 'Friction' Before Election," Breitbart, October 21, 2020, https://www.breitbart.com/tech/2020/10/21/twitter-changes-retweet-functionality-to-add-friction-before-election/.

107 Allum Bokhari, "Google Is Still Erasing Breitbart Stories About Joe Biden from Search," Breitbart, November 3, 2020, https://www.breitbart.com/tech/2020/11/03/google-is-still-erasing-breitbart-stories-about-joe-biden-from-search/.

108 Joel B. Pollak, "NBC Mocked for Still Claiming Hunter Biden Accusations During Campaign 'Unfounded and Baseless,'" Breitbart, December 13, 2020, https://www.breitbart.com/the-media/2020/12/13/nbc-mocked-for-still-claiming-hunter-biden-accusations-during-campaign-unfounded-and-baseless/.

109 Haris Alic, "Joe Biden Refuses to Take Questions from Press on Son's Legal Troubles," Breitbart, December 14, 2020, https://www.breitbart.com/2020-election/2020/12/14/joe-biden-refuses-to-take-questions-from-press-on-sons-legal-troubles/.

110 Mike Allen and David Nather, "Zuckerberg to 'Axios on HBO': 'Just Wrong' to Say Facebook Driven by Conservatives," Axios, September 9, 2020, https://www.axios.com/zuckerberg-facebook-conservatives-algorithm-0ad23698

-7bfe-49cf-9250-fb333edc218e.html; Steven L. Johnson, Brent Kitchens, and Peter Gray, "Opinion: Facebook Serves as an Echo Chamber, Especially for Conservatives. Blame Its Algorithm," *Washington Post*, October 26, 2020, https://www.washingtonpost.com/opinions/2020/10/26/facebook-algorithm -conservative-liberal-extremes/.

111 Hannah Bleau, "Wisconsin: 52 of 400,000 In-Person Primary Voters Diagnosed with Coronavirus, No Fatalities," Breitbart, April 30, 2020, https://www .breitbart.com/politics/2020/04/30/wisconsin-52-of-400000-in-person-pri mary-voters-diagnosed-with-coronavirus-no-fatalities/.

112 Tom Scheck, Geoff Hing, Sabby Robinson, and Gracie Stockton, "How Private Money from Facebook's CEO Saved the 2020 Election," NPR, December 8, 2020, https://www.npr.org/2020/12/08/943242106/how-private-money-from -facebooks-ceo-saved-the-2020-election.

113 Michael Patrick Leahy, "Southern Poverty Law Center Provided Funding to Fulton County, Georgia for 25 Absentee Ballot Drop Boxes," Breitbart, December 17, 2020, https://www.breitbart.com/politics/2020/12/17/south ern-poverty-law-center-paid-for-25-absentee-ballot-drop-boxes-in-fulton -county-georgia/.

114 Amanda House, "Watch Live: Amistad Project Press Conference on Mark Zuckerberg's Alleged Influence in 2020 Election," Breitbart, December 16, 2020, https://www.breitbart.com/politics/2020/12/16/watch-live-amistad -project-press-conference-on-mark-zuckerbergs-alleged-influence-in-2020 -election/.

115 Alex Thompson and Theodoric Meyer, "Biden Transition Elevates Former Facebook Exec as Ethics Arbiter," *Politico*, last updated October 1, 2020, https://www.politico.com/news/2020/09/30/biden-transition-facebook-eth ics-424000; Nandita Bose, "Big Tech's Stealth Push to Influence the Biden Administration," Reuters, December 21, 2020, https://www.reuters.com /article/usa-tech-biden-insight/big-techs-stealth-push-to-influence-the -biden-administration-idUSKBN28V170.

116 Nandita Bose and David Shepardson, "More Tech Executives Than Tech Critics on Biden's Transition Team," Reuters, December 4, 2020, https://www .reuters.com/article/us-usa-biden-tech-change-suite/more-tech-executives -than-tech-critics-on-bidens-transition-team-idUSKBN28E2DN.

117 Brian Schwartz, "Amazon Hires Lobbyist Brother of Biden White House Counselor," CNBC, last updated December 28, 2020, https://www.cnbc.com /2020/12/26/jeff-ricchetti-to-lobby-for-amazon-as-brother-becomes-joe -bidens-counselor.html.

118 John Binder, "Big Tech, Corporate America Lines Up as Donors to Fund Joe Biden's Inauguration," Breitbart, January 10, 2021, https://www.breitbart.com /politics/2021/01/10/big-tech-lines-up-fund-joe-bidens-inauguration/.

119 Byran Bender and Theodoric Meyer, "The Secretive Consulting Firm That's Become Biden's Cabinet in Waiting," *Politico*, November 23, 2020, https:// www.politico.com/news/2020/11/23/westexec-advisors-biden-cabinet

-440072; Lee Fang, "Former Obama Officials Help Silicon Valley Pitch the Pentagon for Lucrative Defense Contracts," *Intercept*, July 22, 2018, https://theintercept.com/2018/07/22/google-westexec-pentagon-defense-contracts/.

120 Fang, "Former Obama Officials Help Silicon Valley Pitch the Pentagon for Lucrative Defense Contracts."

121 Bose, "Big Tech's Stealth Push to Influence the Biden Administration."

122 Jeffrey Dastin and Paresh Dave, "U.S. Commission Cities 'Moral Imperative' to Explore AI Weapons," Reuters, January 26, 2021, https://www.reuters.com/article/us-usa-military-ai/u-s-commission-cites-moral-imperative-to-explore-ai-weapons-idUSKBN29V2M0.

123 Jordan Fabian, Emma Kinery, and Josh Wingrove, "Biden Says He'll Introduce Immigration Bill 'Immediately,'" Bloomberg, January 8, 2021, https://www.bloomberg.com/news/articles/2021-01-08/biden-says-he-ll-introduce-immigration-bill-immediately.

124 Joel B. Pollak, "Biden Kills up to 70,000 Jobs on First Day in Office," Breitbart, January 22, 2021, https://www.breitbart.com/economy/2021/01/22/pollak-biden-kills-up-to-70000-jobs-on-first-day-in-office-job/.

125 Robby Starbuck (@robbystarbuck), " 'When you tear out a man's tongue . . . , '" Twitter, January 9, 2021, 9:51 a.m., https://twitter.com/robbystarbuck/status/1347964223494762499.

126 Pam Key, "Rep. Hakeem Jeffries: Trump Is the 'Grand Wizard of 1600 Pennsylvania Avenue,'" Breitbart, January 21, 2019, https://www.breitbart.com/clips/2019/01/21/rep-hakeem-jeffries-trump-is-the-grand-wizard-of-1600-pennsylvania-avenue/.

127 Jeff Poor, "Ayanna Pressley: I Don't Call Trump the 'President'–'He Is Simply Occupying the Oval Office,'" Breitbart, July 1, 2020, https://www.breitbart.com/politics/2020/07/01/ayanna-pressley-i-dont-call-trump-the-president-he-is-simply-occupying-the-oval-office/.

128 Sarah E. Needleman, "Facebook Says It Is Removing All Content Mentioning 'Stop the Steal,'" *Wall Street Journal*, last updated January 11, 2021, https://www.wsj.com/articles/facebook-says-it-is-removing-all-content-mentioning-stop-the-steal-11610401305.

129 Allum Bokhari, "Twitter Permanently Blacklists General Michael Flynn and Sidney Powell," Breitbart, January 8, 2021, https://www.breitbart.com/tech/2021/01/08/twitter-permanently-blacklists-general-michael-flynn-and-sidney-powell/.

130 Mike Pompeo (@mikepompeo), "This is how you create an echo chamber . . . ," Twitter, January 9, 2021, 10:47 a.m., https://twitter.com/mikepompeo/status/1347978415312433159.

131 David Ng, "Hollywood Celebs Rejoice After Twitter Permanently Bans Trump: 'We Did It' 'We Need to Go Further,'" Breitbart, January 8, 2021, https://www.breitbart.com/entertainment/2021/01/08/hollywood-celebs-rejoice-after-twitter-permanently-bans-trump-we-did-it-we-need-to-go-further/.

132 Kyle Morris, "Democrat Joe Manchin Praises Twitter's Decision to Perma-

nently Suspend Trump," Breitbart, January 8, 2021, https://www.breitbart
.com/politics/2021/01/08/democrat-joe-manchin-praises-twitters-decision
-to-permanently-suspend-trump/.

133 Andy Ngo (MrAndyNgo), "Twitter still allows these Portland antifa groups
to organize, promote, and/or incite violence on the platform . . . ," Twitter,
January 8, 2021, 4:05 p.m., https://twitter.com/MrAndyNgo/status/1347695
893261262848.

134 Alana Mastrangelo, "Google Blacklists Parler App from Play Store," Breitbart,
January 8, 2021, https://www.breitbart.com/tech/2021/01/08/google-black
lists-parler-app-from-play-store/.

135 Alana Mastrangelo, "Apple Joins Google in Blacklisting Parler," Breitbart, January 9, 2021, https://www.breitbart.com/tech/2021/01/09/apple-joins-google
-in-blacklisting-parler/.

136 John Paczkowski and Ryan Mac, "Amazon Will Suspend Hosting for Pro-
Trump Social Network Parler," BuzzFeed News, January 9, 2021, https://www.
buzzfeednews.com/article/johnpaczkowski/amazon-parler-aws.

137 Lucas Nolan, "Glenn Greenwald Blasts Big Tech for Censoring 'Unilaterally,
with No Standard, Accountability or Appeal,'" Breitbart, January 8, 2021,
https://www.breitbart.com/tech/2021/01/08/glenn-greenwald-blasts-big
-tech-for-censoring-unilaterally-with-no-standard-accountability-or-appeal
/; Chris Tomlinson, "German Chancellor Merkel Critical of 'Problematic'
Twitter Trump Ban," Breitbart, January 11, 2021, https://www.breitbart.com
/europe/2021/01/11/german-chancellor-merkel-critical-of-problematic-twitter
-trump-ban/.

138 "A 'Bad Sign': World Leaders and Officials Blast Twitter Trump Ban," Al
Jazeera, last updated January 12, 2021, https://www.aljazeera.com/news/2021
/1/11/a-bad-sign-world-leaders-and-officials-blast-twitter-trump-ban.

139 John Nolte, "ABC News Political Editor Calls for 'Cleansing' of Trump Movement," Breitbart, January 7, 2021, https://www.breitbart.com/the-media/2021
/01/07/nolte-abc-news-political-editor-calls-for-cleansing-of-trump-move
ment/.

140 Joshua Klein, "Wapo: Media Must Shun Republicans Who Don't Accept Biden
as 'President-Elect,'" Breitbart, December 4, 2020, https://www.breitbart.com
/the-media/2020/12/04/wapo-media-must-shun-republicans-who-dont
-accept-biden-as-president-elect/.

141 Elizabeth A. Harris and Alexandra Alter, "Simon & Schuster Cancels Plans
for Senator Hawley's Book," New York Times, last updated January 15, 2021,
https://www.nytimes.com/2021/01/07/books/simon-schuster-josh-hawley
-book.html.

142 Tom Elliott, "Now CNN's @oliverdarcy is going after cable companies for
carrying Fox News," Twitter, January 8, 2021, 12:48 a.m., https://twitter.com
/tomselliott/status/1347465189252341764.

143 AnnaMaria Andriotis, Peter Rudegeair, and Emily Glazer, "Stripe Stops Pro-
cessing Payments for Trump Campaign Website," Wall Street Journal, last

updated January 10, 2021, https://www.wsj.com/articles/stripe-stops-process
ing-payments-for-trump-campaign-website-11610319116.

144 Fadel Allassan, "Major Businesses Say They Will Pause Political Donations
Following Capitol Riots," Axios, January 10, 2021, https://www.axios.com
/capitol-riots-businesses-political-donations-c06b95f6-d03a-4a18-959f
-a4a6bae9631c.html.

145 "Daily Presidential Tracking Poll," Rasmussen Reports, February 19, 2021,
https://www.rasmussenreports.com/public_content/politics/biden_adminis
tration/prez_track_feb19.

Chapter 11: A Time to Heal

1 Emily Badger, "Most Republicans Say They Doubt the Election. How Many
Really Mean It?" New York Times, November 30, 2020, https://www.nytimes
.com/2020/11/30/upshot/republican-voters-election-doubts.html.

2 Domenico Montanaro, "Poll: Just a Quarter of Republicans Accept Election Outcome," NPR, December 9, 2020, https://www.npr.org/2020/12/09
/944385798/poll-just-a-quarter-of-republicans-accept-election-outcome.

3 Dartunorro Clark, "Georgia Hand Count of Votes Affirms Biden's Narrow
Victory over Trump," NBC News, November 19, 2020, https://www.nbcnews
.com/politics/2020-election/georgia-expected-release-results-trump-biden
-hand-recount-n1248234.

4 Vanessa Williams, "Stacey Abrams Lost the Georgia Governor's Race. But Her
Star Is Rising," Washington Post, February 3, 2019, https://www.washington
post.com/lifestyle/style/stacey-abrams-lost-the-georgia-governors-raise-but
-her-star-is-rising/2019/02/02/1c3f4b74-2737-11e9-ad53-824486280311
_story.html.

5 Christina Wilkie, "Biden Calls for Unity and Healing After Electoral College Certifies His Victory," CNBC, December 14, 2020, https://www.cnbc
.com/2020/12/14/biden-calls-for-unity-and-healing-after-electoral-college
-cements-his-victory.html.

6 "Maddow Explains Why Putin's Russia Hacked the 2016 Election," YouTube
video, posted by "MSNBC," October 17, 2019, https://www.youtube.com
/watch?v=Vo8OJVzbuxI.

7 Zachary Keck, "Hacking Elections," Harvard Kennedy School, Belfer Center
for Science and International Affairs, Fall/Winter 2016-2017, https://www
.belfercenter.org/publication/hacking-elections.

8 Matt Vasilogambros, "Mueller Findings Raise Election Hacking Fears in
States," Pew Research Center, May 2, 2019, https://www.pewtrusts.org/en
/research-and-analysis/blogs/stateline/2019/05/02/mueller-findings-raise
-election-hacking-fears-in-states.

9 David E. Sanger and Catie Edmondson, "Russia Targeted Election Systems
in All 50 States, Report Finds," New York Times, July 25, 2019, https://www
.nytimes.com/2019/07/25/us/politics/russian-hacking-elections.html.

10 Alexandra Wolfe, "Why a Data-Security Expert Fears U.S. Voting Will Be Hacked," *Wall Street Journal*, April 24, 2020, https://www.wsj.com/articles /why-a-data-security-expert-fears-u-s-voting-will-be-hacked-11587747159.

11 Kim Zetter, "Software Vendor May Have Opened a Gap for Hackers in 2016 Swing State," *Politico*, June 5, 2019, https://www.politico.com/story/2019/06 /05/vr-systems-russian-hackers-2016-1505582.

12 Nicole Perlroth and David E. Sanger, "Ransomware Attacks Take on New Urgency Ahead of Vote," *New York Times*, last updated November 16, 2020, https://www.nytimes.com/2020/09/27/technology/2020-election-security -threats.html.

13 Rebecca Shabad, "Hillary Clinton Says Biden Should Not Concede the Election 'Under Any Circumstances,'" NBC News, August 26, 2020, https://www .nbcnews.com/politics/2020-election/hillary-clinton-says-biden-should-not -concede-2020-election-under-n1238156.

14 David Leonhardt, "Trump's Refusal to Concede," *New York Times*, November 12, 2020, https://www.nytimes.com/2020/11/12/briefing/ron-klain-jeffrey -toobin-tropical-storm-eta.html.

15 "Biden: Trump Refusal to Concede 'An Embarrassment,'" BBC News, November 11, 2020, https://www.bbc.com/news/election-us-2020-54897627.

16 Noah Pransky, "Postal Service Delays Disenfranchised Thousands of Legally -Cast Ballots This Fall," NBC Lx, December 6, 2020, https://www.lx.com/poli tics/postal-service-delays-disenfranchised-thousands-of-legally-cast-ballots -this-fall/25647/.

17 Sonam Sheth, "'The Bad Guys Can Get In': Hackers at a Cybersecurity Conference Breached Dozens of Voting Machines Within Minutes," *Business Insider*, August 1, 2017, https://www.businessinsider.com/voting-machine-hack-def -con-russia-2017-7.

18 Miles Parks, "Florida Governor Says Russian Hackers Breached 2 Counties in 2016," NPR, May 14, 2019, https://www.npr.org/2019/05/14/723215498/flor ida-governor-says-russian-hackers-breached-two-florida-counties-in-2016.

19 Frank Bajak, "Reliability of Pricey New Voting Machines Questioned," Associated Press, February 23, 2020, https://apnews.com/article/ec2374b 3f4aa6d8e628b75724cb4caeb.

20 "Not Enough Voters Detecting Ballot Errors and Potential Hacks, Study Finds," Michigan Engineer News Center, January 8, 2020, https://news.engin.umich .edu/2020/01/new-study-finds-voters-not-detecting-ballot-errors-potential -hacks/.

21 David Emery, "Did Paul Krugman Say the Internet's Effect on the World Economy Would Be 'No Greater Than the Fax Machine's'?" Snopes, June 7, 2018, https://www.snopes.com/fact-check/paul-krugman-internets-effect-economy/; Paul Krugman, "How to Rig an Election," *New York Times*, November 7, 2016, https://www.nytimes.com/2016/11/07/opinion/how-to-rig-an-election.html.

22 Chris Kahn, "Half of Republicans Say Biden Won Because of a 'Rigged'

Election: Reuters/Ipsos Poll," Reuters, November 18, 2020, https://www
.reuters.com/article/us-usa-election-poll/half-of-republicans-say-biden-won
-because-of-a-rigged-election-reuters-ipsos-poll-idUSKBN27Y1AJ.

23 Hannah Bleau, "GOP Senators Including Cruz, Blackburn to 'Reject the Electors from Disputed States' January 6," Breitbart, January 2, 2021, https://www
.breitbart.com/politics/2021/01/02/gop-senators-including-cruz-blackburn
-to-reject-the-electors-from-disputed-states-january-6/.

24 Ian Hanchett, "Hawley: Dems Exercised 'Right' to Object to Electoral College Certification, Why Can't GOP?" Breitbart, December 30, 2020, https://
www.breitbart.com/clips/2020/12/30/hawley-dems-exercised-right-to-object
-to-electoral-college-certification-why-cant-gop/.

25 Kyle Olson, "Sen. Josh Hawley: I'll Object to Electoral College Votes on January 6," Breitbart, December 30, 2020, https://www.breitbart.com/politics/2020
/12/30/sen-josh-hawley-ill-object-to-electoral-college-votes-on-january-6/.

26 Associated Press, "Sen. Ted Cruz Calls Objection 'Right Thing to Do,' Assures
Peaceful Transition of Power," WFAA, January 7, 2021, https://www.wfaa
.com/article/news/politics/sen-ted-cruz-statement-defends-objection-was
-right-thing-to-do-assures-peaceful-transition-of-power-in-statement/287
-f7081330-0349-43d6-91f1-2485fe56e0d2.

27 Reuters, "Trump Summoned Supports to 'Wild' Protest, and Told Them to
Fight. They Did," U.S. News, January 6, 2021, https://www.usnews.com/news
/top-news/articles/2021-01-06/trump-supporters-crowd-into-washington-to
-protest-congress-certifying-bidens-victory.

28 Charlie Spiering, "President Trump Returns to White House Despite Saying
He Would March to Capitol Hill," Breitbart, January 6, 2021, https://www
.breitbart.com/politics/2021/01/06/president-trump-returns-white-house
-despite-saying-he-would-march-capitol-hill/.

29 Debra J. Saunders, "How to Start a Civil War," Las Vegas Review-Journal, January 8, 2021, https://www.reviewjournal.com/opinion/opinion-columns/debra
-saunders/debra-j-saunders-how-to-start-a-civil-war-2246517/.

30 ABC 7, "The judge noted the rioter bragged about writing . . . ," Facebook,
January 28, 2021, 5:30 p.m., https://www.facebook.com/ABC7/posts/10158
160780207452.

31 "A Man in a Horn Hat Posed for Photos as Violence Unfolded at US Capitol.
He's a QAnon Supporter," News 18, January 7, 2021, https://www.news18.com
/news/buzz/us-capitol-violence-deer-suit-man-viral-3255641.html.

32 Quint Forgey, "Pence Rushed Out of Senate Chamber as Protesters Storm
Capitol," Politico, January 6, 2021, https://www.politico.com/news/2021/01
/06/pence-rushed-out-of-senate-capitol-455483.

33 Donald J. Trump (@realDonaldTrump), "Please support our Capitol Police
and Law Enforcement . . . ," Twitter, January 6, 2021, 7:38 p.m., https://media
-cdn.factba.se/realdonaldtrump-twitter/1346904110969315332.jpg.

34 Justine Coleman, "Most of 120 Arrested or Identified at Capitol Riot Were

Longtime Trump Supporters: AP Analysis," *Hill*, January 10, 2021, https://thehill.com/homenews/news/533579-most-of-120-arrested-or-identified-at-capitol-riot-were-longtime-trump.

35 Matthew Daly and Michael Balsamo, "Deadly Siege Focuses Attention on Capitol Police," Associated Press, January 8, 2021, https://apnews.com/article/capitol-police-death-brian-sicknick-46933a828d7b12de7e3d5620a8a04583.

36 Brian Stelter (@brianstelter), "We were minutes away from a possible massacre . . . ," Twitter, January 10, 2021, 5:37 a.m., https://twitter.com/brianstelter/status/1348262802788655105.

37 Tom Elliott (@tomselliott), ".@JoeNBC: Yes 'we can draw the analogies' between the Capitol Hill riot . . . ," Twitter, January 11, 2021, 3:58 a.m., https://twitter.com/tomselliott/status/1348600081650495489.

38 Tom Elliott (@tomselliott), ".@AOC objecting to Republicans opposed to impeaching Trump over the Capitol Hill riot . . . ," Twitter, January 10, 2021, 12:25 p.m., https://twitter.com/tomselliott/status/1348365394730487808.

39 Zolan Kanno-Youngs and Tracey Tully, "He Dreamed of Being a Police Officer, Then Was Killed by a Pro-Trump Mob," *New York Times*, last updated February 16, 2021, https://www.nytimes.com/2021/01/08/us/politics/police-officer-killed-capitol.html.

40 Pilar Melendez, Ana Lucia Murillo, Will Lennon, and Matt Taylor, "MAGA Mob Kills Capitol Police Officer Brian Sicknick, a Iraq War Veteran Defending Congress from Trump Rioters," Yahoo News, January 7, 2021, https://news.yahoo.com/three-other-people-died-during-214841130.html?guccounter=1.

41 Evan Perez, David Shortell, and Whitney Wild, "Investigators Struggle to Build Murder Cases in Death of US Capitol Police Officer Brian Sicknick," CNN, on Internet Archive, February 2, 2021, https://web.archive.org/web/20210203173544/https:/www.cnn.com/2021/02/02/politics/brian-sicknick-charges/index.html (the screenshot of the site was captured on February 3, 2021).

42 John Nolte, "Investigators Say Blunt Force Trauma Did Not Kill Officer Sicknick at Capitol Riot," Breitbart, February 4, 2021, https://www.breitbart.com/politics/2021/02/04/nolte-investigators-say-blunt-force-trauma-did-not-kill-officer-sicknick-capitol-riot/.

43 Gabrielle Fonroughe and Laura Italiano, "Who Are the Five People Who Died in the DC Protest at the Capitol?" *New York Post*, January 7, 2021, https://nypost.com/2021/01/07/who-are-the-four-who-died-in-the-dc-protest-at-the-capitol/; Michael L. Diamond, Susan Loyer, Suzanne Russell, and Greg Tufaro, "NJ Hometown 'in Shock' After Capitol Police Officer Brian Sicknick Dies in D.C. Riot," *My Central Jersey*, January 8, 2021, https://www.mycentraljersey.com/story/news/local/2021/01/08/brian-sicknick-nj-capitol-police-officer-died-dc-riots/6593972002/.

44 Kanno-Youngs and Tully, "He Dreamed of Being a Police Officer, Then Was Killed by a Pro-Trump Mob."